PLANTING THE UNION FLAG IN TEXAS

NUMBER TWO: *Red River Valley Books*
Sponsored by Texas A&M University–Texarkana
Doris Davis, General Editor

PLANTING THE UNION FLAG IN TEXAS

The Campaigns of Major General Nathaniel P. Banks in the West

STEPHEN A. DUPREE

Texas A&M University Press
College Station

First edition

This paper meets the requirements of ANSI/NISO Z39.48-1992 (Permanence of Paper).
Binding materials have been chosen for durability.

Library of Congress Cataloging-in-Publication Data

Dupree, Stephen A.
Planting the Union flag in Texas : the campaigns of Major General Nathaniel P. Banks in the West / Stephen A. Dupree.
p. cm. — (Red River Valley books ; no. 2)
Includes bibliographical references and index.
ISBN-13: 978-1-58544-641-4 (cloth : alk. paper)
ISBN-10: 1-58544-641-6 (cloth : alk. paper)
1. Banks, Nathaniel Prentiss, 1816–1894. 2. Generals—United States—Biography. 3. United States. Army—Biography. 4. Texas—History—Civil War, 1861–1865—Campaigns. 5. United States—History—Civil War, 1861–1865—Campaigns. 6. United States—History—Civil War, 1861–1865—Biography. I. Title.
E467.1.B23D87 2008
973.7'3092—dc22
[B]

2007026462

In Memoriam

ALLEN CAMILLE DUPREE
1902–1999
who in his youth knew several
of the participants in this narrative

and

JOHN LEWIS DUPREE
1841–1925
Bvt. Capt.
Company H
Debray's 26th Texas Cavalry

CONTENTS

ILLUSTRATIONS

MAPS

PREFACE

Texas remained almost completely free of Union occupation throughout the Civil War. This was not the result of a lack of interest in Texas on the part of the Federal leadership, nor of a lack of effort on the part of the Union military to occupy part of the state, but rather of a combination of factors that were unique to the state. First, Texas was remote from the heavily contested regions of the Confederacy. Because of its remote location the state possessed limited military value as a target for invasion, and in the event of an invasion it presented the special difficulties inherent in any long-range military action. To be successful, a Union invasion of Texas would require careful planning along with exceptional effort in the areas of logistics and communication.

Second, although the quality of the individual soldiers in the opposing armies in both Texas and Louisiana was every bit as good as that of the armies of the east, such was not the case for the senior officer corps of these armies. Competent and effective army commanders were available to the Confederate forces present in these states, but the Union Army of the Gulf suffered from poor military leadership. Thus, in addition to having the advantage of being on the defensive, in general the Southern troops could depend on their commanding officers using them effectively and to good purpose. The Northern troops could not.

For a period of seventeen months, from mid-December 1862 through mid-May 1864—a period during which many crucial and determining events of the war occurred, including the Battles of Stones River, Chancellorsville, Gettysburg, and Chickamauga, plus the capture of Vicksburg—the Army of the Gulf was commanded by Major General of Volunteers Nathaniel P. Banks. During this period, among his other military and political activities, General Banks attempted to invade Texas five times. Two of these attempts were thwarted by Southern forces in Louisiana and failed to reach Texas soil, whereas two reached the coast of Texas only to be soundly repulsed by local Confederate and Texas state troops. The fifth attempt, which was actually the fourth chronologically, was Banks's only successful invasion, though the question of whether it was in fact a success is perhaps moot. Under whichever interpretation one chooses, however, the invasion resulted in the capture and occupation of a small area near the mouth of the Rio Grande and, for a short while, some areas along the coast of south Texas.

All of Banks's invasions of Texas, including his partially successful coastal invasion, have been the subject of scrutiny and assessment by historians, and full-length treatments exist that cover four of the invasions. Each of these assessments treats the invasion it covers as an essentially isolated campaign: the Battle of Galveston, the Texas overland expedition, the Battle of Sabine Pass, and the Red River expedition. None of the extant works that addresses Banks's Texas campaigns has examined them as part of a coordinated whole. In fact, there was a level of consistency in the motivation and intent of the Union government, as well as that of the Gulf Department commander, that lay behind these events. The present work attempts to address this consistency by examining the decisions made in Washington concerning Texas, along with the actions and reactions of General Banks to these decisions and to events in his department.

Unless otherwise noted, all quotations contained in the text reproduce the syntax and spelling used in the document quoted. Thus, there are numerous misspelled words, run-on sentences, and other nonliterary gems in the quotations. Rather than mark these blunders "[*sic*]" to indicate that the errors are in the original, I have chosen to leave them for the reader to discover.

Attrition caused frequent changes in leadership at nearly all levels of both armies during the war, and both the military grades and assignments of some officers changed rapidly. I have attempted to designate the grade of the officers mentioned in the narrative at the time of the action being described. Thus, in some cases the reader will find the same individual referred to by different grades at different points in the narrative because of interim promotions. Frequently no explicit reference is made to such promotions.

Official time zones and their associated standard times—products of the transcontinental railroad—did not exist during the period of this narrative. The times stated for the events presented have been taken from those cited by the various participants. Whether these times were obtained from the position of the sun, taken from an individual's pocket watch, or estimated using some other means, the actual times of the various events that occurred during the Civil War are necessarily uncertain. All times reported herein should be interpreted accordingly.

It is a great pleasure to acknowledge the many libraries and institutions, and their hard-working administrators and staff, who provided repeated, cheerful, and invaluable assistance to me in locating and acquiring the references used in this book. Although I cannot list them all, special thanks are due to the Library of Congress, including the helpful staff of the general reading room, the microfilm division, and the manuscripts division; the U.S. Army Military History Institute in Carlisle, Pennsylvania; the National Archives; the Zimmerman Library of the University of New Mexico; and the Center for American History of the University of Texas at Austin. Special thanks also go to the staff of the Interlibrary Loan desk of the Juan Tabo branch of the Albuquerque Public Library. Finally, I would like to thank my wife, Patricia, for traveling with me to numerous battlefields and museums, for waiting (sometimes patiently) while I roamed through various libraries and bookstores, and for (mostly) tolerating my distraction and crankiness during the preparation of this book.

When one is assembling a large number of facts into a narrative history, it is sometimes difficult to avoid what I might call "transcriptional longiloquence" (that is, the inclusion of gratuitous facts, lengthy descriptions, or nongermane events), the inadvertent introduction of oddities and inconsistencies of presentation, and the inclusion of outright errors. Although I make no claim that the final text is both taut and error free, the number of extraneous perambulations and factual errors is certainly much smaller now than it was before the text was reviewed by a number of very helpful people. I would like to thank John Taylor, Bill McAdams, and Jessalyn Brach for reviewing portions of the text, in one form or another, and for offering many useful comments and suggestions on presentation and factual matters. I would also like to thank my anonymous reviewers for pointing out numerous places where the text needed to be improved, suggesting ways to improve it, and identifying a number of mistakes and typographical errors. As a result of their efforts I believe the product has been much improved. Special thanks go to my copyeditor, Cynthia Lindlof, for her diligence, patience, and perseverance. Her efforts have resulted in innumerable improvements. Finally, I would like to thank Don Frazier for preparing the excellent maps contained herein. Naturally, all remaining errors are my responsibility.

PLANTING THE UNION FLAG IN TEXAS

PROLOGUE

As the end of the year 1862 approached, the military situation prevailing in the politically divided United States of America did not appear favorable to those hoping to reunite the country. Although invasions of Kentucky and Maryland by the South had been repulsed and Northern armies had subsequently advanced, after twenty months of internecine war there was no discernible decline in the defiance offered by the Confederacy to U.S. authority. In the west the fortress at Vicksburg ensured Confederate control of the Mississippi between that point and the fortified position at Port Hudson. The Union blockade of Southern ports was only partially effective, and because Texas shared a border with a neutral, foreign state, the Confederacy had an undisturbed, land-based route for conducting international trade. This trade route, through Brownsville, Texas, and the nearby Mexican towns of Matamoros and Bagdad, was conspicuously active. To one observer the ships waiting off the Mexican shore to trade war goods and other supplies for Southern commodities were so numerous that, as seen from Bagdad, the "Gulf, for three or four miles out, was literally a forest of masts."[1]

The most valuable commodity that the South had to offer for trade was cotton. Raw cotton had become available in quantity following the introduction of Eli Whitney's gin in 1793, and the supply of the product continued to develop in partnership with the growing demand for textiles during the early and mid-nineteenth century. The dominant supplier of high-quality, raw cotton to the world, a supply that was believed essential to the care and feeding of textile factories everywhere, was the American South. Southern cotton constituted more than half the total monetary value of American exports and accounted for 75 percent of all raw cotton imports to England in the years immediately prior to the Civil War.[2]

In response to the rising demand and the consequent rising price of cotton, the slavery-based plantation system in the southern part of the United States turned out vast amounts of the staple. In 1860 production exceeded 4 million bales.[3] By the end of 1862, however, this situation had changed dramatically. Several events had reduced cotton production and export, along with the profits of the growers, the factors, and the shippers. First, because of the Civil War, farmers in the South had been encouraged to replace cotton and tobacco with food crops to support Southern armies. Second, early in the war Jefferson Davis and others in positions of authority or influence, in an attempt to induce England and France to intervene in the war on the side of the South, urged an ill-conceived and only partially effective cotton embargo. Finally, the impact of the Federal blockade of Confederate ports had gradually increased, and both the blockade runners and the Southern war effort were beginning to feel the impact of the Union navy. The result was a significant reduction in the worldwide supply of raw cotton. Some 80 percent of the textile plants in New England were closed at one time or another during 1862 because of the shortage of raw materials.[4]

In the decade of the 1850s the price of cotton on the U.S. market had averaged about eleven and one-half cents per pound. By 1862 the price had risen to as much as one dollar per pound. As might be expected, despite the war and the Confederate attempt to embargo cotton, the incentive for smuggling and other illicit trade in this commodity had grown along with the price. In response to the shortage and high price of cotton in the North, powerful economic interests began to pressure Pres. Abraham Lincoln to correct the supply situation. In the natural course of events, this state of affairs produced aggressive groups of lobbyists that advocated various measures to acquire cotton from the South. In the time-honored tradition of American politics, this horde descended upon Washington, and the president was faced with a seemingly unending series of requests for authority to trade for cotton beyond the Union lines.[5]

One of the early, and recurrent, themes of what can reasonably be described as the "cotton lobby" involved seizing the opportunity presented by the state of Texas. The lobbyists' argument, that the state offered a place for New Englanders to grow cotton, had predated the war. In 1845 Edward Everett Hale, clergyman, prolific author, grandnephew of Nathan Hale, and nephew of Edward Everett, had written a pamphlet advocating the migration of New Englanders to Texas. In this pamphlet he predicted that "even as certain men went from Leyden to Massachusetts Bay in 1620, a body of us would go to Texas in 1845."[6] Before anything could come of Hale's Texas initiative, however, the national debate on the Kansas-Nebraska Act focused attention on the question of whether to allow slavery in the territories. Hale's proposal got nowhere.

Motivated by the Kansas-Nebraska Act, in 1854 Eli Thayer, a member of the lower house of the Massachusetts state legislature, chartered an organization known as the Emigrant Aid Company in the state. The purpose of Thayer's organization was to promote the immigration of New Englanders to Kansas to prevent the latter from becoming a slave state through the self-determination allowed by the act. During this same period Frederick Law Olmsted, future landscape architect and designer of New York City's Central Park, traveled through the South as a special correspondent for Henry J. Raymond, editor of the recently established New York *Daily Times.* In 1854 Olmsted visited several German communities near San Antonio, Texas. He reported that he found widespread antislavery sentiments in the local population, along with "a number of parallelograms of COTTON—FREE-LABOR COTTON."[7] From his visit he got the idea that a series of free-labor colonies in Texas might block the westward expansion of slavery in the state. Hale gave his support to Olmsted's plan, and the two began an effort to convince prospective investors that cotton could be produced profitably by free labor in Texas. It looked for a while as though funds would be forthcoming to support this endeavor; however, the economic fallout from the Panic of 1857 eliminated any hope of raising funds, and once again an antislavery proposal directed at Texas came to nothing.[8]

In 1861 Edward Atkinson, an influential abolitionist from Massachusetts, published an essay entitled "Cheap Cotton by Free Labor" that reiterated the theme of colonizing Texas with free-labor farmers. Atkinson advocated having the Federal government send an army to Texas to emancipate the slaves and to settle those same troops on Texas lands to grow cotton. Massachusetts governor John Andrew was enthusiastic about Atkinson's scheme and in November 1861 recommended the idea in a letter to Assistant Secretary of the Navy Gustavus Fox. In Andrew's opinion, such a move would "flank the whole rebellion" and "open the way out for cotton."[9]

A general consensus began to arise among New Englanders that Texas had large numbers of Union sympathizers ready to support a Federal invasion, that German immigrants to the state successfully and profitably grew cotton without slaves, and that thousands of unused acres of prime cotton land existed in the eastern part of the state. This unused land was available for use by Northern farmers who could be transported there to ensure a free-soil population loyal to the Union. These ideas were enthusiastically carried to Washington by the cotton lobbyists. Finally, in addition to expounding all of these advantages for an expedition to Texas, the lobbyists declared that east Texas was poorly defended and ripe for plunder.

At least some of the arguments advanced by these lobbyists were true.

German settlers had begun immigrating to Texas while the state was still part of Mexico. After Texas achieved its independence from Mexico in 1836, such immigration was encouraged by Pres. Sam Houston, among others. By the time Texas joined the Union, many thousands of German settlers had established themselves in the state. To a large degree these immigrants were not assimilated into the slave culture brought to Texas by settlers from the old South. Thus, in contrast with many of their neighbors, a large fraction of these German settlers were opposed both to slavery and to secession.[10] Typically, the German settlers were not afraid to let their opinions on these subjects be known. As the threat of war approached, such outspokenness created considerable friction between the German Unionists and the local secessionists. One reaction to this internal strife was the so-called Great Hanging at Gainesville.[11] In the North, word of the execution of Union supporters at Gainesville provided ammunition for the cotton lobbyists.

Under different circumstances Lincoln may not have paid much attention to the demands of the cotton lobby concerning Texas. However, by the latter part of 1862 the president was receptive to a military expedition to Texas for several reasons. Perhaps most obvious, it would quiet the cotton critics and get some of the buyers and speculators out of his office. If things did work out as the lobbyists claimed, a steady supply of cotton would help the economy and thus the war effort. Second, an expedition to Texas would have the desirable side effect of reducing or eliminating the active Confederate trade that was taking place through Mexico. Third, a Union presence in Texas would provide support and encouragement to the loyalists in the state who in some cases, according to reports, were being subjected to harsh treatment.[12] Last, an ongoing problem with the French nagged at the president.

In July 1861, in response to a financial crisis in the regime of Pres. Benito Juárez, the Mexican Congress announced that Mexico would defer interest payments on the country's debt.[13] As could have been predicted, this did not sit well with certain financial institutions and wealthy individuals in Europe who had made loans to the Mexican regime. Some European leaders argued that the personal safety of European nationals living in Mexico was at risk because of unstable conditions in the country. These leaders felt something had to be done both to force the resumption of payments on the debts and to protect their citizens. In addition, the European monarchies were keenly interested in expanding their spheres of influence in the Western Hemisphere. As Napoleon III stated in 1862, "We are interested in seeing the United States powerful and prosperous, but we have no interest in seeing that republic acquire the whole of the Gulf of Mexico, dominate from this vantage-point the Antilles and South America, and become the sole dispenser of the products of the New World."[14]

Given that the United States was busy with a war inside its own borders, and with perhaps the end of that ridiculous and radical idea of self-government finally in sight, the time seemed ripe to do something constructive. In pursuance thereof Queen Victoria of Great Britain, Queen Isabella of Spain, and Napoleon III of France signed the Tripartite Treaty. This treaty, which became effective in November 1861, formed the basis for the forcible intervention in Mexico by these European states.[15] On December 7, 1861, twenty-six Spanish vessels arrived at Vera Cruz, Mexico, and 6,000 Spanish troops occupied the city. Later, in the winter of 1861–62, British and French warships entered the Gulf of Mexico and troops from these countries occupied several ports on the Mexican coast. Spain occupied Santo Domingo (the present-day Dominican Republic), blockaded several ports in Peru and Chile, and occupied an island off Peru.

It was questionable from the beginning whether these activities furthered the stated objectives of the European allies. After a time Great Britain and Spain began to suspect ulterior motives on the part of the French, motives with which they were not in sympathy. In particular, Spain had originally thought Napoleon III was interested in placing a Spanish prince on the throne of Mexico. Learning that the French emperor instead favored the Austrian Ferdinand Maximilian Joseph, Spain withdrew its forces from Mexico. The British were more interested in obtaining rights to an interoceanic trade route in Central America than in assisting France in gaining control of Mexico, and they left as well. However, King Leopold of Belgium, Maximilian's father-in-law, supported the installation of Maximilian as emperor of Mexico, which, in his opinion, would "raise a barrier against the United States and provide a support for the monarchical-aristocratic principle in the Southern states."[16]

During the spring of 1862 a French army moved inland from Vera Cruz toward Mexico City, much as Hernán Cortés and Winfield Scott had done previously. The invaders anticipated a swift and easy victory over Juárez. Meeting unexpected resistance, however, the French army fought and lost a battle with the Mexican army under Gen. Ignacio Zaragoza near the town of Puebla on Cinco de Mayo (May 5), 1862. Despite this defeat, and the subsequent retreat of his army from the Valley of Mexico, Napoleon III did not back down from his objective of establishing a suzerainty in Mexico. With such high stakes at risk, Secretary of State William H. Seward and others in the

U.S. government kept a wary eye on this activity south of the border. Numerous Monroe Doctrine leagues and Mexican clubs were organized in the North with the objective of assisting Juárez, but little could be done because of the war at home. Lincoln wanted to stop this French hegemony, but he wanted to do so without starting a fight with France. He declared that the principles of the Monroe Doctrine would be maintained but concluded that he would have to be patient.[17]

In November 1862 the French emperor proposed that a six-month armistice be established between the North American belligerents and that France, Britain, and Russia jointly mediate a peace agreement. The logical inference was that this proposal meant France was seeking an opportunity for recognizing the Confederacy.[18] Although Britain and Russia quickly rejected the proposal and nothing further came of it, rumors soon circulated in Washington that in addition to recognizing the Southern republic, the French, if successful in Mexico, might support the reestablishment of the Republic of Texas. All these events heightened the ongoing domestic criticism of Lincoln's policy toward Mexico and raised Lincoln's interest in initiating some military action within the state of Texas.

Early in the war several proposals were offered for undertaking military campaigns in Texas. General McClellan sent Lincoln his "Memorandum for the Consideration of His Excellency the President" on August 2, 1861, in which he addressed "another independent movement which has often been suggested and which has always recommended itself to my judgment." This movement called for an advance from Kansas and Nebraska, through the Indian Territory, into west Texas. McClellan added that such a movement could possibly be supported by a simultaneous advance from California through New Mexico. An alliance with Mexico might permit use of routes of travel in that country, such as the road from Guaymas to New Mexico or from Tampico to the Rio Grande. McClellan even opened the question of using Mexican soldiers to support military campaigns in Texas.[19] This proposal was not pursued.

A similar idea surfaced in December 1862 in which it was suggested that Brig. Gen. David Hunter or Maj. Gen. James H. Lane be sent through the Indian Territory into west Texas in combination with an invasion of the Gulf Coast. This latter plan was approved by Lincoln and his cabinet but was never executed.[20] Thus, Texas, though an object of attention on the part of the Union leadership, was not selected as a major target for military activities in the first two years of the Civil War.

Despite the fact that there were several legitimate reasons for initiating military operations in Texas, it was clear to the president that the Union had a more important goal in the west than occupying a portion of that state. After weighing the alternatives, Lincoln decided to concentrate on gaining control of the Mississippi River, as originally recommended by the general in chief of the army Winfield Scott in his so-called Anaconda plan.[21] The Mississippi was of more substantial military importance and urgency than Texas, and the cotton lobbyists, the European traders, and the French would just have to wait their turn. Besides, the goal of opening the Mississippi also had powerful political support in Washington. In the antebellum era most of the produce of the states along the Ohio and the upper Mississippi had found its way to market by way of the river. Politicians from those states wanted to see this avenue of commerce reopened. Military forces were already in place to accomplish this goal, but progress had been slow and Lincoln believed that something else was needed: the right man for the job.

LINCOLN'S POLITICAL GENERAL

1 At the time of the Civil War there was a widely held opinion, both in Washington and Richmond, that professional military training was not a prerequisite for a man to become an effective army commander. On the contrary, many believed that the professionals from West Point were excessively defensive minded and would not take the steps necessary to win the war.[1] The West Point generals were seen by some as prejudiced, cliquish, and self-serving. This was confirmed to outside observers because such generals frequently chose to recommend for high command members of the exclusive club of Academy graduates. In the traditional American manner the conclusion was drawn that such selectivity clearly had nothing to do with the ability of those not recommended but was prima facie evidence of prejudice. What the country needed, what the military situation demanded, and what the politics of the war required were some political generals in the service. In addition to showing those stodgy professionals how to make war, a few politicians in positions of military leadership would "unite discordant groups in support of the war and . . . keep down divisions in the North."[2] One of Lincoln's first political generals was Nathaniel Prentice (or Prentiss) Banks.

In 1860 Nathaniel Banks was a successful, forty-four-year-old politician who seemed to epitomize the American dream.[3] Born into a working-class family January 30, 1816, in Waltham, Massachusetts, he began work in a textile mill at the age of eleven. At the mill he was responsible for replacing bobbins on the weaving machines, and every indication is that he bore the responsibility well. Because of this initial job assignment Banks later acquired from his political opponents the demeaning epithet that remained with him the rest of his life: the "Bobbin Boy of Waltham."

Banks had a rich, melodious voice and an aristocratic bearing that he worked hard to improve, and as a young man he became an outstanding orator. His oratorical abilities and commanding stage presence led him naturally into politics. In 1848 Banks was elected to the lower house of the Massachusetts legislature, the Commonwealth's Great and General Court, as a Democrat. He was a successful legislator from the beginning, ultimately serving four terms in the state House. Banks was elected Speaker of the Massachusetts

House in 1851. He showed great skill as Speaker. At various times he was described as "brilliant," "attentive," "tactful," "firm," and "decisive." One colleague concluded that "as a presiding officer he had never been equaled before."[4] One of the reasons for his political success—a technique practiced by countless American politicians both before and after Banks—was his effort to seek the middle ground in all issues while saying little or nothing about his personal convictions.

In 1852 Banks won the first of his ten terms in the U.S. House of Representatives. Then, after being elected but before departing for Washington, he was chosen as a delegate to a constitutional convention to be held in Massachusetts beginning in the spring of 1853. Anticipating a successful session, in a letter to his wife written the day before the convention opened Banks described it as the "greatest meeting ever held in Massachusetts."[5] Banks was elected president of the convention. As expected by his colleagues, in this role he was notably successful. Even delegate Charles Sumner, who was almost always on the opposite side of political questions from that of the presiding officer, declared that Banks had a talent for presiding that was "as marked as Bryant for poetry."[6] At the close of the convention, August 1, Banks praised its members by declaring, with hyperbole that would become a hallmark of his self-evaluations, "I believe no representative assembly ever surpassed that whose labors are now about to close."[7]

As a freshman Democratic member of the U.S. House of Representatives, Banks was appointed to the Committee on Military Affairs, a position from which he might have learned much about the operation of the U.S. military establishment. He paid scant attention to military matters, however, instead focusing on the Kansas-Nebraska Act. Banks, like many other Northern moderates, and in unison with the other ten House members from Massachusetts, was opposed to the act. He adopted the position of accepting slavery where it existed but opposing its spread. After the House passed the act, a number of those contending against passage, consisting mostly of Northern Democrats opposed to the policies of Pres. Franklin Pierce, began to meet and discuss common positions and goals. This disaffected group of politicians ultimately formed the core of the Republican Party. Banks was a charter member of the group and was thus one of the founders of the new party.

Banks was reelected to his seat in the House in 1854. When the 34th Congress assembled for their first legislative session in December 1855, the House proceeded to find itself in a deadlock for a Speaker. The battle for Speaker continued for nine weeks and reflected many of the strains present in the national body politic at that time. Finally, a decision was reached on the same basis as the compromise of 1849, in which a plurality was approved to decide the winner. On February 5, 1856, on the 113th ballot, Nathaniel Banks was elected Speaker of the House. He received 103 votes to 100 for William Aiken, the former governor of South Carolina. The remaining eleven votes were distributed among other candidates.[8] With this victory Banks became the highest-ranking elected, antislavery official in the country in 1856.

As had been the case in the Massachusetts House, Banks proved to be an extraordinarily effective Speaker, and he quickly added to his reputation. Horace Greeley described him as "prompt, vigorous, decided, and just. . . . Abler men may have filled that difficult post; but no man, I judge, ever gave himself more unreservedly to the discharge of his arduous duties."[9] He was an obvious favorite for the presidential nomination by the new Republican Party. However, despite his prominent position and outstanding performance as Speaker, Banks chose not to seize the nomination and became instead a strong supporter of his friend John C. Frémont.

After his reelection to the House in 1856, Banks began to consider the possibility of seeking the governorship of Massachusetts. Perhaps with the governorship and some luck he could become the Republican Party standard-bearer in the presidential race of 1860. Setting his path accordingly, Banks won the Massachusetts gubernatorial election and took office in January 1858. At the same time a pro-Banks majority was installed in the state legislature. As a governor with a supportive legislature Banks extended his reputation for being an effective and innovative executive. However, the Massachusetts governor at that time served a one-year term, and Banks found himself having to run for office almost continuously. In 1859 he ran against, and defeated, a strong Democratic candidate named Benjamin Franklin Butler.

Despite his success in gaining a second term as governor, Banks's hopes for the 1860 presidential nomination were not realized. Banks was thoroughly disappointed by this turn of events. He seemed to take this failure to achieve his dream of the presidency as a sign that it was time for him to make a change in his career. Though assured of another term as governor, Banks, who was chronically short of money, chose to leave politics in 1860. He accepted an offer from William H. Osborn, president of the Illinois Central Railroad, to become the Chicago manager for the railroad. This career change required a move to Chicago, so Banks packed up his family and headed west. He assumed his new position in January 1861, leaving the spoils of the Massachusetts polity to the radicals.

After the Republican presidential candidate, Abraham Lincoln, won the national election in 1860, Banks hoped to receive a cabinet appointment. As he waited, and as the states of the Deep South began seceding, Banks spoke out for compromise. He felt strongly that although secession was legally impossible, initiating a war to prevent it was unthinkable. Concessions must therefore be made and a compromise reached to avoid war. His declarations did not endear him to the Republican radicals, and, at least in part as a result of his public statements, he did not get his cabinet position.[10] But then, without warning, his life changed. Lincoln offered him an appointment as major general of volunteers. The appointment was made June 5, 1861, to date from May 16 of that year. Banks accepted at once. This appointment made Banks one of the senior officers in the army, outranked only by Winfield Scott, George McClellan, John C. Frémont, John A. Dix, and his former political foe, Benjamin Franklin Butler.[11] Thus, after years of single-mindedly building his political future, twice within the period of a year Banks undertook a dramatic change of career.

Banks liked being a major general. He liked the pageantry and the dignity of the office. Banks, with his booming and theatrical voice, was said to be able to address ten thousand men with ease. He selected beautiful horses for himself and became an accomplished rider. He grew a very commanding mustache. Adm. David Dixon Porter, who bore an intense dislike for Banks, wrote a sarcastic description of the general after the war. Despite being filtered through the admiral's personal opinion, the description probably reflects more than an element of truth: "General Banks was a handsome, soldierly-looking man, though rather theatrical in his style of dress, which might be accounted for through the fact that he had at one time been on the stage—so I have been told. He wore yellow gauntlets high up on his wrists, looking as clean as if they had just come from the glove-maker; his hat was picturesque, his long boots and spurs were faultless, and his air was that of one used to command. In short, I never saw a more faultless-looking soldier."[12]

Following his appointment, Banks proceeded to read tirelessly about military matters, including manuals on strategy and books on the campaigns of Napoleon. He mastered the rudiments of military command and applied himself to the task of war much as he had once applied himself to the tasks of public speaking and politics. Unfortunately, one bit of military philosophy that he apparently acquired from his book learning at this time, and by which it was said that he was "very much influenced," was derived from a quote ascribed to Napoleon: "The world belongs to the phlegmatic." As one of his staff officers was to paraphrase later, Banks interpreted this to mean that "those who act in a twinkling are too fast and do mischief, their works cannot stand."[13] The conjecture that this quote formed a part of the new general's military philosophy may or may not be correct, but it is certain that as a field commander he was frequently slow to react to developing circumstances.

Lincoln first assigned his brand-new major general to the command of the Department of Annapolis. Then, after only a few months, the president reassigned him to the command of the Department of the Shenandoah. There, in October 1861, Banks assumed command of the Army of the Shenandoah. This army, which at the time was located in the vicinity of Frederick, Maryland, consisted mostly of poorly trained, unruly, and demoralized volunteer troops who had enlisted for terms as short as ninety days. With much effort and with the guidance and advice of General in Chief George McClellan, by the spring of 1862 Banks had made his little Shenandoah Valley army into a credible organization. More important, showing himself to be good at recruiting, he had successfully reenlisted or replaced most of his short-term volunteers with men who had signed up for three-year tours.

As a field commander Banks deliberately avoided agitating the local populace; instead, he took rather the opposite position. He began working with the resident leadership near Frederick in a successful attempt to install in positions of power local moderates who supported the Union government. Banks's attitude toward the South was one common among Northerners early in the war: that the citizens of the Southern states were errant compeers who were misled by a few rabid secessionists and that these citizens needed to be shown the way back to the fold firmly but gently. Throughout the war Banks's idea for ending secession was to arrange for Union supporters to take power in secessionist areas. As he explained his actions in Maryland, "The secession leaders . . . were replaced and loyal men assigned to . . . their duties. This made Maryland a loyal State. . . . What occurred there will occur in North Carolina, in South Carolina, in Georgia, in Alabama and Mississippi. If . . . those States shall be controlled by men that are loyal . . . we shall then have loyal populations and loyal governments."[14] Banks's attitude toward the seceded states was not much different from that of General McClellan, but unlike McClellan Banks never presumed to tell the president how to set policy.[15] Lincoln rather liked this calm and noncontroversial aspect of his general. He especially appreciated Banks's moderate political position, which was in sharp distinction to the positions of two of his other generals with whom he had problems and disagreements, Frémont and Butler.[16]

From the beginning of his military career Banks was consistently opposed to unauthorized foraging by his troops. He believed that such action hurt Unionists as well as secessionists, that it increased the antagonism of the local population toward the Union, and that it would complicate the reconstruction of the Union after the war was won. He also maintained that foraging promoted straggling, and vice versa. These common evils he sought to eradicate.[17] However, his efforts to end unauthorized foraging, with its attendant looting and destruction, were mostly ineffective. The men under his command developed a reputation for being as efficient and thorough a group of foragers as any in the Union armies.

Early in 1862 Lincoln removed McClellan from his position as general in chief of the Union armies. In consequence, Banks was no longer under McClellan, and the political general assumed his first independent command. Banks wanted very much to succeed in this command, but it was not to be. In his first field campaign he had the misfortune to be pitted against one of the true masters of the art of war, Maj. Gen. Thomas J. "Stonewall" Jackson. Banks soon found himself on the losing end of Jackson's famous Valley campaign. Before this campaign Banks, complacent and overconfident, wrote the secretary of war that there was "nothing more to be done by us in the valley."[18] Rarely has a general been so wrong.

Having sent Brig. Gen. James Shields's division of about 9,000 troops east, as ordered, to join Maj. Gen. Irvin McDowell's force near Washington, Banks remained in the valley with approximately 6,000 men at Strasburg plus another 2,500 strung out along the Manassas Gap Railroad east of Strasburg. Some 1,000 of these troops were stationed at Front Royal. The latter force was soon attacked by Jackson, who had been reinforced by Maj. Gen. Richard Ewell's division and now commanded 16,000 to 17,000 troops.[19] Jackson attacked at Front Royal, along the route of Banks's retreat from Strasburg, and at Winchester. In each engagement Banks was soundly defeated. He suffered roughly 2,800 casualties in the early part of the Valley campaign and abandoned hundreds of wagonloads of supplies to the enemy. Despite these losses, Banks saw his retreat into Maryland as a great military maneuver. He wrote his wife, "Whatever may be said of our recent movement I can assure you that it is one of the most remarkable that has occurred or will occur during the war. It is miraculous almost that my entire command and its train should escape without harm the long matured plans of an enemy five times our number."[20]

During this campaign Banks showed no natural affinity for military command. Furthermore, as has been pointed out by his biographers,[21] his subsequent military actions show that he failed to learn from the mistakes he made in the Shenandoah Valley in 1862. In addition, he exhibited two major weaknesses that would plague him throughout his military career. First, he tended to burden his marches with nonessential supplies, which required a large wagon train. In the valley his train became a major source of supplies for Jackson, and during this campaign Banks earned the title by which he was known in Virginia and other parts of the South: "Commissary" Banks. Second, and more important, he showed a lack of tactical insight and imagination. He could not conceive of the enemy doing anything other than what he expected. He seemed unable to allow for contingencies and was repeatedly caught by surprise.

In the summer of 1862 Banks again ran into Jackson, this time at Cedar Mountain. There he fought a battle that turned out to be a preliminary round of the Second Battle of Bull Run. Unlike his fights in the Shenandoah, however, Banks fought rather well against a numerically superior foe even though he was defeated in this engagement. Jackson, whose 24,000 troops were in the process of moving north from Gordonsville when they encountered the Federals, ultimately was able to engage about 15,000 to Banks's 9,000.[22] Fortunately for Banks, as Jackson's men arrived on the field, he threw them piecemeal into the fray, and the Northern commander was successful in countering these thrusts for much of the fight. During the battle Banks ordered a stirring attack that, for a while, kept the outcome in doubt. Unfortunately, he did not follow this attack with additional force, and the attackers were driven back with heavy losses. Banks then ordered several uncoordinated advances, all of which were roughly handled by the Confederates.

As a result of his performance at Cedar Mountain, Banks was generally praised in the Northern press. Furthermore, during the battle, as always, he was personally brave. He was said to be "as cool and calm as when in the Speaker's chair, while shells or bullets were whizzing around him."[23] According to one of his aids, Jackson always expressed respect for Banks as a military leader, saying at one point, "I think General Banks a better officer than his people think he is. I always found he fought well."[24] Whether Jackson actually said this or not, Banks's record was not totally negative by the end of the second summer of the war. He had gained some respect at Cedar Mountain and had finally earned the right to feel rather good about his performance as a general.

2 A NEW COMMANDER IN LOUISIANA

Toward the end of the Battle of Cedar Mountain, after most of the fighting had ended but while the armies were still partially engaged, Banks was injured when he, Maj. Gen. John Pope, and several other Union officers were charged by Confederate cavalry. In the confusion produced by the enemy charge Banks was struck by a horse and knocked to the ground. He quickly got to his feet, mounted his horse, and escaped, but he was in considerable pain.[1] He returned to Washington to recuperate and to take charge of the defense of the city during McClellan's Antietam campaign.[2] However, he was not given much time to rest. Despite Banks's demonstrated limits of military capacity, the president had a need for his woebegone general. Banks was still quite powerful in national politics and had many friends in Washington. He could not be ignored. Thus, the president decided to substitute the politically moderate and relatively obedient Banks for one of the thorns in his side, Banks's opponent in the Massachusetts gubernatorial campaign of 1859, Benjamin F. Butler. Butler had been serving as commander of the Department of the Gulf since his forces had occupied New Orleans on May 1, 1862, following Capt. David G. Farragut's capture of the city. However, as the department commander, Butler was not making the progress that Lincoln thought he should in addressing the problem of opening the Mississippi River. Sending Banks to try in Butler's stead seemed a good idea.

By the end of the summer of 1862 Lincoln had decided to replace both the troublesome Butler and the dilatory McClellan. Because he did not want to disrupt the Federal elections then in progress, he waited until after election day, November 4, to announce his new assignments. On November 8, 1862, Banks was "assigned to the command of the Department of the Gulf, including the State of Texas."[3] The next day Lincoln's general in chief, Maj. Gen. Henry Wager Halleck, sent Banks specific orders regarding his new assignment. These orders called for Banks to "proceed . . . to New Orleans and relieve Major-General Butler." Once in New Orleans the new commander, with the cooperation of Rear Admiral Farragut, was to concentrate on "the opening of the Mississippi and the reduction of Fort Morgan or Mobile City." Halleck added, "The President regards the opening of the Mississippi River as the first and most important of all our military and naval operations, and it is hoped that you will not lose a moment in accomplishing it." Halleck also told Banks that "as the ranking general in the southwest . . . you will exercise superior authority as far north as you may ascend the river."[4] Thus, the door was open for Banks to become the dominant general in the west and, perhaps, in the entire Union army.

After stating these instructions from the president, Halleck went on to suggest additional military activities that Banks could conduct following the opening of the Mississippi. He suggested "two objects . . . as worthy of your attention." The field commander should first consider moving east from Vicksburg to "cut off all connection by rail between Northern Mississippi and Mobile and Atlanta," and second, to "ascend with a naval and military force the Red river as far as it is navigable, and thus open an outlet for the sugar and cotton of northern Louisiana." Halleck added, for the first but not the last time, his belief that the Red River "would form the best base for operations in Texas." He closed with the reasonable admonition that "you must necessarily exercise your own judgment and discretion in regard to your movements against the enemy. . . . The Government has unlimited confidence not only in your judgment and discretion, but also in your energy and military promptness."[5]

As news of Banks's new assignment surfaced, the cotton lobbyists concluded that Lincoln was responding to their recommendations for an invasion of Texas. They hailed this decision as a bright new day in the economy of the New England textile industry and, of course, of themselves. The speculators prepared to lay siege to the cotton lands of Texas. Meanwhile, Banks's true destination was kept a secret. Neither the governors of the states that were expected to supply troops for Banks's army nor the secretary of the navy, who was to assist in the movement of these troops, was told his destination. Secretary of War Edwin M. Stanton actively contributed to the subterfuge by writing to the governors of the New England states and New York, telling them only that "General Banks has established his headquarters in New York to organize a Southern expedition." He called upon these governors to assist by providing troops for Banks and asked them to "answer his requisition, and render him every aid in [their] power in speedily organizing his command."[6] Nominally this secrecy was maintained in order to confuse the enemy, but it also served to retain the cotton lobby as a source of support for the expedition.

With his usual attention to politics, and with an eye to furthering the impression that Banks's objective was the state of Texas, the president decided to appoint a military governor of Texas to travel with Banks. His choice was one of the most active of the lobbyists for an invasion of Texas, an avid supporter of former Texas president and governor Sam Houston, former U.S. representative and Texas state senator Andrew Jackson "Colossal Jack" Hamilton. For good measure, Hamilton was also appointed brigadier general.[7] On November 16 Secretary of War Stanton notified Banks of Hamilton's appointment, stating in his instructions to Banks that Hamilton had "orders to report to and be subject to your direction." Banks did not like Hamilton, who was closely affiliated with the cotton speculators. In his opinion, Hamilton's whole staff was "organized in New York especially for plunder."[8] Nevertheless, Hamilton and his entourage were now part of the expedition, and Banks accommodated them to the extent he felt he must.

According to the orders he had received from Halleck, Banks was to bring reinforcements with him to the Gulf, including the "troops assembling in transports at Fort Monroe." The troops at Fort Monroe, under the command of Brig. Gen. William Hemsley Emory, were veterans of McClellan's Peninsula campaign. Additional reinforcements were to come from recruiting efforts in New York and elsewhere in the east. Recruiting was something Banks did well, and he began devoting himself to these efforts. As a result he left many of the details involved in the preparation of his expedition to others. It was perhaps this distraction of his attention that led to Requisition No. 40.

Like most of the generals on both sides of the war, Banks frequently complained of being short of men, muskets, artillery, ammunition, wagons, shoes, and other equipment, and he routinely requested more of everything from army headquarters. Having accepted the appointment as commander of the Gulf Department, he almost immediately submitted Requisition No. 40. This document requested from the quartermaster general a vast supply of equipment, including one thousand wagons, for use by his army. When Lincoln learned of this requisition, he replied November 22, 1862, with perhaps feigned astonishment:

> I have just been overwhelmed and confounded with the sight of a requisition made by you, which, I am assured, can not be filled, and got off within an hour short of two months! . . . My dear General, this expanding, and piling up of *impedimenta,* has been, so far, almost our ruin, and will be our final ruin if it is not abandoned. You would be better off any where, and especially where you are going, for not having a thousand wagons, doing nothing but hauling forage to feed the animals that draw them, and taking at least two thousand men to

> care for the wagons and animals. . . . The simple publication of this requisition would ruin you.[9]

Lincoln's warning was prophetic, but in his usual diplomatic manner the president left Banks a way out of the imbroglio by including the statement, "I inclose you a copy of the requisition, in some hope that it is not genuine—that you have never seen it." Lincoln knew his man, and Banks seized upon this excuse. By the time he received Lincoln's missive, Banks had already received a scolding from General Halleck for this same requisition. Halleck had included words similar to Lincoln's regarding the delay inherent in awaiting the accumulation of the supplies requested. From the Astor House in New York City, Banks replied to Halleck, promising that "we shall wait for nothing that is not absolutely necessary, according to your dispatch. I fully share your impatience, and will spare no exertions to get off at the earliest possible moment."[10] To the remonstrance from Lincoln he replied contritely two days later, "I never contemplated waiting supplies referred to in requisition No. 40 one moment. It was drawn up by an officer who did not fully comprehend my instructions, and inadvertently approved by me without sufficient examination and proper explanation."[11] No more was said about Banks's requisition, despite the clear admission of command failure. However, it seemed to be a premonition of actions to follow, and whether a mistake or not, it remained on his record as one more slip of this amateur general.

As the weeks went by, Banks continued to devote himself to recruiting. Unfortunately, he also continued to pay scant attention to his other duties. His inattention possibly contributed to the acquisition of an extraordinary group of vessels by which he intended to transport his new troops and supplies to Louisiana. On Banks's behalf, Cornelius Vanderbilt and others took charge of chartering the vessels. These gentlemen began actively seeking anything that would float. Banks's agents had no minimum standards for the boats, and most of the charters were approved without Banks's personal examination. Many of the boats were rotten and leaky. Furthermore, in some cases arrangements were made that apparently involved kickbacks and other unauthorized exchanges of government money. The resulting collection of floating hardware was not one to inspire confidence in the commanding general.[12]

Fifty charters were arranged in support of Banks's move to Louisiana. Despite the age and condition of the boats, troops and supplies were wedged tightly aboard all of the transports. For example, one of the boats was the *J. Morton,* originally a passenger liner. In civilian service, as a safety precaution, the liner had been limited to 1,632 passengers. Under Banks's purview it was used to carry 4,550 soldiers to Louisiana. Even such crowding was not enough to carry all of the recruits Banks had gathered, so some of the troops had to be left behind and brought later to Louisiana. Fortunately, the old boats somehow held together and made the trip to New Orleans.

To the public and to the cotton speculators, Banks seemed to be gathering his force for the long-awaited invasion of Texas. After all, Banks was from Massachusetts, where the economic pain from the cotton shortage was severe. The new recruits, along with immense quantities of supplies, were being assembled and loaded aboard the transport vessels as though Banks were preparing for an extended expedition into enemy territory. And the newly appointed military governor of Texas was accompanying the general. The obvious conclusion was that their destination must be Texas. This popular belief led to a significant number of cotton speculators squeezing onto the overcrowded transports along with the troops and supplies.

After an elaborate farewell banquet hosted by the New York Chamber of Commerce, the former Massachusetts politico and the military governor of Texas departed New York for the Gulf of Mexico aboard the steamer *North Star* on December 4, 1862. In addition to Governor Hamilton and a small number of staff officers, Banks carried with him a burden of avaricious, cotton-hungry hangers-on. He was on his way to gain military victories, and cotton, for the Union, and coincidentally to gain a bright political future for Mr. Banks.

Entering the Mississippi in the early morning of December 14 after an uneventful voyage, Banks sat with Lt. Col. David Strother of his staff watching the shoreline move slowly past. Banks must have been in a reflective mood because Strother reported that the general began discussing his plans for the upcoming campaign. In this discussion Banks revealed his continuing commitment to the idea that if Union supporters were placed in power in the South, the population would once again be loyal to the government. According to Strother, Banks stated the opinion that "the great moral motive of the expedition was the reunionizing of Louisiana by getting up a counter current of popular feeling against the Secession party." The idea of Yankee colonization of the South must also have been on the general's mind. As the steamer moved past sugar plantations and orange groves, the soldiers on board responded with "bursts of admiration," in response to which Banks "smiled and observed, 'Thus it is that we will possess and regenerate the country. Half of these fellows, who see this blooming land for the first time will never willingly return to their bleak and sterile homes in New England.'"[13]

The *North Star* tied up next to New Orleans' French Quarter about sunset December 14. Banks and some of his staff went ashore to pay their respects to General Butler and to set up residence at the St. Charles Hotel.[14] The duty of informing Major General Butler of the change in command was executed the next day, and the change-of-command ceremony was conducted on the morning of December 16. Formal orders announcing Banks's assumption of the command of the department were issued December 17. For some time there had been rumors of a change of command in New Orleans, and on August 2, 1862, Butler had informed his wife that "they have an absurd story here that Banks is to be sent down here to take my place. I wish to heaven he would come!"[15] Butler got his wish.

Banks, secure in Union-controlled New Orleans, was faced with a myriad of problems. As he described it, he had fewer than 30,000 men, many of whom were raw, nine-month enlistees. "The military positions held by our forces extended from the Floridas to Western Texas, . . . were strongly garrisoned, and threatened constantly with attack by the enemy."[16] To his north Banks found a strong Confederate force located near Baton Rouge. This force, along with the garrison at Vicksburg, effectively blocked his communications with Maj. Gen. Ulysses S. Grant, who was then positioned north of Vicksburg. Thus, Banks was unable to learn of the activities of the Union forces upriver in a timely manner. To his west Banks found a collection of opponents arrayed from the Mississippi to the Rio Grande. He was informed that there were some 8,000 enemy troops in Arkansas, 14,000 in western Louisiana, 7,000 in Texas, and an additional 4,000 in the Indian Territory.[17] Given the geographical extent of his department, it would be difficult to concentrate his forces against any one part of this array of opponents without opening opportunities for others to retake at least some Union positions.

There were not just problems with short-term enlistments and a wide dispersal of forces in the department, however. Banks also inherited a hostile civilian population that had suffered from his predecessor's rule. Banks described the Butler administration to Halleck as "an immense military government, embracing every form of civil administration, . . . in addition to the ordinary affairs of a military department."[18] To his wife Banks added, "Everybody connected with the government has been employed in stealing other people's property."[19] In addition to finding himself inheriting the indignation of the local civilians, Banks was faced with a large number of irate foreigners. Many consuls and naval officers of foreign governments had been insulted and repressed by Butler and were vocal with their complaints. The fact that much of this repression was associated with pro-Confederate activities on the part of certain consuls did not lessen the complaints.

As he had done in Maryland, Banks adopted a liberal and conciliatory policy toward the local citizens in Louisiana. Although he was firm with obvious secessionists, he attempted to accommodate those civilians he considered open to loyalist views. He repealed an order issued by General Butler closing churches whose pastors refused to pray for President Lincoln, and he freed some 120 political prisoners incarcerated by his predecessor. He announced he would investigate illegal seizures of property and other questionable actions perpetrated by Butler and his officials on the local citizens, and he instituted price controls on bread. He continued Butler's policy of providing government employment for the poor on public works. He made himself available to the local people to hear complaints and requests for favors. He offered assistance to loyal citizens but was unsympathetic to people he considered disloyal. He suppressed the publication of several secessionist newspapers in New Orleans and subsidized others that were sympathetic to his policies, including the *Era,* the *Times,* and the *Daily True Delta.*[20]

Banks was not opposed to trading with the local planters since part of his idea for regaining the loyalty of the citizenry was to show the economic advantages of returning to the Union. However, he wanted all such trade to be conducted under government control. Thus, Banks allowed cotton and other produce to be brought into New Orleans for sale but announced early in his tenure that he would not tolerate unauthorized trade in cotton.[21] He consistently attempted to bar private merchants from tagging along on military marches. As far as he was concerned, the army would handle whatever cotton was found. The local traders, however, being used to dealing lavishly with General Butler, sought to continue their lucrative activities. On January 16, 1863, a local citizen brought a contract to Banks that confirmed certain arrangements that had been negotiated with General Butler. The contract was reportedly signed by James Seddon, Confederate secretary of war. It called for the implementation of an exchange rate of one bale of cotton for sixteen sacks of salt. The "citizen offered General Banks a hundred thousand dollars if he would enter into the contract."[22] Banks refused and shortly thereafter reported to his wife, "I thank God every night that I have no desire for dishonest gain. I had one hundred thousand dollars offered me the other day to allow the people to 'continue' the commercial enterprises, but it was no temptation for me."[23]

As commander of the Gulf Department Banks came face-to-face with the issue of the use of black troops in the Union army. Butler had been a major force for the incorporation of both free blacks and former slaves into the army and had recruited several black regiments.[24] Although he delayed action on the matter until May 1, 1863, at that time Banks proposed the addition of three divisions of black soldiers to the Army of the Gulf and formed the Corps d'Afrique as their functional unit.[25] Ultimately Banks incorporated some 10,000 black soldiers into the Army of the Gulf, more than in any other Union department. He made use of these troops in combat on several occasions. However, he discontinued Butler's policy of commissioning black officers in the regiments he raised and drove almost all of those already appointed to resign.[26]

Banks's appointment to the Gulf Department preceded the effective date of Lincoln's Emancipation Proclamation, January 1, 1863, by less than two weeks. The president's proclamation specifically exempted from its terms the slaves located in the area of Federal control in Louisiana. As a result, the status of the large number of fugitives who had taken refuge near the army camps around New Orleans was uncertain. Banks resolved this problem by issuing General Orders No. 12, which established a Sequestration Commission to "establish a yearly system of negro labor."[27] The resulting labor system called for ex-slaves not inducted into the Union army to work on plantations in the Union-controlled areas of Louisiana or on public works. Wages and conditions of employment for both men and women were specified. Although this labor system was heavily criticized by radicals and others, Banks was quite proud of it. One student of the era has termed it "one of the most comprehensive attempts made during the war to solve the problems created by the sudden destruction of slavery."[28]

Consistent with his enjoyment of an active social life, and with his objective of using positive measures to influence the local population, Banks soon began to invite the ladies and gentlemen of New Orleans to dances, concerts, and receptions hosted by him and his wife. Among the other participants, cotton speculators were often conspicuously present at the Banks's soirées. As a result of these activities Banks was called by some of his detractors the "dancing master" and was accused of trying to "dance the fair creoles to loyalty."[29] Such criticism did not sway him, however, because he was convinced that by concession and example New Orleans would become a Union city, and Louisiana a Union state. He wanted to institute a reconstruction program in Louisiana that would be a model for all of the Southern states.

Politically, Banks aligned himself with the moderate Union faction in New Orleans. This faction was headed by Georg Michael Decker Hahn, a local labor politician.[30] The resulting Banks-Hahn political machine quickly grew in power and influence. Banks soon discovered that his measures for restoring loyalty to the Union were opposed by certain civilian and military administrators. These included many of the Treasury Department officials appointed by the radical secretary Salmon P. Chase. However, Treasury opposition was relatively minor compared with that of Brig. Gen. George F. Shepley, the military governor of Louisiana whom Banks had inherited from his predecessor.[31] The politically sensitive Banks believed that despite his own appointment as department commander, Lincoln continued to support Shepley as the political leader of the state. Banks felt constrained not to interfere with the civilian administration that had been constructed prior to his arrival. As a result he concluded that he would have to wait for a more propitious opportunity to implement a civilian program for Louisiana.[32]

THE FIRST INVASION

Galveston

3 The city of New Orleans was occupied by Union forces early in the second year of the war. The feat of capturing the South's most populous city was accomplished by a Southern naval officer who was chosen for the task only after much discussion within the Navy Department about his allegiance to the Union and his capacity for high command. The flag officer selected to lead the expedition was Capt. David Glasgow Farragut. Farragut proved to be a brilliant choice. The new flag officer carefully laid his plans, acquired needed ships and equipment, and prepared his fleet. Then, following an extensive bombardment, with nerves of steel he steamed upstream past the enemy forts located below the city, leaving them occupied by defiant Confederate garrisons, and proceeded to accept the surrender of the city on April 25, 1862. Farragut then moved upstream to Vicksburg, capturing Baton Rouge en route.[1]

Subsequent to these successes along the lower Mississippi, and following Farragut's return to New Orleans, the Confederates fortified a new position on the left bank of the Mississippi upstream from Baton Rouge called Port Hudson. Farragut was hopeful of mounting a combined land and sea operation to destroy this new stronghold. However, when he approached General Butler with this idea, the latter declared that he would be unable to provide assistance. Butler also demurred when Farragut raised the issue of reinforcing a Union naval force that was located at Galveston. Then, in the midst of these discussions, General Banks took command of the Gulf Department and Butler left New Orleans. Banks brought with him a letter from Lincoln introducing him to Farragut and requesting the admiral's cooperation in opening the Mississippi.[2]

Banks and Farragut seemed to get off to a good start. In the fall of 1862 the Confederates had retaken portions of Baton Rouge from the occupying Union forces, and even before he had formally assumed command, Banks took action to change this situation. With Farragut's assistance and concurrence Banks ordered Brig. Gen. Cuvier Grover to use all the troops that were in condition for service to reoccupy the Louisiana capital. On the morning of December 16 Grover, with about 4,500 men, ascended the river on transports, escorted by a portion of Farragut's fleet. The next day, upon the approach of the Union force, the small Confederate garrison at Baton Rouge departed and the city once again came under Union occupation, this time for the duration of the war. Farragut liked the aggressiveness exhibited by Banks in this undertaking. However, the admiral considered the general a bit naive, claiming, "General Banks talks of being at Vicksburg in a fortnight, but of course he does not know the difficulties to be encountered."[3]

Following this success at Baton Rouge, Farragut decided to approach the new department commander regarding the possibility of sending reinforcements to Galveston. The Union navy had been attempting to blockade the port of Galveston since July 1861, but to little effect. In October 1862, in an effort to reduce the rampant blockade running along the Texas coast, Farragut sent a flotilla to capture the city of Galveston. This naval force was placed under the direction of Cdr. William B. Renshaw. Renshaw's flagship was the gunboat *Westfield.* Three other gunboats—*Harriet Lane, Clifton,* and *Owasco*—were included in Renshaw's small fleet along with the *Henry James,* one of the mortar schooners used in the capture of New Orleans. With little opposition these boats entered Galveston Bay and tied up along the Galveston wharves. Renshaw did not actually occupy the city, however. The commander soon discovered that although his men could control the dock without any problem, he had insufficient force to control the city, especially at night. As a result, at night the sailors would withdraw to the waterfront and leave the city to the Confederates.[4] There the situation rested until late December.

Banks responded positively to Farragut's proposal for the army to reinforce the navy garrison at Galveston. After all, by sending a small force to Galveston, he could assuage some of the cotton fever that had surrounded him since his appointment, and perhaps a simple victory at Galveston would open some military opportunities in the state of Texas. A. J. Hamilton, the military governor of Texas, also pressured Banks to support an operation against Galveston. Thus, a plan was formulated to send infantry reinforcements to Renshaw to complete the occupation of the city of Galveston and to expand the sphere of Federal influence into the surrounding area. Banks also hoped that Hamilton, who along with a number of other Texas refugees was to accompany the expedition, could recruit both Union soldiers and Unionist support in the state and thereby further enlarge the Union position.[5]

To begin this, his first invasion of Texas, Banks ordered a force of some 260 men, consisting of Companies D, G, and I of the 42nd Massachusetts, under the command of Col. Isaac S. Burrell, to proceed at once to Galveston.

These troops were new recruits who had just arrived from New York aboard the transport *Saxon.*[6] They were sent to Texas after having spent only four days in Louisiana. The 2nd Vermont Battery was sent along to provide artillery support. An additional force, consisting of Texas Cavalry (Union) Troops A and B, along with the artillery horses of the 2nd Vermont, was to follow in a few days aboard the transport *Cambria.*

The first contingent of Banks's troops arrived at Galveston December 24. Instead of disembarking on Pelican Island, as Renshaw had originally suggested and as Burrell preferred, at the commander's request they went ashore at Kuhn's Wharf, at the north end of 18th Street.[7] Even with these reinforcements, however, the Union troops were still too few in number to take possession of the town. According to Burrell, "During the day we control the city, but at night, owing to our small force (as the balance of my regiment has not yet arrived), I am obliged to draw in the pickets to the wharf on which we are quartered."[8] Although the situation at first appeared stable, there were rumors of an imminent Confederate attack, and in response Burrell did what he could to establish a good defensive position. A barricade was constructed on the wharf at the shore end, in part by taking up planks from the decking of the wharf. This barricade not only improved the defensive line but left behind the equivalent of a moat.

Maj. Gen. John Bankhead Magruder, a career officer who had had both grand and not-so-grand moments in his military life, was in command of the Confederate forces in Texas.[9] A probable alcoholic who spoke with a lisp, Magruder was fond of theatrical productions and of flashy uniforms. He was known as "Prince" John, in part because of his taste in the latter. Flashy uniform or not, when Magruder was at his best, he was a brave and competent commander. Unfortunately, while serving under Robert E. Lee during the Seven Days Battles around Richmond, Magruder showed his less professional side. Poor performance by Prince John, possibly caused by excessive drinking during this period, led Lee to reject Magruder as a commander in his Army of Northern Virginia. Magruder was banished to Texas. However, it was a banishment somewhat to the liking of the flamboyant general. Instead of having to live down his performance while remaining under Lee, in Texas Magruder was hailed as a savior and a hero.

Once in command in Texas, Magruder believed his first duty was to break the incomplete Federal hold on Galveston. He began planning a combined land and sea attack against the Federal occupation force. For this undertaking Magruder scraped together the brigade of Brig. Gen. Henry Hopkins Sibley, which had been re-recruited to near full strength following its return from New Mexico; a regiment of heavy artillery; and a light artillery battery. In addition he had a naval force consisting of two steamboats, *Bayou City* and *Neptune,* plus two tenders, *Lucy Gwinn* and *John F. Carr.* The steamboats had been converted to cottonclad gunboats under the direction of Leon Smith, a volunteer aide to Magruder who was given the honorary title of major or commodore, depending on whether he was ashore or afloat.[10]

A railroad bridge connected Galveston Island with the mainland. Planks had been laid over the ties to facilitate crossing by animals and wagons.[11] The Federals had made no attempt to destroy this bridge. On the contrary, Commander Renshaw allowed supplies from the mainland to be brought over the bridge to prevent undue suffering among the civilians on the island, and he wanted to keep the bridge available to use in the future when Union forces occupied the surrounding area. This decision turned out to be a mistake. In the early morning hours of January 1, 1863, Magruder led his ground force across the railroad bridge and into the city of Galveston. At the same time Magruder's two cottonclad steamers, under the command of Leon Smith and loaded with dismounted Texas cavalrymen under Col. Thomas Green, descended Buffalo Bayou and took a position in the upper part of Galveston Bay. The Texas cavalrymen had volunteered for the mission and afterward were fondly referred to as "Horse Marines." Green, who was a veteran of the Texas Revolution and had commanded the Southern forces in their victory at Valverde in New Mexico, was aboard the *Bayou City* while Col. Arthur Bagby of the 7th Texas Mounted Volunteers commanded the troops aboard the *Neptune.* The boats were to advance when the men aboard heard the sound of artillery, indicating that the ground attack had begun.

Just after 4:00 A.M. Magruder's land attack got under way with the firing of batteries stationed at several points along the waterfront. The Southern infantry then opened with muskets on the barricaded troops as well as on the gunboats anchored just off the wharf. The firing was heavy on both sides as the Union gunboats answered the Southern attack. Burrell was forced to instruct his troops to stay behind cover and fire only when necessary because the supply of ammunition available on the wharf was limited. As dawn approached, the navy gunners were finally able to see their targets and their aim improved. Under this heavy enemy fire Magruder began pulling his troops back in preparation for a retreat.[12] With conditions apparently improving for the Federals, Renshaw tried to move the *Westfield* close to land to get a better field of fire. Unfortunately for the Union forces, in doing so he ran aground.

The commander's attention was thus diverted to the task of attempting to free the flagship, which was now unable to assist the troops on the wharf.

Hearing firing from the island, Leon Smith led his cottonclads forward. The boats were heavily loaded and difficult to steer. Moving slowly across the bay, they arrived near the wharf at dawn. As they approached the Federal fleet, both boats made straight for the nearest Union target, the *Harriet Lane.* Seeing the approaching enemy, Cdr. Jonathan Wainwright, in command of the *Harriet Lane,* attempted to get his boat under way. Before the boat could move, however, it was rammed by the *Neptune.* The collision was fatal to the little cottonclad, which backed off and sank. The deck remained above water, however, and the Texas troopers aboard fired briskly from behind the cotton bales. Although the *Harriet Lane* was not damaged by the collision, its officers and crew were distracted by the impact as well as by the musket fire from the Confederate boats. *Bayou City,* following close behind *Neptune,* was able to take careful aim at the wheelhouse of the Federal gunboat and struck it under full power. The two vessels became locked together, and the Texans boarded the Union vessel. Commander Wainwright was killed, and his second in command, Lt. Edward Lea, was mortally wounded. The survivors soon surrendered.[13]

After the *Harriet Lane* was captured, Capt. Henry S. Lubbock, brother of Texas governor Francis R. Lubbock and commander of the *Bayou City,* went aboard the *Clifton* under a white flag. Addressing the commanding officer of the *Clifton,* Lt. Cdr. Richard Law, Lubbock demanded the surrender of the entire Federal fleet. In the face of this demand Law requested a truce and, being granted three hours by Lubbock, went to consult with Commander Renshaw. Renshaw, who had observed the surrender of the *Harriet Lane,* had by this time decided to destroy his flagship to prevent its capture by the enemy. Renshaw ordered Law to take the remainder of the fleet to safety outside the bay and, transferring his crew to the steamers *Mary Boardman* and *Saxon,* prepared to burn his flagship. Unfortunately, the fuse he used to ignite the gunpowder and turpentine that had been spread aboard the *Westfield* did not work as intended. The boat exploded shortly after eight o'clock, before Renshaw and the four men aboard the gig that was to carry them to safety could pull away. All were killed.

Law assumed command of the Union naval forces and, in response to Renshaw's order, led the remaining Union vessels, still flying flags of truce, to safety outside the harbor.[14] Without support from the navy Burrell was forced to surrender. Magruder's attack was thus completely successful, and the Confederates regained control of both the wharf and Galveston Bay. In addition, the attack resulted in the capture of the gunboat *Harriet Lane* and several small craft, the destruction of the *Westfield,* the death of the Union naval commander, and the capture of all Union forces and supplies ashore. Magruder reported 26 men killed and 117 wounded. For their roles in the victory at Galveston both John B. Magruder and Thomas Green received the thanks of the Confederate Congress.[15] On January 2, after the fighting was over, the second contingent of Banks's troops arrived offshore. The Confederates attempted to entice the *Cambria* into Galveston Bay, where they hoped to capture her, but they were unsuccessful.[16] After two days of fighting wind and high seas, the *Cambria* returned to New Orleans.

When he learned of the result of Magruder's attack on his fleet at Galveston, Farragut was incensed. He sent Commodore Henry H. Bell to the Texas coast to reestablish the blockade. Following his signal victory, Magruder began to bolster Galveston's defenses by stationing infantry in the city and by emplacing several large guns in strategic locations. This work had not progressed far by the time Bell arrived offshore, and the commodore made plans to recapture the city. Then, unfortunately for Bell, shortly after noon on January 11 the notorious Confederate cruiser *Alabama,* under Capt. Raphael Semmes, approached Galveston Island. Spotting the strange sail, and assuming it was a blockade runner, Commodore Bell sent the *Hatteras* in chase. After drawing the *Hatteras* away from the Federal fleet, Semmes turned on his pursuer and sank her. This incident gave Magruder time to complete his fortifications, which effectively ended the opportunity for the Union navy to recapture the city. Galveston remained under Confederate control for the duration of the war, serving as a haven for blockade runners and a source of much-needed goods for the Confederacy.

Banks was undeterred by the loss of his troops at Galveston and proceeded to offer several excuses for the defeat. In a message to Halleck he wrote that sending the army detachment to reinforce Renshaw was the idea of Admiral Farragut, who misinformed him by telling him the occupation was "perfectly secure." Furthermore, such an expedition had already been contemplated by General Butler to assist in recruiting Texas Unionists. Besides, he would not have sent the detachment to Texas at all except for the importunity of Governor Hamilton and his friends, men who were along for "base, speculative purposes and nothing else."[17] Clearly, Banks was not responsible for the defeat.

In the midst of all this activity Banks reorganized his forces in the Department of the Gulf with an order dated January 5, 1863, but retroactive to December 14, 1862. Under this order the XIX Army Corps was formed, consisting of all the forces in the department. The corps was organized into four Divisions: 1st Division, commanded by Brig. Gen. Christopher C. Augur; 2nd Division, Brig. Gen. Thomas W. Sherman; 3rd Division, Brig. Gen. William H. Emory; and 4th Division, Brig. Gen. Cuvier Grover.

At the time Banks arrived in New Orleans, the Confederate army in western Louisiana had in its possession a gunboat, the *Cotton,* that was well armed and partially clad in railroad iron. This gunboat was considered by knowledgeable Union officers to be a major threat to potential Union advances west of the city.[18] A raid up Bayou Teche for the purpose of destroying this gunboat had been planned by twenty-seven-year-old Brig. Gen. Godfrey Weitzel before Banks arrived in New Orleans. Weitzel was a brilliant young officer who had graduated second in his class at West Point in 1855. After the war began Lieutenant Weitzel served as General Butler's chief engineer. Butler, who was fond of Weitzel and who may have invited his subordinate to participate in some of the shady but highly profitable transactions the general undertook in New Orleans, recommended Weitzel's promotion to brigadier general. Soon after the promotion was granted, Butler appointed his new brigadier acting mayor of occupied New Orleans.[19]

Shortly after assuming command of the Gulf Department, Banks consented to Weitzel's plan to destroy the *Cotton.* Assembling his troops and equipment, Weitzel crossed Berwick Bay January 13, 1863, in concert with four of Admiral Farragut's gunboats. The following morning he marched up Bayou Teche in company with the gunboats. The joint force soon encountered the troops of Brig. Gen. Alfred Mouton along with the dreaded *Cotton.* Jean Jacques Alfred Alexandre Mouton was the son of former Louisiana governor and U.S. senator Alexander Mouton. General Mouton, for whom English was a second language learned only after he had reached adulthood, had graduated from West Point in 1850. He had resigned from the army in the downsizing that occurred after the Mexican War and returned to Louisiana, where he worked as a railroad engineer. He joined the Confederate army after Louisiana seceded and was wounded at Shiloh while leading the 18th Louisiana. Returning once again to his home state, Mouton was placed in command of the advance portion of the Confederate army west of New Orleans.[20]

Mouton and his gunboat met the Union force with heavy musket and cannon fire. Against this resistance, and with hard fighting, Weitzel advanced until, near dark, his infantry flanked the *Cotton.* The Confederate gunboat was disabled in the fighting, and that night Mouton ordered the *Cotton*'s crew to turn the boat sideways in the channel and set her afire to block the Union advance. The next morning General Weitzel, satisfied that he had achieved his objective, burned or carried away captured enemy supplies and returned to Berwick Bay. There he announced that "the Confederate States gunboat Cotton is one of the things that were."[21] Thus, Banks's military record in Louisiana, as opposed to that in Texas, continued to be positive.

Although Banks maintained his personal opposition to unnecessary foraging and destruction of civilian property, he was either unable or unwilling to stop such activity. As had been and would continue to be the case during Federal incursions into western Louisiana, unauthorized foraging, plus theft and destruction of private property by Union soldiers, was rampant throughout Weitzel's expedition. During their withdrawal Weitzel's troops looted and burned homes, barns, and most other structures that they encountered along the line of march. A Southern reaction to Weitzel's raid was published in the *Houston Tri-Weekly Telegraph,* where it was stated that "the enemy have retreated to Berwick Bay. . . . The red blaze of incendiarism, the smoldering ruins which mark their backward march, would seem to indicate that they are about to abandon this section and seek to leave cruel remembrances of their fanatical hate behind them."[22] The author of this article was wrong. Banks was just getting started in Acadiana.

A few weeks after the conclusion of Weitzel's successful raid up the Teche, Southern naval forces on the Mississippi destroyed the Union gunboat *Indianola.* Upon learning of the loss, Farragut decided to move upstream past Port Hudson to gain control of the stretch of river between that point and Vicksburg. To assist him in passing Port Hudson, he asked Banks to create a diversion. Banks agreed to do so, stating that Farragut's plan "would of necessity involve the cooperative movement of the land forces upon the rear of Port Hudson, while the Navy should be engaged in passing the enemy's batteries on the river."[23]

In this, the first campaign in Louisiana that the general was to lead in person, Banks marched north out of Baton Rouge March 13 with 12,000 men.[24] After a grueling march with his green troops he advanced to within a few miles of Port Hudson but failed to initiate any diversionary action. He believed he was heavily outnumbered by the enemy garrison, and his maps of the vicinity proved inaccurate. He was unable to find a route by which he could advance his artillery to a position from which it could fire upon the fort. In this failure he showed both a lack of reconnaissance skills and a lack of perseverance, as though he did not really want to support Farragut. Apparently frustrated by the position in which he found himself, and showing a bit of pique, Banks wrote to his wife, "I do not mean to lead my men to a fool's fight and a dog's death."[25] Then, at almost the same time that he was writing this letter to his wife, he sent a message to Farragut indicating that he would begin his diversion at midnight. Farragut's response upon receiving Banks's message is reputed to have been, "He had as well be in New Orleans or Baton Rouge for all the good he is doing us."[26]

Farragut, aboard the *Hartford,* which was lashed to the gunboat *Albatross,* advanced on schedule at 10:00 P.M. on the night of March 14 against a strong current and in a storm of artillery shells from the enemy batteries. Pressing relentlessly forward, he successfully passed Port Hudson before midnight. However, the remainder of his fleet was turned back. One vessel ran aground and had to be destroyed. The army offered no support during this action, and afterward Banks retreated, never having engaged the enemy.[27] As they left the vicinity of Port Hudson, the men of the Gulf army again demonstrated the continuing improvement of their marauding skills. According to one witness, the "soldiers plundered without restraint, keeping up a skirmishing fire all around on pigs, poultry, and cattle. . . . The discipline was very bad, mules and horses were taken everywhere, and some houses wantonly robbed."[28]

After his failure to engage the enemy at Port Hudson, Banks turned his attention, such as it was, to the opening of the Mississippi. Because the direct route from New Orleans to Vicksburg was still blocked by the Confederate garrison at Port Hudson, the general decided to try to bypass this position and open an alternative water route to the upper Mississippi. In this endeavor he elected to follow a plan proposed by General Weitzel.[29] At the time the Atchafalaya River was a distributary of the Mississippi, its headwaters being formed by the mixing of the flows of the Mississippi and Red rivers. By entering the Atchafalaya at the upper end of Grand Lake, Banks believed he could move upstream to the Red and thus into the Mississippi without having to pass Port Hudson. Access to Grand Lake could be via Berwick Bay and the lower Atchafalaya or from the Mississippi above Baton Rouge by way of Bayou Plaquemine and the Grand River. Banks claimed that the Atchafalaya route would enable the navy to cut the Confederate supply line along the Red River and would provide the army with a means for safe communication between New Orleans and the Union forces near Vicksburg.[30]

Although the concept of trying to bypass Port Hudson was militarily reasonable, Banks now had the misfortune to run into an old adversary. By moving into western Louisiana, he faced one of Stonewall Jackson's most outstanding subordinates in the Valley campaign of 1862, Maj. Gen. Richard Taylor.[31] The thirty-seven-year-old Taylor was the son of Mexican War hero and former president Zachary Taylor and erstwhile brother-in-law of Jefferson Davis. As a civilian before the war "Dick" Taylor was undisciplined, stubborn, independent, a bit erratic, and a dallier who liked to hobnob with aristocrats. Unfortunately for General Banks, however, he was also a natural leader and a quick learner. Following the Valley campaign Taylor continued to show superior military leadership and soon became second only to J. E. B. Stuart as the youngest major general then serving in the Confederate army. When Louisiana governor Thomas O. Moore requested from President Davis a general who could take command of the defense of Louisiana, Taylor, who was a prominent resident of that state, was an obvious choice. While recuperating from a bout of rheumatoid arthritis in Richmond in July 1862, Taylor was informed by President Davis of his new assignment as commander of Confederate forces in Louisiana.[32] Taylor left Lee's army shortly after the Seven Days campaign and, as Douglas Southall Freeman has commented, "The Army was poorer for Taylor's departure."[33]

IRISH BEND, ALEXANDRIA, AND PORT HUDSON

4 In early April 1863 Banks traveled to Brashear City with the intent of opening his water route to the upper Mississippi. By that time some 15,000 Union soldiers were stationed at or near the town. Taylor, observing this activity, had positioned his small army, approximately 3,000 in number, at a place called Fort Bisland, about ten miles up Bayou Teche from Berwick City.[1] Although the position could scarcely be called a "fort," the site was well chosen. In addition to a line of barricades prepared under the direction of Col. Valery Sulakowski, who was formerly with the Austrian army, the Confederate defense included a captured Union gunboat, *Diana.* By moving his boat around the bends of the bayou above the earthworks, the captain of

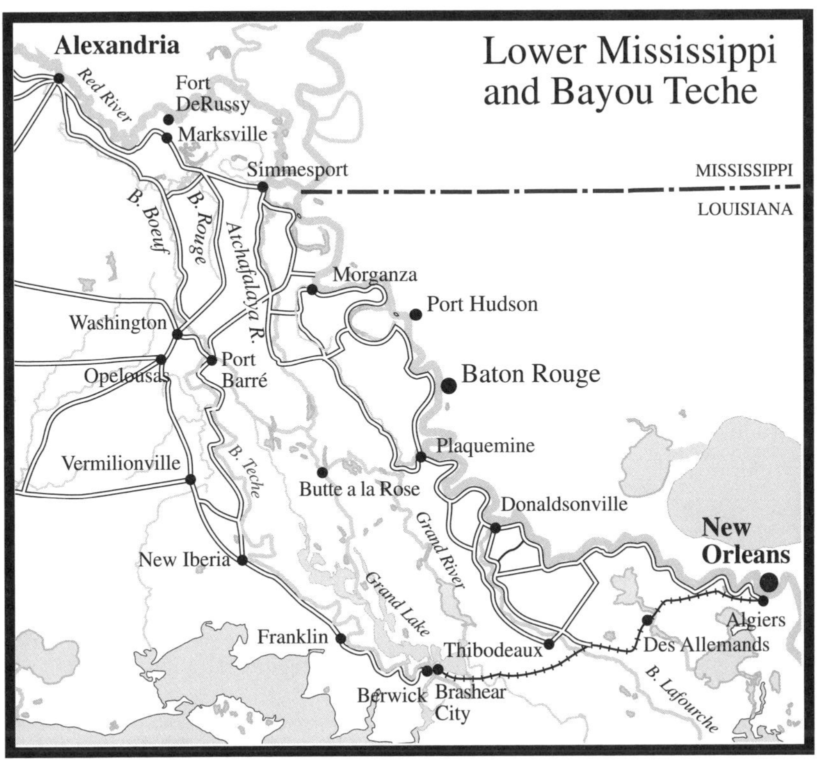

The Lower Mississippi River and Bayou Teche

the *Diana,* Oliver J. Semmes, son of Raphael Semmes, could bring her guns into play as needed to support the troops along the barricade. The Union boats, on the other hand, were unable to maneuver in the straight, narrow channel of the bayou below the Confederate position and thus could offer but little assistance in an attack against that position.

In February General Weitzel had suggested sending a portion of the Union army across Grand Lake to Indian Bend, above Fort Bisland, to cut off Taylor's retreat. This was part of a plan to invade the Teche country and capture the small Confederate fort located at Butte-à-la-Rose, at the upper end of Grand Lake, known as Fort Burton. After this flanking force was in position, the main army would launch an attack up the Teche. This would catch Taylor in a trap from which escape would be difficult.[2] After some consideration Banks accepted Weitzel's plan and, in late March, began to implement it. He ordered Grover, with about 8,000 men, to cross Grand Lake and take a position at Irish Bend, near the town of Franklin. Then, near noon on April 11, Banks began his ground advance on Fort Bisland.

The Union infantry reached Fort Bisland April 12. Instead of waiting to hear from Grover, Banks attacked the next morning. The evening of April 12, the *Diana* had been moved down the bayou in advance of the Confederate line. As a result the gunboat became a target for much of the Union artillery, and soon a fortunate shot penetrated the superstructure and exploded in the engine room. The boat was disabled and, to the cheers of the Union troops, withdrew up the Teche. The boat was subsequently sunk by the Confederates. One member of the 38th Massachusetts, apparently familiar with Banks's political past, described the army commander during this attack as "sitting on his horse, amid the flying missiles in the air, as cool and as calm as if he was presiding over the Legislature."[3]

Meanwhile, Grover had shown little initiative in executing Banks's orders. First, he spent a day and a half packing men and equipment onto his army transports until, as one participant noted, "The men appear to lie two or three deep on deck; while some hang up in the 'shrouds.' . . . We are literally 'as thick' on board 'as three in a bed.'"[4] After finally getting under way, with a four-gunboat escort under Lt. Cdr. Augustus P. Cooke, Grover lost more time trying, but failing, to free the navy escort vessel *Estrella,* which ran aground in Grand Lake. He then used another full day finding a location for his landing. After deciding on a spot, he sent the gunboat *Clifton* to inform Banks. However, because of the low water level he was unable to reach the shore and lost more time as, in the late afternoon of April 13, his men jumped overboard and scrambled through the water and mud to dry land. The artillery was transported to shore in flatboats. Having gotten his men ashore, Grover, with no maps and no wagons, was uncertain what to do. Finally, after driving away some Confederate cavalry, he was able to reach Oaklawn Manor, where he bivouacked for the night. Meanwhile, shortly after four o'clock in the afternoon of April 13, the *Clifton* had arrived in front of Fort Bisland. Banks was told that Grover was ashore and was marching toward Taylor's rear. Expecting Grover to be in position by the following morning, Banks ordered his troops to withdraw and rest for the night. He issued instructions to assault along the entire line at first light.

With the insight of a good general, Richard Taylor had sent a small force to watch the lakeshore in the Confederate rear. He thus learned of Grover's landing about the same time that Banks did.[5] In response to this landing Taylor ordered his wagons to begin a retreat up the bayou. Leaving part of his force at Bisland, he moved north with the remainder of his army and took a concealed position in the woods near Irish Bend, facing east. At first light on April 14, the unsuspecting Grover moved south along the bayou road toward the town of Franklin. After marching about two miles toward Indian Ridge and passing diagonally in front of most of Taylor's force, the front of the Union column ran into the right of Taylor's line. The Confederates opened fire. In response Grover's lead regiments formed a line of battle and advanced across a field of young sugarcane toward the enemy. The cane furrows were deep, and the advance was exhausting. Furthermore, a Confederate battery positioned near the bayou on the Union left opened an enfilade fire into the advancing ranks. Taylor then initiated an attack on the Union right flank, driving it back across the field. By this time the main body of Taylor's army, after abandoning the line at Bisland, had reached Irish Bend. Taylor extricated himself from his engagement with Grover and joined the retreat.

While Grover was feeling the brunt of Taylor's surprise attack, Banks's force advanced on Fort Bisland in the early morning of April 14, as ordered, and found the enemy works empty. Banks at first pushed hard to catch and destroy the retreating Southerners. However, when he reached the battlefield at Irish Bend, he saw that the bridges across the bayou had been destroyed by the retreating enemy. Rather than continue his chase by the roundabout route of the bayou road, Banks elected to rest his men for the night. Later Taylor declared Banks's pursuit from this point to be "without energy or vigor."[6] Whether or not this was a precise description of Banks's actions, the Confederates had successfully eluded the Union trap.

Following his capture of Fort Bisland and advance to Irish Bend, Banks acquired large quantities of corn, sugar, molasses, cotton, and cattle from the surrounding plantations. In addition, thousands of slaves joined the march of the advancing Union army. Finally, as usual, the Union troops carried out widespread looting and marauding. According to Brig. Gen. William Dwight of Grover's division, as the army advanced, "The scenes of disorder and pillage . . . were disgraceful to civilized war. Houses were entered and all in them destroyed in the most wanton manner. Ladies were frightened into delivering their jewels and valuables into the hands of the soldiers by threats of violence toward their husbands. Negro women were ravished in the presence of white women and children."[7]

On April 15 Banks began a mad dash up the Teche. According to one participant, "Our whole force, horse, foot, and artillery were started in rapid pursuit."[8] Some of the men considered this advance a "forced march, such as few soldiers, in any cause or age or clime, have ever been compelled to make. . . . The sun was scalding hot, dust almost thick enough to cut with a knife, and water mostly bad."[9] However, despite the rapid pace of the march, as during previous incursions by the Gulf army into country previously untouched by the war, much looting and destruction of private dwellings took place. Marauders burned plantation houses and stole or destroyed whatever they could find of value, sometimes to the point of absurdity.

> When so much wealth lay within the reach of soldiers, frequently they rendered themselves very ridiculous, and excited the merriment of their comrades by attempting to appropriate articles the most cumbersome and useless. One was seen with a large and elegant clock upon his back, while another was trudging along with a family Bible under his arm. . . . After he has borne them a few miles, he throws them away for others of the same or a different character. . . . Thus it is that the road in the rear of an army is often found encumbered with books, furniture, china ware, portraits, ladies' apparel, farming utensils, and every portable thing that possibly can be imagined. Oftentimes a soldier can be found with such an enormous developement of the organ of destructiveness, that the most severe punishments cannot deter him from indulging in the breaking of mirrors, and pianos, and the most costly furniture.[10]

According to Brig. Gen. John G. Pratt and Col. John E. King, special commissioners to Governor Henry W. Allen of Louisiana, the invading army "robbed the planters . . . sacked private dwellings . . . plundered the rich of their money, the poor of their necessary effects, the women of their jewelry, and even the children of their trinkets . . . fired volleys among passing citizens . . . violated the sanctuary and the tomb . . . arbitrarily arrested peaceful and unoffending citizens . . . unnecessarily occupied private dwellings . . . razed to their foundations, or wantonly burned plantation buildings . . . destroyed not only the poultry, the flocks and herds, the fields, the gardens, and the orchards, . . . but also the medicines and surgical instruments."[11]

When some soldiers were caught plundering private property, Banks said punishing them would delay the march, and the army commander instead took the opportunity to expound publicly on some of his philosophy regarding the proper way to fight the war. Robbing and plundering had "evil consequences," Banks told his men. This was not the way to make war. Instead, they should "march on New Iberia. If the enemy makes a stand there, pitch in without a minute's delay. That is my idea of making war." The guilty men were forthwith returned to ranks. Whether inspired by Banks's impromptu speech or heartened by the lack of punishment dispensed to their comrades, the men responded to Banks's talk with cheers. Seeing the effect of his lecture, "the General was in high spirits" as the advance continued.[12] Unfortunately, whether despite or because of this leniency, the destruction continued, and Banks eventually began to take more drastic measures. On April 21 General Orders No. 29 was issued. This order forbade "pillage and plunder," which it called "inexcusable and atrocious acts" punishable by death.[13] From Opelousas May 2, 1863, Banks informed Halleck that "one soldier has been shot to death for plundering and pillaging, and some others are being tried for the same offense." He acknowledged that "the temptations to plunder and pillage have been so strong, and the disregard of reiterated orders forbidding it such, that severe measures were indispensable."[14]

On April 16, while at New Iberia, Banks took the opportunity to destroy the Avery salt works, which was located on Marsh Island some twelve miles southwest of the town. Since its discovery in May 1862 this important rock-salt deposit had become a major source of salt for the Confederacy, and the works had produced 22 million pounds of salt by the spring of 1863. Because of the nearby salt deposit, a slaughterhouse and meatpacking factory had been established at New Iberia.[15] General Grover ordered Col. John W. Kimball, commander of his 2nd Brigade, to eliminate the salt works. This was done April 18. According to Grover, "Colonel Kimball destroyed the buildings, 18 in number, their steam-engines, windlasses, boiling and mining implements, and 600 barrels of salt."[16]

During the afternoon of April 17, while approaching the town of Vermilionville (now Lafayette), Grover observed Col. Tom Green's cavalry, acting as Taylor's rear guard, retreating across Vermilion Bayou and setting fire to the bridges. Grover immediately instructed Dwight to deploy skirmishers. With the help of artillery Dwight's force drove off the enemy but was too late to save the bridges. Following this "Battle of Vermilion Bayou," Grover rebuilt the main bridge, known as Pinhook Bridge, and crossed the bayou April 18.[17] The next day the army moved across Bayou Carencro to the small town of Grand Coteau, and from there to Opelousas. Once again the troops felt that "it was a forced march. . . . We were a hard-looking crowd, so sunburnt as to look like mulattoes, out at the elbows, out at the knees, out of money, out of patience,—nothing plenty but hard marching, lice, and fleas."[18]

While the army was advancing, Lieutenant Commander Cooke's force, after capturing Fort Burton, steamed up the Atchafalaya to report to Farragut. Banks's water route to the Red River and the Mississippi above Port Hudson was now open. However, Banks did not want to stop his ground advance. Given the ease of his march up the Teche, he anticipated reaching Alexandria before the end of the month. He therefore directed General Augur, who was commanding the troops at Baton Rouge, to send a message to Admiral Farragut asking him to have a fleet meet the army in Alexandria.[19]

Hoping to obtain reinforcements and perhaps practicing his phlegmaticness, after reaching Opelousas Banks halted his advance. He sent Brig. Gen. William Dwight to the town of Washington, Louisiana, to establish a forward position at that location. He also ordered a force to Port Barré, or Barré's Landing, near the intersection of Bayou Teche and Bayou Courtableau, which opened a waterborne Union supply line from Opelousas to the Gulf. The army began transferring the produce of the country to the landing for transport to New Orleans. The scene that evolved over the next few weeks was described by a member of the 52nd Massachusetts: "A mountain of cotton bales is piled upon the river bank, to which hundreds of teams are continually adding. . . . Great barbarities, I fear, have been committed; but of these I have seen but little. They are committed by stragglers. . . . The pile of cotton is a mountain at the landing. All day long teams have brought it in, and now it goes piecemeal through the bayou on little steamers toward New Orleans."[20] Banks was elated. He wrote his wife on May 3, informing her that "all say it is the cleanest, the best conceived and best executed campaign of the war."[21]

During the fall and winter of 1862–63, while Banks was preparing to travel from New York to New Orleans and, after his arrival, learning something about his new assignment, General Grant had been struggling to reach Vicksburg from the north. Repeatedly he had been turned back only to try again—Holly Springs, Chickasaw Bluffs, Yazoo Pass, Steele's Bayou, all failures. By late March 1863, while Banks was attempting to open his proposed water route to the Mississippi above Port Hudson, Grant was ready to try again, and he wanted Banks to help. In retrospect, had he acted quickly to move a portion of his army north to assist Grant, Banks's military career in the west might have experienced a significant improvement. However, Banks was of the opinion that he needed to capture Port Hudson before proceeding to Vicksburg in order to eliminate the risk of having a powerful enemy fortress in his rear. Banks's experience in approaching Port Hudson from the south in early March had apparently led him to conclude that a northern approach, from the vicinity of Bayou Sara, was preferable. To accomplish this, he believed he needed to send transports up the Atchafalaya. Therefore, Banks exchanged several dispatches with Grant and Farragut indicating his desire to have Grant join forces with him to capture Port Hudson. In the event, however, as Grant began another advance on Vicksburg, Banks made no attempt to move to the Mississippi.[22] Instead, he chose to move to Alexandria.

On March 29 Grant ordered Maj. Gen. John A. McClernand to open a road along the west bank of the Mississippi so that his army could bypass Vicksburg and move to a point on the river downstream from the enemy stronghold. During the night of April 16 Rear Admiral Porter successfully got eleven boats past the fortress, losing only one in the attempt. Several nights later six transports and twelve barges passed the batteries to join Porter's fleet downriver. Using these gunboats and transports, Grant's army crossed the river unopposed April 30, and the general prepared to move into Mississippi. As a result of these actions Porter now had a major naval force positioned within the Confederate-controlled section of the Mississippi. This force would be available to aid Farragut in disrupting enemy commerce crossing the river as well as to conduct raids up navigable tributaries.

The same day that Admiral Porter finished ferrying Grant's men across the Mississippi to begin their final and successful movement against Vicksburg, Commander Cooke met with Admiral Farragut. The latter, having been joined by Brig. Gen. Alfred Ellet with the ram *Switzerland,* was blockading the mouth of the Red River. Cooke delivered a message from Banks in which the general requested help from the navy in preventing Confederate forces from reinforcing Alexandria. In response, Farragut wanted to proceed up the Red, cut off the retreating Southern army, and assist in the capture of Alexandria. He sent Ellet up the Mississippi to request the loan of two ironclads from Porter to assist in this endeavor. Porter decided to answer this request in person and proceeded to steam down the river in his flagship, the *Benton.* With him he brought three other gunboats and a tug.

Porter joined Farragut at the mouth of the Red on May 4, two days after Lee and Jackson had launched their surprise flank attack against Joseph Hooker at Chancellorsville in Virginia. By this time Porter had received orders from the secretary of the navy to relieve Admiral Farragut from command of the fleet above Port Hudson and to support Banks's campaign by advancing up the Red River. In consequence Farragut informed Banks that Porter would join him (Banks) at Alexandria. In particular, Farragut expressed the opinion that Porter "will be at Alexandria before you can possibly get there."[23] The admiral boarded the *Sachem* May 8 and headed down Banks's new water route to New Orleans.

Upon receipt of the news from Farragut about Porter meeting him in Alexandria, and the admiral's opinion that the navy would get there first, Banks left Opelousas in a rush. Weitzel marched north at five o'clock on the morning of May 4. Emory's division, temporarily commanded by Col. Charles Jackson Paine while Emory was in New Orleans recovering from an illness, followed the next morning. Banks departed Opelousas on May 6. In good spirits, and with good weather and dry roads, the army maintained a pace of twenty-five to thirty miles per day from Opelousas to Alexandria. Capt. John William De Forest of the 13th Connecticut, who subsequently became a novelist and writer of some repute, said he thought he "would rather take my chance in another battle than chase Texans again from Camp Bisland to Alexandria." For much of the way the army marched through smoke and haze as the retreating enemy burned cotton along the route. "The smoke of burning cotton streaked the day, and the flare of it luridly starred the night; for even in his haste Mouton was determined that no fraction of the financial king should fall to the Yankees."[24] As was becoming the norm, and despite the pace of the advance, Banks's troops marauded and pillaged homes and property and thoroughly cleaned the countryside of provisions.

The army arrived in Alexandria May 9. Banks was pleased, and as he recalled later with a hint of pride, "On May 5, our headquarters at Opelousas were broken up, and the troops moved for Alexandria, a distance of from 90 to 100 miles, making this march in three days and four hours."[25] Perhaps this rapid march was something the commanding general of the Gulf army had learned from Stonewall Jackson in the Shenandoah Valley in 1862, and perhaps by driving his men forward, Banks hoped to catch Taylor. It could have been that the commanding general set the pace in order to prevent the Confederates from having time to burn all of the cotton along the army's route, leaving some for the Yankees to confiscate. Or perhaps the rapid march was motivated by the fact that Banks wanted to get to Alexandria before Porter. In any event, Banks did not catch Taylor, most of the cotton along the route of march was burned before the army could take possession, and Porter got to Alexandria first.

While Banks was marching overland to Alexandria, Porter was moving by water toward the same objective. Easily passing the only Confederate defense on the lower Red River, Fort De Russy, the fleet reached Alexandria May 8, one day ahead of Banks. After Banks arrived, because of the falling level of water in the river, Porter elected to take *Benton, Pittsburg, Price,* and *Ivy* back to the Mississippi. He left *Lafayette, Switzerland, Arizona,* and *Estrella* at Alexandria under the command of Capt. Henry Walke to support the army. En route downstream Porter stopped to destroy what he could of Fort De Russy, but he was able to do major damage only to the water batteries and a few casemates.

Banks and Porter, the politician turned general and the professional naval officer, took an immediate dislike to each other. The aggressive and tireless Porter could not abide a lack of professionalism in military officers, and he saw such a lack in Banks. For his part, Banks felt Porter was pushy, assumed authority, and treated the army with disrespect. With Porter now in command of the waterborne forces of the Union along the inland waterways of the Mississippi above Port Hudson, and Banks in command of the land-based forces along the lower river, the two officers were destined to interact professionally a great deal over the next thirteen months. Their personal opinions and attitudes toward each other were never far below the surface of their interactions, and the animosity that built up between them did not serve to further the cause for which they both fought.

Although a hard and aggressive fighter, Porter was a disruptive element in the navy, criticizing and undermining his superiors and trying to win favor with young officers. Secretary Welles said of him, "I did not always consider David to be depended upon if he had an end to attain." Later he added, "[He] has stirring and positive qualities, is fertile in resources, has great energy, excessive and sometimes unscrupulous ambition, is impressed with and boastful of his own powers, . . . is not generous to older and superior officers, . . . but is kind and patronizing to juniors. . . . Is given to cliquism, but is brave and daring like all his family."[26]

Proud and boastful as ever, General Banks sat secure but immobile in Alexandria. Writing to Secretary of War Stanton from this previously unoccupied enemy city, and conveniently overlooking the work of Farragut and Porter, he declared that he had successfully interrupted the Confederate supply line from the Trans-Mississippi to the eastern battlefields and captured some 4 or 5 million dollars' worth of enemy supplies. He had taken possession of a water route to the upper Mississippi River that bypassed Port Hudson and was forwarding cotton and other produce of the area to New Orleans even as he wrote. Banks declared later that in the ten days he was in Alexandria he brought in "10,000 bales of cotton, a large quantity of sugar, and mules, horses, and forage to a considerable extent." In his estimation, "Colonel Hollabird, the quartermaster of the department, paid into the treasury of the United States two millions of dollars from the cotton, and nearly one million of dollars from the sugar, mules, horses, &c."[27] However, while at Alexandria Banks perhaps began to feel a little removed from the war and chose not to advance farther up the Red.

On the Confederate side, despite concern about the loss of Fort De Russy and much of the Red River valley to the Federal advance, Taylor's superior, Lt. Gen. Edmund Kirby Smith, was pleased that his subordinate was able to keep such a large enemy force occupied. He believed that Taylor had prevented Banks's army from intervening in the important military activities then occurring in the vicinity of Vicksburg. In Smith's opinion, "The decisive battle of the West must soon be fought near Vicksburg. The fate of the Trans-Mississippi Department in a great measure depends on it, and Banks, by operating here, is thrown out of the campaign on the Mississippi."[28]

Smith was right. Banks had maneuvered himself into a dead end as far as the war effort as a whole was concerned. For a month he had taken 15,000 troops out of the battle for control of the Mississippi and dragged them far into the interior of enemy territory on what could only be described as an ineffective raid.[29] He did not draw troops away from Lt. Gen. John C. Pemberton, who commanded the defense of Vicksburg, and thus did not help Grant's advance against that stronghold. On the contrary, while Banks was in western Louisiana, no pressure was being placed on Port Hudson, and its commander,

Maj. Gen. Franklin Gardner, was able to provide reinforcements to Pemberton. The few dollars Banks was able to claim as profit from the acquisition of cotton and supplies from the residents of western Louisiana was a paltry return for the effort expended and opportunities lost.

Banks received a message from General Grant May 12 requesting assistance in capturing Vicksburg and Port Hudson. Probably as a result of this dispatch, Banks decided that it was time for him to get back to the task at hand. Therefore, he issued a stream of orders to his subordinates to collect the spoils he had acquired,[30] both from the country along the Teche and from the vicinity of Alexandria, and prepare to march to the Mississippi. He told Grant on May 13 that although he would like to receive some reinforcements, with or without them he would seize Port Hudson on his way to Vicksburg. According to the Gulf commander the capture of Port Hudson would be a minor affair but would be of great assistance in the capture of Vicksburg:

> I have sent . . . a note of this date, informing you of my determination to join you at all hazards with as little delay as possible. There are great difficulties in the way of our movement, but we shall overcome them all. . . . Port Hudson can be reduced without delay and with perfect certainty if you can assist us with from 10,000 to 20,000 men. . . . I earnestly urge upon you the consideration of this subject in this light, but should it be impossible for you to conform with it, I shall move to you as soon as possible with the force that I have stated. At best the movement against Port Hudson can delay us but a few days. . . . The moral effect of the reduction of Port Hudson upon Vicksburg and the junction of our forces after that will be inappreciably great.[31]

In Banks's eyes all of the military actions he undertook were of extreme urgency and of critical importance to the Union cause. Furthermore, the accomplishment of these actions was perfectly certain despite the fact that great difficulties had always to be overcome.

Grover started the infantry's march down the Red River from Alexandria on May 14.[32] He was followed by Col. Charles Jackson Paine the next day. In wagons and aboard transports the army carried the supplies that had been collected from the vicinity of the town, and behind them the soldiers left destruction and desolation. When the Confederate cavalry entered the Union campsites at Alexandria, they found ample evidence of looting and destruction of civilian property: "At their abandoned camps could be seen, furniture of all kinds, from kitchen to parlor, that they had taken out of privat residences, pianos, large mirrors, every thing, all of which they demolished when they brok camp."[33] A Rapides planter reported to Governor Moore that "the country in many places below is ruined—fences were torn down and burnt—houses and provender destroyed, cattle turned into the fields, and the negroes on many plantations driven off in a body. . . . On the road to Simsport the destruction of property and crops was greater if possible."[34] According to Banks, "The enemy was driven into the pine woods more than 70 miles above Alexandria, and the destruction of foundries and shops, and the seizure of horses, carts, &c., throughout the whole of that district, the advantage of which I am now reaping, has made it impossible to organize and supply a large force from that country."[35] The commanding general left Alexandria May 15 aboard the *Lexington.*

Banks instructed Col. Thomas E. Chickering of the 41st Massachusetts, who was son of the piano magnate and who had been acting as Banks's military governor at Opelousas, to bring the materials and supplies that had been collected along the Teche to Brashear City.[36] By May 20 Chickering was under way. His troops not only looted homes and destroyed property as they moved down the bayou but also seized and carried off all the slaves they could find. "The entire country was deprived of its laboring population. . . . Consternation preceded the movement of the soldiers, and the planters devised every means to conceal their slaves." These efforts were to little avail, however, because "Yankee ingenuity and cunning . . . generally frustrated all their plans."[37]

Unaware of Banks's decision to abandon Alexandria and return to the Mississippi, General Halleck informed Banks May 19 that his operations on the Red "are too eccentric to be pursued. I must again urge that you co-operate as soon as possible with General Grant east of the Mississippi." On May 23, Halleck added, "If these eccentric movements, with the main forces of the enemy on the Mississippi River, does not lead to some serious disaster, it will be because the enemy does not take full advantage of his opportunity. I assure you the Government is exceedingly disappointed that you and General Grant are not acting in conjunction."[38] This scolding by the general in chief did not appear to disturb Banks. Although he had barely gotten away from Alexandria ahead of Halleck's censure, the commander of the Gulf Department could legitimately claim that he had correctly anticipated the government's wishes. Later Banks stated, "I had the strongest possible desire to reach Shreveport when in Alexandria in May, but the necessity of operations on the Mississippi prevented it."[39]

After returning to New Orleans, Banks announced to Halleck that he was going to attack the Confederate garrison at Port Hudson. Halleck was unhappy with this decision, stating that "the success of such important operations on the Mississippi River [the capture of Vicksburg] should not be put in peril by the diversion of troops upon secondary operations." This dispute continued even after Banks had begun his siege at Port Hudson. As late as June 4 the general in chief was still hoping that "you have ere this given up your attack on Port Hudson and sent all your spare forces to Grant." On June 18 Banks told Halleck that if he were to move to Vicksburg, "it would be a source of great danger to New Orleans to leave a garrison of 5,000 men at Port Hudson, as many at Mobile, and a larger number in the Teche country." With this Halleck was at last assuaged, stating simply, "The reasons given by you for moving against Port Hudson are satisfactory."[40]

By May 22 Banks had the Port Hudson garrison of about 4,500 effectives surrounded by some 20,000 to 25,000 troops.[41] Admiral Farragut had five gunboats and a mortar fleet in the river below the fortress, while above the Confederate position Cdr. James S. Palmer had five gunboats. Wishing to take the fortress quickly, Banks ordered an attack for May 27. Unfortunately, he neglected to give detailed orders to his subordinate commanders regarding the timing and sequence of the attack. This resulted in piecemeal advances and bloody repulses everywhere along the Union line. Significantly, because of the lack of coordination in this attack, Banks took an action that was unprecedented for this overly tolerant general. While the fight was raging on the north end of the Union line, Brig. Gen. Thomas W. Sherman, who was in command on the south side, was eating lunch in his tent. Noticing the delay in the advance on his left, Banks ordered his chief of staff, Brig. Gen. George L. Andrews, to relieve Sherman and assume command of his division.[42] When Andrews arrived at Sherman's headquarters, however, the latter claimed he was ready to begin his attack, and as a result Andrews allowed Sherman to retain his command.

Following the failure of the attack of May 27, Banks, like Grant at Vicksburg, decided to resort to a siege. Then, when some deserters told him that Southern morale was low and that the enemy soldiers were near starvation, he ordered another assault. He wrote Farragut June 12, stating with his usual self-confidence, "We are ready for the assault to-morrow, but may postpone it till next day; we shall carry the works without fail when we attempt it."[43] The second attack was in fact delayed, and on the morning of June 14 Banks again ordered his army to advance against the entrenched enemy. Once more the attack was piecemeal, and the Union troops were turned back with great slaughter.[44] Banks then resumed his siege.

As the burning summer sun beat down on the troops at Vicksburg and Port Hudson, the three-day Battle of Gettysburg was fought in Pennsylvania and the Southern hopes for a beneficial outcome of General Lee's second invasion of the North were shattered. General Pemberton realized that help for his beleaguered Vicksburg garrison was probably not going to arrive and thought he could get better terms by surrendering on July 4 than continuing to hold out until he was forced to surrender. Arrangements with Grant for the surrender of Vicksburg were completed July 3. On the morning of July 7 Col. Thomas Kilby Smith brought official news of the surrender to Banks. Much cheering and firing of guns ensued as the men under Banks began a tumultuous celebration. The news was shouted across the lines to the Confederates, who at first refused to believe it. Then, after seeing a copy of the official communication from Grant, General Gardner agreed to surrender, and at seven o'clock on the morning of July 9 Union troops marched into Port Hudson. This was the brightest day of the war for General Banks, and soon thereafter he received the thanks of Congress "for the skill, courage, and endurance which compelled the surrender and thus removed the last obstruction to the free navigation of the Mississippi River."[45]

The victory at Port Hudson never achieved the stature in the North that those of the previous week at Gettysburg and Vicksburg gained. The fall of Port Hudson was considered a necessary consequence of the capture of Vicksburg and therefore was, in a sense, Grant's achievement. Furthermore, the reaction to Banks's victory was diluted by the New York City Draft Riots of July 13–16. Nevertheless, Banks's fame temporarily rose in the victory-starved North.[46]

THE SECOND INVASION

Sabine Pass

5

Following the capture of Port Hudson, Banks proposed to Halleck that he, Banks, either invade Texas or cooperate with General Grant in the capture of Mobile. It is not clear whether Banks believed these objectives to be of equal value militarily, but certainly Lincoln and Halleck knew that the military importance of Mobile was much greater than that of Texas. Nevertheless, the president continued to be pressured to occupy some portion of Texas. In addition to active lobbying by the New England textile interests to have the army take control of east Texas, Texas loyalists continued to urge Lincoln to establish a Union presence in the state.[1] The president was always sympathetic to appeals of the latter sort, believing that the Federal government should provide protection to loyal citizens wherever they resided.

Furthermore, in June 1863 events in Mexico had taken a turn for the worse. That month Pres. Benito Juárez was driven out of Mexico City by the French, and Maximilian accepted the job of emperor of Mexico offered to him by Napoleon III. Though he still felt unable to take direct action to assist Juárez, Lincoln believed the military occupation of a portion of Texas would be a positive step toward resolving the problem of European intervention in Mexico and reducing the possibility of French and Mexican recognition of the Confederacy. However, the general in chief of the U.S. Army, Maj. Gen. Henry Wager Halleck, was perhaps the most important supporter of an invasion of Texas and thus an unintentional ally of the cotton interests.

Halleck, an 1839 graduate of West Point, was an extraordinary individual.[2] Nicknamed "Old Brains," he was made an assistant professor while still an undergraduate. As an engineer, author, and head of a law firm in California, Halleck had accumulated considerable wealth and at one point turned down the offer of a seat in the U.S. Senate. Appointed in 1861 to replace Frémont as commander of the Department of the Missouri, he reorganized that department with great energy and efficiency, and his subordinates proceeded to gain glory on numerous battlefields. However, when he finally assumed a field command, after the Battle of Shiloh, he showed himself to be singularly inept. In July 1862, after observing Halleck's poor performance in the field, Lincoln ordered him to Washington, where he became general in chief of the Union armies.

In his new position Halleck demonstrated no particular strategic ability. He passed along orders to his field generals when instructed to do so by the president or the secretary of war, but he almost never developed plans or issued orders on his own initiative. Although one of his biographers believed the new general in chief "served Lincoln well" and "fought for the principles he had imbibed from Mahan or Jomini, and often dissuaded the President from impractical military operations,"[3] it soon became clear that "Halleck simply refused to command. . . . Halleck would not seize the reins of operational authority. He had become commanding general in name only."[4]

On the other hand, Halleck readily and continually offered advice to Union generals. However, he was always careful to declare that such advice was only a suggestion and that the final decision on whatever matter was under consideration was left to the field commander. He thus avoided the responsibility of giving specific orders, and any failure resulting from either the acceptance or rejection of his "suggestions" could not be laid at Halleck's door. This stratagem created numerous problems between Halleck and the various Union field commanders.

In addition to his continuing avoidance of responsibility for making military decisions, Halleck bickered with and criticized others for his own mistakes. As one of his fellow officers stated, "Unable to command successfully one army, he was ordered to Washington to command all the armies."[5] On July 7, 1863, Gideon Welles wrote an apt description of the general in his diary: "I look upon [Halleck] as a pretty good critic of other men's deeds and acts, but as incapable of originating or directing military operations."[6]

Halleck informed Banks July 24, 1863, that the government considered the occupation of some point in Texas more urgent than the capture of Mobile. Consistent with instructions from the president, on that date he directed the commander of the Gulf Department to prepare for an expedition to Texas. Lincoln subsequently explained his decision by stating to Banks, "Recent events in Mexico, I think, render early action in Texas more important than ever."[7] Halleck added emphasis to this conclusion August 6, declaring that there are "important reasons why our flag should be hoisted" at some point in Texas in the immediate future. "Do this by land, at Galveston, at Indianola, or at any other point you may deem preferable. If by sea, Commodore Farragut will co-operate. There are reasons why the movement should be as prompt as possible."[8]

Halleck followed his dispatch of August 6 with another on August 10. In this latter note he provided some clarification to his previous statements and offered additional comments. In particular, he wanted to make some "suggestions" regarding the correct way to invade Texas. Despite the fact that, as he stated, "it was left entirely to your own discretion to select any point for occupation in Texas" and that "the effect and force of that order are left precisely as they were on its issue," Halleck seemed to feel that the original order allowed too much leeway. Therefore, he set about retracting what he had said four days earlier. In effect, Halleck proceeded to give Banks some not-very-well-concealed instructions on how to do his job and implied that the whole plan was Banks's rather than his own. He even managed to put some of the responsibility for his "suggestions" on Secretary of State Seward:

> In my opinion neither Indianola nor Galveston is the proper point of attack. If it is necessary, as urged by Mr. Seward, that the flag be restored to some one point in Texas, that can be best and most safely effected by a combined military and naval movement up the Red river to Alexandria, Natchitoches, or Shreveport, and the military occupation of northern Texas. This would be merely carrying out the plan proposed by you at the beginning of the campaign, and, in my opinion, far superior in its military character to the occupation of Galveston or Indianola. Nevertheless, your choice is left unrestricted.[9]

Halleck went on to explain that occupying points on the coast would divide Banks's troops and allow the enemy to concentrate on a part of the army. On the other hand, occupying the Red would cut the Trans-Mississippi in two. Then for the third time in this one message he repeated, "I write this simply as a suggestion, and not as a military instruction." Thus, Halleck, as usual, left himself blameless should his advice lead to defeat yet retained the opportunity for future criticism should it not be followed.

Banks was ready to go to Texas, but first he had to solve the problem presented by losses suffered at Port Hudson and by the expiration of the enlistments of his nine-month soldiers.[10] He sent an urgent appeal to Halleck for more men. He also reorganized the XIX Corps. On July 25 Brig. Gen. Charles P. Stone succeeded Andrews as Banks's chief of staff. Sherman's 2nd Division, which had been badly cut up and its commander wounded in the second attack at Port Hudson, was eliminated and its brigades transferred to the 3rd Division. Several other brigades were either combined or transferred to balance the remaining divisions. Finally, Banks chose Maj. Gen. William B. Franklin, who had just arrived from the east, to replace the ailing Augur in command of the 1st Division. Emory and Grover retained command of the 3rd and 4th Divisions.

William Buel Franklin was another of the West Point generals who never seemed to rise to his full potential.[11] A native of York, Pennsylvania, Franklin graduated first in the 1843 class at West Point. This was the class in which Grant graduated in twenty-first place. After being twice breveted for gallantry during the Mexican War, he was given responsibility for construction of the new Capitol dome and for an expansion of the Treasury building in Washington, D.C. On May 14, 1861, Franklin was commissioned colonel of the 12th U.S. Infantry. Three days later he was promoted to brigadier general of volunteers. He fought with distinction during the Seven Days campaign at White Oak Swamp, Savage's Station, and Malvern Hill. Promoted to major general of volunteers July 4, 1862, he commanded the forces that defeated a detachment of Lafayette McLaws's Division at Crampton's Gap in South Mountain in the Maryland campaign of September 1862. However, this victory was tainted by the fact that for five hours Franklin allowed a defensive force of less than 1,000 men to delay the advance of his corps of 12,300 effectives. He would have waited even longer than the five hours before attacking, but his subordinates took the initiative to drive away the Confederate defenders.

After assuming command of the Army of the Potomac, Maj. Gen. Ambrose Burnside named Franklin commander of his "Left Grand Division." Franklin commanded this Grand Division at the Battle of Fredericksburg, where he attacked Stonewall Jackson's line on the Confederate right with only two divisions instead of his whole force. This attack was rather roughly handled by Jackson's men. Subsequently, Burnside blamed Franklin for disobeying orders and held him responsible for the Union loss. The Congressional Joint Committee on the Conduct of the War, a political creature characterized "by the bold ruthlessness of its leaders . . . and by the star-chamber quality of its proceedings,"[12] found Franklin negligent, and his reputation was irreversibly damaged. Rather than shelve Franklin, however, Lincoln let him sit around for a few months and then sent him to Banks. Now Richard Taylor faced two generals who had been humiliated by his mentor.

In response to Banks's appeals for additional troops to support the anticipated move into Texas, Halleck instructed Grant to send a corps of 10,000 to 12,000 men to Banks. Accordingly, Grant, on August 7, 1863, sent Banks a detachment of the reorganized XIII Army Corps.[13] Maj. Gen. E. O. C. Ord, commander of the XIII Corps, took sick leave, and the detachment was placed under the command of Maj. Gen. Cadwallader C. Washburn. The four divisions of the detachment were commanded by Brig. Gen. William P. Benton,

Maj. Gen. Francis J. Herron, Brig. Gen. Albert L. Lee, and Brig. Gen. Michael K. Lawler. Col. John J. Mudd commanded the brigade of cavalry that was included. The effective strength of the detachment was 778 officers and 13,934 enlisted men.[14] Moving from the vicinity of Vicksburg, where they had participated in the capture of that stronghold, these western troops joined Banks's army in Louisiana. With this increase in his forces Banks now had a two-corps army. Therefore, August 15, as the reinforcements from Grant began to arrive, Banks appointed Franklin commander of the XIX Corps; Washburn remained in command of the XIII Corps detachment. Weitzel took over the 1st Division, XIX Corps, and Robert B. Merritt took Weitzel's brigade.

Sherman's men brought with them a bit of mystique, and it was soon apparent that they also brought the well-developed foraging and marauding skills they had learned in Mississippi. According to Surgeon Harris Beecher of the 114th New York, "They had a wonderful disregard of personal appearance. . . . They also took a special delight in destroying every species of rebel property that came within their reach." In addition to raising the art of foraging to new heights, said Beecher, the western soldiers had other bad habits. He believed they had an advanced propensity for gambling, "a vice to which the men of the Nineteenth Corps were much less addicted," and a habitual gasconade. "They were . . . arrant braggarts, continually dilating upon their wonderful achievements, and forever depreciating the laudable efforts of others."[15]

The Gulf veterans reacted with wounded pride, and a certain anxiety regarding the arrival of the men from Vicksburg. As one of the members of the 21st Iowa wrote:

> The 13th Army Corps has a bad name down here, and has the reputation of being composed of the most lawless, undisciplined and predatory troops in the whole army. The boys, indeed, seem to take pride in this reputation, and evince a determination to maintain and deserve it. They are continually coming in collision with the 19th Army Corps' men, from New York and New England, whose precision of dress and conduct they affect to despise. There is a good deal of bad blood between the two corps, and some of it has been spilled already. I am sorry to say that often our men are the aggressors. But it seems that the repute of our amiable disposition does us no harm with the rebels, which even our companions of the 19th admit, for some of their scouting cavalry, who had been 30 or 40 miles out in the country, came in to-day to report a widespread consternation at the news of the 13th Corps, or "Grant's men," being here.[16]

Whether or not the rebels felt "consternation" at the arrival of the detachment of the XIII Corps, many of these troops from the Old Northwest would remain in the Gulf country for the duration of the war.

Following his success at Galveston January 1, 1863, General Magruder had ordered an attack on the blockading vessels at Sabine Pass. This attack took place January 21 and resulted in the capture of the two blockade vessels *Morning Light* and *Velocity.* Learning of the loss of these vessels, Farragut wanted to launch a quick retaliatory strike. He wrote Commander Bell describing a plan for capturing the Confederate position at the pass: "I think . . . that a land force would bag the whole party by taking them in the rear. Look at the beach well and see if there is not a good place for landing 2 or 3 miles to the southward and westward of the town [Sabine City]." It was a good plan, but at the time he wrote his note to Bell, Farragut knew that the army was not ready to support it. Therefore, he added, "But I see no chance just yet of the Army making an attack in that quarter, but it is well to be posted ready for the work when it is to be done."[17]

Sabine Pass is located at the mouth of the Sabine River, on the border between Texas and Louisiana. A portion of Farragut's fleet had raided the pass late in September 1862. At that time three boats commanded by Acting Volunteer Lieutenant Frederick Crocker crossed the bar and shelled the small enemy position, Fort Sabine, at the upper end of the pass. The defenders evacuated the fort and Crocker's men went ashore, destroyed the works, and burned some nearby railroad property. Since that time the Confederates had built a new fort on the pass, Fort Griffin, and the port at Sabine City had become an important facility for blockade runners.[18]

Probably as the result of a suggestion from Farragut, Banks adopted the idea of attacking Sabine Pass as his initial response to Halleck's instructions to hoist the Union flag in Texas. This seemed a reasonable choice given that the pass was close to Berwick Bay and that Lieutenant Crocker had met little opposition in his raid of September 1862. Then on August 1, as the planning for the Sabine Pass expedition was getting under way, Farragut became ill and left for New York City. Commodore Bell was summoned from the Texas coast to take command of the Western Gulf Squadron. Bell supported the idea of an attack on the Confederate position at Sabine Pass, stating that when Banks "requested the cooperation of the navy . . . I most gladly acceded." Knowing that the bar at the mouth of the pass was shallow, he stated that the four gunboats *Clifton, Sachem, Arizona,* and *Granite City* were "the only available vessels of sufficiently light draft at my disposal for that service."[19]

In contemplating his attack on Sabine Pass, Banks soon envisioned a great deal more than the mere capture of the enemy position at that point. As early as the middle of August, in his reply to General Halleck regarding the need for "early action in Texas," Banks stated, "Measures have already been taken to carry into effect your orders. We shall plant the flag in Texas within a week, I hope. . . . We can move 8,000 men at once to the Sabine Pass, and thence concentrate rapidly on Galveston. . . . From Galveston . . . I would move a force of 5,000 or more to the Rio Grande. . . . This has been my view of operations in Texas from the beginning."[20] As the days passed, the undertaking continued to grow in Banks's imagination. It soon became a grand expedition of perhaps 20,000 men that would lead immediately to the occupation of Houston and Galveston. "I regarded it certain . . . that we could concentrate and move upon Houston by land with 15,000 to 17,000 men before it would be possible for the enemy to collect his forces for its defense."[21]

Like a child with a new toy Banks seemed to feel he had found the perfect plan. On August 26 he argued strongly for the Sabine Pass move. In his opinion there were five objects to be gained by a movement to the Sabine. First, it plants the flag "at a prominent and commanding position" in Texas. Second, "it is accomplished by water." Third, it requires but a small force and thus can be accomplished "without attracting attention of the enemy until it is done." Fourth, it "enables us to move against Galveston from the interior." Fifth, it offers flexibility because after occupying Galveston, a small force could be left to garrison the island and the main force could "push on to Indianola, or the Rio Grande, or to return to the Mississippi, as the exigencies of the service may require."

However, at the same time that Banks enumerated the advantages of a move to the Sabine he seemed to feel obligated to refer to Halleck's pet plan for an expedition up the Red River. Perhaps uncertain how to handle the obsessive attention Halleck gave to the Red, Banks almost reluctantly indicated his continuing interest in a campaign up that river. As an excuse for not immediately undertaking a campaign up the Red, he cited his inability to navigate the river during the current season because of low water. Then he added, somewhat gratuitously and in sharp contrast to his heady endorsement of the Sabine Pass expedition, "If the season were different, the northern line would be doubtless preferable on many grounds."[22] A less enthusiastic endorsement of Halleck's Red River plan could hardly have been offered.

On September 2, 1863, while plans for the move against Sabine Pass were being finalized, General Grant traveled to New Orleans to confer with Banks on how he, Grant, could aid the advance into Texas. Although Banks had conducted a grand review of his troops August 29, he ordered another such review for September 4 in honor of his visitor. Unfortunately, while returning to town after the review, the visitor suffered an accident. The horse Grant was riding, which the general had borrowed from Banks, struck a carriage that had apparently gotten out of control because of the noise of a train whistle.[23] Whether or not Grant, who was a superb horseman, was completely sober at the time is moot, but in any case he was knocked unconscious and suffered an injury to his leg along with three cracked ribs. He was bedridden for a week and returned to Vicksburg on crutches. Because of Grant's injuries, not much business was transacted during this visit, but Grant did confirm to Banks that he would loan some troops at an appropriate time to assist in the invasion of Texas.

Banks explained his objective in attacking Sabine Pass in a letter to President Lincoln dated September 5, 1863. In this message he waxed eloquent as his enthusiasm for the expedition continued to grow: "My purpose is to move upon the Sabine Lake, marching to Beaumont, thence to Liberty Houston and Galveston. Galveston will fall by a movement in its rear. In possession of Galveston and Houston the whole state is in our possession." He felt he had found the key to success in the far west and that there was no way he could be stopped. "The Sabine is the weak and the key point of Texas for assault. From thence, if safely landed we can secure every position to the Rio Grande. Let me say that if we land safely your utmost expectations will be realized."[24]

Unfortunately for the commander of the Gulf Department, the final, conditional statement in his optimistic declaration to the president turned out to be prophetic, as did Farragut's response upon learning the details of Banks's plan for the attack. On September 11 Farragut, who was still recuperating from his illness, was in Secretary Welles's office when a dispatch outlining Banks's plan arrived from Commodore Bell. According to Bell, "A squadron of four gunboats, under the command of Acting Lieutenant Crocker, shall make the attack alone . . . and having driven the enemy from his defenses, and destroyed or driven off the rams, the transports are then to advance and land their troops."[25] The plan said nothing about a land force taking the fort from the rear, as originally recommended by Farragut. According to Welles, upon learning the contents of the dispatch, Farragut immediately predicted, "The expedition will be a failure. . . . This call is made for boats to accompany an army expedition; it is expected the navy will capture the batteries. . . . The soldiers should land and attack in the rear, and the vessels aid them in front. But that is not the plan. The soldiers are not to land until the Navy had done an impossibility with such boats. Therefore there will be disaster."[26]

During the summer of 1863 the new fort at Sabine Pass had been strengthened under the direction of the same Col. Valery Sulakowski who had helped prepare General Taylor's defenses at Fort Bisland. Sulakowski was now Magruder's chief of engineers. The colonel was supported in this undertaking by Maj. Julius G. Kellersberger. Neither of these officers was an amateur when it came to building forts.[27] They applied their skill to Fort Griffin, and by September the tiny fort was rather formidable. For armament Fort Griffin had six cannon—two 32-pound smoothbores, two 32-pound howitzers, and two 24-pound smoothbores. The fort was garrisoned by Company E, 1st Texas Heavy Artillery. This was an Irish company, known as the Jeff Davis Guards, consisting of "disorderly characters" and "dockwallopers" from the Houston area. The company was commanded by Capt. Frederick H. Odlum. Under the guidance of the company officers, including in particular 1st Lt. Richard William Dowling, the men of the Jeff Davis Guards had conducted target practice with the fort's artillery against stakes placed in the channels by Kellersberger. By September they had become pretty good shots.[28]

On September 6 Col. William H. Griffin, the commander in Sabine City, was absent and Captain Odlum was in town as acting commander. Odlum's nephew by marriage, the twenty-five-year-old Lieutenant Dowling, was left in command of the fort, which at the time was manned by 42 enlisted men. Dick Dowling, a native of County Galway, Ireland, was the prosperous owner of a successful saloon known as the Bank of Baccus, or just "the Bank," located at the corner of Main and Congress streets in Houston.[29] To assist the fort in defending the pass were two small Confederate cottonclad steamers, *Uncle Ben* and *Josiah Bell,* plus two unarmed river steamers, located upstream in Sabine Lake. Although their resources were limited, Odlum and Dowling had prepared their command as well as they could to resist an enemy attack.

Despite Banks's grandiose expectations for his Sabine Pass campaign, in practice there were but few transport vessels available that could both survive the passage across the Gulf and pass over the bar at the mouth of Sabine Pass. As a result only about 5,000 troops could take part in the first wave of the invasion.[30] This did not deter the enthusiasm of the commanding general. Anticipating great results, he proceeded with the expedition, placing General Franklin in command. General Weitzel was to assist. The troops allotted to the undertaking included George M. Love's 1st Brigade of Weitzel's 1st Division, and Robert B. Merritt's 3rd Brigade of Emory's 3rd Division, XIX Army Corps. For artillery support, Capt. Richard C. Duryea's Company F, 1st U.S. Artillery; Capt. George G. Trull's 4th Massachusetts Battery; and Capt. George T. Hebard's 1st Vermont Battery were brought along. Two squadrons of the 1st Texas Calvary (Union) were included.[31] William P. Benton's 1st Division and Francis J. Herron's 2nd Division, XIII Corps, were to assemble at Berwick Bay to follow Franklin's advance force after the initial assault was completed.

Frederick Crocker was again asked to lead the Union naval vessels in the attack on Sabine Pass. Crocker, a veteran New Bedford whaler captain, had more experience at sea than many of the senior officers of the navy. He had little tolerance for what he termed the "stupidities" of regular navy officers. At one time he had resigned from the service in protest against such stupidities but was coaxed back by Farragut. Thus, he was available when called upon to lead this second Sabine invasion.[32] On August 31 Banks told Franklin to contact Crocker and have him prepare to embark from New Orleans. Because the most important result expected from the expedition was to occupy some position within Texas, in accordance with Lincoln's order, Banks instructed Franklin that "a landing, if found impracticable at the point now contemplated, should be attempted at any place in the vicinity where it may be found practicable to attain the desired result."[33]

Franklin's plan called for the *Granite City* to proceed to the pass ahead of the main invasion fleet and mount a light. General Weitzel, with 1,000 men and one battery, aboard transports accompanied by the gunboat *Arizona,* would leave New Orleans September 4 and join Lieutenant Crocker, who, with the gunboats *Clifton* and *Sachem,* was to wait at Berwick Bay. This flotilla would then proceed to Sabine Pass. These forces were expected to arrive after dark on the evening of September 6 and to use the light from the *Granite City* to position themselves for the invasion. At daylight September 7 they would enter the pass and engage the guns of the fort, landing troops at some appropriate point. These troops would hold a position onshore until Franklin arrived later that day with reinforcements.[34]

On September 6 the blockading vessel at Sabine Pass, *Owasco,* was absent, having gone for supplies. Its replacement, *Cayuga,* had not yet arrived.[35] Thus, Acting Master Charles W. Lamson, commander of *Granite City,* arrived at the mouth of the pass on schedule during the afternoon of September 6 and found no blockade vessel on station. Then, "soon after anchoring, he discovered a large man-of-war steamer, painted lead color, which his fertile imagination transformed into the dreadful *Alabama;* that he thereupon got underway and left, went to the mouth of the Calcasieu River."[36] That afternoon Weitzel and Crocker joined forces as planned and departed for the Sabine, but because the *Granite City* was not at the pass to signal them when they arrived, Crocker's flotilla missed the pass in the dark and, after sailing around in the Gulf most of the night, also wound up at Calcasieu Pass in Louisiana the next morning.

Near eleven o'clock on the morning of September 7 Franklin arrived at the mouth of the Sabine. Neither blockaders nor invaders were to be seen. He entered the pass, but still seeing no activity, he withdrew and awaited events. Crocker and Weitzel finally arrived about 9:00 P.M., after stopping to repair two of their transports. Thus, the invading force was finally assembled in front of the pass twenty-four hours later than planned. The next morning, from the decks of the transports, the troops observed a bare, sandy beach extending to the limit of sight in both directions. The blockade vessel *Cayuga* had arrived and was anchored nearby. "Opposite the fleet was a narrow inlet, called 'Sabine Pass,' near which, upon a sandy knoll, could be seen an earthwork, a light-house, and a few shanties." The earthwork exhibited a few cannon, but no enemy was visible either around the fort or along the shore. "Such was the uninviting prospect that greeted our boys' arrival at Texas."[37]

Early on the morning of September 8, Franklin, Weitzel, and Crocker entered the pass to reconnoiter. Franklin found that his boat grounded some 125 feet from shore and that the bottom of the pass was soft mud in which a man could sink to his knees. Furthermore, the fort commanded both land and water approaches and, in Franklin's opinion, was heavily armed. Because of the lack of a good landing site, he concluded that his men could not go ashore outside the range of the guns of the fort. Therefore, he developed a new plan on the spot. Under Franklin's new plan *Sachem* and *Arizona* would move up the Louisiana channel of the pass, drawing the fire from the fort, while *Clifton* moved rapidly up the Texas channel and engaged the fort at close quarters. *Granite City* and *General Banks,* the latter with Weitzel and 500 men aboard, would follow *Clifton* up the Texas channel. While *Granite City* provided cover, Weitzel's troops would land at the old fort and "advance upon the fort as skirmishers, endeavoring to drive the enemy from his guns, while the Clifton engaged the fort at close quarters."[38] The old fort was one thousand yards or so below the new, both being on the Texas side of the pass. Franklin anticipated that the *Clifton* would eventually run aground as she approached the fort, and in that case the troops were to protect the boat from the guns of the fort by firing at the enemy artillerymen.

About three o'clock in the afternoon of September 8 the gunboats began crossing the bar. As they entered the pass, *Sachem* and *Clifton,* the latter under the personal command of Lieutenant Crocker, opened fire on the fort. In accord with the plan of Odlum and Dowling, the fort remained silent while the invaders' shells were exploding over it, and "the opinion began to increase among spectators that the work was evacuated." Then, when the first boat, the *Sachem,* reached the marker stakes in the Louisiana channel, the defenders leaped from their places of concealment and opened fire.[39] "Now, between gunboats and fort, the engagement became general, and very warm." The careful target practice conducted by the Davis Guards stood the defenders in good stead, and the leading gunboat was swiftly disabled. "In a few moments, the poor *Sachem* was seen enveloped in a cloud . . . and steam floated lazily out of her hull. When the thick volume of steam had partly cleared . . . the spectators observed with pain that her flag was down, and a white one was in its place."[40] The *Uncle Ben,* steaming down from Sabine Lake, accepted the surrender.

The *Arizona* had grounded some distance behind the lead boat. After the surrender of the *Sachem* the *Arizona* managed to break free and immediately began backing down the channel. Ignoring the retreating *Arizona,* Dowling's men now turned their guns on the *Clifton,* which by this time had reached the stakes in the near channel. With heavy and accurate fire they destroyed her tiller ropes and blew up the boiler, leaving the boat disabled in the mud. The *Granite City* and the *General Banks* did not advance in support of the *Clifton.* Instead, they joined the *Arizona* in a hasty retreat from this destructive fire. Undaunted, the sailors aboard the stranded *Clifton* fought until the flag was ordered lowered by an officer. Crocker countermanded the order when he learned of it, but by then all but one gun was disabled. With no help forthcoming, Crocker surrendered. The lieutenant was singularly unhappy about the lack of support provided by the rest of his fleet as well as by the army, and he concluded in his report that "the conduct of the commanders of the Arizona and Granite City, or of my officer who hauled down the flag, I am not now called upon to characterize; nor that of General Franklin in failing so utterly to cooperate; but I trust my Government will soon place me in a position to ask an inquiry into the facts."[41]

As the navy vessels struggled back across the bar in full retreat, Franklin, unwilling to step in where the navy now feared to tread, ordered his transports back to New Orleans. As he explained later, "The day's experience had taught me that no attack which I could make with the troops which I had been able to get across the bar could possibly succeed."[42] In their haste to recross the bar and get away from Dowling's artillery, the commanders of some of the transports that had run aground in the mud threw several hundred mules and horses overboard, along with wagons, ammunition, and some two hundred thousand rations. The defenders of the fort had suffered only minor injuries from wood splinters and from burns caused by touching the hot guns.[43]

After a speedy return trip, Franklin landed at Algiers, Louisiana, September 11. Banks's "weak and key point of Texas" was left behind, unconquered and defiant. The commanding general, exhibiting his usual proficiency for transferring blame, stated, "The immediate cause of the failure was the misapprehension of the naval authorities of the real strength of the enemy's position, and the insufficient naval force with which the attempt was made." He then added, rather gratuitously, "Had we the requisite naval force or transportation, I would renew the attempt on the Sabine, or strike at the Rio Grande. But we have neither."[44]

The blame for the failure of the Sabine Pass expedition must rest on General Franklin,[45] who had now topped his performance at Crampton's Gap with this ignominious retreat in the face of an overwhelmingly inferior enemy force (5,000 Unionists to 42 Confederates, the first number not counting the Union naval force and the second not counting Dick Dowling and 4 volunteers). A few accurate artillery shots and two retreating gunboats seem to have unnerved him completely. Following Weitzel's withdrawal in the *General Banks,* Franklin did not attempt a landing, either at Sabine Pass or elsewhere, as his orders from General Banks required. Even General Grover, who was not the most imaginative of military commanders, had succeeded in getting his men ashore at Irish Bend and thus shown himself to be a more determined commander than General Franklin. In his report of the engagement Franklin stated that he was able to move to within 125 feet of the shore at points outside the range of the guns of the fort. From this distance a landing would appear to have been completely feasible, even given the muddy bottom. This is especially true since there was no observable defense present in the vicinity other than the fort itself.

Although Banks did not know the full story of Franklin's fiasco at the time he wrote his initial report, and undoubtedly Franklin provided exaggerated estimates of the size of the Texas garrison in his unofficial communications with his commanding officer, it is hard to see why a commander would ever give another important assignment to a subordinate who so miserably failed to carry out his instructions.

THE THIRD INVASION

The Great Texas Overland Expedition

6 Two days before Franklin's abortive attack on Sabine Pass, Gen. Braxton Bragg abandoned Chattanooga to Maj. Gen. William Rosecrans. Rosecrans pressed the advantage gained by his opponent's retreat, dividing his army while following Bragg into Georgia. However, as he retired, Bragg gained strength. Maj. Gen. Simon B. Buckner abandoned Knoxville to General Burnside and joined Bragg in Georgia. Additional reinforcements arrived from Mississippi, and Robert E. Lee sent Lt. Gen. James Longstreet's corps from the Army of Northern Virginia. Rosecrans finally realized the risk he ran by keeping his army divided and reunited it along Chickamauga Creek. There, on September 19 and 20, 1863, the combined Southern forces attacked and defeated the Army of the Cumberland, driving Rosecrans back to Chattanooga in panic. Not much about the battle could make the Union proud, but the highlight for the North was the stand made by Maj. Gen. George H. Thomas at Horseshoe Ridge. For this stand General Thomas was thereafter known as the "Rock of Chickamauga."

President Lincoln responded to the Union loss at Chickamauga by sending reinforcements to the Army of the Cumberland in the form of two corps of the Army of the Potomac under Maj. Gen. Joseph Hooker. These troops strengthened the Northern army stationed in Chattanooga, but Rosecrans failed to take advantage of this fact. He seemed able only to sit in stunned inactivity. Bragg, who had failed to pursue his retreating foe after the Battle of Chickamauga, thus depriving his army of much of the fruits of their victory, decided to besiege the city. He occupied the hills that formed an arc around the southern boundary of Chattanooga and interrupted the rail and river traffic that brought supplies to Rosecrans's army. Supplies grew short, and the situation grew critical for the Army of the Cumberland until Lincoln created the Military Division of the Mississippi October 16 and named General Grant its commander. Grant immediately relieved Rosecrans from duty and replaced him with General Thomas. Grant opened his "Cracker Line" into Chattanooga October 26, and Bragg's siege was effectively broken.

Meanwhile, far to the west, Banks was undeterred by Franklin's failure at Sabine Pass. Furthermore, there was no indication that he placed any blame on, or had any reduced confidence in, General Franklin. Instead, as was his wont, Banks quickly discarded the strategic concept for which he had so recently argued—that Sabine Pass was the key to the occupation of Texas—and turned his attention elsewhere. Perhaps recalling the brief success of his spring adventure up the Teche, or perhaps thinking to placate General Halleck somewhat, he now decided to move up that bayou for a second time and enter Texas from the east. Then, in an astounding decision that was seemingly made without hesitation or reflection, Banks proceeded to place General Franklin in command of this new offensive. It was as though the commanding general wanted the campaign to fail. According to Banks's orders, Franklin was to advance to Vermilionville. At this point he was to turn west toward Niblett's Bluff on the Sabine River.

Before beginning this new advance, Banks once again issued orders against straggling and marauding. In these instructions he repeated his belief that reconciliation and peace could best be achieved through equitable treatment of the local population.[1] As usual, his orders were mostly ignored, and wanton destruction continued unabated throughout the campaign. Meanwhile, on the Confederate side, Lt. Gen. Kirby Smith issued a call "to the people of Arkansas, Louisiana, and Texas" urging them to oppose the imminent Yankee advance any way they could. He informed the populace that "you should contest the advance of the enemy at every thicket, gully, and stream. . . . Endure awhile longer; victory and peace must crown our efforts."[2] Thousands of copies of Smith's statement were published and distributed.

General Franklin began his move up the Teche from the vicinity of Fort Bisland October 3, 1863. At the same time General Ord, returning from sick leave and assuming command of the two divisions of the XIII Corps that were included in the advance, moved from Berwick Bay, a day's march behind Franklin. As they advanced, the troops encountered continuing harassment by Taylor's force. They also began to suffer from the shortage of supplies available in the devastated country along the bayou. On October 9, at the town of Vermilionville, the army found that the retreating Confederates had burned the newly reconstructed Pinhook Bridge over Vermilion Bayou and appeared ready to contest the crossing. On the north bank, portions of Brig. Gen. James P. Major's cavalry were arrayed along a knoll. Franklin ordered his men into position for an assault, and the artillery opened fire. Then, as the infantry advanced, the Texas cavalrymen departed, resulting in a bloodless victory for the Union.[3]

Banks departed from New Orleans with his staff October 7, moving through New Iberia toward Vermilionville to join Franklin's army. He arrived on the scene as this second "Battle of Vermilion Bayou" was winding down. Seeing a glorious victory in the brief standoff, he immediately sent a telegram to Halleck stating, "As soon as we cross the Vermilion I will inform you of my plans. . . . No time will be lost in raising the flag as directed."[4] However, after observing the condition of the country around Vermilionville, Banks changed his mind about turning west toward Texas. Reconnaissance details from Banks's cavalry, which was now under the command of Brig. Gen. Albert L. Lee, indicated that Taylor, with Green's troopers, was ready for such a move and would be a major obstruction. Union supporters from west of the village of Vermilionville reported that General Magruder was on his way from Texas with a large army. Finally, opportunities for obtaining forage and supplies from the region west of Vermilionville were even worse than those along the Teche. There was little water, and the army's line of communication would be subject to harassment by both the enemy cavalry and a largely hostile population. It appeared to Banks that little was to be gained by a move in that direction.

Rather than make haste in "raising the flag" in Texas, as he had promised Halleck, Banks now had to backpedal. In a letter to Lincoln he tried to justify canceling his plans to move toward Texas from his current position on the Teche. As though he had never thought of the matter before arriving in Vermilionville, he explained to the president that "to the Sabine, we have a march from Opelousas and Vermilion of between 100 and 200 miles, without water, without supplies, and without other transportation than by wagons." As far as the other alternative, to move to Marshall, Texas, "we have a march of from 350 to 400 miles in that direction, without other communication than by wagon train, and through a country utterly depleted of all its material resources." Furthermore, the enemy will collect all of his forces to stop the advance, "hanging upon our rear throughout the whole march." He concluded, "It is not good policy to fight an absent enemy in a desert country, if it can be avoided."[5] Surely the president would understand that, despite Banks's previous bravado, he simply could not invade Texas by this overland route.

Banks remained with his army in or near Vermilionville until October 11. On that day Franklin moved north and crossed what was described by Beecher as "a dirty little brook, dignified by the name of bayou."[6] This stream, known as Bayou Carencro, which both the Yankees and Confederates called Carrion Crow (termed by the same New York critic an "appropriate and classic name"), was located twelve miles south of Opelousas. Before he departed, Banks ordered Franklin to continue his advance toward Opelousas, Barré's

Landing, and Washington, Louisiana. Off to plan yet another campaign for the invasion of Texas, Banks left Franklin in command of all the Union forces in western Louisiana. Instead of advancing any farther, however, Franklin decided to take advantage of the mild fall weather and rest his troops. The men seemed to appreciate the rest, one describing the weather as "delightful. No one who ever saw such an autumn could ever forget it."[7] Franklin ordered his men into camp on the Carencro in a location used earlier by the retreating Confederates.

After resting his army for three days, Franklin finally began his advance north from Bayou Carencro. The head of the column almost immediately ran into Tom Green's cavalry, which was defending a prepared position near Bayou Bourbeau. There the two forces briefly collided and fought the Battle of Buzzard's Prairie. Shortly after the engagement began, Franklin ordered Weitzel's division to advance and drive the enemy from the field. As this movement got under way, Green ordered a charge by the old Sibley Brigade, veterans of the battles in New Mexico, consisting of the 4th, 5th, and 7th Texas Mounted Volunteers. For a brief period the Confederate charge turned Weitzel's right. This enemy advance was countered by Capt. Ormand F. Nims's 2nd Massachusetts Battery, which General Franklin reportedly once described as "the finest battery in the United States," and by Col. Edmund J. Davis's Texas Cavalry (Union).[8] For a while Texans fought Texans on the Louisiana prairie, as the Confederates repeatedly withdrew only to charge again. The overly cautious Franklin seemed unwilling to avail himself of his overwhelming manpower to resolve the affair, but finally Brig. Gen. Stephen Gano Burbridge's division was sent into the fray and the issue was settled.[9]

The battle must have tired Franklin because he proceeded to order a few more days of rest on Bayou Bourbeau before resuming his advance toward Opelousas. Taylor, who was operating out of Opelousas, longed to tear into the Yankee legions but was restrained from doing so by Kirby Smith. On October 20 Smith reminded Taylor, "In the present state of the public mind, a defeat to your little army would be ruinous in its effects. When you strike, you must do so only with strong hopes of success."[10] Resenting, but obeying, these orders, Taylor continued to withdraw his men before the advancing Yankees. Franklin's lead troops finally reached Opelousas near noon October 21. At the same time Lee's cavalry occupied Barré's Landing.

A Union supply depot had been established at Barré's Landing the previous April to support the army that was then operating in western Louisiana. Unfortunately for Franklin, low water now prevented the use of the landing for such purpose. Then, to make matters worse, shortly after the advancing army arrived at Opelousas, a cold front hit and torrential rain dampened the bodies and spirits of the invaders. Despite the rain, the water level in the Courtableau remained too low for steamboats to bring in supplies. Foraging was poor, and the army's animals were suffering. Franklin informed Banks's chief of staff that "my troops hold Opelousas and Barre's Landing." However, "On account of a violent storm now raging, movements must be delayed some time. . . . Forage is very scarce here and higher up." Franklin could see that he would have to stop his advance until he could obtain additional supplies and it would be difficult even to remain in Opelousas without such supplies. Woefully, he pleaded that he would be "very glad to get definite instructions."[11] Ironically, Banks ignored Franklin's plea for "definite instructions." In a few months the commanding general would find himself in a similar situation begging for definite instructions.

Receiving no instructions from his commanding officer, Franklin scattered his force of 27,000 men in a half-dozen camps around Opelousas. The weather prevented effective reconnaissance but did not discourage marauding by the troops, and the men continued to abuse civilians and take whatever they wanted from the surrounding homes and farms. Meanwhile, the supply problem continued to worsen as Franklin remained stationary. Then, when the weather improved, Franklin began to be inundated by runaway slaves. Many of the able-bodied black men who entered the Union lines were mustered into the Corps d'Afrique and sent to Brashear City for training. However, large numbers of desperate men, women, and children arrived daily, and not all could be sent downstream. As they took up residence in or near the Union camps, they began to pose health problems and their presence aggravated the supply situation of the army. Finally, Franklin decided to return to Bayou Carencro, where he believed forage would be better than around Opelousas. The army began its retreat from Opelousas November 1, and by the next day most of the troops were back in their old camp on Bayou Carencro. As one of the participants later stated, "We turned our heads south & it was plainly to be seen that the Great Texan Overlan Expedition was a failure, all owing to too much strategy by Gen Banks."[12]

Being the type of man who sees a glass half full instead of half empty, Taylor took Kirby Smith's instructions of October 20 to mean he could "assume the offensive" whenever he felt he could do so to advantage. Thus, as Franklin withdrew from Opelousas, Taylor began consolidating his scattered forces to challenge the Yankee invaders.[13] On the night of November 2 General Burbridge was assigned as rear guard for Franklin's army. Burbridge's force, totaling about 1,625 men, was positioned north of Bayou Bourbeau.[14] Although Camp Carrion Crow, where the main force was located, was but a few miles away across Buzzard's Prairie, Burbridge was badly exposed.

Shortly after noon November 3 Burbridge received a report that a heavy column of enemy cavalry was forming in line of battle to his left. Burbridge had little time to make preparations and soon found himself under attack. He was outnumbered by the two brigades of infantry and cavalry that had been assembled under Brig. Gen. Tom Green, and after only a brief resistance, his line began to break. Most of the 67th Indiana were captured as "the fierce cavalry sweep like a whirlwind among them with gleaming sabres. The swift riders enfold them and, almost without resistance, march them away captive before our eyes."[15] The retreating Federals splashed across the Bourbeau with Green's Texans right behind. Meanwhile, Col. Thomas H. Bringhurst of the 46th Indiana had heard the sound of the fighting from his nearby campsite, had formed up his regiment, and was moving toward the sound of battle. The 46th Indiana was soon followed by the whole 3rd Division of the XIII Corps.

Colonel Bringhurst recalled later that his men "marched on rapidly for two miles, when men, wagon trains and artillery were seen dashing out of the woods. Rebel cavalrymen were seen striking teamsters and artillerymen with their sabers." An incredible scene ensued in which mules and horses, men and wagons, rushed from the woods followed closely by the Texans. The latter were yelling, firing sidearms, swinging sabers, and running down the retreating Yankee soldiers. The Indiana reinforcements were quickly formed into a line. "The men laid on the ground and went to work. . . . The rapid firing of the regiment and the two guns checked the rebels and drove them to the woods."[16] A counterattack soon swept across the prairie, driving the Confederates back to Bayou Bourbeau. There, according to General Green, "Deeming it imprudent to fight this large additional force, after a warm skirmish, I withdrew slowly and without loss, the enemy not attempting to follow me."[17]

Union losses in this Battle of Bayou Bourbeau were reported as 716 killed, wounded, or captured, almost all from Burbridge's 1st Brigade. The Confederates reported 180 casualties. After the enemy was driven back across Bayou Bourbeau, the Federals gathered their wounded, buried their dead, and on November 5 departed for Vermilionville. The retreat from Camp Carrion Crow did not sit well with the Union troops. Col. Alvin P. Hovey, of the 24th Indiana, stated that "if we had had Generals with as much spunk as a mouse we would have turned about and whipt them soundly."[18] In the wake of the battle the Houston *Tri-Weekly Telegraph* described Franklin as a "Yankee Sancho Panza" and reported that "if a crazy set of fools had broken loose from Bedlam . . . they could not have acted in a more ridiculous manner, or more like natural-born fools." Wistfully the reporter added, "Adoo Yankee General, Adoo, and next time you come bring along your knitting."[19]

It was not until November 13 that Franklin received his much-longed-for definite instructions from New Orleans. These directed him to "make such arrangements as you think will best secure the occupation of as much of the Teche country as your present force can hold."[20] Franklin decided that he would have to entrench somewhere, but he was uncertain where. He idled around Vermilionville until November 16, when he decided to retreat toward his base of supplies. He turned south and headed for New Iberia. At New Iberia Franklin dug in, planning to stay put for the winter. As usual, the army left desolation and destruction in its wake. Moving into the area around Vermilionville after the departure of the Yankee invaders, Pvt. John R. Cox of Gould's Texas Battalion described the scene: "If you were ondley hear to look round and see the distruction. All of the fences burnt up, corn riunt, house burnt, cattle shot down. ther air plenty of family hear that has not got a ear of corn. No pin can discribe it."[21]

The failure of the Texas overland expedition in the fall of 1863, in addition to humiliating the soldiers under General Franklin and demonstrating once again the poor leadership in the Gulf Department, had serious long-term consequences. As one historian has said, "If the Overland Expedition had succeeded, there would have been no need for the Red River Campaign a few months later. And if there had been no Red River Campaign in 1864, many of the Union divisions sent off on that hapless adventure would have been available for the capture of Mobile and for Sherman's march from Chattanooga to Atlanta. . . . Who knows what Generals Sherman or Grant might have done with two or three extra corps of tough veterans in their 1864 campaigns?"[22] Once again Franklin had shown himself unequal to the task of leading an army in the face of an enemy. Although his force significantly outnumbered that of his opponent, his reaction to the aggressiveness of the latter was much the same as at Crampton's Gap and Sabine Pass. It appeared that his willingness to fight had been completely lost. Perhaps he had been psychologically destroyed by the charges brought against him by General Burnside after the Battle of Fredericksburg, or perhaps he was never capable of being a good, independent fighting general. In any case General Banks was starting to pay the penalty for keeping his timorous subordinate in a position of command.

THE FOURTH INVASION

The Texas Coast

7 General Sherman came to Chattanooga, Tennessee, with 17,000 reinforcements for General Grant on November 14, 1863. With these additional troops, and with his friend and subordinate Sherman to help him, Grant was ready to attack Bragg's army. Bragg, who had spread his men over the hills surrounding the town of Chattanooga, had lost the services of General Longstreet. After much bickering and arguing within the Southern command, Longstreet had taken his corps and marched to Knoxville to attack General Burnside. With his army weakened and dispersed, Bragg was vulnerable to attack. On the morning of November 24 General Hooker's divisions attacked Lookout Mountain and drove the defenders off the mountain in the aptly named Battle above the Clouds. At the same time Sherman attacked the north end of Missionary Ridge. Finally, on the afternoon of November 25 General Thomas's troops charged up Missionary Ridge and routed the Con-

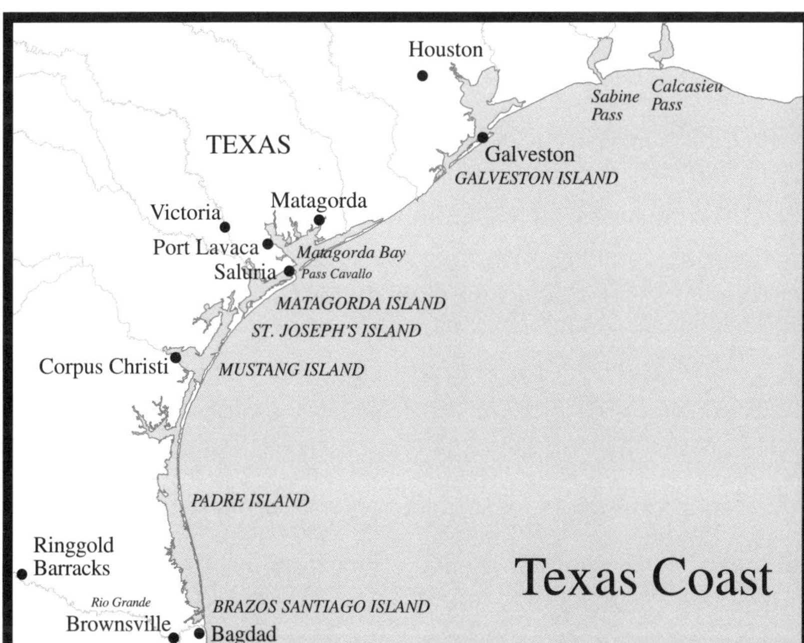

The Texas Gulf Coast in 1863

federate defenders. Bragg retreated toward Dalton, Georgia, leaving the victorious Federals in control of the country as far as Chickamauga Creek.

Meanwhile, as Franklin bungled his way along the upper reaches of Bayou Teche and eventually decided to settle in one spot for a while, General Banks initiated a move that seemed to show some strategic insight. Leaving Franklin's overland invasion force to occupy Taylor's army, Banks proceeded a third time to attempt to invade the Texas coast. This time his move caused both the department commander, Gen. Kirby Smith and Smith's subordinate in Texas, Gen. J. B. Magruder, considerable distress. The Southerners were now faced with defending a broad area against a numerically superior foe, and the Southern advantage of interior lines was eliminated by the mobility afforded the Northern troops by the army transports and their navy escorts. In a nineteenth-century version of Adm. Chester Nimitz's island hopping against the Japanese in the Pacific during World War II, Banks had an opportunity to catch the Texans flat-footed by striking without warning at any landing point along the coast. Under better leadership, and with proper backing from Washington, Banks's invasion of the coast of Texas in the fall of 1863 might have resulted in a successful Union occupation of the populated regions of the state. Unfortunately for the Union cause, little leadership was available in the Gulf Department, and support from Washington, at least as far as General Halleck was concerned, was nonexistent.

Banks's new plan for invasion was to occupy Brownsville, sever the Confederate trade through Mexico, and then move up the coast to capture Galveston from the southwest. On October 26, 1863, after three days' delay because of weather, he began this endeavor by sailing from New Orleans with some 6,000 troops. The troops were mostly infantry from the XIII Corps—about 4,000 effectives from the 2nd Division augmented by the 13th and 15th Maine, the 1st Engineers and 16th Infantry of the Corps d'Afrique, and the 1st Texas Cavalry (Union). The troops were under the command of Maj. Gen. Napoleon Jackson Tecumseh Dana, a native of Maine and an 1842 graduate of West Point.[1]

Dana's force was bound for Brazos Santiago, a village at the north end of Brazos Island near the mouth of the Rio Grande. The army transports, as usual overloaded with men, horses, mules, artillery, and supplies, were escorted across the Gulf by the gunboats *Monongahela, Owasco,* and *Virginia.*[2] After assembling at the southwest pass of the Mississippi, Banks's fleet headed into the Gulf October 27. The first three days of the passage across the Gulf were uneventful, but the invading army was soon to learn something about autumn weather off the Texas coast.

Precisely "at half-past four o'clock" on the morning of October 30, as the convoy approached Aransas Pass, "a 'heavy norther' struck us. . . . Many vessels being compelled to separate and run before the wind, which soon blew a gale."[3] By dawn several of the transports had become separated from the fleet. Aboard some of these boats orders were given to lighten the load, and mules, horses, caissons, and other equipment were thrown overboard.[4] "For nearly twelve hours the storm raged, and long after the wind had ceased to blow, the waves ran 'mountains high.'"[5] The transport *Zephyr* lost power and had to be taken in tow by the *Owasco,* while the *Monongahela* assisted another transport, the *Bagley.* On the day after the storm the *General Banks* ran out of coal and was taken in tow by *Empire City.* Arranging a tow in heavy seas is a dangerous undertaking, and aboard the *General Banks* there were anxious moments as the *Empire City* attempted to get a line to the distressed vessel. The fact that no loss of life occurred speaks well for the nautical skills of the commanders and crews.[6] Three vessels—a small steamer, one schooner, and one launch—were lost in the storm, but, by heroic efforts, "though three vessels have sunk, not a life has been lost nor a man injured."[7]

The *Monongahela* and the *Owasco* remained with the damaged transports while the *Virginia,* though temporarily disabled, was able to continue with the main part of the fleet. The *Virginia* and her entourage arrived off Brazos Island November 1. Continuing high seas and strong winds prevented a landing that day, but the next day the fleet passed through the Boca Chica to reach the sheltered side of the island. There Banks, who was aboard the first transport to cross the bar, stepped onto Brazos Island at noon. The general immediately sent a dispatch to Washington. With more than a bit of pride, a great deal of premature judgment, and a somewhat theatrical view of his success, he stated, "The flag of the Union floated over Texas to-day at meridian precisely." He concluded, "Our enterprise has been a complete success."[8] The dispersed portion of the fleet arrived safely November 3. Several of the vessels were unable to enter the channel, and men and equipment had to be shuttled ashore. In some cases horses and mules were thrown overboard to fend for themselves. Most did not make it to shore. "The whole island is covered with heaps and piles of broken pieces of ships, furniture, boxes, barrels, and hundreds of other things and much resembling a vast drift pile."[9] Banks now had his army of invasion positioned to take control of Texas. The first step in his plan was complete.

The landing on Brazos Island was unopposed, the few enemy cavalrymen in the vicinity having withdrawn as the Union troops came ashore. Although he had suffered no losses, once ashore Banks seemed to decide that the task of conquering Texas was going to be somewhat more difficult than he had anticipated. Despite the fact that he had just declared the enterprise a "complete success," Banks proceeded to ask for reinforcements. He wrote Halleck from his flagship *McClellan* on November 4: "Unless we are strengthened, we may have to abandon the great advantage we have gained."[10] Reinforcements or not, however, Banks was convinced that all of Texas would soon be in his hands. Crossing a pontoon bridge constructed between the island and the mainland, the army occupied Point Isabel and Brownsville November 6.

Brig. Gen. Hamilton Prioleau Bee, elder brother of Brig. Gen. Barnard E. Bee who was responsible for giving "Stonewall" Jackson his nickname, was in command of the Texas forces in Brownsville. The forty-one-year-old Bee, a native of Charleston, South Carolina, was a veteran of the Mexican War and former Speaker of the Texas House of Representatives. After Texas seceded, he was made a brigadier general in the Confederate army and, in 1863, went to Brownsville, where he assumed command of the outpost at that location. His main task there was to facilitate the trading of cotton and other produce for munitions from Europe by way of Mexico.[11]

Bee's force of about 100 was heavily outnumbered by the invading Federals, and as Dana's men approached Brownsville, Bee elected to retreat. Before leaving the town, he ordered the destruction of the large stock of cotton and supplies on hand. Sparks from the burning cotton were carried by the wind, and a block of buildings caught fire and was burned. Some powder exploded, spreading panic among the populace. Bee declared that "terror was around me on all sides." Judge Israel Bigelow requested help from Matamoros, and some 200 Mexican soldiers, under Gen. José María Cobos, were dispatched to help restore order. Despite this confusion, the Texans managed to destroy most of the supplies and escape without losing a man.[12] Thus, as at Brazos Island, the Federal army met with no resistance and quickly occupied Brownsville and the surrounding area. Once in the town, Dana began to collect whatever undamaged cotton he could find. By November 21 he had accumulated over five hundred bales, which he forwarded to New Orleans. At least part of this cotton was acquired from trains arriving from the interior. In some cases, as the trains approached Brownsville, "the teamsters were somewhat astonished at finding themselves within Union lines and Gen Banks authorized to receive it and their teams pressed into Point Isabel service to hawl commissary goods for the benefit of the soldiers of Brownsville."[13]

Shortly after discovering that Banks planned to occupy Brownsville, Secretary of State Seward instructed the political general not to enter Mexico "unless it be temporarily." Nor should he create any "unnecessary and unlawful enlargement of the present field of war."[14] However, within these constraints he was free to conduct discussions with Mexican authorities for the purpose of encouraging the latter to sever the Confederate trade passing through their borders. With his political instincts coming to the fore, Banks quickly availed himself of this opportunity, and working with the U.S. consul in Matamoros, he began negotiating with the local Mexican leadership across the Rio Grande. During this period the shifts in Mexican politics were rapid and difficult to follow, and the Yankees referred to the frequent changes in leadership across the border as "revolutions."[15]

After numerous exchanges of memoranda, and several face-to-face meetings with leaders of various Mexican factions, Banks reported to Lincoln that once again he had been completely successful. He stated that his "most sanguine expectations are more than realized," despite the fact that "three revolutions have occurred in Matamoras, affecting the government of Tamaulipas." With success following success, statesman and military commander Banks proudly claimed that "everything is now as favorable as could be desired."[16] In a letter to his wife he added, "I have always known that there was a protecting Hand above us but I never *felt* it until now. I have experienced the sensation of deliverance. I may say for the first time in my life, I believe our success to have one of great importance to the Country."[17]

By occupying Brownsville, Banks temporarily interrupted the Confederate trade through Mexico. The trade quickly resumed, however, using river crossings at Eagle Pass, Laredo, and other points upstream. As one historian described the result, "At times great trains of wagons rolled across the Texas plains in clouds of dust, whips cracking and mules braying."[18] For the Southerners the route to Mexico was now less convenient than before, but the trading of cotton for weapons and other supplies continued.

Once established in Brownsville, Banks moved rapidly to expand his toehold in Texas. Col. Edmund J. Davis was sent up the Rio Grande to Ringgold Barracks with his 1st Texas Cavalry. Davis occupied that site November 20.[19] A large amount of cotton and other stores were captured there. Another Texas Unionist, Col. John L. Haynes, advanced fifteen miles farther upriver, to the town of Roma. Although not many Texas recruits were added to Banks's army, a sizable number of Union sympathizers and refugees sought shelter within the Union lines in Brownsville.[20] Meanwhile, on November 16, leaving General Dana in charge at Brownsville, Banks reembarked with the intent of occupying points up the coast. With his usual perspective and insight, he informed his wife that this would be the "finest campaign of the war."[21] He took with him about 1,500 men, including the 13th and 15th Maine, 26th and 34th Iowa, and the 8th Indiana, plus one battery of artillery. These five regiments of the 2nd Division were under the command of Brig. Gen. Thomas Edward Greenfield Ransom.

Ransom was born in Vermont and educated at the military school in Norwich.[22] With the rank of colonel he served as chief of staff for Maj. Gen. John A. McClernand during the Corinth campaign and was subsequently named inspector general of the Army of the Tennessee. He commanded a brigade of John McArthur's division of James McPherson's XVII Corps at Vicksburg. After the capture of that fortress he was transferred to the Gulf with the XIII Corps detachment. General Grant, volunteering rare high praise, once said of Ransom, "He has always proved himself the best man I have ever had to send on expeditions. He is a live man and of good judgment."[23]

Wading ashore through the surf at Aransas Pass, Ransom's force occupied Corpus Christi and moved up Mustang Island. After a brief skirmish they captured most of the island's defense force of about 100 men. With this success Banks apparently believed he had earned the right to taunt Halleck a bit about the general in chief's beloved Red River campaign. In reporting his new move, Banks took the opportunity to retract his previous tepid endorsement of the Red River being the best line of defense for Louisiana and base for operations in Texas. After all, his troops already controlled Berwick Bay and the Atchafalaya, and he was sanguine about his activities along the Texas coast leading to the occupation of that state in its entirety. Therefore, he boldly declared, "The success of our expedition will very likely transfer our operations to the coast. The best line of defense for Louisiana, as well as for operations against Texas, is by Berwick Bay and the Atchafalaya."[24] In this message Banks did not mention the Red River.

Governor Hamilton, who had remained in New Orleans at Banks's suggestion "until the practicability of re-establishing the flag of the Union in Texas could be determined," joined Banks at Aransas Pass November 25. The last thing Banks wanted was to have to worry with the mercurial Hamilton, so he now suggested that the governor make his headquarters at Brownsville, "where our position would be permanent, and his official communication with the interior of the State uninterrupted and easy." Somewhat surprisingly the governor agreed to this proposal and departed the next day for the isolated and remote Rio Grande post. Banks subsequently bragged to the president that "General Hamilton expressed unqualified satisfaction with the success which had been attained, and said that the occupation of Matagorda Bay placed in the control of the Government the entire State of Texas."[25]

After reaching the north end of Mustang Island, Ransom's troops crossed the pass to St. Joseph's Island and continued their advance. A few days later, following a brief skirmish, the lead brigades crossed Cedar Bayou, the pass between St. Joseph's and Matagorda islands, and Ransom was soon ready to move toward Pass Cavallo, the entrance to Matagorda Bay. Meanwhile, a portion of the 1st Brigade, 1st Division, XIII Army Corps, under the command of Col. Henry D. Washburn, had been sent to New Orleans by General Franklin in response to Banks's request for reinforcements. Washburn's force arrived in Texas during Ransom's advance up the coastal islands. Along with the colonel's troops came Maj. Gen. Cadwallader C. Washburn (no relation to Henry D.), and on November 13 General Washburn assumed command of Ransom's expedition. At that time Ransom's regiments were reorganized into the 3rd Brigade, 2nd Division, XIII Army Corps. With the arrival of Washburn, Banks decided it was time for him to return to Louisiana.

At the north end of Matagorda Island was the tiny village of Saluria, where Col. Earl Van Dorn had accepted the surrender of some 500 Union troops in April 1861.[26] Between this village, on the bay side of the island, and a lighthouse and abandoned fort on the Gulf side, the Texas defenders had constructed a substantial earthen fort called Fort Esperanza with which to defend the entrance to Matagorda Bay. A short distance to the west of Saluria the island was separated from the mainland by a narrow strip of water known as McHenry's Bayou. Communications between the island and the mainland were maintained by a floating bridge across the bayou. In the latter part of November 1863 Fort Esperanza was defended by some 500 men of the 1st Regiment, Texas Heavy Artillery, under the command of Col. William R. Bradfute.[27] Washburn carefully planned his attack against the fort, expecting to encounter stiff resistance by the defenders.

Accompanied by 2,800 men, and escorted by the gunboats *Monongahela* and *Granite City*, Washburn started up Matagorda Island November 26. One force, under Henry D. Washburn, moved along the beach on the Gulf side of the island, while another, under General Ransom, trudged through the sand dunes along the center of the island. Colonel Washburn's force reached the lighthouse and abandoned fort on the Gulf side of Pass Cavallo November 27, then turned northwest toward the outer works of Fort Esperanza. These works stretched along a northeast-southwest line between the waters of the pass and a small lagoon that connected with Matagorda Bay. After driving the enemy pickets before them, Colonel Washburn's force took shelter behind some sand dunes about three hundred yards from the Confederate outer works. The latter position was described as "a heavy earthwork, . . . regularly laid out, about 15 feet in thickness, and from 10 to 15 feet in height."[28] Skirmishing and sharp-shooting between the attackers and the defenders were continuous. An occasional round of artillery was fired from the fort, but the shells generally fell harmlessly behind the Union troops. Ransom's force joined that of Washburn in front of the Confederate line November 28.

During the night of November 28 the men of the 8th Indiana and the 99th Illinois, having had considerable experience in building entrenchments at Vicksburg, were set to digging rifle pits and trenches parallel to the enemy's works. While these positions were being prepared, a norther struck, making the soldiers miserable but not stopping the work. Then, early on the very cold morning of the November 29, Washburn's men filed into the entrenchments. After a brief cannonade the Union force rushed forward and took possession of the outer works. Artillery was soon brought up and began to fire on the fort. The naval gunboats were to assist in the bombardment, but this proved impossible because of the weather. However, the navy guns were not needed. Return fire from the fort was not very accurate, and the Union artillery soon drove the enemy from their guns. Meanwhile, the infantry continued to push the Confederate skirmishers back toward the fort. During the fighting an old work several hundred yards in front of the main Union line and to the south of the fort was occupied by a company of the 8th Indiana. During the night of November 29 this position was reinforced, and four pieces from the 7th Michigan Battery were emplaced there. A general advance was planned for daylight November 30.

The Texans in the fort observed the buildup of the Union forces on the evening of November 29, and Colonel Bradfute decided resistance was futile. He elected to abandon his position. About 10:00 P.M. the garrison began retreating across McHenry's Bayou. After midnight, as the last of the garrison was ready to retreat to the mainland, Bradfute ordered the guns he had not been able to remove to be spiked and the magazines destroyed. A short time after midnight on the morning of November 30 an explosion of gunpowder in the fort alerted the Union forces to the fact that the enemy was retreating. Advancing in the dark, the Union skirmishers found the works abandoned. The advance quickly pushed on to the edge of the bayou but arrived too late to intercept the escaping Confederates. Six Texans, left behind to burn the floating bridge, were captured. General Washburn, with the loss of 2 killed and 10 wounded, now had possession of Fort Esperanza and therefore of Pass Cavallo.

Washburn was optimistic that his victory presaged a triumphal advance up the coast. With a little help from some reinforcements and a bit of luck he expected to move rapidly to Houston. At about 4:00 A.M. on November 30 he wrote to Banks, who by then was en route to New Orleans, informing him that "the rebels evacuated Fort Esperanza at about 10 o'clock last night, and blew it up at 1 o'clock this morning. Our troops entered it at 2 o'clock." The next day he declared, "I have determined to move up the Matagorda Peninsula to the mouth of the Brazos River. . . . That will be my base of supply from which to move to Houston and Galveston. . . . If you will send the Third Division, Thirteenth Army Corps, here, with that and the First, I will ask no more to go to Houston and take Galveston."[29] At the time the Union troops arrived on the south end of Matagorda Island, there were less than 1,000 enemy soldiers in the vicinity of Matagorda Bay. Even by the end of November General Magruder had only about 6,700 men available for the defense of the upper Texas coast.[30] An opportunity to complete his plan for the occupation of Texas was thus placed in front of Banks, but it remained to be seen whether he could screw up enough courage to accept the challenge, and the risk, offered by Washburn.

Banks arrived in New Orleans December 2. He received the notes from Washburn a few days later, and showing his usual propensity for overestimating the number of enemy troops arrayed against him, decided he did not want Washburn to cross Pass Cavallo without reinforcements. By the time Washburn received word of this decision, however, some 1,000 men had already crossed to the north side of the pass. In response to Banks's order not to cross the pass, Washburn replied that conditions, including fuel for fires, were better on the north side of the pass than on the south side. After weighing Washburn's arguments, Banks agreed to allow the occupation of Decros Point, at the southwest tip of Matagorda peninsula, but he would not let his subordinate proceed with plans to move immediately up the peninsula to the mouth of the Brazos.

Instead, on December 5 Brig. Gen. Charles P. Stone, Banks's chief of staff, informed Washburn that "the commanding general desires that you scout actively all the country in your front." It would be okay to make demonstrations to "amuse and confuse the enemy as to your intentions," but that is all. Banks was fearful that an advance would "bring down upon you the concentrated forces of the enemy," and "you must be largely re enforced before such advance is made." Thus, Washburn's suddenly timid commanding officer decided that his field commander would "be well employed in strengthening your present position, rendering your men as comfortable as possible,"[31] rather than advancing against the enemy.

In response to these orders, after leaving troops at Fort Esperanza, Washburn sent detachments by water to occupy the towns of Indianola, Port Lavaca, and Matagorda. These detachments faced little opposition upon landing, and small contingents of troops were left at each location. Meanwhile, he sent more troops across Pass Cavallo to join the encampment on Decros Point. At Washburn's order, Ransom traveled up the coast by gunboat to observe the enemy defensive works that were being prepared. These works, at the base of Matagorda peninsula near the Confederate headquarters at Velasco, were judged to be quite formidable.[32]

Magruder had hoped to hold the position at Pass Cavallo. In September 1863 he had told General Bee that Saluria must be held at all costs, for its loss would endanger Galveston and the rest of east Texas.[33] Now that Fort Esperanza had fallen and the Yankees controlled Pass Cavallo, Magruder decided to concentrate his forces on the line of the Brazos, San Bernard, and Caney rivers and attempt to defend the coast between the Brazos and the Sabine. He appealed to Kirby Smith and Richard Taylor for reinforcements. The only response he received to this request was that the cavalry of Brig. Gen. Tom Green—the same cavalry that Magruder had sent previously to support Taylor in Louisiana—was ordered back to Texas. Even then, Magruder was told not to disperse Green's troopers because they might be needed again in Louisiana. Ultimately, Magruder had to depend on his own limited resources for his attempt to stop Banks. In December 1863 he moved his headquarters to Velasco to direct the defense of east Texas personally. There he began making preparations to repel an attack by the invaders.

At Banks's order, in early December Franklin began forwarding still more troops from New Iberia to New Orleans for service in Texas. The movement of these troops was necessarily slow because of the weather in Louisiana. The winter storms there seemed to combine the worst of mud and cold. Nevertheless, frequently in inclement weather and under trying conditions, a steady line of troops struggled down the Teche to Berwick Bay. After crossing the bay to Brashear City, the men got a respite from slogging through the mud as they moved by rail to Algiers. Then, boarding transports, the reinforcements proceeded down the Mississippi and across the Gulf to Texas. The last, open-water portion of the trip was frequently the roughest part, as many of the men suffered from seasickness during the voyage.[34]

The first of Franklin's reinforcements began arriving in Texas in mid-December. The newcomers joined those troops already in camp on the tip of Matagorda peninsula. One new arrival described the site as "a dreary, desolate sand bank, known as DeCrow's Point." He added that "while vast stores of 'hard-tack,' and kindred luxuries were piled up at New Orleans, Gen. Banks, with a foresight for which his military administration was famous, failed to furnish his troops in Texas with the much-needed supplies." Furthermore, the weather was cold, and the wind howled unimpeded across the peninsula. "It was no uncommon thing to see the whole encampment lying prostrate on the sand."[35]

On December 24, 1863, Maj. Gen. Francis J. Herron was ordered to Brownsville to take command of the Union forces there. With Herron now in command in Brownsville, Dana was ordered to Fort Esperanza, where on January 12 he relieved Washburn, who had requested a leave of absence.[36] Dana was now commander of all of the U.S. troops on the coast of Texas. Ransom was assigned command of the 4th Division, XIII Corps, located at Decros Point. After the arrival of the reinforcements from Louisiana, Dana was ready to undertake the advance up the coast that had been planned by Washburn after the capture of Fort Esperanza.[37] By the time the reinforcements arrived, however, heavy concentrations of enemy troops had gathered near the mouth of the Brazos, and any advance was expected to be met with a vigorous defense. To assess the enemy strength, Dana ordered General Ransom to conduct a ground-based reconnaissance of the Confederate positions at the upper end of the Matagorda peninsula. Ransom marched up the peninsula as far as the Southern works on Caney Creek, where he again observed Magruder's forces. He found that the Southerners were entrenched and well prepared to meet the Union advance. Any movement up the coast would have to be planned carefully.[38]

From New Orleans Banks could see that a clash between Dana and Magruder was shaping up on the Caney. With reinforcements now in place Banks believed his army in Texas would soon be able to destroy or disperse the enemy at that point, after which there would be a clear road to Galveston. Soon after reaching Galveston, Banks's expeditionary force should be able to complete the occupation of the Texas coast from the Rio Grande to Sabine Pass, and all of Texas would once again be Union. This goal was soon circumvented, however, by decisions in Washington.

Even though he had successfully, though belatedly, planted the Union flag in Texas, Banks could not shake the persistent Halleck from the latter's desire to have him, Banks, send a force up the Red River. Almost hypnotically the commander in the field kept falling into Halleck's trap. After Banks sent his note to Halleck November 18, stating that "the best line of defense of Louisiana, as well as for operations against Texas, is by Berwick's bay and the Atchafalaya," Halleck professed to agree. On December 7 the general in chief wrote Banks with some disingenuousness, "I fully concur with you in this opinion. It is the line which I advised you from the beginning to adopt." Yet Halleck continued his querulous nagging about Banks's activities. In this December 7 message he warned that "the danger . . . of dividing your army, with the enemy between the two posts, ready to fall upon either with his entire force, was pointed out from the first."[39]

Banks was growing tired of always getting the same "suggestion" from Halleck whenever he revealed his military plans to the general in chief. Therefore, as though he were hoping to keep his new plan a secret until he had achieved some spectacular success, Banks had begun his coastal invasion of Texas without notifying Halleck. In his December 7 message to Banks, Halleck complained about this. Banks replied December 23, 1863. Following his failure to capture Sabine Pass, he said, "I immediately concentrated all my disposable force upon the Teche, with a view to enter Texas by the way of Niblett's Bluff, on the Sabine, or by Alexandria." However, the low water level in the Louisiana rivers and bayous, and the lack of supplies available in the country along the Teche, defeated this plan. "I concluded to make another effort to effect a landing at some point upon the coast of Texas, in the execution of what I understood to be imperative orders." Then, apparently assuming a weak excuse would be better than none at all, he added, "It is my purpose always to keep you informed of all movements that are contemplated in this department, but it did not seem to me to be possible to do more in this instance."[40]

Banks was obeying Halleck's orders of August 6 by invading the Texas coast, and he now had a string of victories, from the Rio Grande to Pass Cavallo, to show for it. Would this constant harping about the risks to his forces incurred by his expedition to the Texas coast, and about the desirability of a campaign up the Red River, never stop? It appeared that it would not. By January Halleck was becoming testy. On January 4 he wrote again to Banks, now implicating both Sherman and Maj. Gen. Frederick Steele, commander of the Department of Arkansas, in his monomaniacal obsession:

> Generals Sherman and Steele agree with me in opinion that the Red river is the shortest and best line of defense for Louisiana and Arkansas, and as a base of operations against Texas. If this line can be adopted, most of the troops in Arkansas can be concentrated on it. But, as before remarked, Steele cannot alone attempt its occupation. His movements must therefore be dependent, in a great measure, upon yours. If, as soon as you have sufficient water in the Atchafalaya and Red rivers, you operate in that direction, Steele's army and such forces as Sherman can detach should be directed to the same object. The gunboats should also co-operate. If, on the other hand, your operations are mainly confined to the coast of Texas, Steele must make the Arkansas river his line of defense, and most of Sherman's force may be required to keep open the Mississippi.[41]

Pressure like this played heavily on the mind of the major general commanding the Gulf Department. As his troops marched about on the Matagorda peninsula and watched the Confederates fortify their position at the mouth of the Caney and in the town of Velasco, Banks continued to mull over what he should do next.

By early January, having watched regiment after regiment of the XIII Corps leave his force in New Iberia to travel to Texas, Franklin found himself with little more than 5,000 infantry and 3,500 cavalry with which to hold his position against the ever-belligerent Taylor. Believing he was in an exposed position and at risk of being attacked, on January 5 he issued orders for his troops to prepare to march south. That night a freezing rain fell, and the Louisiana mud became coated with a glaze of ice. Because of the weather Franklin put the march off for a day, then started down the Teche the morning of January 7 in the midst of a biting norther. Many of the cutoff roads across the bends of the bayou were in such bad condition that they could not be used; as a result the army had to march nearly the full length of the watercourse. One member of the 114th New York, after leaving the regiment's comfortable camp in New Iberia, claimed that "the English language is inadequate, the powers of rhetoric too feeble, to describe the march of that day." As the soldiers and animals struggled through the ice and mud, wagons were abandoned and "mules and horses dropped dead in the harness, from exhaustion and inhuman beating. . . . A confused mass of struggling, wallowing, dirty, half-concealed-in-the-mud humanity, all day slowly labored along the roads and across the fields."[42] Some of the men found or made rafts and floated down the bayou ahead of their plodding comrades.

Finally, the army arrived at the town of Franklin on January 9. There, most of the men whose enlistments were expiring consented to reenlist, and the XIX Corps was reinforced by the arrival of four new regiments. Three, the 29th and 30th Maine and the 153rd New York, joined Franklin's army in the field; and a fourth, the 14th New Hampshire, was assigned to temporary duty near New Orleans. Capt. Benjamin Nields's 1st Delaware Battery and Capt. Newman W. Storer's 7th Massachusetts Battery also joined the corps. With these additions to his force, Franklin finally felt secure and decided to settle down for the remainder of the winter. The next move was up to General Banks.

At the same time that Banks was trying to respond to Halleck's incessant suggestion for a campaign up the Red River, he was communicating with the president regarding the political situation in his department. For almost a year Lincoln had wanted to see progress in the matter of a local election to establish a loyalist state government in Louisiana. Banks was in agreement; however, as the general saw it, he had not been assigned the responsibility for forming such a government. Instead, the assignment had been given to the military governor of Louisiana, Brig. Gen. George F. Shepley. When the president urged Banks to give Governor Shepley's efforts to hold an election "a hearty sympathy and support,"[43] Banks replied, "I have regarded reorganization of the government here as of the highest importance." However, "I found most of these gentlemen [Governor Shepley and his supporters] so interested in topics, that seemed to me disconnected with the general subject, and so slightly disposed to encourage my participation in the affair that I . . . turned my attention . . . to matters more likely to be accomplished"; that is, his invasion of the Texas coast. He added, "I have had neither authority, influence, or recognition as an officer entrusted with this duty," and promised that "had the organization of a *free* state in Louisiana been committed to me under general instructions only, it would have been complete before this day. It can be effected now in sixty days—let me say, even in thirty days, if necessary."[44]

This letter to the president was answered diplomatically on December 24:

> I deeply regret to have said or done anything which could give you pain, or uneasiness. . . . I have all the while intended you to be *master,* as well in regard to

> re-organizing a State government for Louisiana, as in regard to the military matters of the Department. . . . I now tell you that in every dispute, with whomsoever, you are master. Gov. Shepley was appointed to *assist* the Commander of the Department, and not to thwart him, or act independently of him. . . . I now distinctly tell you that you are master of all, and that I wish you to take the case as you find it, and give us a free-state re-organization of Louisiana, in the shortest possible time. . . . I do not mean that you are to withdraw from Texas, or abandon any other military measure which you may deem important. Nor do I mean that you are to throw away available work already done for re-construction; or that war is to be made upon Gov. Shepley, or upon any one else, unless it be found that they will not co-operate with you, in which case, and in all cases, you are master while you remain in command of the Department.[45]

The repetition used by Lincoln in this message is almost that of a parent to a slow child. Four times he used the word *master* to describe Banks's role in Louisiana. From this message even General Banks should understand the president's intent. The last clause, "while you remain in command of the Department," was premonitory. Lincoln was growing tired of the inability of his department commander to control his own department. There was a veiled and ominous threat to Banks's military future in this statement, and Banks would do well to pay attention.

In the fall of 1863 controversy was growing over the process by which the Southern states were to be restored to their proper place in the Union. During his recovery from a bout of varioloid, a mild form of smallpox, Lincoln took the opportunity to craft a reconstruction policy that would avoid extremes and allow for the early resumption of the participation of the seceded states in the political activities of the Union. In his message to Congress December 8 the president presented the policy he had decided upon: the Proclamation of Amnesty and Reconstruction. This was a generous policy based on the premise that the Southern states were misguided sisters who should be welcomed back into the Union once they mended their ways. On the other hand, while stating his own preference, the president kept the door open to other suggestions: "Saying that reconstruction will be accepted if presented in a specified way, it is not said it will never be accepted in any other way."[46]

Lincoln's carefully considered road map for the restoration of the Union was his Ten Percent Plan. In it he stated that, with a few exceptions, "a full pardon is hereby granted to them and each of them [who have participated in the rebellion] . . . upon the condition that every such person shall take and subscribe an oath" of allegiance to the United States. Furthermore, when 10 percent or more of the number of white males of a seceded state that had voted in the 1860 election took such an oath, the eligible voters would be allowed to write a new state constitution and establish a state government. After these actions the state could resume its place in the Union. The Ten Percent Plan was quite controversial at the time and received much criticism from both radical Republicans and Democrats. The New England cotton interests liked the plan, however. They suggested that it would not be difficult for a small number of Northern immigrants to gain political control of a state under the circumstances stipulated by the president.[47]

Banks learned of Lincoln's Ten Percent Plan in late December. He liked the plan. It was consistent with his idea that when a loyalist group became organized in each of the seceded states, the opposition to the Federal government would rapidly disappear and the state would return to the fold. On December 30, after receiving the new instructions and authority contained in the president's letter of December 24, he wrote to Lincoln, "Your message and proclamation can not fail to produce great national results." He was ready to implement the plan and suggested that to guarantee a "*speedy and certain*" result, he be allowed to proceed under the existing constitution of the state of Louisiana, "except so much thereof as recognizes and relates to slavery."[48]

Banks's stated preference for using the existing Louisiana constitution as a basis for filling elective offices in a new, free-state government rather than first holding a constitutional convention was met with numerous objections in Washington and New Orleans. Banks supported the goal of a new constitution but believed a convention to create one should follow and not precede an election for state offices. Because Banks's decision effectively terminated plans already under way by Governor Shepley and others for election of delegates to a constitutional convention, it has been interpreted by many students of this era of Louisiana politics as a petty effort by the commanding general to exert his new authority.[49] However, it seems more likely that this decision was based on his experience in the Massachusetts constitutional convention of 1853. That convention was in session for three months. Banks realized that a Louisiana convention would likely require months of deliberation over and above the time required for the election and seating of delegates, and he told Lincoln on December 30 that he "feared that delegates would debate 'every theory connected with human legislation,' occasioning 'dangerous if not fatal delay.'"[50] In light of Lincoln's sense of urgency it is probable Banks felt that the installation of a loyalist civilian government could be accomplished more quickly if it preceded rather than followed the preparation and approval of a new state constitution.

The president continued to impel Banks forward. "I am much in hope that, on the authority of my letter, of December 24th. you have already begun the work." If not, "on receiving this, proceed with all possible despatch." The only constraints the president placed on Banks's actions to establish a Unionist government in Louisiana was that he not stray from the conditions he, Banks, had specified regarding the use of the extant state constitution, "nor from those of the Message and Proclamation of December 8th."[51] With the receipt of this letter Banks proceeded to authorize elections under the antebellum state constitution, regarding which he declared all provisions relating to slavery to be inoperative and void. He scheduled the election for February 22, 1864, the anniversary of George Washington's birth.[52]

In Banks's opinion a moderate position, which called for continued support for his labor policies for the freedmen but opposed suffrage for the former slaves, would be the most likely to gain the support of the local population. He stated in a letter to George Boutwell that "if the policy proposed be too conservative or too radical it will bring a counter-revolution, which will bear the seeds of infinite revolutions and anarchy." But to Banks the moderate approach did not mean that emancipation would be abandoned. "Those who have been slaveholders in this state will gladly consent to a government upon the basis of immediate freedom . . . if urged upon them, in a spirit not unfriendly."[53]

The election results were as Banks anticipated, and the new, moderate Republican governor of loyalist Louisiana was Banks's political associate from New Orleans, Michael Hahn. The election safely met Lincoln's 10 percent requirement. In the rosy glow of success, and employing his customary overblown rhetoric, Banks saw the results of his political efforts in Louisiana as "without parallel in history. It [the effects of the election] has been far greater than could have been anticipated with reason." Banks was certain that Louisiana would soon become "one of the most loyal and prosperous States that the world has ever seen."[54] Then, following his promise to pursue the construction of a new, free-state constitution after the election was over, on March 11 Banks announced that March 28 there would be an election of delegates to a constitutional convention.

BEGINNING OF THE FIFTH INVASION

Halleck's Red River Expedition

8 Responding to the wishes of President Lincoln to establish a military presence in Texas, Halleck had encouraged Banks to "hoist the flag" in that state. Although he had not ordered Banks to conduct any specific military operations to accomplish that objective, Halleck was displeased with Banks's choice of invasion route. He obviously expected his suggestion about the Red River being "the shortest and best line of defense, and as a base of operations against Texas" to be accepted by Banks as though it were an order. As Banks stated later, "That movement had always been pressed upon me by General Halleck before I left Washington to assume command of that department."[1]

To counter the general in chief's persistent references to the Red River, Banks reminded Halleck on December 30, 1863, that "it is impossible, at this time, to move as far north as Alexandria by water. The Red river is not open to the navigation of our gunboats, and it is commanded by Fort De Russy, which has been remounted since our occupation of Alexandria."[2] Disregarding this rational counterargument, Halleck continued to put forward the same suggestion. In his complaints to Banks, Halleck took no notice of the fact that his field general had diligently and with modest success followed the instructions, if not the advice, of the general in chief.

Banks, for his part, wanted to receive something more than a suggestion from Washington before beginning a campaign up the Red. He repeatedly asked Halleck for "instructions." Undoubtedly Banks would have attempted to execute any instructions that Halleck sent, but the wily general in chief made sure that he never issued any. Instead, he just provided more arguments in support of an advance up the Red. On January 11 Halleck again goaded Banks toward the Red, at the same time tempting him by promising help not only from Generals Sherman and Steele but also from Admiral Porter. He pointedly asked Banks to confer with these gentlemen concerning a joint operation on the Red: "I am assured by the Navy Department that Admiral Porter will be prepared to co-operate with you as soon as the stage of the water in the southwest will admit of the use of his flotilla there." Furthermore, a movement up the Red, according to Halleck, would provide not only a better line of defense for Louisiana and a base for invading Texas but also provide a "shorter and better line of defense for Arkansas and Missouri." Finally, such a move would "open to us the cotton and slaves of northeastern Louisiana and southern Arkansas."[3] How many more points of argument would his field commander demand before yielding to such irrefutable logic?

Sherman indeed did support a move up the Red, but this support was only in the context of related actions on both sides of the Mississippi. Now that the Union had regained control of the river, one of Sherman's concerns was the continuing guerrilla activity directed against river shipping. He believed that quick strikes against enemy facilities and resources along the river would help reduce such activity. In pursuit of this idea he suggested, and Grant approved, a quick strike against Meridian, Mississippi. Sherman's purpose in this raid was to destroy railroads and anything else of value to the enemy along the route between that town and the river. In January 1864 Sherman ordered Brig. Gen. Andrew J. Smith to move from Columbus, Kentucky, into western Tennessee to support this forthcoming Meridian expedition. He told Smith to "punish the country well for permitting the guerrillas among them. Take freely the horses, mules, cattle, &c., of the hostile or indifferent inhabitants, and let them all understand that if from design or weakness they permit their country to be used by the public enemy they must bear the expense of the troops sent to expel them; also notify them that we will soon begin to banish all people who are deemed opposed to the re-establishment of civil order. . . . The people must expect us to treat them as enemies, unless they assist us in our efforts to restore civil order."[4] Smith enthusiastically adopted the philosophy of his commander as expressed in this dispatch and applied the recommended procedure freely to the areas of the South in which he operated.

On January 16 General Sherman sent a message to Banks in which he declared that he would "like nothing better than to unite with you" in a raid up the Red. "I think this movement [on Meridian], and one similar on Shreveport, as soon as the Red river rises, would pretty well settle the main question in the southwest."[5] The Meridian raid took place in February 1864. General Sherman considered it to be a great success and was motivated to make strikes on other enemy strongholds along the Mississippi. He stated to Halleck, "If Red River will admit of a similar prompt and decisive movement on Shreveport, I see no reason why Grant should not be re-enforced in all April with 20,000 men from this quarter."[6] As far as Sherman was concerned, an expedition up the Red River would complement his Meridian raid and constitute an application of the same tactics—a series of quick strikes against rebel strongholds to eliminate the ability of the enemy to support guerrilla movements against traffic on the river.[7]

The messages from Halleck and Sherman began having an effect on Banks. In a letter to Halleck dated January 23 Banks backed down from his position that Berwick Bay and the Atchafalaya formed the best line of defense for Louisiana and Arkansas. He now stated that he agreed with Halleck's position concerning the Red River. However, he indicated that alone he could operate only on the coast without hope of moving far into the interior of Texas. With Sherman and Porter's cooperation, on the other hand, things would be different and he would "cordially co-operate" with them. He reiterated his long-standing, conciliatory position that after Union forces secured the region along the Red, "their people will gladly renew their allegiance to the Government." Furthermore, in his opinion, "The occupation of Shreveport will be to the country west of the Mississippi what that of Chattanooga is to the east."[8]

Still seeking instructions from the general in chief, Banks added that he proposed to operate "in the direction of Shreveport, and from thence await your instructions." In his testimony to the Congressional Joint Committee on the Conduct of the War in January 1865 Banks stated, "My idea was to move rapidly upon that point [Shreveport], leaving no line of communication to be interrupted by the enemy anywhere."[9] Despite this statement, Banks's concept of a move on Shreveport was vastly different from that of Sherman. He also stated to the committee that as he understood it, "it was the purpose of the expedition to occupy Shreveport, and hold it. General Steele's forces were to hold it if we occupied it." In his orders to General Grover at Alexandria, dated March 31, 1864, Banks indicated his belief that the Red River expedition was intended to take and hold at least some territory. In referring to Alexandria, he informed Grover that "it is probable that this will be a permanent post."[10] This was not a description of the quick strike that Sherman envisioned.

Banks wrote Halleck again January 29, indicating that he was ready to cooperate with Sherman and Steele in a campaign up the Red. However, in any such campaign major support from the navy would be essential. "I can take possession of Alexandria at any time, but could not maintain the position without the support of forces on the river." Then he added, almost pleading for directions from the general in chief, "Anxiously, awaiting information and instructions in regard to operations on the Red River, I have done nothing in Texas, except to provide for the security of the positions held."[11]

General Sherman sent another note to Banks January 31, shortly before departing for Jackson and Meridian, regarding his desire for cooperation in a move up the Red. He was enthusiastic about the campaign: "My orders from General Grant will not, as yet, justify me in embarking for Red River, though I am very anxious to move in that direction." However, he added, "I understand that Red River is still low. . . . You cannot do anything till Red River has twelve feet of water on the rapids at Alexandria. That will be from March to June."[12] Sherman, who lived near Alexandria before the war, knew the characteristics of the Red. He promised Banks that, if allowed, he would furnish 10,000 men for the expedition. He clearly was at cross purposes with Banks, however, as he again emphasized the quick-strike nature of the movement he envisioned and said nothing about any "occupation" of Shreveport or taking "possession" of Alexandria. He did say, however, "I do not believe the enemy will fight a force of 30,000 men acting in concert with gun-boats."[13]

Though greatly encouraged by Sherman's expression of support, and perhaps taking to heart Sherman's belief that the enemy would not fight a force of 30,000 men, Banks still hesitated because he received no positive orders from Halleck. In his next missive to Banks, dated February 1, Halleck again practiced the art of duplicity. He admitted that "if the Red River is not navigable . . . there seems very little prospect of the requisite co-operation or transportation of supplies. It has, therefore, been left entirely to your discretion . . . to adopt this line or substitute any other."[14] The implication that Halleck made by his use of the word *therefore* was false and probably deliberately misleading. He implied that were the river navigable, the decision regarding an expedition up the Red would not have been left "entirely to your discretion" but would have been the subject of direct orders. It is certain, however, that Halleck would never have issued such orders unless instructed to do so by Lincoln or Stanton.

In another attempt to prod his reluctant field general into taking the action he desired without ordering him to do so, Halleck mentioned in the same message that Steele had been placed under Grant's command and that Grant might order a portion of the forces in Arkansas to move east to provide assistance for military activities in the state of Mississippi. This "might" reduce the support that Steele could provide for a move up the Red. Furthermore, Halleck explained, Sherman "may" have modified his plans. As the general in chief saw it, the coalition supporting his cherished Red River expedition was beginning to fall apart. "So many delays have already occurred, and the winter is now so far advanced, that I greatly fear no important operations west of the Mississippi will be concluded in time for General Grant's proposed campaign in the spring." This newfound concern for the passing of the season was nothing more than a display of frustration and a figurative wringing of hands on General Halleck's part. The statement was in direct contradiction to his previous admission that an expedition up the Red would not be possible until the river had risen from its winter low. It was just another way to needle his field general.[15]

Banks's head was undoubtedly spinning from the war of words between himself and Halleck. It was clear to him by now that Halleck would not back down. The general in chief wanted Banks to move up the Red but was not about to take the responsibility for ordering such a move. Banks wanted positive instructions from Halleck before beginning the campaign and figuratively dragged his feet through the Louisiana mud awaiting such. The Union flag was securely planted in Texas, and Banks wanted to attack Mobile and thereby support some of the impending military activities in the Confederate heartland. A major campaign up the Red, with the objective of taking and holding Shreveport, made no sense militarily at this point in the war and was purely a figment of Halleck's desk-bound imagination.

On February 11 Halleck finally explained to Banks in no uncertain terms that he, Halleck, was not about to order a move up the Red, or anything else for that matter:

> Your dispatches of January 29 and February 2 are received. In the former you speak of awaiting orders and instructions in regard to operations on Red River. If by this it is meant that you are waiting for orders from Washington, there must be some misapprehension. The substance of my dispatches to you on this subject was communicated to the President and Secretary of War, and it was understood that while stating my own views in regard to operations, I should leave you free to adopt such lines and plans of campaign as you might, after a full consideration of the subject, deem best. Such, I am confident, is the purport of my dispatches, and it certainly was not intended that any of your movements should be delayed to await instructions from here.[16]

Halleck was a master at this game. Five days later he wrote to Grant and placed all responsibility for any move up the Red on Banks. Without specifying by whom it was "understood," and without reference to the fact that General Steele had as yet received no orders to advance against Shreveport, he told Grant that after Sherman completed his Meridian expedition, "it was understood that he and General Banks would move up Red river to meet Steele's advance against Shreveport." Then to make it clear that he, Halleck, bore no responsibility for such an expedition, he added, "This was General Banks's plan, if Sherman and Steele could co-operate with him." He implicated Sherman as well by adding, "Will not the probable delay in expelling Longstreet from East Tennessee justify the adoption of this plan of Banks and Sherman?"[17] Then, just to reinforce the fact that his own hands were clean on the issue, on February 17 Halleck added, "I have given no orders to General Sherman in regard to his movements."[18]

Banks wrote Admiral Porter three days later: "The Government inclines to a movement upon Shreveport, rather than to any other line of operations west of the Mississippi." He claimed that the combination of the forces of Steele, Sherman, and himself (Banks) "would make a quick and decisive campaign." However, the lack of explicit orders from Halleck was also on his mind, and he conspiratorially hinted that maybe Porter, unlike himself, had received instructions from Washington to conduct an expedition up the Red. He told Porter, "I shall be ready to move by the first week in March for Opelousas and Alexandria and hope to clear the Red River to that point. I shall expect your cooperation and suppose you have received instructions from the Government at Washington in regard to the movement."[19]

As late as February 25 Banks was still pettish about not receiving orders from Halleck. In a message to the general in chief on that date he stated, "I understand that I am to move against Shreveport, and am unable to divide my command by any demonstration against Mobile, which must take some weeks before I could get them to this point again." In this dispatch Banks seemed to be seeking permission to move against Mobile: "This would be my desire, if it were consistent with my orders from the government." However, he now admitted, "I do not expect instructions from Washington beyond what I have received, except it relate to the movements of General Sherman or General Steele." He informed Halleck that he was now preparing for a campaign up the Red and claimed, "I can be at Alexandria or Natchitoches on the 15th of March, if either of the other commands shall co-operate with me in time."[20]

Banks had finally yielded to Halleck's pressure, and thus he began his fifth, and last, attempt to invade Texas. In preparation he withdrew almost all of his troops from the coast of Texas and sent them to join General Franklin, who was still ensconced at Franklin, Louisiana. With the help of Admiral Porter's gunboats, troops from Arkansas, and additional reinforcements from the Army of the Tennessee, Banks looked forward to the capture and occupation of the Confederate Trans-Mississippi headquarters. Once Shreveport was captured, it could be used as a base from which an invasion of east Texas could be launched.

On March 2, 1864, General Sherman visited New Orleans to meet with

Banks and discuss both the impending campaign up the Red and the possible loan of troops. There he learned of the plans Banks had made for the inauguration of Michael Hahn.[21] Banks invited Sherman to stay for the ceremonies, which according to Sherman "would include the performance of the 'Anvil Chorus' by all the bands of his army, and during the performance the church-bells were to be rung, and cannons were to be fired by electricity. I regarded all such ceremonies as out of place at a time when it seemed to me every hour and every minute were due to the war."[22] Sherman was of the opinion that all attempts to reinstate loyalist state governments in the South should wait until the war was won, and he declined Banks's invitation.

In addition, Sherman learned that Banks had decided to command the expedition up the Red personally. If there was to be a Red River campaign, Grant wanted Sherman to lead it. However, Banks outranked both Grant and Sherman at this point in the war. Placing Sherman in command of the expedition was not possible in light of Banks's decision. Grant certainly did not want Sherman serving under Banks. Thus, Sherman departed, disgusted with Banks's pompous inauguration plans and forgoing any personal role in the impending endeavor.[23] However, he still agreed to loan some troops to Banks to support the expedition, as long as Grant agreed.

Grant did not want to loan troops to Banks, but he felt obligated to do so. He told Sherman he hoped the number of troops diverted to Banks would be kept to a minimum and that the troops would be returned as soon as possible. On March 4 Sherman told Banks that with Grant's permission, he would select two divisions, of about 10,000 men total, and send them up the Red River to join Banks at Alexandria March 17. He added, "I have calculated, and so reported to General Grant, that this detachment of his forces in no event is to go beyond Shreveport, and that you will spare them the moment you can, trying to get them back to the Mississippi River in thirty days from the time they actually enter Red River."[24]

To meet his commitment to support Banks, Sherman selected one division each from James B. McPherson's and Stephen A. Hurlbut's commands, the 1st and 3rd Divisions, XVI Corps, plus a portion of the Provisional Division, XVII Corps. The five regiments selected from the 1st Division, XVI Corps, were under the command of Brig. Gen. Joseph A. Mower; ten regiments of infantry and two batteries of light artillery selected from the 3rd Division were under the command of Brig. Gen. Andrew Jackson Smith; and six regiments of infantry and one battery of light artillery from the Provisional Division, XVII Corps, were under the command of Brig. Gen. Thomas Kilby

Smith. These units were to be accompanied by Brig. Gen. Alfred W. Ellet's marine brigade. Sherman assigned command of his detachment to General Smith. Smith, of like mind with Sherman, saw the coming campaign as a raid intended to reduce the will of the South to fight. Thus, from the start Smith's attitude diverged from that of Banks.

To the extent that there was a plan for the upcoming expedition to Shreveport, it called for three Union armies, or portions thereof (Banks's Army of the Gulf, Sherman's detachment, and Frederick Steele's VI Corps), and a fleet (a major portion of Porter's Mississippi Squadron), each under independent command, to advance from their respective locations along routes to be chosen by their individual commanders, to meet at some remote point well inside enemy lines, and from that point to advance on and capture the enemy headquarters. Initially the four organizations making up the expedition were located hundreds of miles apart. Communications among the field commanders of these four units at times were slow and uncertain, and communications between Banks and Steele were never good. There was no common command authority lower than the president for the army and navy organizations involved, and for the army contingents there was none below General Halleck.

None of the military high command—the president, secretary of war, secretary of the navy, and general in chief—issued orders to any of the participants concerning the expedition. Although A. J. Smith was told to proceed to Alexandria "from which point Major-General Banks would assume the command and direction of the expedition in person,"[25] if the four independent military forces did successfully combine, Banks apparently did not believe that he would be in overall command. When asked whether he was subject to Banks's command, Admiral Porter stated, "Not at all. I was perfectly independent of him."[26] After the war Banks stated, "I should have acted under either one of them [Sherman or Steele] with perfect satisfaction." This was probably true since Banks had already shown himself willing to serve under an officer junior in rank to himself. At the time of the Battle of Cedar Mountain he was serving in the Army of Virginia in a position subordinate to the army commander, Maj. Gen. John Pope. However, because no one was given clear command authority, virtually every aspect of the Red River campaign would have to be improvised.[27]

In the original conception of a campaign up the Red, Banks and Halleck had both described the Red River as both a line of defense for Louisiana and a base from which to operate against Texas. On the other hand, once he captured Shreveport, Banks knew he would have to return Sherman's troops.

This would handicap any immediate attempt to use Shreveport as the base for an invasion of Texas. Furthermore, it is unlikely that Banks believed he could live off the country west of the Red because one reason he had abandoned his move into Texas from western Louisiana in the fall of 1863 was the lack of supplies and water available between the Red and the Sabine. Conditions would not likely have improved much in this regard during the intervening four months. Therefore, a move west from Shreveport would require a large wagon train to carry forage and provisions for the army. Whether Banks considered such a move viable following the occupation of Shreveport is uncertain, although he definitely made provisions for a large wagon train. Finally, Halleck had indicated that once Shreveport was captured, Banks was to turn the city over to Steele, after which it would serve as a line of defense for Arkansas and Missouri. Without Banks and Porter to help him, it was not obvious how Steele was to hold this position. Army transports could use the Red River to provide supplies and support to the troops remaining in Shreveport only for the period of the spring runoff. Without water access to the Mississippi, Steele's supply line to Shreveport would be tenuous indeed.

The success of a Red River expedition would depend heavily on the U.S. Navy. The commanding officer of the Mississippi Squadron, and the officer whose support was essential for the expedition, was Rear Adm. David Dixon Porter. For some time Porter had known that the idea for a campaign up the Red was brewing. He was not confident about the value, or enthusiastic about the prospects, of such an expedition, but if there was to be one, he wanted his friend Sherman to lead it. When he learned that Banks, not Sherman, was to lead the expedition, he was disappointed but felt obligated to participate since Sherman had promised to have Brig. Gen. A. J. Smith's troops at Alexandria by March 17, but only if Porter agreed to support the campaign.[28] Porter thus joined the expedition reluctantly but with every intention of making it a military success.

The force from the Army of the Gulf that Banks committed to the expedition consisted of just over 21,500 men, including 4,635 cavalry and mounted infantry under General Lee. The two XIX Corps infantry divisions under General Franklin plus the 3rd and 4th Divisions of the XIII Corps under Brig. Gens. Robert A. Cameron and Thomas E. G. Ransom, totaled 15,392. Finally, the four regiments of the Corps d'Afrique numbered 1,535. On March 7 the XIII Corps began the expedition by boarding transports and starting up Bayou Teche from their camp at Berwick.

Sherman's detachment from the Army of the Tennessee left Vicksburg

March 10 aboard a fleet of more than thirty transports. They joined Admiral Porter at the mouth of the Red River the next day. The divisions under Brig. Gen. A. J. Smith numbered approximately 10,000 men to which Ellet's marine brigade added roughly another 3,000. From the mouth of the Red, Smith's troops were to advance up the river in company with Porter's flotilla of thirteen ironclads and four tinclads. In addition there were tugs, pumps, and quartermaster, commissary, and hospital boats. This combination of navy warships, army transports, and support vessels constituted the largest waterborne military force ever assembled in the west.[29] The result was a vast aggregation of floating craft of various types and sizes that required a high degree of command leadership and interservice cooperation in order to move at all.

While this fleet was preparing to advance from the mouth of the Red, some of Smith's troops took the opportunity to go ashore. There they offered a preview of what was to occur continuously during the upcoming expedition as they proceeded to practice the art of pillaging and destruction mastered during the Meridian expedition. A reporter from the St. Louis *Daily Missouri Republican* was shocked and disturbed by what he saw:

> I should not be a faithful historian if I omitted to mention that the conduct of the troops since the late raid of General Sherman, is becoming very prejudicial to our good name and to their efficiency. A spirit of destruction and wanton ferocity seems to have seized upon many of them, which is quite incredible. At Red River landing they robbed a house of several thousand dollars in specie, and then fired the house to conceal their crime. At Simmsport, a party of them stole out, and robbed and insulted a family two miles distant. In fact, unless checked by summary example, there is danger of our whole noble army degenerating into a band of cut-throats and robbers.[30]

Although many Northerners had a low opinion of Southerners, some considering them dirty and ignorant barbarians,[31] the "spirit of destruction and wanton ferocity" described by this reporter was likely not generally something the soldiers brought with them when they enlisted in the army. Rather, it was often undoubtedly the product of frustration and pent-up anger against the Southern soldiers and the civilian population that supported them. Some of the Northern soldiers may have blamed these civilians for precipitating the war and considered the destruction of their property as just punishment; others may have seen the acts of plundering as justified by attacks on the troops committed by irregulars or civilians.[32] In any case, many of the hapless residents who found themselves in the line of march of the Union army suffered the loss of their personal possessions, their stock, their buildings and implements, and in many cases their homes.

Maj. Gen. Frederick Steele was to move from Arkansas toward Shreveport with a portion of his 13,000-man VII Corps in concert with the advances of Banks, Smith, and Porter. However, despite his instructions to support Banks, Steele initially did not see how he could assist the Red River expedition. He saw himself beset by near-insurmountable military and political difficulties in Arkansas. When urged by Halleck to move south in March, Steele seemed able to think only of reasons why such a move was not possible. On March 12, the day Porter's fleet with its complement of army transports started its advance up the Red, Steele explained to Halleck that "General Banks, with 17,000 and 10,000 of Sherman's, will be at Alexandria on the 17th instant. This is more than equal for anything Kirby Smith can bring against them." Steele's army was therefore not needed and would be better used by keeping them where they were, "holding the line of the Arkansas secure" so he could "soon free this State of armed rebels." Steele argued that the roads were bad, the country was destitute of provisions, and besides, the president had instructed him to conduct an election. Furthermore, many of his veterans had been given furloughs. It seemed there was just no way he could move in March. Instead, he suggested to Halleck that he might "threaten the enemy's flank and rear with all my cavalry and to make a feint with infantry on the Washington road."[33] Unfortunately for Banks, Steele was beginning to position himself successfully out of the campaign.

On the Confederate side, in response to Kirby Smith's request for some Texas troops to support the defense of Shreveport, Magruder sent the cavalry troops of Tom Green and Hamilton Bee along with several smaller units. Then, drawing on his last available resources, Smith requested that Maj. Gen. Sterling Price send reinforcements from Arkansas. Price proceeded to forward some 5,000 Missouri and Arkansas troops toward Shreveport. Unfortunately, these troops would not arrive for some time; in the interim Smith had available only Taylor's command to counter the force that the Union was about to field against him. Taylor's army consisted of about 5,300 infantry, plus 500 cavalry and mounted infantry, and 300 artillerymen.[34] As he had done in the fall of 1863, Smith ordered Taylor to harass the enemy as they advanced but to preserve his army and avoid major conflict. When all of the reinforcements arrived on the scene, the Confederate force in front of Banks would number about 17,000.

Nathaniel Prentice Banks / Library of Congress

David Glasgow Farragut / Library of Congress

David Dixon Porter / Library of Congress

William Buel Franklin / Library of Congress

Andrew Jackson Smith / Randy Beck Collection, U.S. Army Military History Institute

Joseph Bailey / Library of Congress

Henry Wager Halleck / Library of Congress

Richard Taylor / Library of Congress

Red River dam during construction. / Library of Congress, *OR Navies* 26, 130

Steamboat *Signal* towing material for the Red River dam / Library of Congress

Federal fleet at Alexandria / Library of Congress, *OR Navies* 26, 124

THE ADVANCE TO ALEXANDRIA

9 Late in the afternoon of March 13, 1864, Banks's cavalry under Brig. Gen. Albert L. Lee left the town of Franklin to begin the march to Alexandria. The last of Lee's troopers did not depart until the morning of March 14. The column of cavalry, with its baggage train, stretched some nine miles along the road up Bayou Teche. As the last of the cavalry wagons got under way, Emory's division of the XIX Corps moved into column behind them and started up the road toward Shreveport.[1] Both Robert A. Cameron's 3rd Division and Thomas E. G. Ransom's 4th Division of the XIII Corps had by this time returned from the Texas coast and gone into camp at Franklin. There, on March 15, Ransom assumed command of the two divisions, and in an unusual assignment for a colonel, William Jennings Landram took command of the 4th Division. Under this new command structure the XIII Corps detachment followed Emory out of town, forming the rear of the column. General Franklin was in overall command of the troops.

In support of Banks's long-standing policy against the theft and destruc-

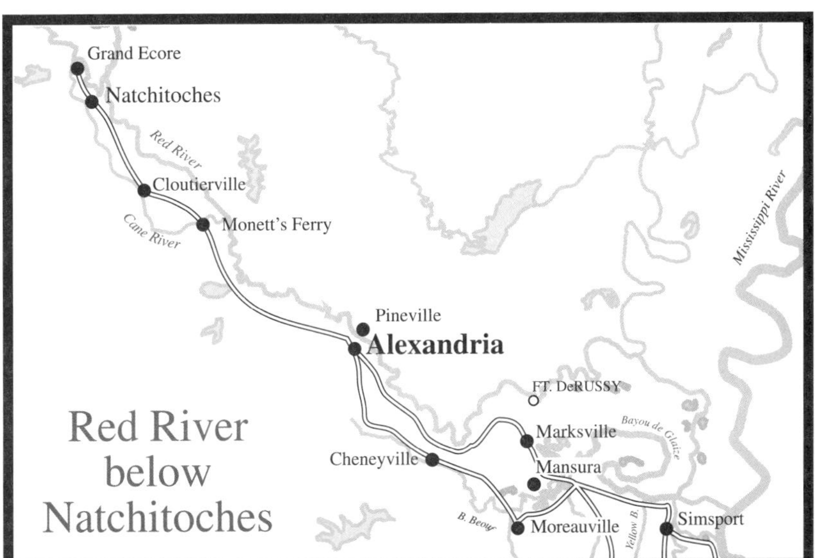

The Red River below Natchitoches, Louisiana

tion of civilian property by the army, General Franklin issued specific orders March 16 forbidding private foraging. However, as described by one reviewer, "His usual orders against private foraging were, as usual, ignored."[2] As the march progressed, the foragers began to suffer some casualties, whether from disgruntled residents, freelance Jayhawkers, or Confederate stragglers competing for the spoils, and as a result the distaste of the soldiers for the local population grew. The men saw no reason to respect the private property of the local residents when "the flanks and rear of our army were constantly annoyed by these cowardly sneaks—men who had not the courage to enlist and fight like soldiers, but stood at their gates and bowed as the army passed, and then, seeking the cover of the brush, acted their mean contemptible part in the capture or killing of our men." Some of the plantation houses flew the French flag and carried signs declaring "NEUTRALITY—FRENCH PROTECTION HERE." Such efforts availed little, however, "for the boys showed their contempt for all such claims, by acts of wholesale destruction as they passed along."[3]

Taylor watched as the two wings of the Union invasion advanced up the Red River and Bayou Teche. He could do little to obstruct their advance; however, he could and did see to it that all of the cotton he could find along the enemy's route of travel was destroyed. He did this with great efficiency, and as a result the Yankees, "like the Israelites of old," traveled in company with "a cloud (of smoke) by day, and a pillar of fire by night."[4]

The Federal fleet arrived at Alexandria March 15 after the rebuilt Fort De Russy was captured and destroyed. As the lead boat, the *Ouachita,* steamed into view of the town, "the last of a fleet of transports passed over the falls." The enemy troops had made good their escape and had saved all the river transportation they could. Because of the low water, one large ferryboat, the *Countess,* ran aground while trying to pass the falls and was burned by the retreating Confederates. Porter was forced to halt at Alexandria because "no reliable pilot could be procured to take our boats across the falls." Thus, he remarked, "The transports will have to escape for the present, but are sure to be captured or destroyed before the month is over."[5]

As the army transports tied up to the Alexandria docks and the Union men came ashore, they found a city that was uncertain of how to receive them. Many residents had left their homes and traveled with the retreating army, while others stayed indoors as the troops began wandering the streets. The departing Confederates had taken supplies, horses, and other material of potential use to an army, leaving little for the Yankees. Nevertheless, scavenging was rampant. According to Thomas C. Manning, Governor Allen's commissioner for Rapides Parish, Smith's men were given the run of the town. "So soon as the men of General A. J. Smith landed from the boats, for a full twenty-four hours they were left free to do as they pleased, and well did they employ their time. Every store in the town was at once forcibly entered and robbed of every article, and the cases, windows, iron chests, shelves, etc., broken to a thousand fragments. I was on Front Street and saw these scenes. Officers of all grades were present and took a part in it, and did their share of the plundering. Private houses were entered in like manner, and robbed and desecreated in the most infamous manner."[6]

According to Lt. Charles W. Kennedy of the 156th New York, writing from Alexandria on March 27, 1864, the town

> was full of soldiers, wagon trains loading up with supplies, officers and mounted orderlies galloping about in every direction . . . the stores and houses were shut up and hardly one of the inhabitants to be seen in the streets. The 16th and 17th Army Corps marched out the day we arrived. They are Western men who came down the river from Vicksburg, good for fighting, but awfully rough. The inhabitants were in a sad state of tribulation while they remained here. They committed all sorts of outrages, ransacking stores and dwelling houses, and carrying off whatever they took a fancy to and destroying more than they took.[7]

Two weeks into the Federal occupation, on March 28, Lt. Col. Frank Peck of the 13th Connecticut wrote, "I have just been through the town trying to find something to eat but nothing can be found. A more desolate deserted looking place I never saw."[8]

Porter, finding himself in possession of Alexandria and its environs, availed himself of the opportunity to collect cotton from the countryside without interference by, or competition from, General Banks. "While waiting for General Banks to appear, Porter's seamen cleaned the Alexandria warehouses of cotton. They tugged flatboats up both sides of the river and piled them with bales they had rolled down end over end to the water's edge."[9] Not satisfied with the indigenous ground transportation, the sailors impressed Kilby Smith's army wagons, along with their teams of mules, into the service of hauling cotton from distant plantations. On March 24 Porter reported that his sailors had collected 2,129 bales of cotton.[10]

Gen. Kilby Smith saw nothing wrong with the theft and destruction of civilian property. The same day of Porter's report, Smith wrote in a letter to his mother, "The inhabitants hereabouts are pretty tolerably frightened; our Western troops are tired of shilly shally, and this year will deal their blows very heavily." In his opinion conciliation had been tried and had failed, and because "past kindness and forbearance has not been appreciated or understood," it was time to change policy. From now on the Southern civilians "will be terribly scourged. Quick, sharp, decisive, or, if not decisive, staggering blows will soon show them that we mean business."[11]

At the time Porter and A. J. Smith arrived in Alexandria, Taylor had only a small cavalry force available to him because the reinforcements from Magruder had not yet arrived from Texas. In response to the Federal occupation of Alexandria he ordered his best, the 2nd Louisiana Cavalry under Col. William G. Vincent, to serve as a rear guard. Vincent took an excellent defensive position on Henderson's Hill, twenty-three miles upstream from Alexandria. There, because of the natural defense offered by the site, the Confederates relaxed, feeling assured that their position was unassailable. Smith had other ideas, however. He ordered General Mower to take some troops and drive the Confederates from this position. Using a local inhabitant as a guide and the countersign provided by a captured enemy courier,[12] General Mower's men surrounded Vincent's camp on the cold and stormy evening of March 21. After getting into position near midnight, the Union men charged. The surprise was total, and with little loss Mower's force captured some 250 prisoners, plus many horses and a battery of artillery.[13]

The loss of most of the 2nd Louisiana was a serious blow to the Confederates. When informed of the Union action by some of the Louisianans who had escaped Mower's attack, including Colonel Vincent, Taylor ordered his remaining force to retreat toward Natchitoches. On March 22, in miserable weather, they retreated about thirty miles to the town of Kisatchie. The next day Taylor continued north to Carroll Jones's plantation, south of Natchitoches, where he had previously established a depot. Here he hoped to remain until Green's cavalry arrived from Texas. He informed Kirby Smith that "as soon as Green joins me I shall assume the offensive, and hope to be able to do so without the assistance of Price, as I do not doubt the intention of the enemy to move from Arkansas."[14]

Kirby Smith, who was in a quandary from not knowing whether the bigger threat was that of Banks or Steele, continued to advise Taylor to remain on the defensive and be prepared to support Price in Arkansas if necessary. Stating the obvious, Smith advised Taylor, "A general engagement should not be risked without hopes of success." Partly in defense of his own indecision

Smith went on to say, "Our role must be a defensive policy where the enemy is largely our superior, and where our columns come within a practical distance of each other, concentrating rapidly upon and crushing one or the other of the enemy's columns."[15] The two divisions that Smith had obtained from Price, those of Brig. Gens. Thomas J. Churchill and Mosby M. Parsons, arrived in Shreveport March 24. Not knowing where to send these reinforcements from Arkansas, Smith kept them in Shreveport.

While the XIII and XIX Corps were advancing toward Alexandria, General Steele was still in Little Rock making excuses why he would be unable to assist in the campaign along the Red. Seeing his long-anticipated Red River campaign at risk, Halleck wrote to Steele March 13. With his usual verbal evasion the general in chief told his field commander, "I advise that you proceed to co-operate in the movement of Banks and Sherman on Shreveport, unless General Grant orders differently."[16] This "advice" had no effect on the recalcitrant general. Then on March 15 an angry Grant, reconciled to a movement that he did not personally favor, sent Steele a direct order: "Move your force in full co-operation with General N. P. Banks' attack on Shreveport. A mere demonstration will not be sufficient. Now that a large force has gone up Red River it is necessary that Shreveport and the Red River should come into our possession"[17] After receiving these orders, Steele reluctantly marched south out of Little Rock with the 3rd Division, VII Corps, plus two cavalry brigades, totaling about 8,500 men. His advance was opposed by the remaining troops of Maj. Gen. Sterling Price, who retreated before Steele in a running skirmish, much like Taylor's retreat before Banks.

On March 23 General Banks departed New Orleans for Alexandria aboard the transport steamer *Black Hawk.* He arrived in Alexandria the next day. With him on the steamer was reported to be a "host of hungry-eyed cotton speculators,"[18] loaded with rope and bagging and eager to go after cotton. One observer noted, "I meet quite a number of persons here who have Gen. Banks' passes, who are dealing in cotton, sugar, &c. In fact, the boat upon which General Banks came to this place, the Black Hawk, brought up 150 coils of rope, and 50 bales of bagging, to be used in baling cotton."[19] The smoke from burning cotton formed a haze in the sky to the north of the city, and it looked as though the speculators had better hurry or all of the cotton would go up in smoke. The lead units of Banks's infantry column, under Emory, entered Alexandria March 25, one day later than Banks and eight days later than planned. As the XIX Corps units marched into Alexandria, "Generals Banks, Franklin, Emory, Smith, Mower and staffs, reviewed us as we passed, amid the huzzas of the men. The inhabitants, unwilling spectators of the scene, looked on in grave silence."[20]

In Alexandria, the men of the XIX Corps encountered for the first time the veteran troops of A. J. Smith. Banks's soldiers considered Smith's troops coarse, uncouth chicken thieves, and braggarts, and they gave these rather disreputable and disheveled men from Sherman's army the epithet "Smith's Guerrillas." In their turn Smith's men sneered at the Gulf soldiers, considering them "holiday soldiers," paper-collar and white-glove gentlemen who could neither shoot nor forage. Col. Lucius F. Hubbard of the 5th Minnesota said of Banks's men: "Their arms were of the most approved pattern and their uniforms were new. . . . It was the proudest army, in bearing and appearance, that graced the Valley of the Mississippi during the war." On the other hand, Sherman's XVI Corps "had been hurried from one campaign or expedition to another so rapidly that it had been given no opportunity to exchange its soiled and much-worn uniforms for fresh ones, and as a consequence its tout ensemble was positively shabby in comparison." However, the men of the XVI Corps "accepted rather as a compliment than otherwise the designation of 'Smith's Guerrillas' given it by the tony fellows of Banks's command."[21]

The men from Sherman's army raised the already high standards of marauding and destruction that the area in and around Alexandria had been experiencing. A New York *World* correspondent reported wholesale plunder and abuse, noting that "every mule, every horse, every ox, every cow, every hog, and every sheep have been driven off. . . . The victims do not know whose troops it is who do this destructive work; but it is asserted here that it is all done by the Western men who were out with Sherman in his raid through Mississippi."[22] On March 23 David C. Ashley of the 2nd New York Veteran Cavalry reported to his family that "I am well and am living high, for the chickens, geese &c. are very plenty in this region and our officers allow us to forage as much as we like."[23]

The military force assembled at Alexandria was the greatest in the history of the west. Even with losses from sickness and other causes, the ground force consisted of about 30,000 men with a total of 90 guns. Added to this were Porter's gunboats plus some thirty-eight army transports and quartermaster boats with a total of 210 guns.[24] With this impressive array of military strength, how could Banks fail to capture Shreveport?

The army was ready to begin its triumphant advance to capture the rebel general's stronghold. However, there was a problem. The Red River had not risen by its usual amount for the month of March.[25] To the dismay of both Admiral Porter and General Banks, there was enough water for only the shallow-draft tinclads to pass above the falls. Thus, it appeared that only a few navy boats, and those generally the least valuable of the fleet, would be able to accompany the army north from Alexandria. Banks urged Admiral Porter to use every effort to get his ironclads above the rapids. Porter, because he had agreed to support Banks, and with an eye to the vast stores of cotton rumored to be upstream, promised to do his best. After the fact, in January 1865, Banks stated, "It was conceded by everybody that it was impossible to navigate the river in the condition it was then in. But Admiral Porter thought the river would rise; and he used this expression until our officers were indisposed to talk about it: He said, 'that wherever the sand was damp he could run his boats.'"[26]

In February 1864 Congress passed a bill authorizing the grade of lieutenant general for the U.S. Army. Lincoln signed the bill into law February 29. On the same day he sent the name of Maj. Gen. Ulysses S. Grant to the Senate to fill the position. Grant's appointment was confirmed March 2. At last there would be a military leader who was an effective general in chief, and who was a grade above Halleck, Banks, Butler, and the other Union major generals. Grant traveled to Washington and accepted his appointment March 9. The new commanding officer quickly began formulating a strategic plan for winning the war. The plan pointedly did not include a Red River expedition; however, such an expedition was already under way. Grant believed it should be brought to a successful conclusion as soon as possible.

Banks received instructions from Lieutenant General Grant March 26. This message informed him that Shreveport should be taken as soon as possible. Afterward Gen. A. J. Smith's troops were to be returned to Memphis. If it appeared that Shreveport could not be taken according to Sherman's original schedule, Smith's detachment was to be returned even if it meant abandoning the expedition. Should the expedition prove successful, Shreveport and the Red River should be held "with such force as you many deem necessary." Although Banks was to commence no move to acquire additional territory, he was not restrained from "going anywhere to meet and fight the enemy." Thus, the Gulf Department commander was granted permission to pursue Taylor's army into Texas, should he wish to do so. Finally, Grant indicated that his plans may call for Banks to move on Mobile after completing the current expedition.[27]

Banks had a tight time schedule within which to complete his expedition. However, the river continued to refuse to cooperate, and its usual ample spring runoff did not materialize. Nevertheless, without hesitation, and perhaps with an unjustified bravado, Banks elected to continue, counting on General Steele's cooperation to help him to victory.[28] On March 27, while the navy was busy dragging gunboats over the falls, he ordered Lee's cavalry to move up the stage road that paralleled the Red, toward Natchitoches. The same day, under orders from Maj. Gen. James McPherson, Ellet and his marines, whose heavy rams could not pass over the falls, left for the Mississippi.[29] The next day, in hot, dry weather that contrasted sharply with the conditions encountered only one week earlier, the lead elements of the army left Alexandria for Natchitoches.

Skirmishing was more or less continuous as the army advanced from Alexandria, but following Kirby Smith's instructions, Taylor avoided a major engagement. After his retreat following Mower's capture of the 2nd Louisiana Cavalry, Taylor had positioned his main force some twenty-five miles below Natchitoches. On March 29, as Lee's advance approached his position, Taylor withdrew to the vicinity of Pleasant Hill, thirty-six miles northwest of Natchitoches. Then, to Taylor's relief, that night the first of Gen. Tom Green's cavalry units arrived from Texas.[30] Meanwhile, the sailors in Alexandria continued to work muscle, wood, and steel against rock and water to get the fleet above the falls. Eventually, twelve gunboats and thirty transports were dragged over the falls, and although seven gunboats and several large transports remained below the rapids, Porter decided that he had done enough.[31] He departed for Cotile Landing April 2 while the last few boats were still being pulled up the falls.

Twenty miles above Cotile Landing the Red River divides, and for sixty miles its waters flow in two unequal channels. The south channel, along which the road runs, is known as Cane River, or Old Red River. The new, north channel was formed in 1838 when the river overran the levee on its left bank during a storm. This channel, called the Rigolets du Bon Dieu, was less tortuous than the old channel and was the only navigable channel. Banks's cavalry entered the island formed by the two channels March 29. Lee had to brush aside some minor opposition from Confederate skirmishers while crossing the Cane onto the island at Monett's Ferry, and again at Cloutierville March 30, but he generally proceeded without difficulty. He entered Natchitoches March 31. Franklin's infantry, following the same route, arrived at Natchitoches two days later.

From Natchitoches, on April 2 Banks told Halleck, "Our troops now occupy Natchitoches, and we hope to be in Shreveport by the 10th of April. I do not fear concentration of the enemy at that point. My fear is that they may not be willing to meet us there." The continuing retreat of the enemy forces in his front had inspired Banks with visions of an immediate advance into Texas, as had been authorized by General Grant. "I shall pursue the enemy into the interior of Texas, for the sole purpose of destroying or dispersing his forces." Even though prior to reaching Shreveport "it will be impossible to form any definite plan of operations, . . . I am confident of an immediate and successful issue."[32] John Hay, Lincoln's secretary, showed this letter to the president. Hay recorded in his diary that "Mr. Lincoln, with that instinct of the approach of bad news which seemed like a sixth sense in him, said, 'I am sorry to see this tone of confidence; the next news we shall hear from there will be of a defeat.'"[33]

Not only was the tone of this April 2 message from Banks indicative of overconfidence but there may well have been some justifiable consternation in the War Department over the fact that as of this date, Banks was admitting that he had no "definite plan of operations."[34] Furthermore, in contrast to the ebullient confidence of the army commander that the enemy would not fight, a war correspondent traveling with Banks, John Russell Young, managing editor of the Philadelphia *Press,* wrote on April 2 that "the rebels are concentrating at Pleasant Hill . . . where it is expected . . . there will be a heavy battle."[35] The newspaper editor apparently had more insight into the military situation than the general commanding the army.

Grant again wrote to Banks March 31. By this time the new general in chief had firmed up his plans for the spring of 1864. In this message, which Banks did not receive until after the latter's dispatch to Halleck dated April 2, Grant stated that after Shreveport was captured, Banks was to turn the defense of the Red over to General Steele and the navy. He was to limit his occupation of Texas to the mouth of the Rio Grande and to fortify along the Mississippi from Port Hudson to New Orleans. Then with the troops that would be freed by these actions, plus 5,000 additional men Grant would supply from Missouri, he was to move against Mobile. "With these, and such additions as I can give you from elsewhere, lose no time in making a demonstration, to be followed by an attack upon Mobile. Two or more iron-clads will be ordered to report to Admiral Farragut. This gives him a strong naval fleet with which to co-operate." Then the ever-impatient Grant added, "Start at the earliest possible moment."[36]

The continuing reference by the new lieutenant general of the U.S. Army to the capture of Mobile, and to Banks's role in such capture, was to the liking of the commander of the Gulf Department. Once Steele's troops arrived,

Banks was confident that he would have force enough to overwhelm anything Gen. Kirby Smith might have in the way of defenses at Shreveport. Then, per Grant's instructions, he could turn the city over to Steele, return to the Mississippi, and capture Mobile. However, in light of these new instructions from General Grant it was clear that making use of the army's new base on the Red to pursue Taylor's army, much less to initiate an invasion of north Texas, would have to be delayed. Given the Gulf Department commander's past disinclination to advance into Texas from any of the towns previously occupied by his army in western Louisiana, forgoing such an invasion may not have been disappointing to him, despite the brave words to the contrary he had sent only a few days previously to General Halleck.

Instead of moving swiftly to aid in the capture of Shreveport, General Steele was encountering continuing problems in Arkansas. After evacuating Camden, Price moved west to Prairie d'Ane and prepared his defenses to stop Steele's advance. There the two armies skirmished indecisively for several days until April 11, when Price ordered a retreat to a position some eight miles north of the town of Washington, Arkansas. Steele advanced a few miles but, instead of attacking Price in earnest, merely continued to skirmish with his opponent. Finally, to the surprise of both friend and foe, the Union commander turned east toward Camden.[37] Once there, Steele found his army could not live off the exhausted countryside around the town, and raids by Confederate cavalry on his wagon trains made all attempts at obtaining supplies unreliable.

From Camden, Steele informed Sherman that Southern reinforcements, said to be en route from Kirby Smith, would place his force at risk. He wondered why Banks had allowed enemy troops to be shifted from the Red River into Arkansas.[38] Instead of admitting that he, Steele, had failed in his mission to support Banks, he believed Banks was responsible for his current predicament. Steele abandoned Camden April 27, moving north toward Little Rock. Thus, although he did succeed in holding some of Price's troops in Arkansas and away from Taylor, Prairie d'Ane was the closest he came to supporting Banks's attempt to capture Shreveport. In a statement reminiscent of Farragut's declaration about Banks following the admiral's passing of Port Hudson on the night of March 14, 1863, Banks declared later that Steele "was of no earthly assistance to us at all."[39]

THE ADVANCE TO SABINE CROSSROADS

10 General Banks boarded his headquarters boat April 2 and, in convoy with the army transports carrying Gen. A. J. Smith's troops and the portion of Porter's fleet that had passed the falls, moved upstream from Alexandria.[1] This contingent of the expeditionary force arrived at Grand Ecore, eight miles above Natchitoches, on April 3. The tiny village overlooked the point at which the Cane and the Red separate into two channels. The same day, Franklin's lead regiments marched into Grand Ecore to join Banks, Smith, and Porter. Getting to this point had been relatively easy and straightforward. The commanding general now had the responsibility of deciding which route to take out of Grand Ecore in order to continue on to Shreveport. At least three roads led out of the village. The stage road to Shreveport turned west-southwest, away from the river. Another road proceeded north from Grand Ecore along the right bank of the Red. Finally, there was a road across the river that led northeast toward the town of Campti.

The river road along the right bank apparently serviced a number of plantations and farms upstream from the town. Admiral Porter saw this road as he proceeded up the river from Grand Ecore, and after the fact he wrote to

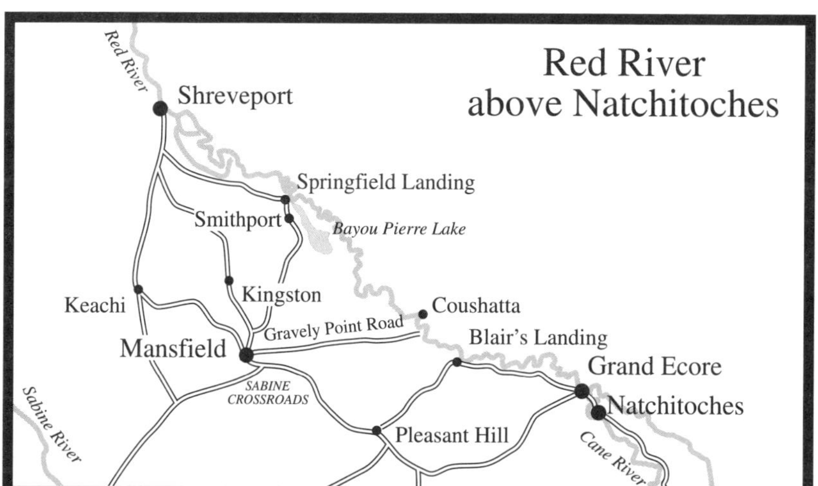

The Red River above Natchitoches, Louisiana

General Sherman: "It struck me very forcibly that this would have been the route for the army, where they could have traveled without all that immense train, the country supporting them as they proceeded along. The roads are good, wide fields on all sides, a river protecting the right flank of the army, and gunboats in company. An army would have no difficulty in marching to Shreveport in this way."[2]

Porter's comments about the river road must be taken in the context in which they were written: at the time of writing he was in Alexandria, having just struggled downstream from Loggy Bayou. His anxiety for the safety of his fleet and his disgust for Banks were at their maximum. Elsewhere in his letter Porter did not mince words in his criticism of the army general. However, he had not traveled the river all the way to Shreveport, so, even giving him the benefit of the doubt regarding the total veracity of his statement, his testimony that an army "would have no difficulty in marching to Shreveport in this way" cannot be considered definitive. Furthermore, there is apparently no record of any attempt on the part of Porter or any other naval officer to encourage Banks to use this road. Since the navy's tugs and gunboats had been moving back and forth along this stretch of the river for at least several days prior to the army's departure from Grand Ecore, if it was known that the road would lead to Shreveport, it seems strange that this fact was not communicated to the army commander.

General Franklin claimed after the fact, "Before we left Grand Ecore for Shreveport I tried to have a reconnoissance made directly up the Red River, with a view to taking that route, instead of going off to Mansfield, because I thought we would have a better chance on the Red river to obtain corn. . . . The answer that I received was that it would take time to reconnoitre that river, and therefore it could not be done."[3] Franklin's statement may or may not be either accurate or complete, but in any case it is possible that Banks was told, or believed, that the road along the river above Grand Ecore did not continue all the way to Shreveport.

Wellington W. Withenbury, a self-professed Union man of somewhat questionable character and a pilot on the Red, testified to the Joint Committee in 1865 that while Banks was at Grand Ecore, he (Withenbury) had pointed out on a map to General Stone, Banks's chief of staff, the location of Pleasant Hill. According to him, "the words 'Pleasant Hill' were not on [Stone's map]. I traced out the different roads leading from point to point." Withenbury also claimed to have provided Stone with "my own maps for his guidance." Then he stated that in a separate meeting "during that same day, perhaps," he had answered questions from both Banks and Stone about the possibility of the army traveling to Shreveport on the east, as opposed to the west, side of the river. Withenbury claimed he told them such a route, that is, the route through Campti, would "take them about two days longer to reach Shreveport. . . . They then decided not to go that way." He also stated that he told them, "When you get above Pleasant Hill, on the road to Mansfield, you will not see the river any more."[4] The latter statement is curious because the road to Mansfield leaves the river at Grand Ecore, long before reaching Pleasant Hill. The statement may indicate that Withenbury knew less about the roads in the area than he claimed. In any case Withenbury, in reporting his discussions with Banks and Stone to the Joint Committee, made no reference to a road that followed the right bank of the river upstream from Grand Ecore.

In his premier study of the campaign Ludwell Johnson concludes that Withenbury must have known about the road along the west bank of the river but for his own reasons chose not to tell the generals about it.[5] Gary Joiner, who apparently agrees with Johnson, elaborates on Withenbury's possible reasons for concealing the existence of this road and proposes that it was the result of his desire to prevent the Federals from confiscating cotton he owned that was located above Grand Ecore. He declares Banks's decision to take the stage road west of the river instead of that east of the river "correct," given the absence of further information, but terms Banks's refusal to require a reconnaissance of the area to the north and west of Grand Ecore before selecting the route for his advance "unforgivable."[6] William Brooksher argues that although the river road did not appear on Union maps, "there was a better route [than that through Mansfield] available along the river . . . but that was missed through ignorance and a failure to conduct a reconnaissance."[7] Thomas Ayres states that Banks was assured that the Mansfield road was "a much better road than the one that followed the river," and hence Banks chose it.[8] Curt Anders argues that Banks had both the resources and opportunity to scout the river road and calls Banks's decision to take the Mansfield road "the most critical blunder he made during the entire campaign."[9]

In all of this speculation it appears the following assumptions have been made: (1) the river road in fact did continue to Shreveport, as claimed by Porter, and that for its entire length it remained in good enough condition for an army to use; and (2) Withenbury knew about this road and deliberately concealed it from the Union army commanders. Although the contention that Withenbury deliberately concealed from Banks the fact that a practical route to Shreveport along the river existed might be correct, Withenbury may have failed to mention such a road because he knew it did not lead all the way to Shreveport. There was certainly some kind of road along the river above Grand Ecore, but it is not clear how far upriver this road continued and for what distance it remained in good condition.

Taylor, who was surely familiar with the roads in the area, stated, "Though lateral roads existed, his [Banks's] column marched by the main one."[10] Taylor's statement does not make clear whether the destination of these "lateral" roads was Shreveport or Mansfield, but Taylor apparently never considered the possibility that Banks would proceed to Shreveport by any route other than that through Mansfield. One might thus infer that the river road north of Grand Ecore did not provide a serviceable route to Shreveport, though it may have left the river upstream to join the road to Mansfield. Whether this was the case or not, Banks probably knew about a road along the river north of Grand Ecore but perhaps did not believe it provided a practical route to Shreveport.

In any event, apparently without scouting for possible alternatives, and rejecting the long route east of the river pointed out by Withenbury, the commanding general elected to stay on the main road. This meant leaving the protection of Porter's gunboats.[11] The main road, though the primary route to Shreveport, was a wretched, sunken trail through the forest, described as more like a red ditch than a road. There were few structures and little water between Grand Ecore and Shreveport. For most of the distance trees and brambles grew right up to the road. There was little space for a courier to pass an infantry column, much less room to turn a wagon around. Banks did not appear to be disturbed either by the fact that he would be leaving the river or by the condition of the road. Before departing from Grand Ecore, he stated sanguinely in a letter to his wife that "the enemy retreats before [us] & will not fight a battle this side of Shreveport if then."[12] Later Banks justified his decision to follow this route away from the river when he wrote to Stanton: "The shortest and only practicable road from Natchitoches to Shreveport was the stage road through Pleasant Hill and Mansfield . . . through a barren, sandy country, with little water and less forage, the greater portion an unbroken pine forest."[13]

Given the requirement of his being in Shreveport by April 10, as set by Sherman and Grant, Banks gave Franklin orders to begin the march out of Grand Ecore on April 5. Franklin, in turn, ordered General Lee to "move out on the Shreveport road, attack the enemy wherever [he] could find him, but not to bring on a general engagement."[14] Exactly what his cavalry commander was expected to do to avoid a general engagement in that tangle of forest was never clarified by Franklin. General Banks was once again risking his whole enterprise by incautiously relying on a subordinate who had repeatedly demonstrated incompetence.

Banks planned to reestablish contact with Porter at or near Loggy Bayou, not far from Springfield Landing, some 110 river miles upstream from Grand Ecore. Kilby Smith's men, numbering about 1,700, were to remain with Porter. By the first week of April 1864 the Red River was slowly rising. Even so, Porter decided to leave behind at Grand Ecore six of his heavy ironclads and ten of the transports he had struggled to get over the falls. He took with him upstream only *Cricket, Fort Hindman, Lexington, Osage, Neosho,* and *Chillicothe,* plus a fleet of twenty transports bearing Kilby Smith's division and a large quantity of military stores.[15] Porter departed from Grand Ecore April 7 expecting to reach Loggy Bayou by April 9. The trip involved more effort than the admiral had anticipated, however, as the boats struggled over sandbars and around sharp bends. "We had no pilots of any account, and got along by main strength and nonsense. If one got on a bank, another would haul him off." Thus, the reduced fleet moved slowly up the Red toward Loggy Bayou. Regarding the latter, according to Porter, "The name is significant enough without saying any more in regard to it."[16]

On the morning of April 6 General Lee, leading the brigades of Cols. Thomas J. Lucas, Harai Robinson, and Nathan A. M. "Gold-Lace" Dudley, with a total of about 3,300 men plus three small batteries,[17] left Grand Ecore to form the vanguard of the army's advance. Conditions were dry, and the dust was thick. The cavalry covered twenty-three miles before stopping for the night at Crump's Corners. The troopers were followed by Lee's train of between 250 and 350 wagons. These wagons, which contained ten days' rations for Lee's men, three days' forage for the animals, plus a large supply of ammunition and camp equipment, extended about five miles along the narrow road.[18] Ransom's infantry followed the cavalry train, with Cameron's 3rd Division in the lead. The XIII Corps divisions were, in turn, followed by the XIX Corps led by Emory. Cameron advanced some sixteen miles before stopping for the night.

Behind the Gulf troops, occupying eleven or twelve miles of road, was the infantry baggage train of about 700 wagons.[19] Whether true or not, it was the opinion of many of the men that of this rather large number of wagons, "those of the general's staff formed no inconsiderable portion." A. J. Smith's forces were to take up the march in the rear of Banks's wagon train. Because of the slow movement of the column, Smith did not leave Grand Ecore until

April 7. Banks also remained in Grand Ecore until that date. Then, passing the infantry train and most of the marching column, Banks and his staff joined Franklin late that night.[20]

After leaving garrisons at Alexandria, Natchitoches, and Grand Ecore and sending part of Smith's troops with Porter, Banks departed Grand Ecore with about 16,000 men. Given the approximately 1,000 wagons included in the march, he thus employed something approaching 1 wagon for each 16 men effective and present for duty, or an average of more than 62 wagons per 1,000 men. In addition, the transports being escorted upstream by Porter were loaded with supplies. Even without the presence of the supplies on the transports and the plan for the army to rejoin the fleet in front of Shreveport, it was hard for some of the veterans to understand the need for the wagon train they observed. The wagons became a target for the wits among A. J. Smith's veterans, who declared that they were loaded largely with paper collars and linen dusters for Banks's dandies.[21] They joked that Banks's tactics called for the wagons to be used for skirmish and scouting duty.

By 1864 most generals, North and South, had learned what Lincoln told Banks back in November 1862: "You would be better off any where, and especially where you are going, for not having a thousand wagons, doing nothing but hauling forage to feed the animals that draw them, and taking at least two thousand men to care for the wagons and animals."[22] However, specifying the minimum number of wagons required by an army when undertaking a given campaign is not an easy task. In addition to being a function of the number of troops involved, the size of the train depends on factors such as the makeup of the army (that is, the relative sizes of the infantry, cavalry, and artillery components), expected duration of the campaign, expected enemy resistance to the advance, the distances involved, and opportunities foreseen for resupply either from one's own resources or from enemy resources. The Army of the Potomac used 4,300 wagons, or about 51 wagons per 1,000 men, in its advance into the Wilderness of Virginia in May 1864.[23] In November 1864, when retreating to Nashville in front of Gen. John B. Hood, Maj. Gen. John M. Schofield's army of about 22,000 men of the IV and XXIII Corps included a train of some 800 wagons, or about 36 wagons per 1,000 men.[24] Napoleon's standard was 12.5 wagons per 1,000 men.[25]

In 1862 Halleck issued General Orders No. 160, which addressed the number of wagons to be used by different army organizations and what the wagons could carry. For example, a "full" infantry regiment was permitted 6 wagons, "proportionally reduced according to the number of officers and men actually present." These wagons were to carry only "forage for the teams, cooking utensils, and rations for the troops, hospital stores, and officers' baggage."[26] Grant issued standing orders allowing for baggage and camp equipage 3 wagons to a regiment of over 700 men, 2 wagons to a regiment of from 350 to 700 men, 1 wagon to a regiment of less than 350 men, and 1 wagon to a field battery.[27]

Asked later by New York congressman Moses F. Odell, a war Democrat and member of the Joint Committee on the Conduct of the War, whether his wagon train was excessively large, Banks could not make up his mind. Besides, it was not his fault:

> Question. Was the wagon train accompanying your expedition out of proportion to the number of troops?
>
> Answer. It was not unreasonably large, but it was larger than I would have made it had I taken the direction of that myself; and I tried very hard to reduce it while we were at Grand Ecore, but the general officers with whom I consulted said that all the subordinate officers, the company and regimental officers, had made all their arrangements, and the reduction could only be made in the wagons for their accommodation, and it would create a great deal of dissatisfaction. I therefore gave it up. I tried very hard to reduce my headquarters' train; but I had the engineer corps, the signal corps, and the telegraph corps with my own train, so that my headquarters train numbered thirty-five wagons. I could have reduced it to fifteen wagons if I had the organization of the train at first; but that was left to General Franklin. The President had given me instructions at New Orleans which required my attention there at that time.[28]

One may conclude that the number of wagons was unusually large for a Union force this late in the war, particularly given the fact that a large amount of supplies was left on the transports, but the number was not unprecedented. Given the narrow road and the single line of advance, the real problem was not the number of wagons but their placement in the advancing column.

The movement that Banks was undertaking in leaving the river and advancing against an opponent who had shown himself to be astute, resourceful, and aggressive was fraught with peril. Like Hooker's movement into the Wilderness in 1863, or Grant's similar movement in 1864, Banks's advance into the Louisiana piney woods was militarily risky even without the baggage train that was dispersed among the troops. The head of the column was an easy target for a concealed attack. Having ridden past the infantry wagon train and the

XIX and XIII Corps column on April 7, Banks was certainly aware of Franklin's arrangements for the infantry advance from Grand Ecore. Knowing that the cavalry train preceded the XIII Corps, Banks must have noticed that the three components of the column—the cavalry, his Gulf Department infantry, and A. J. Smith's infantry—were isolated from one another. However, he issued no orders to modify these arrangements. Colonel Hubbard noticed that "the Sixteenth Corps was not within supporting distance of the head of the column." However, as Hubbard went on to note, "Dick Taylor . . . soon relieved [Banks] of a large part of this train, and thereafter the relations between the front and the rear of the column were not so distant, and perhaps not quite so strained."[29]

Taylor chose to await the arrival of the Federal column at a place called Sabine Crossroads, which was located about three miles south of the town of Mansfield. The crossroads, named for the intersection of the Mansfield road with a road leading to the Sabine River, included one of the few large clearings in the region. The mostly open ground at the crossroads measured roughly twelve hundred yards east to west and eight hundred to nine hundred yards north to south.[30] Without having necessarily planned to lure Banks into a trap, Taylor was doing so quite effectively.

On April 6 Gen. Kirby Smith visited Taylor at Mansfield. The two generals continued to disagree on whether Taylor should fight or retreat. Smith did not want Taylor to place his small army at risk by forcing a battle, but he compromised by instructing his subordinate "to select a position in which to give battle should Banks advance, and by a reconnaissance in force to compel the enemy to display his infantry."[31] Smith then returned to Shreveport. Given the certain fact that Banks was going to advance, Taylor was to inform Smith when an engagement was imminent so the latter could take command in the field. Smith wrote later that he "hoped to derive an element of *morale* from the arrival of Churchill's command and my own presence at the moment of action."[32] Taylor, who had little respect for Smith's military prowess, was not strongly inclined to make this happen.

Lee's cavalry brigades resumed their advance from Crump's Corners April 7. A member of the 67th Indiana noted that "the enemy fell back and took advantage of the best positions, from which they would pour a volley into our skirmish line, then drop back to another position and await our coming."[33] Despite this intermittent opposition Lee's men easily pushed the enemy skirmishers ahead of them. A heavy rain began that afternoon, continuing until midnight and turning the Louisiana dust into thick, red mud.

The infantry column continued to slog slowly along the narrow road, but the wagons came almost to a stop in the mucilaginous mire. By two o'clock in the afternoon Ransom had overtaken the rear of the cavalry train at Pleasant Hill and, to avoid passing it, went into bivouac at that point. According to Sgt. Charles Oscar Torrey of the 27th Iowa, "Roads very bad, traveled in mud till dark. Camped in fine timber close to big white house. Oh dear how it did pour down."[34] Emory arrived about three hours later and also stopped. The army's train did not arrive until far into the night.

As Ransom was approaching Pleasant Hill, Lee's lead cavalry brigade found a strong force of enemy cavalry at Wilson's plantation, about three miles beyond the town. General Major's brigade of Green's division, under the command of Walter P. Lane, had taken a strong position on rising ground at the far side of a clearing. For the first time in the campaign Lee's cavalry met something more than token opposition. Robinson dismounted his brigade and attempted without success to push back the enemy. Lucas then moved forward to support Robinson, and together they repulsed a determined enemy attack. The Union cavalry counterattacked and, after hard fighting, drove Lane from the field.[35] Banks reported that the fighting had lasted two hours, with the enemy suffering heavy losses. "The enemy made his first stand at Wilson's farm, near Pleasant Hill, on the afternoon of the 7th . . . [where] he was driven from the field, with considerable loss in killed, wounded, and prisoners."[36]

Although Lane, who was badly outnumbered, was successfully driven off, the strong enemy action at Wilson's plantation had shaken Lee. The cavalry commander had been uncomfortable with the manner in which the column was configured. He realized that if infantry were needed to support his advance, they would suffer significant delay in attempting to reach him because of the cavalry wagon train located immediately in the rear of his troopers. He had previously requested permission from General Franklin to place his wagons with the infantry train. This would allow the infantry ready access to the front should such be needed. However, Lee wanted his train to precede the infantry train, and this Franklin would not tolerate. Franklin denied Lee's request, arguing that the infantry train should remain directly in the rear of the infantry column. Furthermore, "I told him that it was his business to take care of his own train." If the cavalry wagons had been placed in the front of the infantry train, "my infantry wagons would never have got into camp the day of my march. . . . The cavalry would have had their wagons up, but at the expense of the infantry. I therefore told General Lee that he must take care of his own wagons."[37] The line of march would stay as it was.

During the fight at Wilson's plantation Lee requested infantry support from General Franklin. Franklin ordered a brigade to move forward, but the firing ceased before the brigade arrived at the front, and the men were ordered back to camp. A peeved Franklin had by then noticed that Ransom's lead brigade had overtaken the cavalry train. This was unconscionable. The column was bunching up. The cavalry should speed up its march. From Pleasant Hill, during the afternoon of April 7, Franklin sent orders to Lee to "proceed to-night as far as possible with your whole train in order to give the infantry room to advance to-morrow."[38]

In response to Franklin's order, in the late evening of April 7 Lee slowly and carefully pursued Lane's force. The cavalry advanced to Carroll's sawmill on Ten Mile Bayou, the southerly tributary of Bayou St. Patrice (or San Patricio), about seven miles beyond Pleasant Hill. There, toward nightfall, the Southerners made another strong stand, and Lee's advance came to a halt. From Ten Mile Bayou Lee sent another request to Franklin for infantry support to be forwarded early the next morning to assist in the advance on April 8. Franklin denied this request. He did not like the idea of mixing infantry and cavalry on the march. Revealing his opinion of the fighting qualities of cavalry, he stated later, "Any order of march which involves sending a force of infantry . . . with . . . cavalry is entirely wrong. If any fighting occurs, it is most likely that the infantry will do it while the cavalry looks on; and if there be merely a march, the cavalry exhausts the infantry."[39]

Lee's request was carried to General Franklin by Col. John S. Clark of Banks's staff. After Franklin refused to help, Clark returned to Lee to report this decision. According to Clark, Lee's response to Franklin was to declare that "I shall move on the enemy's works in the morning." Clark returned to Pleasant Hill with this message and found that General Banks had arrived. He explained to Banks that, in his opinion, General Lee was "in a very dangerous position; . . . would probably be attacked at daylight."[40] In response, Banks sent Maj. George B. Drake of his staff to General Franklin instructing the general to send infantry forward to support Lee. Later, Banks explained that he ordered the infantry support forward because "the advance guard should be composed of cavalry for celerity, artillery for force, and infantry for solidity."[41]

In the face of Banks's direct order, Franklin, with less than total enthusiasm, sent a message to General Ransom "You may use your discretion as to sending a brigade or division" to Lee at or before 5:00 A.M. on April 8.[42] A reporter for the Lacon, Illinois, *Gazette* believed that Ransom, like Franklin, objected to sending even a brigade forward. He quoted Ransom as saying that the plan should be to "remain in camp here until General Smith comes up, and then move on them in force."[43] In any case, under Franklin's halfhearted and discretionary instruction Ransom ordered Colonel Landram to "move to-morrow, with the First Brigade of your division, and report to General Lee, 8 miles in front, at daylight or as soon thereafter as possible."[44] Landram ordered Col. Frank Emerson, commander of the 1st Brigade, 4th Division, to prepare to join Lee early in the morning. Emerson's brigade consisted of the 77th Illinois, the 67th Indiana, the 19th Kentucky, and the 23rd Wisconsin, totaling about 1,200 men. The battery of Capt. Ormand F. Nims, 2nd Massachusetts Light Artillery, was ordered to accompany Emerson.

In testimony to the Joint Committee Franklin later argued that sending infantry forward to support the cavalry, as ordered by Banks on the evening of April 7, was the cause of the disaster at Mansfield. He maintained that the order of march, with the wagon trains interspersed among the troops, was a proper one. In Franklin's opinion, the infantry support sent forward to General Lee merely tempted the latter to "persist in pressing forward until it was too late to retire in safety."[45] Franklin claimed that if the cavalry had been left by itself to lead the advance, the march would have been short and "the whole army would have been in as compact condition as it could have been." However, with the infantry support "the cavalry got on much faster than it would otherwise, and its fast progress was a temptation to General Banks and to the cavalry to bring on a general battle."[46]

Franklin contradicts himself here. He first instructed Lee to speed his advance to prevent the column from bunching up, then claimed that because of enemy resistance Lee's advance without infantry support would be slower than if accompanied by infantry, and thus the column would be in a "compact condition." It is not clear why Franklin believed anything would have changed had Lee not advanced as far as he did April 7. It was not just the distance between Lee and the head of the infantry column that prevented an effective defense or orderly retreat by the cavalry, but the fact that Lee's wagon train was immediately behind his troopers on the narrow lane along which the army was advancing. In his testimony Franklin appears to have been rationalizing his own bad judgment.

At Pleasant Hill on April 7 Banks had another opportunity to rethink the structure of his advancing column. He knew the lead cavalry units had encountered an enemy force of some size and had suffered a significant number of casualties. He knew that General Franklin opposed forwarding infantry to support Lee's cavalry and that Lee felt he could not advance safely without such support. He knew the infantry column was separated from the cavalry by a long line of wagons, although he may not have known exactly how long that line was. However, having just ridden past the infantry wagons strung out along the road from Grand Ecore to Pleasant Hill, he also knew that each wagon almost completely blocked the narrow roadway and that the movement of sizable numbers of men past the wagons would be time-consuming. He must also have noticed that there was no hope of finding paths through the woods for the cavalry to use to retreat or the infantry to advance en masse around the wagons.

In addition to the foregoing, known conditions, Banks and Franklin had information about the size and location of the enemy army. They had been informed of an enemy troop buildup near Pleasant Hill on or before April 2, and Franklin was told April 7 that an estimated 20,175 Confederate infantry and cavalry with seventy-six artillery pieces were located between the present position of the army and the town of Shreveport.[47] With this intelligence added to the known configuration of the line of march, and with an opportunity at hand to modify the structure of the advancing column, perhaps a wise military leader would have planned for some contingencies not originally considered when structuring the marching column. However, the prevailing opinion at Banks's headquarters continued to be that the enemy would not fight before the army reached Shreveport, if then. According to his original biographer, "Banks could have won a limited victory on the Red River had he possessed real military competence. That he lacked, as he would demonstrate during the expedition."[48] Again, despite everything he had experienced in Virginia and Louisiana, Banks showed himself unable to allow for any enemy action other than what he had convinced himself would occur. No change was made in the line of march.

It would seem appropriate to address the question of the proper response of a militarily competent army commander to the conditions encountered at Pleasant Hill. Without addressing the question of how the disposition of the column could have been improved, one student of the campaign has argued that under the conditions Lee found himself in on the evening of April 7, Banks was correct in ordering Franklin to forward infantry support to Lee. Indeed, Banks's "mistake was in not putting the entire Thirteenth Corps detachment forward."[49] Although correct, given what actually happened, this contention presumes advance knowledge on the part of the army commanders. Had either Franklin or Banks been prescient and known that a battle was imminent, ordering the entire XIII Corps forward would have been the correct thing to do. However, Shreveport was still several days' march away, and sending half of their men forward past the cavalry train without otherwise restructuring the column would not allow for the contingency that no battle would occur. In the latter case the disrupted structure of the column would eventually have had to be corrected, an action that would have required a great deal of time and effort. Because any decision to forward infantry support to Lee had to be based on the information Banks and Franklin had at the time, sending the entire XIII Corps was something neither general would have considered on April 7.

Although not commenting directly on the virtue of sending infantry reinforcements forward to support Lee on the evening of April 7, another student of the events of that day has judged the response by Banks and Franklin to Lee's situation to be insufficient given the circumstances of which the generals were aware. "Had either of Lee's superiors taken the possibility of a Confederate ambush seriously, they might also have ordered Lee's horses and wagons to the rear: the horses were worse than useless on wooded terrain, serving only to reduce the cavalry's tactical flexibility, while the two-mile wagon train strung behind Lee effectively isolated his 4,700 bluecoats from the rest of the army."[50] The dismounted cavalry should then have led the advance. This change would indeed have improved the communication between the advance cavalry units and the main body of infantry and probably have changed the outcome of the engagement at Sabine Crossroads. However, once again this change in the column of march does not allow for the possibility of no battle occurring, and under the best of circumstances it could not have been maintained for long. Cavalrymen afoot were generally not able to make the hard marches borne by the infantry, and eventually the army would have needed the services of its mounted arm. Therefore, it is likely that neither Banks nor Franklin would have considered such a revision to the troop dispositions.

The proper response to the situation, given the information available to the army commanders on April 7, was proposed by Ludwell Johnson. According to Johnson, Banks and Franklin should have "(1) reduced the advance guard to not more than one brigade of cavalry; (2) placed the wagons of all but the leading brigade of cavalry in the rear of the infantry train; (3) placed the wagons of the leading brigade ahead of the infantry train."[51] If this recommendation had been followed, there would have been no wagons between the cavalry brigade leading the march and the infantry units following, and communication along this part of the column would have been quick and easy. About one-third of the cavalry train would have been in front of the infantry train, which would have irritated Franklin but would have placed little additional hardship on the XIII and XIX Corps troops. Therefore, this change would have been reasonable to make as a contingency in the event of unexpected enemy action and could have been maintained all the way to Shreveport in the event there was no battle.

If, under Johnson's suggested line of march, Lee's single, leading brigade met significant enemy resistance, it could retreat to the infantry or the infantry could advance to support it. Either option obviates the question of whether a single brigade of cavalry could have driven Green's troopers in their front. Furthermore, the possibility of the enemy entrapping and destroying or capturing a single lead brigade was small given the inability of enemy troops to move through the woods with any dispatch. In any case the possibility of entrapment could have been minimized by keeping the lead cavalry within ready support distance of the infantry column.

After the war Landram indicated he agreed with the position expounded by Franklin at Pleasant Hill. At that time Landram stated that he "told Ransom that his reinforcements would lead to evil results; that the presence of the infantry would embolden Lee to push on beyond support."[52] However, whatever Landram's opinion, he marched forward with Emerson from the camp just north of Pleasant Hill at three o'clock on the morning of April 8, a day designated by the Confederate Congress and President Jefferson Davis as one of "humiliation, fasting, and prayer." They arrived at Lee's camp, after a rapid march of seven or eight miles, at about 5:00 A.M. As one of the men in the 67th Indiana saw it: "The cavalry advanced on the Mansfield road and we had scarcely bivouacked for the night when we were ordered into line, as it was reported that the cavalry had struck the enemy in force. We lay in line of battle until daylight on the morning of the 8th when our regiment with a section of artillery, were ordered forward in double quick time."[53]

Shortly after five o'clock Lee, now with the assistance of Emerson's brigade, moved forward from Bayou St. Patrice. This combined force quickly ran into three of Green's regiments. The cavalry was forced to dismount and join the infantry in driving back the enemy skirmishers. The slow and dangerous process of driving the enemy cavalry from one position to the next continued through the morning hours. "These units fought their way slowly forward, with almost constant skirmishing, for some six miles. This advance was through a heavy pine country, quite undulating, and as the enemy—which seemed to be only a force of cavalry—were driven from one hill, they would take a position on the next."[54]

About noon Lee and Landram arrived at the Sabine Crossroads clearing. One of the soldiers of the 67th Indiana wrote the following in his diary for April 8: "We left camp at 3 A.M. & marched 6 miles and catched up with rear of the rebels where unslung knapsacks. 16th Ind was deployed as skirmished here. 67th Ind & 23 Wis, 19th Ky, 77 Ill supported them. We drove the rebels through the woods untill 1 1/2 P.M. when they made a stand."[55] In front of the Union advance force was an area of gently rolling, mostly cleared land. A shallow ravine crossed the clearing from right to left, and to the left of the road partway across the clearing was a low hill, known locally as Honeycutt Hill. The enemy line of battle, located within the edge of the woods on the far side of the clearing, appeared formidable. Lee sent a request to Franklin for additional infantry to relieve Emerson's brigade and ordered Landram to move his men forward and take possession of the hill. A line of Confederate skirmishers crouched among some trees on the crest, seemingly ready to contest the advance. Though tired from their morning's work, and depleted in number from their hard marching and nearly continuous skirmishing along the line of march, the men moved forward and, to their surprise, occupied Honeycutt Hill without encountering much resistance.

THE BATTLES AT SABINE CROSSROADS AND PLEASANT GROVE

11

During the morning of April 8, Franklin, with Banks's permission, planned to move his troops past Pleasant Hill about ten miles and then stop for the day. His purpose for scheduling such a short march was to allow the rear of the column to close up, rest the men, allow Emory to take the lead, and free the ground around Pleasant Hill for Smith's men to camp. Franklin may also have had some residual concern about the slow advance of the cavalry train and wished to give them additional time to clear the road. He clearly foresaw no danger to the head of the column. Ransom advanced slowly behind the cavalry wagons and by about 10:30 A.M. had reached the northern branch of Bayou St. Patrice. According to instructions from Franklin, he was to remain near this location overnight. He therefore stopped his column and began setting up camp. Shortly thereafter Emory arrived at the southern branch of the bayou, where he also prepared to go into

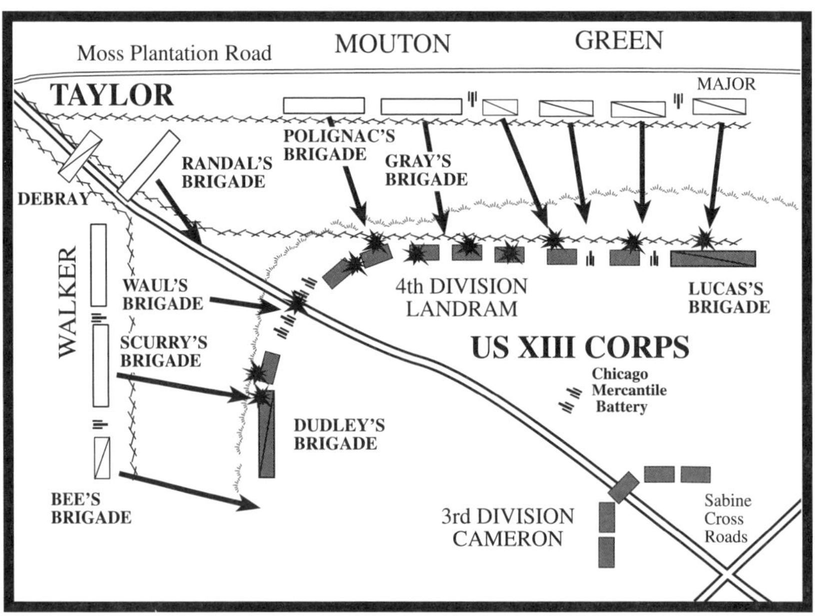

The battle at Sabine Crossroads, or Mansfield

camp. A. J. Smith was still south of Pleasant Hill, behind the long line of infantry wagons.

Upon receiving Lee's request for troops to relieve Emerson, Franklin ordered Ransom to send forward the 2nd Brigade, under Col. Joseph W. Vance. The 2nd Brigade, consisting of approximately 1,500 men of the 97th and 130th Illinois, and the 48th, 83rd, and 96th Ohio, left Bayou St. Patrice around 11:00 A.M. for the front, about five miles ahead. General Ransom chose to accompany these troops.[1] The brigade marched "almost on the run" to get to the front. As they approached the clearing at Sabine Crossroads, the men saw sure signs of preparation for a battle. "Artillery was being hurried up and put in place, lines of cavalry were fronting on every side, . . . the volleys of musketry and the playing of the flying artillery showed that the ball had really opened."[2]

Before noon Banks stopped at General Franklin's camp near Carroll's Mill. While there, according to Banks, Franklin said to him in passing, "There will be no fighting." To this Banks replied, "I will go forward and see."[3] Banks then proceeded to the front, en route passing Ransom and Vance, who were struggling to get their men around the cavalry wagons. Banks arrived at the clearing about one o'clock in the afternoon. By this time the Union force had been exchanging artillery fire with Taylor's men for an hour, but to little effect. At first Banks misunderstood the situation. Although it was clear to him that "the enemy are apparently prepared to make a strong stand at this point," he did not believe there would be a serious engagement. He saw the open field in front of him as a good campsite. From the front he sent a brief dispatch to Franklin, whom he requested to "make arrangements to bring up your infantry, and to pass everything on the road." He added that Franklin had "better send back and push up the trains, as manifestly we shall be able to rest here."[4]

Shortly after sending this dispatch to Franklin, Banks began to understand the state of affairs at the crossroads. Lee informed Banks that they were facing 15,000 to 20,000 Confederates, and Banks stated later that there were, "according to the statements of prisoners and intercepted letters, about 25,000 men, with seventy-six guns,"[5] and "I felt instinctively, for no reason that I can give, that we were in the presence of the whole force of the enemy."[6] He directed another member of his staff to ride back, find Franklin, inform him of conditions at the front, and order him to send forward reinforcements as fast as possible. Franklin received Banks's first dispatch near three o'clock, followed some ten minutes later by the second message. He reacted quickly and soon started toward the front with Cameron's 3rd Division. These reinforcements consisted of about 1,300 men of the 29th Wisconsin, 46th Indiana, 24th and 28th Iowa, and 56th Ohio.[7]

Pushing forward, and leaving Vance and Emory in charge of the brigade, which continued to struggle around the cavalry wagons that clogged the road for miles, Ransom arrived on the field about 1:30. After observing the situation, Ransom reported to Banks, advising him "of the position and apparent strength of the enemy." Ransom judged that when he arrived on the field, there were 2,413 infantry in the Union line.[8] The Union forces occupied the southeast corner and the center of the crossroads clearing, including Honeycutt Hill and a slight rise that extended to the northeast. Taylor's army occupied the northwest corner and north edge of the clearing.

About 3:30 in the afternoon Vance, with Emory's 2nd Brigade of the 4th Division, XIII Corps, arrived at the front. As the men reached the field, they were fed into the line. Frank McGregor of the 83rd Ohio described the situation: "Our regiment was marched to the right of the Division skirting a small woods of scrubby pines, forming our line to prevent a flank movement by the enemy." As the brigade was being placed into position, McGregor noticed the presence of General Ransom, "and I could not but admire how cool and collected he was, attending to all the little minutiae himself. He said at the time he thought the enemy was going to make a stand and that our regiment would have to protect the right flank."[9]

Taylor's line consisted of Maj. Gen. John G. Walker on the right and Mouton on the left. Walker, who was a veteran commander in the Army of Northern Virginia, had been transferred to the Trans-Mississippi in 1862. There he assumed command of a division of Texas soldiers that, under Walker's leadership, became known as the "Greyhound Division." Because the reinforcements from Arkansas had not yet arrived, the Confederates had about 8,500 men on the field. With the arrival of Vance the Union forces present now totaled almost 6,000 cavalry and infantry. Shortly after Vance's arrival, Taylor, chafing from Banks's inaction and desiring to press the issue, ordered Mouton to attack. At approximately 4:00 P.M., after brief preparations, the left of Taylor's line charged into the clearing. T. C. Prescott of the 2nd New Hampshire Cavalry described Mouton's advance: "Masses of rebels, no less than four lines in depth, emerged from the woods and charged with impetuous force, while yelling like crazed demons."[10] A reporter observed "the Rebels suddenly opening with artillery and musketry, charging our surprised and panic-stricken columns with terrific yells, evincing a daring and determination worthy of a better cause."[11]

The Louisianans and Texans pressed forward in the face of artillery and musket fire, reaching and crossing the ravine in front of Ransom's troops, some two hundred yards from the Union line. At a rail fence between the ravine and the Union line the Confederate advance was stopped amid great slaughter. General Mouton was killed in this Confederate charge against the Union right.[12] Taylor, assuming Banks had weakened his left to defend against Mouton's attack, now ordered Walker to attack the Union left. Walker's men, moving forward against enemy musket and artillery fire, charged up Honeycutt Hill and slammed into the flank of the 23rd Wisconsin. Driving that regiment back, they captured three guns.

Bee's Confederate cavalry meanwhile moved around the left flank of the Union line and got into the Union rear. One of the Yankee gunners recalled seeing "men coming out of the woods much nearer than those down the road, so we fired to the front and right until they came to point-blank range and then we fed it to them with double-shotted canister." Despite this murderous fire the Southerners drove around and past the guns, "leaving the hill on which our six guns were planted with our support of 23rd Wisconsin and 19th Kentucky to fight nearly alone." Finally, the "infantry and cavalry had become completely routed and were fleeing to the rear. . . . Finding it impossible to save the guns, our officers ordered us to slip our traces and save our lives if possible, which the men did reluctantly."[13]

As Walker's attack proceeded on the Confederate right, Brig. Gen. Camille Armand Jules Marie, Prince de Polignac, veteran of the Crimean War, and known affectionately as General "Polecat" to the Texans he commanded, assumed command of Mouton's division. He ordered the division forward once again.[14] Mirroring Bee's advance on the Union left, Major's troopers flanked the enemy right and, charging furiously, turned the Union flank. The entire line was crumbling. Ransom issued an order to retire to the woods at the southeast corner of the clearing. Landram and Vance passed the order down the line, but several regiments on the right, including the 130th Illinois and 48th Ohio, apparently did not receive the order. These regiments were surrounded and captured almost to a man.[15] "The rebels seeing their advantage were on the charge, 'twas a fearful sight, our little division fought bravely, but the numbers against them were so much superior, again they were flushed with victory. . . . By this time the artillery was in full retreat, it appeared almost a panic, or the better word would be a *route.*"[16]

On the right, after a short retreat, the Union troops rallied briefly. "General Banks and General Franklin with their staff and escort came up to the rear of our colors. This is the first time I knew he was on the field at all. He almost redeemed himself in my eyes by coming to the post of danger. He looked cool and calm, though rather perplexed I should judge."[17] Banks exhorted the troops to stop the advancing enemy, declaring that the XIX Corps was coming up, but to no avail. With his whole line dissolving, Ransom rode to the edge of the woods in the southeast corner of the crossroads clearing. There the men, retreating in confusion, came pouring from the battlefield and converged onto the road leading to Pleasant Hill. The triumphant Confederates were close behind them. In his report Ransom stated, "In company with Colonel Landram, I was, as the troops arrived, reforming the line in the edge of the woods, when I was severely wounded in the knee and carried to the rear. I found the woods and road filled with mounted men, flying in confusion from the field."[18]

Since shortly after receiving Banks's orders, about three o'clock in the afternoon, General Franklin had been working his way forward past the cavalry wagons. Franklin arrived at the southeast corner of the crossroads clearing just as Landram was struggling to rally his men at the edge of the woods. Observing the extreme danger of the situation, Franklin immediately sent a staff officer to order Emory to hurry forward with his 1st Division, XIX Corps, and to attempt to form a defensive line "at a place which I indicated, about two miles in rear."[19] Meanwhile, scarcely had Franklin and the XIII Corps reinforcements arrived on the field when Franklin's horse was killed and he and two members of his staff were wounded.[20]

As the Union forces continued to retreat in disarray from the battlefield, and with the sound of battle rapidly approaching, General Cameron hastily deployed his men to support the rally begun by Ransom and Landram. His line of battle was formed with the 46th Indiana and five companies of the 29th Wisconsin of the 1st Brigade, under Lt. Col. Aaron M. Flory, on the right of the road. On the left Cameron placed Col. William H. Raynor's 2nd Brigade, which consisted of the 24th and 28th Iowa and the 56th Ohio. With these dispositions Cameron proceeded to move forward to occupy the woods at the edge of the clearing. There his force awaited the arrival of the victorious Southerners. Remnants of Landram's division joined Cameron's line, and some of Dudley's men formed on Raynor's left.

Soon "the rebels, elated with their success, came pouring over the clearing in successive lines and closely massed columns." The enemy was permitted to approach the line "within close rifle range" before the men opened fire. "The

Federal position was such that, concealed behind logs and fences, it could not be located by the rebels, giving an unusually fine opportunity for deliberate aim." A sheet of flame erupted from the concealed Federal troops, and the Confederate advance faltered, "leaving the ground strewn with their dead and wounded. The rattle of the deadly rifle was unceasing, and the rebel slaughter terrible."[21] This was but a temporary setback, however. The Southerners quickly re-formed and charged again. For almost an hour Cameron's makeshift defensive line held the enemy in check, but the victorious Confederates were not to be denied. Cameron's line began to break.

A reporter from the Chicago *Tribune* wrote, "For a short time, it seemed as if a successful rally would be made at this point; but the effort was in vain. The entire strength of the 3d division on the field was only 1,600 men, and, after a short and courageous resistance, the line gave way." Although the makeshift Union line was finally broken, a check had been delivered to the enemy. Observing the discipline of Cameron's men, many of the Federal troops fleeing the battlefield "formed into squads and continued the retreat in better order. Efficient aid was also rendered by Col. Robinson . . . who, hearing the rapidly approaching firing, hastened with a large portion of his command to the front, and wheeling into line in perfect order, delivered a most destructive volley into the Rebels, who were swarming in the road, and then fell back in good order."[22]

The "good order" of the retreat did not last long. Cameron's withdrawal quickly accelerated as the urge to flee became pandemic among the soldiers. In the fading daylight the entire Union force was soon in full flight down the road. All attempts by officers to halt them failed. The Confederate advance was inexorable. "Everything now was in full retreat, there was no such a thing as trying to make a stand, 'twas running and loading, every opportunity returning a shot."[23] The retreat became a panic as the troops, about a mile from the battlefield, ran headlong into the cavalry wagons. Lee had ordered the wagons to be withdrawn, and many were in the process of being turned around. Some of the wagons had been abandoned by their drivers, and the teams, frightened and out of control, reared in their traces. "The road was completely blocked up, drivers . . . *ran* leaving their teams . . . batteries of artillery rushing on the retreat crushing before it. The large force of cavalry on a perfect stampede. Now it was a *complete route.* Self preservation was all that was to be thought of."[24] The soldiers streamed past the wagons and through the edge of the woods on both sides of the road. A newspaper correspondent who observed the scene agreed that panic had infected the army. "Literally oblivious to any thing but the danger behind, men on foot and men on horseback, promiscuously intermingled with negroes on foot and negroes on mules, charged into the forest and through the thicket in a manner that would have utterly routed the foe if the tide had only set the other way."[25]

The Confederates captured twenty guns, three on the field and seventeen at the traffic jam along the road.[26] A member of the 2nd New Hampshire Cavalry noted that "several of the guns of Carruth's, Nims' and the Mercantile batteries came thundering down the road on to the head of the train. A company of rebel cavalry dashed in from the woods on the left and began firing on them; the cannoneers cut traces, mounted the mules, and some got away." The same soldier also noted the bravery of Banks as he attempted to rally his troops. "We soon overtook Gen. Banks, who was endeavoring to check the tide by saying, 'Don't hurry, boys: we are all right. Fall back on Franklin, and form in his rear.'"[27]

As the infantry forced their way around the wagons, no semblance of order survived. One soldier said later, "It was every man for himself and 'Dick' Taylor take the hindmost."[28] Banks, who as always showed great personal courage, tried to form a new line but failed. John Russell Young, the reporter for the *Philadelphia Press* and an admirer of Banks, wrote that "Gen. Banks personally directed the fight. Every thing that man could do he did. Occupying a position so exposed that nearly every horse ridden by his staff was wounded, and many killed, he constantly disregarded the entreaties of those around, who begged that he would retire to some less exposed position." However, the commanding officer and his staff were "swallowed up, as it were, in a hissing, seething, bubbling whirlpool of agitated men," and there was nothing to do but move with the tide. "Gen. Banks took off his hat and implored his men to remain; his staff-officers did the same, but it was of no avail."[29]

The rout at Sabine Crossroads was one of the major panics of the war.[30] Some observers believed the spectacle of the fleeing Federals at Mansfield exceeded that at Bull Run. Sgt. William Barr of the 33rd Wisconsin wrote that the disaster was "worse than any Bullrun stampede you ever read of some never stoped till they reached Grandecore."[31] A member of the 77th Illinois felt that "no one will ever know the depth of shame our hearts experienced over this defeat. For it was a manifest display of the profoundest ignorance of the proper management of a battle."[32] Banks wrote later, "It appeared that the entire cavalry train, with its artillery, occupied the road nearly to the line of skirmishers. The fatal consequences of this most incautious advance of trains and artillery were apparent upon the breaking of our lines in front of the enemy's position."[33]

When he received Franklin's order, shortly before four o'clock on the afternoon of April 8, General Emory was in camp at Ten Mile Bayou, near Carroll's Mill. There was no indication of an impending battle and no sense of urgency apparent in the camp. The wagons of the XIII Corps were passing along the road, on the way to join their command. Emory's wagons had been with him for some time, and several of the division quartermasters were engaged in issuing clothing. When the summons from Franklin intruded into this deceptively peaceful milieu, Emory reacted immediately. Within fifteen minutes of receiving Franklin's message he started forward with some 5,100 men of the 1st Division, XIX Corps. Only after he had been on the road for three-quarters of an hour did Emory receive any indication that an engagement was in progress. At that time a courier arrived from Banks with orders for Emory to hasten forward.

After advancing another mile, Emory met an ambulance carrying Ransom to the rear. The two officers exchanged a few words, after which Emory ordered his division to move at the double-quick. A member of the 30th Maine recalled, "We obeyed the order to 'double-quick,' which was given us about two miles from where we took up our line of battle in rear of the Thirteenth Corps. . . . The road was blocked by wagons, crowded with cavalry, teamsters and negroes, and all were wild with excitement; wagons had been abandoned and drivers were riding their animals furiously to the rear."[34] Emory's column advanced against this current of fugitives, many of whom cried out to the fresh troops that the day was lost.[35]

About three miles from the battlefield Emory entered a clearing at a place called Pleasant Grove, also known as Chatman's (or Chapman's) Hill or Chatman's Peach Orchard. At this point there was a narrow lane leading off the main road to a fenced farm nearby. A small stream, known as Chatman's Bayou, crossed the clearing.[36] Emory decided to deploy his division along the east side of the stream. He ordered William Dwight's 1st Brigade, which had led the march to this point, to form a line directly across the road. Dwight placed the 29th Maine on the left, the 114th New York in the center, and the 116th New York on the right.

In the face of "the retreating cavalry and troops of the Thirteenth Corps [that] were rushing frantically across the field, and endeavoring to break through our lines in the precipitate flight," Emory calmly continued to direct his arriving troops into the line. He sent James W. McMillan's 2nd Brigade to Dwight's right, and Lewis Benedict's 3rd Brigade to the left. Lucas's partially re-formed cavalry brigade, joining Emory directly from the battlefield, was positioned on the right. In their front the men in this line could see "a cleared field of nearly five hundred yards in depth, then a thick wood. . . . The enemy had not yet emerged from the woods, nevertheless, he was pouring well directed vollies" into the Federal line.[37] As the line of battle was being prepared, Emory sent Lt. Col. William B. Kinsey's 161st New York forward to hold the enemy in check until the full division was in position.

In the gathering darkness the men of the XIX Corps stood as the retreating Union troops streamed past them. In passing through Emory's line, McGregor noted, "They were all in line finely. Indeed all knew if *they* did not check them our army was lost."[38] Behind the retreating Federals the victorious Southern troops continued to surge down the narrow road, capturing stragglers and wounded Union soldiers as they advanced. Then Taylor's men encountered General Emory. Heavy skirmishing began as the Confederates moved into the clearing. The Union line was hurriedly completed, and the men of the 161st New York retreated in front of the enemy advance. "It became a serious question whether friend and foe might not enter the Union lines together."[39] As the 161st rejoined their comrades, the enemy were but a few steps behind. Then Emory's line opened fire at point-blank range, and the advancing Southerners were first halted in their tracks and then driven back. The scene was described by a reporter from the Chicago *Tribune:*

> Opening their ranks to permit the retreating forces to pass through, each regiment of this fine division, closing up on the double-quick, quietly awaited the approach of the Rebels; and, within less than five minutes, on they came, screaming and firing as they advanced but still in good order and with closed ranks. All at once, from that firm line of gallant soldiers that now stood so bravely between us and our pursuing foes, there came forth a course of reverberating thunders that rolled from flank to flank in one continuous peal, sending a storm of leaden hail into the Rebel ranks that swept them back in dismay, and left the ground covered with their killed and wounded.[40]

As more of Taylor's men arrived, they were directed toward Emory's right in an attempt to turn the Union line. The 47th Pennsylvania of McMillan's 2nd Brigade began to give way in the face of the Confederate pressure. Emory ordered McMillan to form a line at right angles to the main position to counter this enemy thrust. There, in the twilight of the spring afternoon, and with the help of the hard-fought 116th New York, McMillan was able to check the Confederate advance. In a period of twenty minutes, as darkness fell, the main line turned back two more charges by the Confederates. In his diary, James Sherwood of the 114th New York caught the drama of this engagement as he reported in near stream-of-consciousness prose:

> Apr 8. Their is hevey canonading, musketry. went about 7 miles. found the Rebs had atacked our Cavalry & the 13th Corps in force & are driving them in. Hav taken som of our Artillry. it is in a clearing. the Rebels are in the edg of the woods. our Division is formed on a little hill on one side of the clearing. our Regt is in the front with a few log buildings back of us. it is a tuff looking sight down in the vally. our Cavalry & Infantry all mixed up with the enemy halowing shouting with clouds of dirt & smoke rising. our Troops falls back slowley in side where where we are forming. now the bullets begins to fly around us like haile. they com on yelling but our Division pors in a volly & keeps it up for an houre. we hav stoped them—Gens Banks & Emory rode down the lines & incuraged the men.[41]

Emory's prompt action had effectively halted the Southern advance and had perhaps saved Banks's army. Later Banks stated, "The First Division of the Nineteenth Corps, by its great bravery in this action, saved the army and navy."[42] Unable to tell friend from foe in the darkness, the men stopped fighting. The Union troops dropped to the ground virtually where they stood, still in line of battle. For most, rest was prevented by thirst, by the cold, and by the cries of the wounded. After the fighting stopped, James Sherwood recorded: "It is dark. can hear the wounded calling for help on the field. lay down but P [?] have no blankets & it is so cold canot sleepe."[43]

Banks's initial response to the engagement at Pleasant Grove was to make plans to resume the advance the next day. According to Col. J. G. Wilson, after Emory's successful stand Banks sent a staff officer to General Smith with orders for him to push forward as rapidly as possible in hopes of his joining the army at Pleasant Grove by daylight the next morning.[44] However, by this time it appears that Banks was losing confidence in his own decisions. He began deferring increasingly to the recommendations of his subordinates, most important perhaps to those of his personal friend William Dwight.[45] About nine o'clock on the evening of April 8 Banks called his generals together for a council of war. The council recommended retreat, and Banks so ordered. General Dwight claimed that he concurred in recommending this retreat but stated that he did so on the assumption that Smith would be unable to arrive by the next morning and on the poor condition of the troops that were present. Emory, the last of the Union commanders to leave Pleasant Grove, gathered his men and marched away at midnight, leaving the field to the Confederates.

The battles at Sabine Crossroads and Pleasant Grove had been hard fought, and many brave men had fallen on both sides. According to one of the Federal veterans, "Our men loaded and fired with such rapidity, that it seemed not like the usual tremulous rattling of musketry, but like one continuous explosion. . . . The musketry of Champion Hill and Shiloh did not exceed that of Sabine Cross Roads."[46] Union forces on the field during the early part of the battle included those of Lee, Emerson, and Vance. Lee started with about 3,300 men on the morning of April 8. Losses and straggling during the skirmishing and advance to Sabine Crossroads are unknown but were probably small. Emerson left camp early on the same morning with about 1,200 men. Losses from this command because of straggling during the rapid march from Bayou St. Patrice, followed by the nearly continuous skirmishing during the further advance with Lee's cavalry, are unknown but probably were significant. A reduction of 5 to 10 percent in effective strength by the time the brigade reached Sabine Crossroads is not unreasonable, although many of these losses were undoubtedly temporary pending the men catching up with the main body. Vance had about 1,500 men initially but undoubtedly lost a few percent from straggling during his advance to the edge of the Sabine Crossroads clearing. Thus, the Union force present during the initial Confederate attack at Sabine Crossroads probably consisted of between 5,700 and 5,800 effectives.

Cameron started forward from Carroll's Mill with about 1,300 men. Losses from straggling en route were probably a few percent. Some men retreating from the initial part of the battle joined Cameron's line as it was being formed. Since the Union loss during the fight in the Crossroads clearing was about 1,500, there were some 4,200 men remaining to retreat through Cameron's line. Probably less than half of these joined the line of battle. Thus, Cameron's line consisted of perhaps between 3,000 and 3,200 men.[47] Finally, Emory left camp with about 5,100 men. Again, some losses must be assumed on the march to Pleasant Grove because of straggling. This may have been in the range of 3 to 5 percent. With the addition of some cavalry and a few hearty men from Ransom's corps, Emory's line at Pleasant Grove probably consisted of about 5,000 men. The total Union force involved on April 8 thus probably consisted of approximately 11,500 men. Out of this force Banks had 2,235 casualties. Landram lost almost half of his force, and in the last repulse Emory lost 347 killed, wounded, and missing. The Union death toll may have reached 700. In addition to his abandoned artillery, Banks lost about two hundred wagons plus eleven ambulances and over one thousand horses and mules.[48]

Taylor had about 8,500 men on the field at the time of his attack at Sabine Crossroads. Southern casualties during the early fighting may have been about 500 to 700, leaving between 7,800 and 8,000 to attack Cameron. While passing the wagons en route to Pleasant Grove, many of the Southerners stopped to rummage for food or supplies. Thus, with additional losses from straggling, Taylor's attack on Emory probably included no more than 6,500 rather exhausted men. Taylor's losses are uncertain, but out of roughly 8,500 men engaged, probably some 1,500 were killed, wounded, or captured.

THE BATTLE AT PLEASANT HILL

12 Gen. A. J. Smith and his detachment camped about two miles southeast of Pleasant Hill on the night of April 8, having marched some twenty-one miles that day. Smith reported that he had "heard heavy cannonading in front during the afternoon," which he subsequently learned was "an attack by the enemy upon the cavalry and the Thirteenth Army Corps." After stopping for the night, he notified Banks of his location, set pickets around his position, and ordered his men to "bivouac upon their arms." According to Adolphus P. Wolfe, a member of the 117th Illinois, after Smith learned of the battle at Sabine Crossroads, he decided that "if there was fighting to be done, he wanted to have a hand in it. We poor soldiers were to be pitied, nearly tired out, but still a double quick of about 7 miles before there could be any rest for us. . . . We were left to enjoy a night's sleep such sleep as a soldier enjoys the eve before a battle."[1] The next morning Smith again pushed his troops forward and, along with Oliver P. Gooding's 5th Cav-

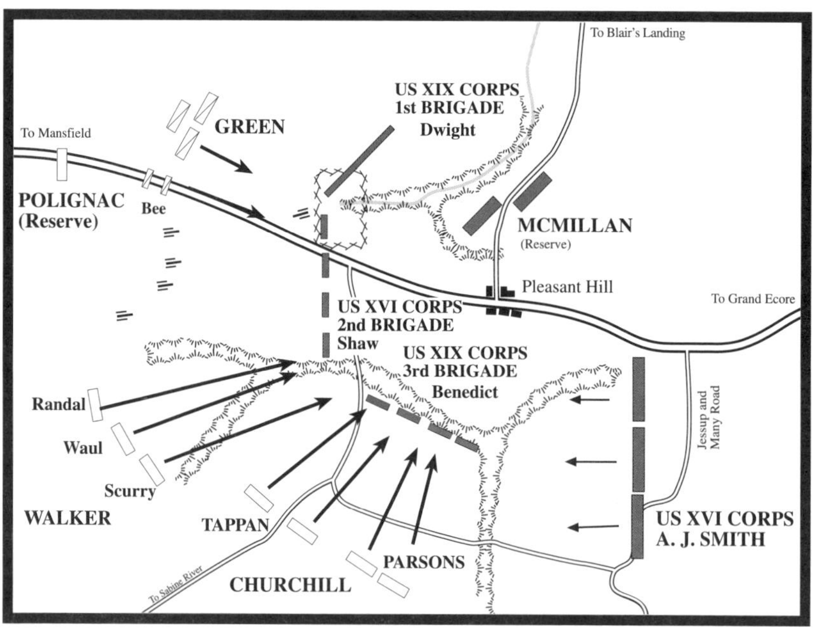

The battle at Pleasant Hill

alry Brigade, arrived at Pleasant Hill early on April 9. There he "formed a line of battle across the Mansfield road."[2]

Banks sent a courier to inform Smith of his decision to retreat from Pleasant Grove and to instruct him to wait for the retreating army to join him at Pleasant Hill.[3] After the battles near Mansfield, the weary troops of the XIII and XIX Corps struggled through the woods in the dark. The first of the retreating troops reached Pleasant Hill shortly after Smith arrived. The fatigued men were glad to find reinforcements, and some were particularly glad that General Smith was in charge of the reinforcements: "As daylight came we reached Pleasant Hill—and were delighted to hear that our old division commander, A. J. Smith was camped on the hill. A few minutes more and our eyes were gladdened—with the sight of them. It was clear that A. J. Smith was going to try them here."[4]

After his arrival at Pleasant Hill on the morning of April 9, Banks held another council of war. John Russell Young apparently observed this council. According to Young, the scene he observed "might have been a parade; it might have been a fair-day, and these men around us so many plain farmers who came to receive medals for their cattle and swine, and hear the county lawyer deliver the agricultural address. It certainly could not be war." Offering an insightful description of the Union high command, Young wrote:

> In an inclosure near the roadside was a small cluster of gentlemen to whom all this phantasmagoria had the meaning of life, and death, and power, and fame. General Banks, with his light-blue overcoat buttoned closely around his chin, was strolling up and down, occasionally conversing with a member of his staff, or returning the salute of a passing subaltern. Near him was General William B. Franklin, his face as rough and rugged as when he rode through the storms of the Peninsula, the ideal of a bold, daring, imperturbable soldier. . . . There was General Smith, with his bushy, grayish beard, and his eager eye, as it looks through spectacles, giving him the appearance of a schoolmaster.[5]

Several relevant points were raised, including that the navy could not provide support to the army at its present location and that numerous reports had been received that General Magruder intended to "come up from Texas and cut off our communications."[6] The recommendation was to continue the retreat. As a result, Banks ordered his wagons to proceed to Grand Ecore. Meanwhile, the army would take a defensive position in case the enemy chose to attack. The wagon train left Pleasant Hill at about ten o'clock escorted by

Dickey's brigade of the Corps d'Afrique and by most of Lee's cavalry division. Banks stated later that he sent the wagon train to Grand Ecore "so in the event of disaster there might be a chance of its safety. . . . A portion of the cavalry of the 19th army corps was sent to protect it."[7]

The army was put into line at Pleasant Hill apparently with little or no regard for any overall tactical defensive plan. The brigades were dispersed almost haphazardly, with units aligned in various directions, sometimes making contact with adjacent units and sometimes not. The generals knew that a victorious enemy force, which they believed to be of immense size, would soon arrive, yet they appeared to pay little attention to maximizing the strength of their defensive position. Col. William T. Shaw's 2nd Brigade moved from their position near the Pleasant Hill cemetery at about 9:00 A.M. The movement was anything but simple in the face of the troops and wagons then arriving from Sabine Crossroads.

> It was near 9 o'clock before we actually moved out of that graveyard camp. As we march out to the road, a scene of indescribable confusion presented itself. It was impossible for infantry to get into the road without being trampled under foot. The road was a "jam" of six-mule teams, each striving to make the most speed to the rear. The mules were entangled each with their feet in the harness of the other. The drivers were whipping and swearing; and, as an accompaniment of the music of their whip-lashes, was their fearful cursings of General Banks and other officers.[8]

As the soldiers and teamsters continued to stream down the Mansfield road, Charles Oscar Torrey of the 27th Iowa reported, "Banks force in full retreat. Corps trains passing all the time. Road lined [with] straglers."[9]

Moving by Banks's orders, and forcing his way through the thick underbrush along the roadside, Shaw reported to Emory about 10:30 A.M.[10] Emory directed him to relieve McMillan's brigade, which at that time was in line perpendicular to the Mansfield road about one-half mile northwest of the village of Pleasant Hill and just beyond a turnoff leading west toward Logansport and the Sabine River. As McMillan's men retired, Shaw moved the 14th, 27th, and 32nd Iowa into the existing line. Irving D. Southworth's 25th Battery, New York Light Artillery, was positioned on some high ground in front, and to the right, of Shaw's center.[11] In front of Shaw's regiments was "a large, open field, which had once been cultivated, but is now overgrown with weeds and bushes."[12] Instead of limiting himself to the front established by McMillan,

Shaw sent his fourth regiment, the 24th Missouri, to his right to hold some high ground northeast of the road.

Col. Lewis Benedict's 3rd Brigade of Emory's division was originally positioned to Shaw's left, southwest of the road to Mansfield. In the middle of the afternoon Benedict was ordered to move back from his position about three hundred yards to occupy the dry bed of a stream that formed a shallow depression some four hundred yards in front of the village. In this new position Benedict's line was nearly perpendicular to the Logansport road, with his right near that road. Battery L, 1st U.S. Artillery, under Franck E. Taylor, was placed on high ground to Benedict's rear and was to fire over the heads of Benedict's men. Thus, the brigades of Benedict and Shaw were formed into nearly parallel lines, but Benedict was located about three hundred yards behind and seven hundred yards to the left of Shaw. The ends of both Shaw's and Benedict's lines were in the air.

Brig. Gen. William Dwight's brigade was positioned on the extreme right of the Union position along a ravine north of, and nearly parallel to, the Mansfield road. His force was thus almost at a right angle to Shaw's line. However, instead of joining Shaw's line, the left of Dwight's line ended well to the rear of Shaw's right. Southworth's battery was located between Shaw and Dwight. Shaw noticed the disadvantages in this troop alignment across and to the right of the Mansfield road and consulted with Generals Dwight and Stone. He claimed later that both of these generals agreed that there was a problem and offered their support to try to fix it. Shaw quoted Stone as saying, "I will see that your flanks are properly supported." However, subsequent to this promise of support, in Shaw's words, "no orders came," and the alignment of the Union defensive position remained broken.[13]

Cameron's XIII Corps was sent out on the Fort Jesup road to watch the left flank of the army. This movement was countermanded, however, when "some person to me now unknown," but purporting to be either from General Stone or General Banks, ordered Cameron to "guard the train . . . until it had passed out of the way of danger." In response to this verbal order, about noon Cameron abandoned his position on the left of the army and moved toward the rear, leaving the Union left uncovered.[14]

Almost a mile behind Shaw's line, and approximately four hundred yards behind Benedict, the remainder of the two XVI Corps divisions lined up in a wooded area more or less parallel to and west of the road to Many and Fort Jesup. At the right end of this line, Lucius F. Hubbard's 2nd Brigade, of Mower's 1st Division, was north of the Mansfield road at the southern edge of the village of Pleasant Hill. To Hubbard's left, south of the Mansfield road and in front of the road to Many, in order right to left, were Risdon M. Moore's 3rd Brigade, 3rd Division; Sylvester G. Hill's 3rd Brigade, 1st Division; and William F. Lynch's 1st Brigade, 3rd Division. Hubbard saw determination in the faces of both his commanding officer and his men and later wrote: "Old A. J. Smith, with his 'Guerrillas' in line, presented an obstacle that Dick Taylor could not brush from his path. . . . If he could have looked into old A. J. Smith's face as he sat astride that black charger, and into the eyes of the line of veterans that had never been whipped, he might have read his fate, and by a timely movement to the rear have saved himself a most painful experience."[15]

The Confederate reinforcements from Arkansas, under the command of Brig. Gen. Thomas J. Churchill, arrived at Mansfield during the night following the battle at Sabine Crossroads. Churchill brought two small divisions: his own Arkansas Division, commanded by James C. Tappan, and the Missouri Division of Mosby M. Parsons. This detachment from Price's army included about 4,300 men. Churchill was immediately ordered to advance to Pleasant Grove, despite the fact that his men had just marched twenty-two miles from the town of Keatchie. They departed from Mansfield at about 2:00 A.M.

Taylor discovered Banks's absence from Pleasant Grove at first light April 9 and, with Green's cavalry, immediately started in pursuit of the retreating Yankees. Churchill's detachment, arriving shortly thereafter, was ordered to follow the cavalry. Last, the victorious but hard-fought divisions of Walker and Polignac fell into line behind Churchill. Taylor's men passed dead and wounded Union soldiers, plus burning wagons and other detritus left by the fleeing army. They captured scores of stragglers as they progressed through the forest.

The lead elements of Green's cavalry approached Pleasant Hill about nine o'clock on the morning of April 9 and, after a brief skirmish with Dwight's rear guard, found the Union army getting into position near the town. Rather than press the Federals with the force he had, Taylor fell back a short distance to wait until all of his army had arrived on the scene. Only light skirmishing occurred on the field through most of the day. Churchill and Parsons arrived at Pleasant Hill around one o'clock in the afternoon, followed about three o'clock by Walker and Polignac. Now Taylor had his entire force present, totaling about 11,500 men. He prepared to attack once again. He directed Churchill, with his fresh troops, to flank the Union left by marching south through the woods to the Fort Jesup road. There he was to form a line of battle facing northeast and move toward Pleasant Hill. Churchill executed this move without detection by the enemy but arrived at the Logansport road, not the Fort Jesup road.

At the Logansport road Churchill formed Parsons's division on the right and Tappan's division on the left, straddling the road. Meanwhile, northwest of the village, Taylor deployed Walker to the right of the Mansfield road and Polignac to the left. Bee, with the cavalry brigades of Debray and Buchel, was placed on the Mansfield road, and the dismounted brigades of Major and Bagby were placed to Polignac's left. Mouton's division, now also under Polignac, was held in reserve. Taylor's plan called for Walker to advance and connect with Churchill's left when he heard the sound of the latter's assault. Then "Major, with two brigades of horse dismounted, was to drive back the enemy's skirmishers, turn his right, and gain the road to Blair's Landing. As no offensive movement by the enemy was anticipated, he would be turned on both flanks, subjected to a concentric fire, and overwhelmed."[16]

At about 4:30 Taylor opened the battle with artillery fire directed toward Southworth's battery. The Union artillery replied for a period, then limbered up and retired, to the chagrin of Colonel Shaw.[17] After driving off this battery, the Southern guns began to fire on Shaw's line. Finally, after half an hour of this warm-up, Churchill began his advance. The 30th Maine had been thrown forward as skirmishers to Benedict's front and left. As the Confederates moved out of the woods and formed their line, one officer of that regiment recalled that "they threw up their hats and yelled, and seemed eager for battle."[18] Advancing rapidly, Parsons struck the left of Benedict's line. Tappan's brigade, close on Parsons's left, was soon engaged as well. Benedict was heavily outnumbered, and Churchill's attack drove the brigade out of the dry streambed. Benedict's men scattered, some moving toward Shaw and others moving toward the woods in which Mower was located.

When the sound of Churchill's attack reached them, the rest of the Southern army charged forward. Shaw was quickly forced to withdraw from his advanced position. Reinforcements were brought up, but soon they also were swept away along with the general retreat of the Union front line. Churchill's forces entered the town limits, and the Federal line appeared to be crumbling. At this point the 58th Illinois, of Lynch's 1st Brigade, 3rd Division, under the command of Maj. Thomas Newlan, moved out of the woods on Smith's extreme left and well to the rear of Benedict's original line. Newlan was followed by the 89th Indiana and the 119th Illinois. These farm boys from the Old Northwest charged Parsons's right flank, taking the Confederates by surprise and driving them back into the dry ravine that had originally been part of Benedict's line. A. J. Smith then ordered his whole line forward. Capt. W. S. Burns of General Smith's staff recalled, "When the order was given, our troops rose to their feet and poured upon the advancing foe a most murderous volley, and then with General Mower at their head sprung forward in a grand charge."[19] According to Sgt. William Barr of the 33rd Wisconsin, Smith "let them have with artillery—infintery just slaying them by hundreds they took 2 Divisions of Prices old army either in killed wounded or prisoners and drove the balance 5 miles."[20]

The Union charge on the left, coming late in the day and following the apparent Confederate success, reversed the tide of the battle. The fighting was severe as Churchill's and Walker's troops fought for every hillock and clump of trees. "The field was a hard contested one, sometimes the enemy driving our troops and then we would drive them."[21] Dusk came, then darkness, and both sides continued to fight, sometimes without being able to tell friend from foe in the darkness. "The mingled roar of artillery and musketry; the shouts of the exultant, as volley after volley was fired with fearful effect; the groans of the wounded; the sulphurous smoke, and the day fading into darkness, all tended to heighten the effect of the thrilling scene."[22]

Fighting hand to hand in some parts of the field, the Federals swept the exhausted Southerners back into the woods to the north and west of the clearing. Five Confederate guns were captured, including three that the enemy had captured the previous day. The 58th Illinois, along with other regiments from the XVI Corps, drove Churchill's men up the road along which they had charged. "In this pursuit so close were we to the rebels that our men seized them by the collars, bayoneting some and capturing others while in the very act of firing their pieces."[23]

Finally, well after dark, Taylor ordered his troops to withdraw and the fighting ended. The closest water was a small stream about six miles to the north, and Taylor sent most of his troops there.[24] According to Maj. William T. Mechling of General Bee's staff, all of Taylor's forces left the battlefield except General Bee, who remained on picket with two companies of Debray's and two companies of Buchel's regiments.[25] Many of the exhausted Union soldiers rested but a few hundred yards from the battlefield. They did not have access to the stream to the north, and except for the few wells or cisterns in the village that had not already been emptied, there was no water available. The cries for water from the wounded, left lying on the field, were said to be particularly distressing that night.

Again James Sherwood of the 114th New York was in the action and recorded his experiences in his diary in a gripping stream of prose.

> 9 Apr. Past our Campe ground about 5 am everything has gon on. we or goin on to Mount Pleasant. we ar very tired. just before we got there the Rebs attacked our rear guard. we formed a line of battle in a clearing behind our Cavalry suporting a Battry. we cant get them out of the woods. went on to our old campe. stayed there abou 1 hr [?]. house was then sent out to the left to prevent being out flanked. staitioned us on a hill. their is skirmishing on hed all the time. 4 pm their is hevey cannonading. they ar returning it. their shells ar bursting over & around us. the Infantry ar geting engaged. the Rebs hav charged on us & have been repulsed a number of times. our Regts has been ordered into a little grove of pines with orders to hold it at all hazards. their is now a perfect storm of musketry. the whole woods seam in a blaze. it is now dark. the woods is full of smoke. they ar trying to out flank us & charging in every direction but we are enough for them. we have taken a lot of Prisoners & had some taken. we have taken the Artillery back that they took from us last night. our Regt held out to take the place of the 153 [New York] & 29th [Maine]. we advance & fire it in to them. they hav fallen back. our Boys are clearing. the firing has stoped. we lay in line of battle. it is very cold.[26]

The carnage at Pleasant Hill was severe for the size of the forces engaged. Taylor lost about 1,600 men killed, wounded, or captured; Banks suffered 152 men killed, 859 wounded, and 495 captured from about 12,200 engaged.[27] One of the Iowa soldiers under Smith subsequently wrote, "My prayer is that I may never witness another such site. Dead men & horses literally covered the ground for rod after rod, while the grones and cries of the wounded were too awful to listen to."[28]

Unfortunately for Richard Taylor, General Churchill, who was ordered to flank the Union line on the Confederate right, did not advance far enough to get behind A. J. Smith's line of defenders before turning toward the enemy. As a result, instead of charging the left flank of Smith's position, Churchill passed in front of Smith's line to strike the left of Benedict's position. Taylor later chided himself, saying that he made a mistake in sending Churchill to flank the Union left. "I should have conducted it myself. . . . All this flashed upon me the instant I learned of the disorder on my right. Herein lies the vast difference between genius and commonplace: one anticipates errors, the other discovers them too late."[29]

Banks apparently believed that A. J. Smith deserved the credit for the Union victory at Pleasant Hill. Smith reported that after the battle, Banks rode up to him and said, "God bless you, General, you have saved the army."[30] Most students of the battle report this fact without elaboration, implying that they agree with Banks's conclusion. Others have taken the position that the Confederate loss should be charged to Taylor because of his faulty execution.[31] However, despite the inadvertent error of Churchill's line of attack, and despite the poor layout of the Union lines, the credit for the tactical Union victory must go to A. J. Smith. General Smith reacted correctly and aggressively to the situation he observed developing and, with hard and determined fighting, drove the enemy from the field.

Banks, who was never known to underestimate the size of an enemy force pitted against him, and was never shy about declaring the immensity of his successes, was deluded into thinking he had just faced the entire Confederate army west of the Mississippi. He claimed that "the enemy we encountered numbered from 22,000 to 25,000, embracing all the troops west of the Mississippi, excepting a small force on the Texas coast and a small portion of cavalry on the north side of the river." He also incorrectly believed that Kirby Smith had commanded the Confederate forces in person, "supported by Price, Green, and the most distinguished generals of the rebel army."[32]

Following the departure of the enemy from the field at Pleasant Hill, A. J. Smith began efforts to gather the wounded and bury the dead. However, Banks had other ideas. Although at one point during the late evening of April 9 he had sent orders for his wagon train to return, he soon reversed himself and ordered the train to continue to Grand Ecore. Then, after consultation with Franklin, Emory, and Dwight, all of whom favored a retreat to the river, Banks decided to "fall back to Grand Ecore and reorganize."[33] Irwin argued many years later that Banks chose to retreat because Grant had ordered him to send A. J. Smith back to Vicksburg and had ordered Banks to move against Mobile by May 1: "Such were his orders from Grant, peremptory and repeated. Therefore Banks at once made up his mind to retreat to Grand Ecore."[34] Be that as it may, it seems likely that Taylor's Confederates had a great deal to do with Banks's decision to retreat.

Judgments of historians about whether this decision to retreat was correct under the circumstances, and interpretations of Banks's actions following the battle at Pleasant Hill, vary widely. Several students of the affair have maintained that the withdrawal was ill advised, arguing that Banks's army was still intact, that Taylor's army was in disarray, and that the Union troops outnumbered the Confederates on the scene.[35] Others argue that the retreat was proper given the poor leadership exhibited by Banks and the absence of the supply train, which the commander had sent to Grand Ecore.[36] Although the latter points are certainly true, the bulk of the evidence appears to be in favor of the first conclusion. Taylor had had to throw everything he had into the fight at Pleasant Hill and even so had been forced to withdraw. Kirby Smith was preoccupied with General Steele's force in Arkansas and was unlikely to summon the rest of Price's army to assist in the defense of Shreveport in a timely manner. Had Banks overruled his subordinates, recalled Cameron and Lee to the field, and aggressively pursued Taylor's army beginning April 10, he may well have reached Shreveport in a few days despite his military ineptness. Occupying that city permanently, with Steele preparing to retreat to Little Rock rather than advancing to help, would not have been possible, of course, but the Red River raid, as Sherman had envisioned it, would have been at least a partial success. Instead, with Banks's decision to retreat, the Union tactical victory at Pleasant Hill was turned into a Confederate strategic victory.[37]

Banks placed part of the blame for his retreat after the battle at Pleasant Hill on the navy, claiming he was "uncertain what had been the success of the fleet. The probabilities were that, on account of the difficulties of navigation, it had been unable to get up." Therefore, he could not count on obtaining supplies from his transports, and he was forced, "against my own judgment, [to retreat and] perhaps find another route on the opposite side of the river, where we might possibly join General Steele."[38] After the fact, in his own defense, Banks offered a dozen or more reasons for the retreat, such as there was a lack of drinking water and rations, the water level in the river was low, General Steele had not arrived to help, some of his men had had to be left at Alexandria, and last but not least Lieutenant General Grant had issued orders for him to move against Mobile. "Upon these general considerations . . . I countermanded the order for the return of the train, and directed preparations to be made for the return of the army to Grand Ecore."[39] It is unknown to what extent the opinions of his subordinates influenced the commander in this decision, but in his apparent confusion, their impact was probably significant.

When told of the decision to retreat, Smith, knowing a victory when he saw one, objected vigorously. He was overruled. He asked for a day to care for the wounded, but this was denied. He asked for four hours and was again refused. A. J. Smith then went to the wounded Franklin, who was second in command, and suggested the latter relieve Banks of command. Franklin pointed out that this would be mutiny, an action that neither general could condone.[40] Smith therefore reluctantly obeyed the army commander's orders. However, in his report on the battle, Smith made sure his vehement objection to Banks's orders was made clear:

> About 12 o'clock on the night of the 9th I received orders from General Banks to have my command in readiness to move at 2 o'clock in the morning. . . . I presented to him that the dead of my command were not buried, and that I had not the means of transporting my wounded; that many of the wounded had not yet been gathered in from the field; and asked of him permission to remain until noon the next day to give me an opportunity to bury my dead, and leave the wounded as well provided for as the circumstances would permit. . . . The permission to remain, however, was refused, and the order to move made peremptory.[41]

After gathering what wounded they could into makeshift hospitals and asking some of the army surgeons to remain behind to tend them, but leaving the Union dead and many of the wounded on the field, the army began its retreat from Pleasant Hill. Charles Oscar Torrey of the 27th Iowa, who was wounded in the battle but able to march with the army, was disgusted by the orders to retreat. Torrey wrote his wife that "we commenced a general retreat . . . which will be an everlasting disgrace on Gen Banks." In his diary he noted on April 10: "Sad affair this leaving the dead unburried on the field."[42] Irwin, who was often an apologist for Banks and who did not participate in the expedition, reported after the fact: "Unfortunately by some mistake the ambulances had gone off with the wagon train, so that there were no adequate means of relieving the wounded on the field. . . . From each corps a detail of surgeons was ordered to stay behind, with such hospital stores as they had at hand."[43]

Emory's division marched away first, followed by Mower. During this retreat, General Smith apparently both freely and continuously expressed his opinion of Banks and Banks's orders: "[Smith's] indignation could not be restrained, and his profane characterization of the cowardly business seemed to give the atmosphere a sulphurous taint all the way to Grand Ecore. . . . Smith's ebullition of wrath . . . seemed to prematurely illumine the horizon as we march to the rear on that early, frosty April morning."[44] According to William Wiley of the 77th Illinois, "We lost all respect for Gen Banks and during our retreat he was hooted whenever he came near the 13th corps and would doubtless have been killed by some reckless yank if he had not made himself pretty scare."[45] Taylor did not let the Yankees depart in peace. Early in the morning of April 10 he sent his cavalry after the invaders. Banks's rear guard fought to delay their pursuers as the Union men moved numbly along the road to Grand Ecore.

Late in the evening of April 9 Kirby Smith arrived in Mansfield, too late to take command of the battle. Taylor and Smith met about midnight to decide their next action. Taylor wanted to pursue and attempt to destroy Banks's army, but Smith wanted to send Churchill and Walker to Sterling Price for use against Steele. As Smith stated later, "I deemed it imprudent to follow Banks below Grand Ecore with my whole force, and leave Steele so near Shreveport."[46] Taylor's counterarguments were to no avail, and as a result of Smith's decision Taylor soon lost more than half of his force. Churchill and Walker started north to Arkansas April 14. Taylor expected these troops to be returned to him as soon as Steele began to retreat; however, Kirby Smith had other ideas. These divisions were not returned to Taylor until the middle of May.

THE RETREAT TO ALEXANDRIA AND THE AFFAIR AT MONETT'S FERRY

13 Porter reported that he reached Loggy Bayou about two o'clock in the afternoon of April 10. A few miles above the point at which Loggy Bayou enters the Red River, the Southerners had blocked the river channel by sinking a large steamer, the *New Falls City,* filled with sand and stones, crosswise in the river. Porter claimed later that the presence and position of this boat was an accident,[1] but at the time he expressed considerable respect for the enemy in devising this rather formidable obstruction. "Across the side of the vessel they had pasted in huge characters an invitation to the 'Yankees' to attend a ball in Shreveport. . . . It was the smartest thing I ever knew the rebels to do," wrote Porter.[2]

While the admiral began wrestling with the problem of clearing the channel of this obstruction, Kilby Smith went ashore to attempt to open communications with Banks by way of Springfield, as ordered. As usual, his men took the opportunity to plunder the surrounding countryside. Then about 4:00 a cavalry detachment arrived with news of the army's defeat at Sabine Crossroads and the intended retreat to Grand Ecore. Banks suggested that Porter should "make your dispositions accordingly," and "if possible send a communication to General Steele."[3] Porter, thoroughly disgusted with Banks but perhaps in part relieved that he would not have to travel farther up the river in its present state of low water, elected to return to Grand Ecore.[4] The trip downstream was difficult. "The river was not wide enough to turn the boats around, so they backed up" until a place could be found to reverse their direction.[5] Taylor sent Green's cavalry to harass Porter, and the boats were attacked repeatedly by artillery and musket fire from the shoreline.

Banks's army reached Grand Ecore on the evening of April 11. Although once again safely encamped on the Red River, Banks continued to worry about being attacked. While waiting for Porter to arrive, he entrenched on the right bank.[6] He also ordered a pontoon bridge constructed across the river and placed a strong detachment from Smith's command on the left bank. At Grand Ecore, many of the wounded who had been evacuated with the army or had been transported in ambulances were loaded aboard transports and sent downriver to New Orleans. J. E. Hayes, correspondent for the New York

Tribune, volunteered to act as a nurse on one of these transports, the steamer *Laurel Hill.* Some 430 badly wounded men were placed on board. In his report of the trip Hayes cited the "greatest incompetency . . . manifested in providing for the care of our sick and wounded on the Red River Expedition. Not one ounce of any sort of medicine was placed on board, and there was no supply of bedding, sheets, clothing, or other articles to relieve the suffering on board."[7]

Banks saw his position at Grand Ecore as precarious in the extreme. He therefore sent urgent orders to Alexandria, New Orleans, and even to Texas, for reinforcements.[8] In response, Henry W. Birge embarked April 12 to move upstream from Alexandria with his 2nd Brigade, plus the 38th Massachusetts and the 128th New York of Jacob Sharpe's 3rd Brigade, Grover's division, XIX Corps. Birge arrived at Grand Ecore to reinforce Banks's beleaguered army on April 13. Frank S. Nickerson's 1st Brigade, Grover's division, had embarked at New Orleans on the previous day, bound for Alexandria. In addition to his concerns about manpower, Banks was faced with the fact that forage was in short supply on the south bank of the river. In an attempt to remedy this situation he ordered his cavalry to scour the region across the river for forage.[9]

Even though he had assumed a defensive position at Grand Ecore, Banks sent Grant a message April 13 stating that he would resume the advance on Shreveport immediately. He indicated that he would be using a somewhat different route of approach, however, and "rendering the column less dependent upon a river proverbially as treacherous as the enemies we fight."[10] Banks was clearly rattled and, far from preparing for another offensive, continued shoring up his defenses around the town. Elias Porter Pellet of the 114th New York commented April 12, "It seems to be an anxious time for all, and the General commanding looks careworn and distressed."[11]

On April 12 and 13 the troops at Grand Ecore heard the sound of heavy cannonading coming from upstream.[12] Worried about the fate of the fleet and of Kilby Smith's brigade, Gen. A. J. Smith moved with two brigades up the left bank of the river to meet and escort Porter's boats downstream.[13] Smith reached Campti, twelve miles above Grand Ecore, the evening of April 14. There he met the first of the fleet arriving from upstream. Smith expressed great admiration for Porter's achievement in getting his fleet down the river, "having by energy, good judgment and rare good fortune succeeded in running the batteries and land forces of the enemy without the loss of a boat, though some were completely riddled with shot."[14] Traveling under Smith's escort from Campti, the last of Porter's fleet finally reached Grand Ecore near midnight April 15.

Banks and Porter met on April 15 to discuss the situation. Banks apparently still had delusions of reaching Shreveport, but Porter adamantly refused to return upriver because of the low water. He was already concerned about getting his boats over the rapids at Alexandria. To minimize the problem of crossing the bar below Grand Ecore in the falling water, he immediately started his large gunboats downriver to Alexandria. Porter himself departed Grand Ecore April 16, leaving only *Osage* and *Lexington* behind with Banks.

Also on April 15 Banks had received a message from General Sherman ordering Smith's troops back to Vicksburg immediately. Sherman, who was planning his Atlanta campaign at the time, was concerned about his long supply line, which stretched from Nashville to Chattanooga. He saw Maj. Gen. Nathan B. Forrest and his cavalry troop as a serious threat to his army's supplies. Sherman planned to have A. J. Smith operate against Forrest to protect the supply line.[15] As he stated in his message to Banks, "I must have A. J. Smith's troops now, as soon as possible."[16] Unaware that Kirby Smith had sent most of Taylor's troops to Arkansas, leaving Taylor with but 5,000 men, Banks refused to release A. J. Smith's men. He declared that he needed them to defend the fleet. As a result Sherman was forced to recruit infantry where he could, including the use of returning furloughed soldiers and cavalry recruits for whom no horses were available.[17]

Banks wrote to Grant April 17 requesting reinforcements from Missouri and Kansas and stating that his campaign was "a defense of Missouri."[18] He followed this with another message to Grant the next day. In this latter dispatch, with either a bit of duplicity or self-delusion, and with his usual flair for self-importance, he added, "This campaign is not of my suggestion, but its results are so much more important than I first thought, and so certain to be attained, that I hesitate to withdraw my forces without positive orders."[19]

Taylor went to Shreveport April 15 to argue again with Kirby Smith for the retention of Walker's and Churchill's forces, with which he was certain he could destroy Banks's army. Again his efforts were in vain. Far from allowing Taylor to retain these units for use against Banks, Smith decided he would go with them to Arkansas and assume personal command of the forces opposed to Steele. Perhaps Smith was angry with Taylor for not informing him of the impending Battle of Mansfield, despite the fact that he, Smith, had made it clear he wanted to assume command of the army in case of a battle. Perhaps he did not want another major battle to occur in his department without his personal leadership. In any case Smith departed April 16 for Arkansas with the divisions of Walker and Churchill. Taylor remained in Shreveport until April

19, writing his report of the campaign, and then rejoined what was left of his army at Grand Ecore.

While at Grand Ecore, Banks decided to make some changes in his department's command structure, perhaps in an attempt to prepare scapegoats for the defeat at Sabine Crossroads and lay the foundation for his own future defense. He relieved Albert L. Lee of command of the cavalry April 18 and reassigned him to the cavalry depot at New Orleans. Colonel Dudley was relieved from command of the 4th Cavalry Brigade and ordered to report to Lee at New Orleans to assist in "reorganizing the cavalry of the department." Richard Arnold, formerly chief of artillery, was assigned temporary command of all cavalry, to report to General Franklin.[20] On the infantry side, Birge was assigned to command a temporary division consisting of his own, Col. Francis Fessenden's brigade, and part of Sharpe's brigade. As Frank McGregor of the 83rd Ohio observed, "Our generals appear to be in a dilemma how to act. I guess they are rather frightened out of their senses. The troops have no confidence in them, and they have as little confidence in themselves."[21]

On April 18 General Banks received a dispatch from Grant instructing him to "turn over the defense of the Red River to General Steele and the navy"; to return Sherman's troops; to move his army to New Orleans; "to abandon all of Texas except the Rio Grande, and to hold that with not to exceed 4,000 men; to reduce the number of troops on the Mississippi to the lowest number necessary to hold it; . . . [and] to commence operations against Mobile."[22] These instructions from the lieutenant general were of great importance to Banks's military future. They described Grant's vision of Banks's role in the grand strategy for ending the war. This strategy involved the movements of the "great armies" of the North: the Army of the Potomac commanded by Maj. Gen. George G. Meade; the combined Army of the Cumberland, Army of the Tennessee, and Army of the Ohio commanded by Maj. Gen. William T. Sherman; as well as the lesser armies of Banks, Sigel, Burnside, and Butler.[23]

The capture of Mobile was an integral part of Grant's strategy to end the war by consolidating the scattered forces of the Union armies and initiating "a simultaneous movement all along the line" that was aimed at the heart of the Confederacy.[24] As he stated to Major General Meade in April 1864, "So far as practicable all the armies are to move together, and toward one common center."[25] After taking Mobile, Banks was to draw Lt. Gen. Leonidas Polk's army south so that army could not assist Johnston against Sherman; then he was to combine with the latter and move east from Atlanta. In the absence of a Union force moving inland from Mobile, Sherman's flank would be open to attack by Confederate forces in Alabama and Mississippi and the army in his front would have no Union force in its rear to be concerned about. Sherman's task of capturing Atlanta would be considerably more difficult if a Union force were not present at Mobile than if Mobile were under Union control.

Despite all his failures to this point in the war, had General Banks recognized the importance of these instructions from Grant, and had he had the ability to execute them, he might have saved some of the reputation he had gained after his capture of Port Hudson and thereby have obtained for himself a modicum of military glory in which to bask after the war. Unfortunately for him, the circumstances he would shortly encounter in Alexandria would ensure that this would not happen.

Banks continued to show bewilderment. However, faced with overwhelming evidence of the impossibility of resuming his advance on Shreveport—including the low water level in the river and consequent lack of support from the navy, Grant's demand for Smith's return, and the lack of cooperation by Steele—Banks finally seemed to agree with his senior officers that the campaign must be abandoned.[26] On April 19 he ordered A. J. Smith, with his entire command, to move to Natchitoches in preparation for a retreat to the Mississippi. Despite ordering a resumption of the retreat, Banks apparently still harbored hopes, or delusions, that something would happen to reinvigorate the expedition. The day Smith departed, April 20, Banks wrote to his wife: "The low water of the River threatens to defeat our campaign as it is only by the River that we can get our supplies."[27]

During the afternoon of April 21 Banks left Grand Ecore with the remainder of his army. He again put Franklin in charge of the marching column. According to Franklin's instructions, Birge's temporary division was to take the lead, followed by the army's wagons, then the troops of Emory, Cameron, and A. J. Smith in that order.[28] Before departing, the last of the Union troops burned the supplies that the army was unable to take along. They also set fire to the few buildings that constituted the town. About two miles below Grand Ecore the army crossed the Cane River and entered the island between the Cane and the Bon Dieu. The wagons completed the crossing about 1:30 A.M., but the rear of the column did not get across the river until midmorning the next day.

At Natchitoches the column passed Smith's troops, which then took their place at the rear of the army. Mower occupied the place of honor, at the tail of the column, where he faced the continuing harassment of Taylor's forces.[29] The Union cavalry was dispersed to the front, rear, and right flank of the column. Before leaving Natchitoches Mower's men set fire to most of the buildings in the town. However, the Confederate cavalry arrived in time to save the town from complete destruction.

As they moved down the island between the Cane and the Bon Dieu, the troops of the XVI Corps, apparently acting under orders, proceeded to pillage across the countryside and burn virtually every structure they encountered. A New York surgeon noted that during the retreat the army was "guided by a pillar of fire by night and a pillar of cloud by day."[30] James Ewer, of the 3rd Massachusetts Cavalry, stated, "One of the distinguishing characteristics of the Red River Campaign was the tremendous wreckage of life and property involved. This began at Sabine Cross Roads, and ceased not until the army had reached the banks of the Mississippi."[31] John Weik, correspondent for the Philadelphia *Press,* reported that "not a building, shanty, or chicken-coop was spared. . . . They went miles out of the way to burn and destroy. They made no distinction between Union and rebel [sympathizers]; were heard glorying in styling themselves the cotton-burners of the 16th Corps."[32]

Another participant reported, "Destruction and devastation follow on the trail of the retreating column. At night, the burning buildings mark out our pathway. As far as the eye can reach, we see in front new fires breaking out, and in the rear the dying embers tell the tale of war. Hardly a building is left unharmed."[33] According to Gov. Henry W. Allen, who visited the area after the Yankee retreat, "The fine estates on Cane and Red rivers, on bayous Rapides, Robert, and De Glaize, were all devastated. . . . You can travel for miles, in many portions of Louisiana, through a once thickly-settled country, and not see a man, nor a woman, nor a child, nor a four-footed beast. . . . A painful melancholy, a death-like silence, broods over the land, and desolation reigns supreme."[34]

By the time the army crossed the Cane River and entered the island between the Old Red and the Bon Dieu, Banks's imagination had conjured up enemy forces in overwhelming numbers opposing him from every direction. He continued to be concerned about a direct attack on his column, but he was even more concerned that Taylor would cut him off from the ford at Monett's Ferry. This ford was the only practical crossing point on the lower Cane River. Because of his concern, Banks drove his men forward at a grinding pace, making this portion of the march the most severe of the campaign. According to Captain De Forest of the 13th Connecticut, "The truth is that Banks was the most merciless marcher of men that I ever knew."[35] One member of the 67th Indiana wrote in his diary that his regiment marched thirty-five miles on April 22.[36] Unable to keep up the killing pace, many men fell out of the line of march and were taken prisoner by the pursuing Confederate cavalry. Once again Banks had managed to get himself into a situation in which his army was fleeing the enemy and, as one historian described it, "The retreat was perilously close to becoming a headlong flight."[37]

Despite the rapidity with which the column proceeded down the river, in its wake the army continued to leave almost total destruction. Everything of value within the reach of the soldiers was stolen or destroyed. The only restraint appeared to be the pace of the march, which limited the time available for the marauders to do their work. Lt. T. C. Prescott of the 2nd New Hampshire Cavalry noted, "This portion of the Red River valley was fair to look upon before any military force marched through it. . . . But as our army passed down, this beautiful valley was transformed into a smoking ruin." The destruction left hundreds of residents homeless in the wake of the army. "The people still remaining, and especially the colored portion, left the burning houses and cabins with such household effects as they could carry, and hundreds of them fell in the rear of our column vainly endeavoring to keep up with the army."[38] In his pursuit, Taylor described passing "the smoking ruins of homesteads, by which stood weeping women and children. Time for the removal of the most necessary articles of furniture had been refused. It was difficult to restrain one's inclination to punish the ruffians engaged in this work; but they asserted, and doubtless with truth, that they were acting under orders."[39]

Convinced that Banks was going to retreat to Alexandria, on April 19 Taylor sent General Bee and most of his cavalry to occupy the Cane River valley downstream from Banks's army. As Banks advanced against him, Bee was to fall back to Monett's Ferry and block the Federal retreat at that point. There, where the Union fleet could not offer support, Taylor hoped to catch what he believed was a demoralized Union army. Bee's force totaled some 1,600 troopers, plus four batteries of artillery mounting twenty-four guns.[40] Reaching the crossing of the Cane, Bee set up a strong defensive line on Monett's Bluff on the far side of the river and prepared to contest the Federal crossing. Bee posted his subordinate, Col. George Wythe Baylor, on his left with a small force of dismounted cavalry and a battery of artillery.[41]

Around 3:00 A.M. April 23 Banks's advance cavalry force, under Gooding, neared the Cane River crossing and discovered Bee's cavalry blocking the ford.

With the force he had, Gooding could do little other than observe the enemy. Then at about 4:30 the main body of cavalry, followed closely by Emory's lead infantry units, arrived at the ford. This force engaged Bee's skirmishers and soon drove them across the river. However, when the cavalry moved into open ground near the crossing, the troopers came under the fire of the enemy artillery and were stopped. General Franklin rode forward to reconnoiter. On the bluff opposite the ford Bee's force was partially visible among the trees. Observing the situation, Franklin made plans to flank the enemy by searching for another river crossing while mounting a demonstration to hold the opposing force in place at the ferry. Before he could implement this plan, however, Franklin's wound became so painful to him that he had to retire. He turned his command over to Emory. McMillan assumed command of Emory's division.

Banks believed it was essential that the enemy be driven from his strong position overlooking the Cane River crossing so the retreat could continue along the south bank of the Red. In his subsequent report Banks wrote, "If we failed to dislodge the enemy at the Ferry, the only alternative open to us was to attempt a crossing to the north side of Red River, an exceedingly difficult and dangerous movement."[42] Emory decided to adopt Franklin's plan. He ordered McMillan to deploy the 1st and 2nd Brigades, now commanded by George Beal and Henry Rust Jr., to threaten the crossing and keep Bee pinned down. In response to this order McMillan placed the 13th and 15th Maine, 1st Brigade, in a line facing the ford, and the 160th New York and 47th Pennsylvania, 2nd Brigade, in support. At the same time Henry W. Closson, commanding the artillery reserve of the XIX Corps, advanced and opened fire on the enemy position. Colonel Rust reported, "For a time [these troops] were subject to quite a sharp fire from the enemies batteries, several shells exploding directly over or in front of the right of the Brig lines. Our batteries silencing the enemies fire our position remained unchanged until about 2 P.M."[43] Meanwhile, Birge and Cameron arrived and halted in the rear of Emory's forces.

Lt. Col. Joseph Bailey of the 4th Wisconsin Cavalry was sent downstream along with Col. E. J. Davis and a small cavalry detachment to search for a possible crossing point. Upon returning, Bailey reported that "the river was not fordable below the Ferry, and that owing to the impassable swamps on one side and the high bluffs on the other, it would not be possible to cross Cane River at any point below the Ferry."[44] It looked like any flanking movement would have to start by moving upstream.

Birge, with two brigades of his temporary division plus portions of

Raynor's 3rd Division, XIII Corps, was then sent to the right, upstream, to see if he could find a place to ford the river. Birge trekked three or four miles up the left bank of the Cane through swampy ground and canebrakes. Then, with the assistance of a local black woman, he found a spot at which his unit could cross the river. Fortuitously this crossing was located well upstream from Colonel Baylor's position. Birge and his men struck through the swamp and cane and successfully crossed in chest-deep water. They then began to double back through the rough country to the west of the river.

With Col. William O. Fiske of the 1st Louisiana (Union) in the lead, Birge's men struggled through bayous, swamps, and tangled woods, moving always determinedly toward the enemy. Finally, late in the afternoon, Birge found Baylor and the left flank of the Confederate force in a formidable position atop a rise. After brief preparation the Union force advanced toward the rise under the fire of the Confederate skirmishers. A sharp battle ensued as the Yankees forced their way slowly up the incline. After being driven back some distance, and in the face of the continuing, determined Union advance, Baylor requested reinforcements from Bee. Surprisingly, instead of providing reinforcements to Colonel Baylor, General Bee ordered Baylor to retreat. A courier, arriving from downstream, told Bee that Porter had landed 6,000 men in his rear and that these troops were marching rapidly up the Alexandria road. Bee believed he had to retreat to save his detachment. In response to Bee's order, Baylor reluctantly withdrew his force and joined his commanding officer in retreating some twenty-eight miles west to Beaseley's Station, where a supply depot had previously been established.[45] Bee stated later that his men desperately needed food and supplies. Whether or not this lengthy retreat by Bee was justified, it removed his force from contact with the Union army for an extended period.

After Bee withdrew from his defensive position, a pontoon bridge was laid across the Cane; as darkness fell, Banks's army began to cross the river. They continued to cross all that night and into the next day. After dark, Taylor attacked the rear of the units that were still on the island. However, this night action was ineffective in slowing the Federal withdrawal. Finally, by two o'clock in the afternoon of April 24 the last of Smith's troops had crossed the Cane. Banks now had a clear route to Alexandria. His army had suffered more than 300 casualties in the engagement at Monett's Ferry, two-thirds of which occurred in the flanking maneuver. Bee lost about 50 men and one artillery wagon.[46]

Once across the Cane, Banks resumed his killing pace, driving his men headlong toward Alexandria. Meanwhile, along the route the destruction of the countryside continued. Cloutierville was burned as the last of the Union troops departed the town. Many of the enlisted men and officers of the army, especially those in the XIX Corps, did not approve of such activities and maintained that "the wanton and useless destruction of property has well earned his [Smith's] command a lasting disgrace. The true American soldier turns in disgust from this war on inoffensive persons; and when a man wearing the livery of the United States so far forgets himself as to become a common robber and incendiary, he sinks the patriot's cause in the ruffians baseness."[47]

The head of Banks's column entered Alexandria on the afternoon of April 25. The troops of Gen. A. J. Smith, having served as rear guard throughout the retreat, did not arrive until late the next day. As Smith entered the town, he was accompanied by crowds of contrabands that had joined him along the route.[48] Franklin was rather proud of the army's successful retreat but did not excuse the acts of destruction committed along the line of march. He reported: "The troops performed the whole of this harassing and tedious march from Grand Ecore in good order and without demoralization, the only exception being such acts of marauding and incendiarism by stragglers in advance of the column as are incident to the retreat of a large army. Every effort has been and is being made to discover the perpetrators of these outrages, to whom the severest punishment will be awarded upon detection."[49] Despite this bold statement, it is not clear that any of the culprits were identified or any punishment imposed for the "marauding and incendiarism." Taylor reported: "The destruction of this country by the enemy exceeds anything in history. For many miles every dwelling-house, every negro cabin, every cotton-gin, every corn-crib, and even chicken-houses, have been burned to the ground."[50]

On May 2 Franklin declared himself disabled by the wound he had received at Sabine Crossroads and left for New Orleans. Between his medical disability and official disfavor, General Franklin was removed from active campaigning for the remainder of the war. Emory officially assumed command of the XIX Corps in Franklin's place, and McMillan assumed command of Emory's 1st Division. Rust took charge of McMillan's 2nd Brigade, 1st Division. A. J. Smith was promoted to major general May 14.

THE RED RIVER DAMS

14

Admiral Porter continued to experience enemy attacks from the shore during his trip downstream from Grand Ecore. He lost two boats en route but brought his battered fleet into Alexandria April 27. There he discovered that while the fleet was upriver, the water level in the Red had fallen more than three feet. It was continuing to fall at the rate of two inches per day. Because of the low water, the rapids above Alexandria, called the "falls," now consisted of two rocky cataracts about one and one-half miles apart, connected by a stretch of relatively deep water. The total fall of the river over this length was thirteen feet, seven feet of which occurred at the upper rapids and six feet at the lower rapids. Within the falls the water foamed and roared through a narrow and crooked channel barely twenty feet wide. The water in the channel was only forty-two inches deep, and there seemed no prospect for a rise.

To some observers, this final obstruction to further retreat down the river seemed to drain the strength and determination from the sailors. "Worn out and exhausted with the work already done, disheartened and discouraged at the prospect before it presented by this natural and apparently insurmountable obstacle to its further progress, for once, and for the only time in its history, the fleet lost heart."[1] Only the shallowest-draft boats and the army transports were able to pass below the falls in their current state, and even then such passage entailed considerable effort and risk of damage. The most powerful boats in the fleet—*Mound City, Louisville, Pittsburg, Carondelet, Chillicothe, Osage, Neosho, Ozark, Lexington,* and *Fort Hindman*—were stuck in the narrow channel above the city.[2]

On April 28 Admiral Porter sent Secretary of the Navy Gideon Welles a message describing the position of the fleet at Alexandria. Thoroughly frustrated with Banks, he told Welles that "I have no confidence in his [Banks's] promises. . . . If left here by the army, I will be obliged to destroy this fleet."[3] Porter felt that his fleet had protected the army in its advance up the river, and now it was the army's turn to protect the fleet: "I do not see why a fleet should not have the protection of an army as well as an army have the protection of a fleet." However, regardless of what Banks did, Porter did not intend to abandon his accepted role of providing protection for Banks's army. Although, in his opinion, "The army should hold this place until the last man can stand. . . . I must confess that I feel a little uncertain how to act. I could not leave this army now without disgracing myself forever."[4] Despite Porter's distrust of Banks, the commanding general was, in fact, in the process of deciding that he could not and would not abandon the fleet.

Banks received another dispatch from General Grant by messenger April 27 reinforcing the latter's instructions of March 31 to end the Red River campaign, return Sherman's troops, and move to New Orleans to undertake a campaign against Mobile. Grant told his messenger, Maj. Gen. David Hunter, that he, Grant, intended in his prior dispatch to impress upon General Banks "the importance of commencing operations at the very earliest possible moment against Mobile" and to "take with him the greatest number of troops possible." The garrisons that Banks still had in place along the coast of Texas should be reduced to a minimum. And with regard to Banks's previous suggestion that he pursue Taylor into Texas should that enemy general continue to retreat before him, Grant offered a succinct reply: "If you have commenced to move from Shreveport to the interior of Texas, or away from the Red River in any direction, retrace your steps on receipt of this. No matter what you may have in contemplation, commence your concentration . . . on Mobile."[5] There would be no more invasions of Texas, and the troops already stationed there would soon be so reduced in number they would be forced to withdraw from the mainland and limit their occupation to Brazos Island.

Although Grant instructed him to release Sherman's troops immediately, Banks was unwilling to do so. In his reply to Grant April 30 he stated that it was "indispensable that the army should remain at Alexandria for the protection of the fleet." In his opinion the enemy force "numbers from 30,000 to 35,000 men. It is indispensable that all the force of this command should be retained here, and the orders given to General Smith by General Sherman to rejoin his command east of the Mississippi were countermanded." Banks also seemed worried about the impression his campaign might be making on General Grant. He began preparing a list of what he apparently hoped would be considered some credible achievements for the expedition. He told the general in chief that he needed more troops, not less, "5,000 to 10,000 men if possible." With this additional force he could "make certain the destruction of the organized army of the enemy west of the Mississippi, the whole of which is here." Meanwhile, it was a good thing he was here to engage this titanic enemy army because otherwise "it is nearly certain that the whole of this force would have been directed against New Orleans." And maybe it was a good thing that he had not taken his army to Mobile. "If we had become inextricably involved in operations east of the Mississippi; or in the event of our remaining at New Orleans, it is certain that the invasion of Arkansas and Missouri by this force would have occurred." Banks was apparently uncertain which excuse would carry more weight with Grant—preventing Taylor's army from attacking New Orleans or preventing it from invading Arkansas and Missouri—so he decided to take credit for both. "Both of these dangers have been avoided by the campaign which we have made."[6]

After Grant sent General Hunter with instructions for Banks to commence his concentration on Mobile, he learned of Banks's defeat at Mansfield and the disastrous situation in northwestern Louisiana. In light of this information Grant urged General Halleck to get President Lincoln to replace Banks.[7] However, Halleck understood the political problems facing the president in this election year, and he told Grant in no uncertain terms that this was not likely to happen soon. "General Banks is a personal friend of the President, and has strong political supporters in and out of Congress. There will undoubtedly be a very strong opposition to his being removed or superseded."[8] It appeared that, once again, military decisions were to be overruled by politics and that Banks would have to be left in command in Louisiana for the time being.

General Hunter, though disgusted with what he saw happening in Alexandria, agreed that the departure of Smith's troops would endanger Porter's fleet. He informed Grant that he supported Banks's position that the army should be left at Alexandria until the fleet could be moved below the rapids.[9] As a result Grant reluctantly agreed to leave Smith's detachment where it was. He also said nothing further regarding relieving Banks, but the latter's days as a field general were numbered. To implement Grant's plans for an attack on Mobile, Halleck sent an order to Banks April 27 instructing the latter to "return yourself immediately to New Orleans, and make preparations to carry out his [Grant's] previous instructions. . . . The troops in the field will be left under command of the senior officer." This order apparently never reached Banks. It may have been lost along with other dispatches that were aboard the transport *City Belle,* which was captured by enemy cavalry below Alexandria on May 4.[10]

Banks set up a double-perimeter defense around Alexandria, including construction of breastworks, redoubts, gun emplacements, and abatis. Along the perimeter the XIII Corps was assigned to the right and A. J. Smith's veterans to the left, with Emory in reserve. Banks was momentarily expecting an attack from an overwhelming force of the enemy. However, although skirmishing was almost continuous at one point or another along the perimeter during the period that the Union army was in Alexandria, the anticipated attack never came. Taylor, still with only about 5,000 men, continued his tactics of harassment. According to Brig. Gen. Xavier B. Debray, the Southern commander's standing order was "to attack every day, and annoy the enemy by every possible means."[11] Taylor knew he could not defeat the Union army by attacking the fortifications constructed around the city, but he believed he could capture the fleet that was stuck above the rapids merely by persevering.

While awaiting a resolution of the predicament in which he found himself and his fleet, Porter sent some of his shallow-draft boats downstream to patrol the river between Alexandria and Fort De Russy. He also sent five of the gunboats that had remained below the falls during the expedition back to the Mississippi to support operations at Fort Pillow following the raid on that fort by Confederate major general Nathan B. Forrest. As Porter explained, "I am bringing up light-draught vessels to take the place of the heavy boats during the low water."[12] The shallow-draft boats that replaced the heavy gunboats increased the maneuverability of the fleet below the falls, but the resulting naval force was relatively weak. Nevertheless, the small fleet that was now positioned below the rapids began the labor of convoying transports up and down the river. This was "severe work, and the men, already worn out with the labor and exposure of the expedition, began to suffer in health." The river was full of "putrefying bodies of dead alligators, horses and mules, negroes and soldiers, that in all stages of decomposition were constantly floating past."[13]

Taylor continued to take risks in the face of a largely quiescent foe. He sent Brig. Gen. James P. Major's cavalry downstream with orders to stop any riverboats attempting to reach Alexandria from below. Major reached David's Ferry near Marksville, about thirty-five miles below Alexandria, on the last day of April. He positioned his forces to begin interfering with the river traffic at that point.[14] The situation favored the Southerners because the river was low and the banks were high. The guns of Porter's tinclads could not be elevated sufficiently to reach the Southern forces. On the first of May. Col. George Wythe Baylor was establishing a position at Wilson's Landing when the Federal transport *Emma* passed. Part of Baylor's cavalry gave chase and captured the transport after a pursuit of several miles. Then on May 4 Major captured the transport *City Belle,* bound from Baton Rouge to Alexandria, with the 120th Ohio Regiment and a courier with dispatches from Washington on board. The Confederates took 276 prisoners in the action.[15] With this and other exploits in which boats traveling below Alexandria were lost to the enemy, for a period of several days the river was effectively closed to Union shipping.

Taylor's demonstrations along Banks's defensive perimeter, by giving the appearance of his having many more men than he actually had, were designed to keep the Union general on the defensive pending the return of the divisions of Churchill and Walker.[16] In addition, to prevent Banks from retreating toward Arkansas or Vicksburg, Taylor ordered all roads and bridges blocked to the north and east of Pineville, a village across the river from Alexandria. Because of the shortage of forage for his animals, Banks sent columns out to seek grain from nearby plantations. Colonel Hubbard of the 5th Minnesota noted that "Banks' supplies, particularly for his animals, became reduced to an extent that compelled the army to attack and drive the enemy back at several points, for the sole purpose of occupying localities where corn and forage could be obtained."[17] However, wherever possible Taylor removed supplies from the surrounding area, and even though Banks's efforts resulted in several sharp engagements as Taylor attacked the far-ranging columns, they produced little forage. Taylor stated, "Forage and subsistence of every kind have been removed beyond the enemy's reach. Rigid orders are given to destroy anything useful that can fall into his hands. We will play the game the Russians played in the retreat from Moscow."[18]

By the end of April, the situation on the Red River looked bad for the Union. Banks was isolated and entrenched at Alexandria, anticipating an imminent attack by 35,000 enemy troops. Admiral Porter's fleet was stuck above the rapids, and the level of water in the river was falling daily. Rocks were exposed for more than a mile below the fleet, and only three feet of water was passing over the falls. The supply line down the river from Alexandria had been interrupted by enemy action, and fodder for the animals was getting scarce. Porter despaired of getting Banks to stay in place to protect his fleet and was fearful that he would have to order his boats destroyed. Then into this picture of confusion and gloom stepped Lt. Col. Joseph Bailey of the 4th Wisconsin Cavalry. Bailey was not at all disheartened by the situation.

Before the war Joseph Bailey was involved in the lumber business in Wisconsin. Specializing in solving problems associated with floating logs down a river, he became proficient in the art of building rough, temporary dams that would raise the water level in log-choked rivers, thereby breaking the jams and allowing the logs to continue downstream. Early in the war he joined the

4th Wisconsin Infantry, which later became the 4th Wisconsin Cavalry. In this capacity, following the capture of Port Hudson, he supervised construction of a dam to free the Southern steamers *Starlight* and *Red Chief,* which were stranded in Thompson's Creek by low water. Following this exploit he was promoted to lieutenant colonel.[19] Bailey joined the Red River expedition as acting military engineer, XIX Army Corps, attached to Franklin's headquarters. In this capacity he performed various duties during the campaign, none of which particularly exercised his engineering skills. When he noticed that the water level in the Red was falling, however, Bailey saw his chance. Knowing that Porter's fleet would have difficulty crossing the rapids at Alexandria, he offered a suggestion.

On April 9, prior to the battle at Pleasant Hill, Bailey told General Franklin that a temporary dam, similar to the one he constructed on Thompson's Creek, could be built to enable Admiral Porter's fleet to pass over the falls at Alexandria. Possibly because he was distracted by his wound and the military activities that were under way at the time, Franklin, though favorably impressed, took no action on the suggestion. Then at Grand Ecore April 17, after learning of the sinking of Porter's gunboat *Eastport* following the boat striking a torpedo in the Red, Franklin thought Bailey might help with the recovery of that vessel. He gave Bailey a letter of introduction to Admiral Porter, requesting him to "do all in my power to assist in raising the Eastport, and to communicate to the admiral my plan of constructing a dam to relieve the fleet, with his belief in its practicability."[20]

Bailey approached Porter while the latter was involved in trying to save the *Eastport.* Porter's initial response to Bailey's suggestions, both concerning raising the *Eastport* and moving the fleet over the rapids, was less than enthusiastic. It can be summed up in the comment that the admiral, well known for his strong and profane language, made to Col. James Grant Wilson, Banks's aide de camp: "If *damning* would get the fleet over, it would have been afloat long ago!"[21] Bailey was not permitted to help save the *Eastport,* and the boat was destroyed to prevent its capture. However, after Porter arrived at Alexandria and saw the condition of the rapids, his attitude toward his potential benefactor changed. In a message to Secretary Welles he summarized Bailey's scheme and stated, "There seems to have been an especial Providence looking out for us in providing a man equal to the emergency. . . . This proposition looked like madness, and the best engineers ridiculed it; but Col. Bailey was so sanguine of success that I requested to have it done, and he entered heartily into the work."[22]

Bailey proceeded to put his proposal in writing and submit it formally through Colonel Wilson. As Wilson described it some twenty-three years after the incident, to his written proposal Bailey added the verbal endorsement, "I wish I was as sure of heaven as I am that I can save the fleet."[23] Despite his own supreme confidence in the plan, Bailey claimed after completion of the dam that "the only supporter of my proposition to save the fleet by means of a dam, and whose persevering efforts caused its adoption," was General Franklin.[24] Actually, in addition to General Franklin, a number of army engineers favored the idea. Lt. Col. Uri B. Pearsall, Corps d'Afrique, formerly 1st sergeant and then 2nd lieutenant of the 4th Wisconsin, and Capt. J. C. Palfrey, Corps of Engineers, both believed the idea sound. Pearsall said that "the project of building a dam across the Red River, although difficult, could never have been pronounced impracticable by any man who followed a similar avocation in civil life."[25] Palfrey reported that, in his judgment, the plan was entirely feasible.[26]

On April 29, after submitting his proposal, Bailey met with General Banks and General Hunter. Bailey reported later that at this meeting Hunter remarked, "Although he [Hunter] had little confidence in its feasibility, he nevertheless thought it better to try the experiment, especially as General Franklin, who is an engineer, advised it."[27] After some discussion, Banks approved the project and provided the necessary orders for work details, teams, and supplies. Bailey was designated engineer in charge, with Pearsall as his assistant.[28]

According to Bailey's design, the wings of the dam would extend from the banks of the river to the edges of the channel. At this point they would bracket the deepest part of the river and form a spillway through which the boats could pass. Despite agreeing that damming the river was feasible, both Col. G. D. Robinson, commander of the engineering brigade, and Pearsall argued that a single dam would not be able to withstand the pressure of the water required to move the boats over both of the falls. They recommended two dams, one at the upper and one at the lower falls. However, Bailey decided one dam would be sufficient, and that settled the issue for the moment.

The project would be a colossal enterprise, given the resources available to the army in Alexandria. General Banks placed 3,000 men and three hundred wagons at Bailey's disposal, including the Engineers of the Corps d'Afrique and the Pioneers of the XIII Corps. The work commenced April 30. Banks watched with great interest and said later, "The men worked in that operation as you have probably never seen men work anywhere. They were in the water night and day. I have seen them working in the water by squads naked or with light clothes."[29] The troops assigned to support the construction project were divided into groups and worked day and night in six-hour shifts. Working in the chilly nights and the burning sun, sometimes up to their necks in the swirling water, the men created the dam. Probably not one of the thousands of troops involved in the project believed initially that the scheme would work, and at first Bailey had difficulty filling work details; however, enthusiasm for the scheme soon grew. Col. James G. Wilson described the hurly-burly that he witnessed during the construction.

> Oak, elm, and pine trees, whose gigantic growth dated from the days of the daring De Soto, were falling to the ground under the blows of the stalwart pioneers of Maine . . . mules and oxen were dragging the trees, denuded of their branches, to the river's bank; wagons heavily loaded were moving in every direction; flat-boats carrying stone were floating with the current, while others were being drawn up the stream in the manner of canal-boats. Meanwhile hundreds of men were at work at each end of the dam, moving heavy logs to the outer end of the tree dam, throwing in brushwood and branches of trees to make it tight, wheeling brick out to the cribs, carrying bars of railway iron to the barges . . . while on each bank of the river were to be seen thousands of spectators, consisting of officers of both services, groups of sailors, soldiers, camp-followers, and citizens of Alexandria, all eagerly watching our progress and discussing the chances of success.[30]

Before long the wings of the dam began to extend from the shorelines out toward the center of the river. On the left bank trees were felled, trimmed, dragged into the river, and aligned with the current. Timber cross ties were used to raise and position the boles. Brick and stone were brought from the surrounding area, and structures in town were torn down to obtain materials to weight the timbers and hold them in place.[31] On the right bank, where large trees were scarce, log cribs measuring roughly fourteen by twenty-two feet were built. The cribs were fabricated on the shore and towed into position. As Bailey described it, "The cribs were placed by means of hawsers. As soon as this was done, bars of iron, taken from sugar houses, were driven from 1 to 3 feet into the bottom, which was of soft stone. The cribs were then filled with old iron, brick, and stone having a layer of fine brush between them."[32] The rows of weighted cribs soon were backing up water from the right bank.

The channel, where the spillway for the dam was to be located, was not in the center of the river but was located well toward the right bank. Thus, the left wing of the dam would have to be significantly longer than the right. As the wings began to stretch into the river from each bank, four navy coal barges, loaded with rocks and oriented parallel to the current, were sunk side by side on the left side of the channel. These barges, which were to be used to anchor the end of the tree dam that was being built from the left bank, would help extend that wing of the dam and balance the amount of time required to complete the two unequal structures. The rightmost barge would define the left edge of the spillway.

While General Banks, General Smith, and Admiral Porter were trapped in Alexandria, the war in the east began a new phase. General Grant initiated his 1864 spring campaign in Virginia by sending the Army of the Potomac across the Rapidan River on May 4. The next day Lee attacked, and for two days the principal armies of the North and South fought each other in the thick gloom of the Wilderness. This was the beginning of a continuous, forty-day period of fighting during which Grant repeatedly tried to maneuver around Lee's right. The fighting was desperate and deadly, and Grant's casualties would exceed the number of soldiers in Lee's army. Meanwhile, following Grant's orders to "move against Johnston's army, to break it up, and to get into the interior of the enemy's country,"[33] General Sherman started his Atlanta campaign with an advance from Chattanooga into Georgia May 7. In a series of maneuvers and battles, Sherman would force Gen. Joseph E. Johnston to retreat until a frustrated Jefferson Davis replaced Johnston with John B. Hood. Hood would abandon Atlanta to Sherman September 1.

Far to the west of these momentous events in Virginia and Georgia, the work on the Red River dam was declared to be complete on May 8. Although the short wing dam on the right bank was sturdy and continuous all the way to the spillway, the long wing extending from the left bank suffered from the fact that the four coal barges at its end were positioned such that chutes of water, each about twenty feet wide, ran between them.[34] Planks had been placed across the gaps, providing a walkway for the workers. The main spillway, between the rightmost barge and the left end of the crib dam, was about sixty feet wide. Unlike the other barges, which were firmly grounded on the bottom of the river, the second barge from the spillway was partially afloat, with a swift flow of water running underneath it. It was held in place against the current by large braces set diagonally upstream, and by large hawsers.

The dam raised the level of the river between the two rapids some five feet, four and one-half inches, producing a chute of water over the lower falls that was about eight and one-half feet deep. Three transports passed through the gap May 8, and three light-draft gunboats, *Fort Hindman, Osage,* and *Neosho,* passed the upper rapids into the pool behind the dam. According to Banks and Pearsall, all the boats could have safely passed the upper falls that day had steps been taken prior to the completion of the dam to lighten the deep-draft vessels by removing their ordnance and armor plating. Surprisingly, this had not been done.

THE END OF THE FIFTH INVASION

15

On the evening of May 8 the naval officers and sailors of Porter's fleet retired pleasantly for the night, leaving the final effort to pass the rapids for the morrow. Banks was restless, however, and later stated that "I went over the dam at eleven o'clock. It was completed, and two gunboats had passed the [upper] rapids to the dam the evening before. . . . I went over the dam and felt conscious that it could not long stand the pressure of the water. Every moment increasing in depth and weight above, I knew it could not stand." Having received this insight Banks claimed he rode upstream to see whether the navy was preparing to move at daylight. "There was not a light to be seen; not a man was stirring; not a ship had been lightened. I could not arouse anybody there."[1] Failing to gain satisfaction in person, Banks proceeded to write Porter a note and send Colonel Wilson to deliver it. Wilson had Porter awakened and successfully delivered Banks's note at one o'clock on the morning of May 9. The note informed Porter that the pressure on the dam is "terrific" and that the navy should prepare their boats to take advantage of the high water. "Every exertion ought to be made to get them ready tonight, so that they may pass the falls to-morrow."[2] Porter was ill at the time and apparently did not respond to Banks's note.

At 5 o'clock on the morning of May 9 the partially floating barge broke loose from its moorings and washed down the river, dragging with it the barge to its right that had defined the left side of the spillway. Both of these barges lodged against a ledge of rocks on the left below the dam. The torrent rushing through the gap that resulted from the loss of the barges produced a rapid drop in the water level behind the dam. At the time the barges were washed away, one gunboat, located above the upper rapids, was ready to try to pass the falls. This boat, the *Lexington,* a converted, wooden river steamer, was one of the first three Union gunboats produced on the western rivers. It was a side-wheeler measuring 180 feet in length with a 42-foot beam and a 6-foot draft.[3] Admiral Porter described what happened next:

> Seeing this unfortunate accident [the barges washing downstream], I jumped on a horse and rode up to where the upper vessels were anchored, and ordered

> the Lexington to pass the upper falls if possible, and immediately attempt to go through the dam. I thought I might be able to save the four vessels below, not knowing whether the persons employed on the work would ever have the heart to renew their enterprise.
>
> The Lexington succeeded in getting over the upper falls just in time, the water rapidly falling as she was passing over. She then steered directly for the opening in the dam, through which the water was rushing so furiously that it seemed as if nothing but destruction awaited her. Thousands of beating hearts looked on anxious for the result. The silence was so great as the Lexington approached the dam that a pin might almost be heard to fall. She entered the gap with a full head of steam on, pitched down the roaring torrent, made two or three spasmodic rolls, hung for a moment on the rocks below, was then swept into deep water by the current, and rounded-to safely into the bank. Thirty thousand voices rose in one deafening cheer, and universal joy seemed to pervade the face of every man present.[4]

The *Lexington* was followed over the lower falls by the three gunboats that had passed the upper falls the previous day. The *Neosho,* leading the way, "all her hatches battened down and every precaution taken against accident," was approaching the lower spillway when the pilot stopped the engine. It was too late to avoid entering the chute, however. Swept along by the rapid current, the boat slipped down the spillway and "disappeared from sight under the water." She quickly reappeared, slightly damaged but still in one piece. Porter then watched *Fort Hindman* and *Osage* pass over the spillway in their turn, "and I thought if I was only fortunate enough to get my large vessels as well over the falls, my fleet once more would do good service on the Mississippi."[5] Six gunboats, along with several tugs and transports, remained trapped above the upper falls by the drop in the water level behind the dam.

Although the two barges washing down the river appeared to be disastrous at the time it occurred, it was generally concluded later to be a fortunate circumstance. In their new positions these two barges lengthened the chute of water over the dam and confined the flow passing through the gap to the region between them and the right bank. This created a greater depth of water at the bottom of the chute than was previously available, and the two barges helped prevent the boats from turning or striking the rocks after passing through the chute.

Bailey, who apparently did not want to share any of the glory associated with the design of the dam, went back to work but was unsuccessful in his attempts to plug the gap. He was then ready to try the idea of a second dam. Adopting the plan of Pearsall and Robinson, he had a second wing dam built near the upper falls, at a point at which the river was now over one thousand feet wide. Again he used stone cribs and logs, but of a lighter construction than that used in the lower dam. This work was completed May 10 and produced a rise of fourteen inches in the water level over the upper falls.

While the new construction was under way, the sailors finally began to lighten their vessels. However, this effort initially seemed to be limited to the removal of armor plating, anchors, naval artillery, and other massive ordnance and materiel. Until the last minute cotton was kept aboard the boats, the naval officers seemingly reluctant to remove it in front of Banks's men. Colonel Wilson of Banks's staff, discovering the cotton, stated later "that every one of the gunboats had cotton in their holds." He told Banks that it was not right that the army "should be working there like beavers, night and day, to construct a dam to float these vessels when they were loaded down with cotton." Banks reported this finding to Porter and "as a result of his expostulations with the admiral they were compelled to disgorge."[6] In the final analysis artillery, iron, and ultimately the confiscated cotton that was aboard were removed from the gunboats to get them over the falls.

Admiral Porter was still blaming the army for most of his troubles. After lightening his boats, he said, "I was obliged to destroy 11 32-pounders, not having time to haul them from above the falls to Alexandria, the army having moved and drawn in all their pickets." To get rid of these guns as well as the iron plates removed from the sides of the gunboats, Porter sent boats "up the river at night to a point where they could find from 5 to 6 fathoms of water, where the iron was thrown overboard."[7] Presumably if Porter had started removing the guns earlier than he did, he could have hauled them overland around the rapids and would not have had to discard them.

During the afternoon of May 10 the *Chillicothe* got through both spillways successfully. However, the next boat that attempted the passage, the *Carondelet* was forced to one side by the current below the upper dam and was grounded just below the dam. There she lay, bow below the left wing of the upper dam and stern pointed partly downstream, diagonally in the channel. Despite this unfortunate situation, the naval officers decided there was space for another boat to pass, and the commander of the *Mound City* was ordered to proceed. Belching smoke and steam, and with paddles churning, the *Mound City* ran through the upper spillway and promptly grounded abreast of the *Carondelet*

let. The channel was now completely blocked. All attempts to move the two boats, using "all sorts of mechanical contrivances," failed.[8]

Bailey and Pearsall met with Banks to discuss the mess in the upper channel. Bailey turned to Pearsall for help. Pearsall, in his report, states that he replied to Bailey, "If you will allow me to build a dam where I please, on my own plan, and give me the men and materials I require, I will agree to put a foot of water under those boats by tomorrow night." Bailey then asked Pearsall what supplies he would need for the work. The self-confident Pearsall claimed that he replied: "The pioneer corps of the Thirteenth Army Corps to report to me at midnight to cross to the left bank, and 10,000 feet of 2-inch plank," which he wanted to be delivered to the upper dam by nine o'clock the next morning. According to Pearsall, "Colonel Bailey agreed to this proposition."[9]

The XIII Corps Pioneers arrived at the upper dam at one o'clock on the morning of May 11, but the navy refused to transport them across the river until daylight. Starting at sunrise that morning, Pearsall supervised the construction of a "bracket" dam just below the left wing of Bailey's upper dam. Pearsall's dam extended from the left bank of the river to the edge of the channel and directed a flow of water toward the grounded *Carondelet* and *Mound City.* The bracket design consisted of log trestles that were to be emplaced at an angle to the current, side by side from the shore to the channel. The trestles had half-inch bolts inset in each leg by which they were to be attached to the bottom of the river. A cap piece for the brackets was anchored to the riverbed a rod or so upstream from, and parallel to, the trestles. Finally, planks, laid parallel to the current and stretching between the cap piece and the tops of the trestles, formed the brackets.

The trestles were built on the shore, and all were completed by 9:00 A.M. These and the cap pieces were wrestled into position under Pearsall's direction. The spikes were driven into the bottom by using "sets." Despite the swift current and slippery bottom, this foundation work was completed by 10:00. Finally, two-inch planks were laid side by side and attached to the upstream cap pieces and the tops of the trestles. This formed a sloped obstruction that directed the water toward the channel. The new wing was completed by 11:00 A.M., just six hours after the project was begun. Even before completing the installation of the planks, and before the water was completely backed up by Pearsall's dam, enough depth had been added to the channel to float the two grounded gunboats. Once free, these boats passed easily through the lower spillway. Then, with this final structure in place, on May 12 the *Louis-*

ville, the *Pittsburgh,* and two tugs passed safely over both of the rapids and into the deep water below the town. However, by this time fog had set in, and the last of the boats, *Chillicothe* and *Ozark,* remained above the upper rapids. These boats were not moved below the falls until the next morning. This was easily accomplished, and by early in the morning of May 13 the battle with the river had been won. Losses were few: some boats suffered minor damage, and one sailor drowned after being washed overboard during the passage of his boat through the spillway.

Assistance provided by the navy for the construction of the dam had been important but limited. In his report Pearsall was critical of the navy participation, though he acknowledged that Capt. Amos R. Langthorne of the *Mound City* and his subordinate officers and men, who were responsible for positioning the cribs, contributed greatly to the enterprise. He also confirmed that the navy assisted the quartermaster's department with ropes, bolts, and other hardware. However, he stated that he had observed no other support to or participation in the construction of the dams by navy personnel. He concluded that the navy did little for itself. The reason for the limited naval participation in the task of building the dam is unclear, although it may have been the result of the friction between Porter and Banks. According to Pearsall, there is no question "that the army of General Banks saved the fleet of Admiral Porter."[10] Nevertheless, Porter was personally interested in the work, and Colonel Bailey states in his report of the operation, "All his [Porter's] officers and men were constantly present, and to their extraordinary exertions and to the well-known energy and ability of the admiral much of the success of the undertaking is due."[11]

Whether or not Pearsall observed all of the efforts by the navy to assist in preparation of the dam, it was certainly not all work for the sailors as the boats were running the gauntlet of the falls. Furthermore, not all of the ladies of Alexandria were die-hard Confederates, at least not while in the presence of the Northern men. As one of Porter's sailors described the evening of May 12: "The balance of the boats came over the falls today with the exception of Chillicothe and Ozark. Went up and invited the ladies to walk down in the evening and see the rest come over. Walked up to the dam. . . . We found it so foggy the boats could not get over. Went back and stopped at the Cricket where the Admiral was receiving a serenade. Treated the ladies to wine and walked home with them. Bade them good bye."[12]

Confederate scouts watched the progress on the construction of the dam, but with his small army, General Taylor had no practical means to interfere with the work. Besides, the prevailing opinion of the Southerners was that no such wild idea as the construction of dams on the river to float boats over rapids could possibly work. The fleet was the property of the Confederate army, and nothing the Yankees could do to the river would change that.[13] When the boats began passing over the falls, the Southerners realized they had lost the opportunity to capture the fleet. Taylor blamed Kirby Smith for the loss of the fleet, Smith having taken away the bulk of his force in order to advance into Arkansas. However, given the size of Banks's army and the firepower of Porter's fleet, the outcome of the affair at Alexandria would probably have been the same even without Kirby Smith's actions.[14] As the Union army departed from Alexandria, "the enemy took possession of the town, and, with rueful and elongated countenances, gazed sadly upon the work of a Northern Army, whereby a fleet worth several millions of dollars, with a magnificent armament of powerful guns, which they had looked upon as their certain prize, had been successfully rescued."[15]

There was easy sailing for the fleet after crossing the falls, and on May 15 Porter wrote Welles, "I am clear of my troubles, and my fleet is safe out in the broad Mississippi. I have had a hard and anxious time of it." He waxed eloquent in his praise for Colonel Bailey: "I do not believe that there ever was a case where such difficulties were overcome in so short a space of time, and without any previous preparation."[16] The next day Porter once more wrote to the secretary of the navy, describing the building of the dam and the freeing of the vessels from their captivity above the falls. He again praised Bailey and, on the side, offered his opinion of military contractors. "Words are inadequate to express the admiration I feel for the abilities of Lieutenant-Colonel Bailey. This is without doubt the best engineering feat performed. Under the best circumstances a private company would not have completed this work under one year." He declared that Bailey had saved the government "a valuable fleet, worth nearly $2,000,000" and had "deprived the enemy of a triumph which would have emboldened them to carry on this war a year or two longer."

> The highest honors the Government can bestow upon Colonel Bailey can never repay him for the service he has rendered the country. . . .
>
> I trust some future historian will treat this matter as it deserves to be treated, because it is a subject in which the whole country should feel an interest, and the noble men who succeeded so admirably in this arduous task should not lose one atom of credit so justly due them. The Mississippi Squadron will never forget the obligations it is under to Lieutenant-Colonel Bailey.

> If this expedition has not been so successful as the country hoped for, it has exhibited the indomitable spirit of Eastern and Western men to overcome obstacles deemed by most people insurmountable. It has presented a new feature in the war, nothing like which has ever been accomplished before.[17]

In his May 17 report on the dam to Maj. Wickham Hoffman, assistant adjutant general of the XIX Army Corps, Lieutenant Colonel Bailey stated, "I presume it is sufficient in this report to say that the dam was constructed entirely on the plan first given to General Franklin, and approved by him."[18] He goes on to make clear that this statement refers to both the lower dam and the upper dam. This point is disputed by several reputable officers. For example, with all the praise for the dam going to Bailey, Colonel Robinson made a special point of citing Pearsall in a report to the chief engineer, Department of the Gulf, dated June 13. He felt that the praise should be shared by Pearsall, who in his opinion was as responsible as Bailey for the success of the dams. "Throughout the whole campaign he labored with unceasing toil and devotion. The plan for building two dams across Red River, which from necessity was finally adopted, was originally proposed by him, and the success of the dam was, in my opinion, mainly due to his efforts."[19]

Bailey's efforts to design and build the Red River dams have been universally praised by both his contemporaries and by historians. In fact, when describing the construction of the dams, most writers have given all credit for both dams to Bailey while Pearsall's role has generally been omitted.[20] Although Pearsall's description of the events surrounding the construction of the dams is probably colored by his personal opinion of Bailey, the testimony of Robinson and others confirms his vital role in that undertaking.

Previous discussions of the building of the Red River dams have also failed to mention the ongoing friction between Bailey and the other officers of the XIX Corps. Bailey described some of his perspective on the work of building the dams in a letter dated July 12, 1864, from Headquarters, Engineering Brigade, Vicksburg, to his friend Perry G. Stroud: "I have received my commission. It is the first and only Brevet Commission that has been issued [to me] sinse the commencement of the war. I have also received officially the thanks of Congress from Old Abe. . . . All this is very grattifying to me and especially as I have labored under the obligations and many disadvantages that you know I have."[21]

Bailey, who proved himself to be innovative and a competent engineer, was not a West Point graduate and appears to have had a chip on his shoulder.

He certainly had his disagreements with the West Pointers. He was described by one observer as "one of those serious men, who . . . require a surgical operation to get a joke into their heads."[22] It appears that this talented engineer officer was not quite the gentleman one might wish given the hero status he attained after the success of the dams. Bailey was apparently egotistical, self-righteous, paranoid about his position in the army, and disdainful of efforts made by others. He wrote to his friend Stroud: "It's enough for me to say that Jo Bailey knew whether he belonged to the army or not, and by keeping his own secrets he found out what paper and what men was his friend. . . . When I left with the army for the Red River I was determined to make or brake. My pride was with Cavalry consequently I was constantly in advance with from 50 to 1000 Cavalry and got all the information and in fact done all that was done with Cavalry on the expidition. This being the case, Banks staff officers and others become as geleous as the devil of me."[23] In the same letter Bailey wrote: "There was many amusing senses transpired whilst building this dam. And when I meet officers that was there we have our own fun. Fun, yes fun, such as hewing [?] Negroes down with a shovel, tying up some Banks politician Niger officers by the thumbs &c. No pen can picture the many funny scenes that happened during the construction of this emence work." It is not clear whether these statements contain elements of truth, are the products of a disturbed mind, or depict an arrant braggadocio.

Bailey was promoted to colonel June 1 and breveted brigadier general six days later. Porter reiterated his appreciation on June 13: "Congratulating him on his promotion, so well deserved, and hoping that the brave officers and men associated with him will appreciate the kind feelings we shall ever entertain for them."[24] Bailey was made a brigadier general of volunteers in November 1864 and was subsequently breveted major general of volunteers. After the war he became sheriff of Newton County, Missouri. In that capacity he was killed by bushwhackers in 1867.

According to Thomas C. Manning, associate justice of the Supreme Court of Louisiana, appointed by Gov. Henry W. Allen to investigate federal atrocities in Rapides Parish after the war, "It became soon generally known throughout the town that the enemy designed to devote the place to pillage and burning on the day they should evacuate it. Threats to this effect were publicly made by the privates as they walked the streets; and the citizens were warned by those of the army less fanatical and brutal, to provide against such a contingency."[25] The residents, fearing they would be thrown out of their homes and left destitute, pleaded with General Banks to save their town. On May 8, in response to this plea, General Banks ordered Brig. Gen. Richard Arnold to station a detachment of cavalry in the town as the evacuation took place. This cavalry troop was to prevent any "conflagration or other act which would give notice to the enemy of the movements of the army."[26]

As the last of Porter's fleet was passing the falls at Alexandria, Banks prepared to evacuate the town. He loaded as much equipment and supplies as possible onto the army transports and was ready to resume his retreat May 13. To the chagrin of the cotton speculators, much of their merchandise, so tediously acquired, was thrown off the boats to make room for military equipment. As Banks stated, "Where cotton or other property interfered with the transportation of any material of the army . . . it was thrown from the boats and abandoned upon the river levee to the enemy." Banks never did ingratiate himself to the cotton speculators.[27] On May 13 Lawler led the army out of Alexandria with his XIII Corps. Behind Lawler came Emory and the XIX Corps, with A. J. Smith again serving as rear guard. Despite Banks's orders and apparent intent to spare the town, with their customary enthusiasm Smith's men set fire to several buildings as they were leaving. Frank Church, a marine 2nd lieutenant, wrote that "some of the soldiers set the town on fire in the lower part. . . . At [illegible] o'clock the fleet got under way and we left Alexandria, the front street being a mass of ruins."[28]

Although by May 13 Banks knew that a portion of Taylor's army had been sent to Arkansas to support Price against Steele, he still envisioned hordes of enemy troops ready to attack his army without warning.[29] Another forced march began as Banks sought to put as many miles as possible between himself and Taylor's army. "The march from Alexandria to the Atchafalaya was continuous. . . . Day and night the columns pressed on, stopping a minute or an hour, as compelled by circumstances."[30] Soldiers, mules, and horses fell out of the march as the column advanced. Despite the pace, both the familiar enemy attacks on the rear of the column and the theft and destruction of private property by the Union troops continued. As they marched down the river toward Fort De Russy, the men of the XVI Corps, bringing up the rear, wreaked devastation on the countryside. James Ewer of the 3rd Massachusetts Cavalry reported, "The country was in flames. Burning buildings could be seen as far as the eye could reach." The column left behind "great clouds of smoke" and "the burning embers mingled with the roar of guns and the report of rifles, made up a picture that was impressive in the extreme."[31]

Banks moved along the right bank of the Red River, providing protection for Porter's fleet and the army transports as he marched. Porter, who was still ill, had gone ahead to the mouth of the Red. With the cavalry regiments of Major, Bagby, and William Steele on the right bank, plus that of Isaac F. Harrison on the left, Taylor used hit-and-run tactics to harass the Federals yet avoid major engagements. Then, in another attempt to stop Banks, Taylor ordered Polignac to move to Avoyelles Prairie, near Marksville, and there to take a position in front of the Union army. At this point a minor engagement occurred May 15 in which the van of Banks's army was turned back for a brief period. By the evening additional Union troops were brought up, and the Confederates were flanked out of their position. Many of his soldiers did not understand why Banks continued to retreat from the Confederates. Daniel Buchwalter, of the 120th Ohio, wrote in his diary May 15, 1864: "Why dont Banks alow us to turn and clean out those rebels. We have enough men to do it, all that we need is A Commander with as much confidence as the men of his army have."[32]

Taylor again tried to stop Banks's retreat on the morning of May 16. At Smith's plantation, in an open area called Belle Prairie near the town of Mansura, about six miles south of Marksville, Taylor placed virtually his entire army, such as it was, across Banks's path. In response, Banks deployed his army in line of battle, Smith on the right, Cameron in the center, Emory on the left, and Arnold's cavalry on the flanks. The result was a nearly picture-perfect battle scene, of the type envisioned early in the war, in which soldiers stood bravely facing the enemy in lines of battle. All who saw it agreed that it was a unique sight for two armies to be drawn up where all their components were visible to every soldier. Harris Beecher, of the 114th New York, was awed by the scene, calling it "transcendently imposing—a sight at once grand and inspiring."[33]

After facing off with the enemy for a while, the Union army wheeled to the left, pivoting on the road near the village of Cocoville, and approached Mansura from the west. "The approach to the enemy's position led across cleared and level ground that gave an unobstructed view from both flanks of the army. The deployment and advance of that line of battle on that clear and balmy May morning was a most inspiriting spectacle." As the line passed Mansura, it halted and the artillery opened fire. Taylor responded, and the ensuing artillery duel, lasting about four hours, was resplendent in the sunshine, on the open prairie, with flags flying and troops in lines of battle. "The flashes of fire from the enemy's artillery and the bursting of shells along our front, together with the responsive volleys from our batteries, gave life and force to the picture. Viewed from the enemy's position, it must have been a most animated and impressive scene."[34] Finally, Banks sent Smith forward to attack Taylor's left. Greatly outnumbered, Taylor withdrew, only to resume his hit-and-run tactics.[35] Banks moved on, bivouacking that night eight miles from the Atchafalaya River.

The head of Banks's column reached Simmesport May 17. Porter's fleet was waiting in the Atchafalaya River. As the front of the column went into camp at Simmesport, the Confederate cavalry pressed the rear at Bayou de Glaize, but to little effect. There was also an unsuccessful attack on the rear of the Union wagon train near Moreauville by Lt. Col. William O. Yager. Following this latter affair the troops of A. J. Smith took a position near Yellow Bayou to protect the rear of the army.

Having no means at hand to cross the river, Banks turned to Lieutenant Colonel Bailey The latter once more showed his ingenuity by quickly solving the problem. He first had the crews of twenty-two transports anchor their craft side by side across the river, bows upstream. When the boats were positioned such that they stretched completely between the banks of the river, he had them tied into place and planks laid across the bows. "String pieces were bolted down across the decks, and, upon them, a floor of the flat cypress rails of the country was laid. It made a good bridge, but exceedingly crooked from the unequal height and length of the boats." The traffic across Bailey's plank "bridge" was heavy. "Wagons, mules and men crossed on it. The artillery was ferried over."[36] The army crossed for two days and nights, the soldiers frequently pushing wagons by hand because of lack of space on the bridge for the teams to pull them. According to one observer, "Across the bows of these [boats] the artillery, cavalry and wagons were passing in a continuous stream, and infantry was crossing through and among them as best they could . . . such getting across a river I never saw."[37] A fleet of small boats assisted by carrying some of the troops across.

In a final effort to destroy part of Banks's army before it crossed the Atchafalaya and moved out of reach, Taylor attacked the Union rear guard at Yellow Bayou May 18. As skirmishing began to the west, Mower ordered his three brigades to cross Yellow Bayou and engage the enemy. His men scrambled across the bayou and began driving the Confederates back. After advancing about two miles and emerging from some woods, the Federals found a strong force of the enemy behind rail breastworks on the far side of a field on Norwood's plantation. The Southerners opened fire with artillery while Mower formed a line of battle.

Maj. Gen. John A. Wharton, a brigade commander from Joseph Wheeler's cavalry corps of the Army of Tennessee, had been appointed by Taylor to replace Green, who had been killed in a fight with Porter's gunboats.[38] Following a heavy cannonade by his artillery, General Wharton ordered his and Polignac's men forward against the Union front and left flank. The Union line countercharged and drove the Southerners back. Colonel Harrison of the 15th Texas reported that as the Yankees charged, they yelled, "Surrender you damned Rebels or we'll Kill you all."[39] Col. Thomas J. Kinney, temporarily in charge of Lynch's brigade, noted that the day became "excessively warm, and many of our men fell from sunstroke and exhaustion. There being no water in our reach, the men suffered exceedingly for want of it."[40] Finally, about 4:00 P.M. Mower ordered a general advance, and with sharp fighting, his troops drove the enemy across the open field. A. J. Smith noted, "The firing during the second charge set the thicket on fire, so that it formed a barrier impassable for either party."[41] The field was heavily contested, and the battle moved back and forth across the prairie. The dry vegetation burned rapidly, adding to the heat of the day and to the smoke from cannon and musket. Then, at dark, Mower withdrew from the field.

Hubbard called the battle "one of the prettiest fights of the campaign, we wound it up, if not in a 'blaze of glory,' certainly with infinite credit to 'Smith's Guerrillas.' Taylor was handsomely whipped and troubled us no more."[42] Although the Southerners held the field at the end of the battle, they had suffered about 450 casualties and had failed once again to halt Banks's retreat.[43] The Union lost about 350 men in this action. Banks's crossing of the Atchafalaya had proceeded even while the battle raged and afterward continued without further harassment. Even when the Union army was mostly across the river, and those forces remaining on the west bank may have been vulnerable to attack in detail, Taylor did not have the resources to take the offensive. Banks had at last escaped from his nightmare of tens of thousands of Confederate troops lurking about his column, ready to attack without warning.

Halleck had told Grant May 3 that Banks could not be relieved of command because he "[is] a personal friend of the President, and has strong political supporters in and out of Congress." However, after writing this note, Halleck must have pondered the question of whether Banks could be moved aside in a way that would be acceptable to both Lincoln and Congress. Within a few days he had found a way. He would not relieve Banks; he would appoint a new commander over him. Thus, May 7, 1864, while the Red River dam was nearing completion, under instructions from General Grant and with President Lincoln's approval General Halleck informed Brig. Gen. Edward Richard Sprigg Canby that he had been promoted to major general of volunteers and given command of the newly organized Military Division of West Mississippi. Although he was junior in rank to Banks, Canby was to take charge of all military affairs in both the Department of the Gulf and the Department of Arkansas. Specifically, so that there would be no confusion about the chain of command, Halleck told Canby that Banks was to be his subordinate. Canby set out immediately for Cairo, Illinois, where he assumed his new command May 11.[44] Although technically Banks retained his position as commander of the Department of the Gulf, his days as a field commander were over.

A SUMMATION

16

During his tour of duty as commanding officer of the Department of the Gulf, Maj. Gen. Nathaniel P. Banks was given three assignments: open the Mississippi River to Union control and reduce Fort Morgan or Mobile City, establish Union control at some point in Texas, and institute a loyalist state government in Louisiana. Although he never got a chance to attack Mobile, in one way or another Banks successfully completed the other assignments he was given. However, because of the manner in which he completed them, which included wasting time, resources, and lives, his tour of duty in the Gulf was a failure.[1]

Halleck's instructions of November 9, 1862, given to Banks coincident with his appointment as commander of the Gulf Department, stated that while he was charged with the tasks both to open the Mississippi to Union control and to reduce Mobile, the task of opening the Mississippi was "first and most important." Banks was also told that should he choose to unite his army with that of Grant, he would be in command of both armies.[2] Thus, Banks had the opportunity to become the commanding general of all of the Union infantry along the Mississippi River. However, the new Gulf Department commander seemed deliberately to avoid uniting with Grant, and he never undertook any military action in unison with the army to the north of his department. Although he did complete the opening of the Mississippi by his capture of the secondary objective, Port Hudson, he failed to capitalize on his opportunity to position himself to assist in the attack on the primary objective, Vicksburg.

His second assignment, given to him July 24, 1863, left Banks a choice of which point in Texas to occupy. His first choice was Sabine Pass. This was not a bad selection, and had his invasion attempt been successful, it is possible that he could have soon occupied the most populous parts of the state. However, the failure of the Sabine Pass invasion in September 1863, followed by the failure of the overland expedition to Texas through western Louisiana in the fall of that year, cast a negative pall over Banks's eventual landing at Brazos Island. Therefore, although he did occupy a part of Texas and thus successfully completed his second assignment, this success was an anticlimax marred by two prior failures as well as the disaster at Galveston in January 1863. In addition, he ultimately squandered this success by allowing Halleck to goad him into undertaking the Red River expedition.

In fulfilling his third assignment, as expounded by Lincoln in his letter of December 24, 1863, Banks rejected the option of beginning with a state constitutional convention. This decision was probably driven by the urgency expressed by the president for inaugurating a loyalist government in Louisiana. Banks's experience in the Massachusetts constitutional convention of 1853 gave him insight into the typically lengthy machinations of such proceedings, insight not shared by most of the politicians in Louisiana or in the U.S. Congress. He therefore chose to delay the writing of a new state constitution and instead to use the existing constitution as the basis for his new government. Unfortunately, even with Banks's declaration that the portions of the document that recognized and related to slavery were null and void, the references thereto were still present, so the use of this document as a basis for establishing a Unionist government in Louisiana provided an opportunity for perhaps unwarranted criticism. Although Banks's efforts produced a state government that met the requirements of Lincoln's Ten Percent Plan, and a few months later produced a free-state constitution, these political structures did not survive the subsequent onslaught of the radicals in Congress.

During his tenure as commander of the Gulf Department, Banks extended the area of Union control from the environs of New Orleans to a significant portion of central and southern Louisiana. He recruited, trained, and made effective military use of many thousands of free blacks and escaped slaves, and he provided for decent if limited employment and educational opportunities for many other ex-slaves. Banks was a compassionate man who consistently attempted to minimize the brutalizing influence of war and to prevent the abuse of the indigenous civilian population by his troops. He opposed private dealings in cotton in the territory that was under his control, and despite numerous opportunities for personal gain, he neither participated in cotton speculation nor accepted bribes in return for granting permission for others to trade in cotton. Unfortunately, all of this was outweighed by his dismal military performance.

The successful projection of military force over long distances into enemy-controlled territory is a difficult matter, and history is replete with examples of the failure of such attempts. Unlike Grant and Sherman, Banks never appreciated the risks involved in such undertakings, and almost all of his campaigns into enemy-held territory turned out to be partial or total failures. Although he won most of the battles he fought while commander of the Gulf Department, apart from the surrender of Port Hudson he failed to reduce significantly the fighting capability, much less destroy, the enemy armies with which he had to contend. Except for a few areas close to his home base of New Orleans and accessible by water, such as Brashear City, Baton Rouge, and Port Hudson, and the single exception of Brazos Island, he was unable to convert his campaigns into either militarily productive raids or long-term occupations of enemy territory.

After Banks assumed command in New Orleans, Farragut, who ceaselessly sought to gain advantage over the enemy, agreed to cooperate in a move against the Confederate forces at Baton Rouge. Banks acted quickly, and as a result of the effective collaboration between the army and navy commanders on the scene, the capital city of Louisiana was soon in Union possession. This move against Baton Rouge boded well for what Banks might accomplish in Louisiana and Texas.

Banks's second military move as commander of the Gulf Department was considerably less auspicious than his first. In this, his first invasion of Texas, Banks sent Colonel Burrell with a small contingent of troops to Galveston to assist Commander Renshaw in the occupation of the city. He anticipated that Union control of the area would soon be extended to the adjacent mainland. Burrell feared an attack and prepared as best he could, but he and Renshaw were unable to fend off the combined sea and land assault mounted by General Magruder. The navy leadership on the scene was poor, and two gunboats were lost. The troops ashore were captured, and the second contingent of Banks's force of occupation arrived only after the shore position was lost.

It seems certain that Banks had no insight whatsoever into the plans of his enemy at Galveston, and no awareness of the risk to which his troops would be exposed. He did not foresee any significant, aggressive move by Magruder, and the Union infantry contingent was woefully undersized for its assignment. The Battle of Galveston was thus but another example of an uncoordinated advance against the enemy. As it turned out, Banks's reputation would have suffered less if he had not reinforced Renshaw rather than provide the inadequate reinforcements that were sent. By his action he merely provided Magruder with more prisoners than he would otherwise have had. On the other hand, had he not suffered the loss of the first contingent of troops sent to Galveston, it is possible that Banks soon would have effected a long-term occupation of the town and surrounding area. Had such an operation happened early in Banks's tenure as commander of the Gulf Department, the history of his military career might have been quite different from what it turned out to be.

Continuing the high level of activity begun in December, in January 1863 Banks sent General Weitzel on a raid up Bayou Teche to destroy the Confederate gunboat *Cotton.* This advance into enemy territory was well orchestrated, and though met with strong resistance, the mission was accomplished with speed and daring. The support provided to the army troops by the navy was effective, and the two services worked well together. It appeared that Banks had found a winning combination. Perhaps now was the time to build on this success, destroy Richard Taylor's army, and find a water route around Port Hudson to the upper Mississippi. An excellent opportunity to achieve these goals lay in front of him.

Banks, however, repeatedly underestimated the military skill and daring of his Confederate opponent in western Louisiana. As Taylor's biographer concluded, "Taylor had achieved a lustrous record as a southern officer. . . . Among non-West Pointers Taylor's reputation as a battlefield commander was surpassed only by Forrest, Hampton, and Patrick R. Cleburne. He surely would have rivaled them and perhaps even eclipsed them had not his fragile health cut short a promising career as a combat officer in the Army of Northern Virginia."[3] To destroy or capture the army of a leader of this caliber would not be easy. Nevertheless, Weitzel offered a good plan in an attempt to do so. Banks pondered and eventually accepted Weitzel's plan. The initial part of the plan worked well. Unfortunately, as seemed to happen often in the Gulf Department, Banks's subordinate in command of a critical part of the plan, General Grover, was not equal to the role to which he had been assigned. Rather than proceed in a timely manner to execute his mission, Grover stopped for four hours in an attempt to aid one of his gunboat escorts and then lost another twelve hours or more searching for a place to land his troops. After finally selecting a landing site, he was forced to expend additional hours hauling equipment ashore through shallow water. Once ashore, more time was lost while the general decided what to do.

Some of Grover's problems, such as the shallow water that prevented his transports from approaching the shore, may have been unavoidable, although with advanced warning from a good pilot or with proper reconnaissance, better plans might have been made for this amphibious landing. To compound the errors committed in finding a landing point and getting his force ashore, when Grover finally got around to advancing toward Taylor's rear, he failed to use a screen of skirmishers adequate to avoid surprise. He was stunned by a flank attack and was stopped in his tracks. Because of his own shortcomings as a commander he failed to perform the movement assigned to him. After the battles at Fort Bisland and Irish Bend he should have been relieved from duty for the good of the army.

There were important lessons to be learned from the action at Irish Bend. Had the commanding general been sufficiently alert to observe the fighting style and military skills of his opponent, he would have noticed that Richard Taylor was not the type of general to retreat in panic from an enemy advance. Although hard pressed in front by Banks's attack at Bisland, Taylor had divided his army and launched a surprise attack against Grover. Here was an opponent who was not easy to push around and who would fight back in unexpected directions when given the opportunity. If Banks had been able to learn from experience, he might have warned Franklin to be more careful than he was during the advance up the Teche in the fall of 1863 and during the expedition up the Red River the following year. However, as was pointed out by his second biographer, Banks's "major flaw was an inability to learn from his mistakes."[4]

After his failure to capture Taylor's army at Fort Bisland, Banks moved rapidly to Opelousas. There his periodic indecisiveness seemed to strike. He halted his advance and simply waited. Then, when he learned of Porter's intention to move up the Red, he took off again at breakneck speed toward Alexandria. The lengthy delay at Opelousas made the subsequent rapid march to Alexandria meaningless. The entire history of the expedition to Alexandria in the spring of 1863 pointed to a lack of planning and a complete absence of military strategy on the part of the army commander.

At Port Hudson Banks finally focused on a clear military objective. With his overwhelming ground force and the help of the navy even he could not fail to capture the fortress. However, Banks seemed compelled to mimic Grant in the latter's attacks on the Vicksburg fortifications despite the fact that, unlike Grant, Banks had no enemy force in his rear. As a result many lives were wasted in uncoordinated and fruitless attacks against the entrenched enemy. Once he settled into a siege, the fate of the garrison was assured and the capture of this fortress became the brightest star in Banks's military crown.

With the opening of the Mississippi following the capture of Port Hudson the Trans-Mississippi South could no longer contribute men and supplies in significant quantities to the fighting forces east of the river. It might have made sense to ignore this remote portion of the Confederacy and concentrate on making gains in the eastern theater; however, the Lincoln administration had important reasons to initiate a move against Texas. Therefore, Banks was not allowed to attack Mobile, as he wished, and instead was instructed to plant the Union flag in Texas. In following these orders, Banks decided to try to capture Sabine Pass. However, in this, his second invasion of Texas, he once again made the mistake of sending an unqualified subordinate to perform an important duty. Occupation of the pass by the joint army-navy expedition should have been a simple matter. Instead, Franklin's ridiculous failure to capture tiny Fort Griffin was one of the major fiascoes of the war. From the Union perspective, allowing an enemy commander with 42 men and 4 volunteers to drive away four gunboats and 5,000 troops, much less to capture two of the gunboats, was ludicrous.

The engagement at Sabine Pass in September 1863 is a prime example of the outcome of a battle hinging on a struggle between two commanders rather than a struggle between two armies. The bravery and determination of Lieutenant Dowling so overshadowed the willpower and ability of General Franklin that the overwhelming manpower and weapons of the latter were of no avail. That Franklin was allowed to remain in command following this engagement was inexcusable and reflects Banks's total inability to recognize incompetence in his subordinates. It is astounding that any commander would allow such a subordinate as General Franklin showed himself to be at Sabine Pass to retain a command position.

But retain a command position Franklin did, and next Banks sent his incompetent subordinate up the Teche with the intent of initiating a third invasion of Texas from some appropriate point in western Louisiana. As long as the commanding general traveled with the advance, the army moved forward at a lively pace and soon reached New Iberia. Banks then chose to return to New Orleans, leaving the army under Franklin's command. The advance came to a halt. Franklin loitered at Bayou Carencro, then moved to Opelousas. After remaining there for a while, he decided to return to the Carencro. At Bayou Bourbeau he left part of his army in an exposed position, and it was thoroughly beaten by General Green. Following this lesson Franklin retreated, first to New Iberia and then to the town of Franklin. Much as they would do after the battles at Mansfield and Pleasant Hill, the men grumbled as they marched away from the enemy, placing the blame for the defeat on General Franklin.[5] Just as at Sabine Pass, Banks was able to accomplish nothing in this attempt to invade Texas. However, once again, against all logic, Franklin was allowed to retain his command.

In October 1863 Banks undertook a fourth invasion of Texas. This time the army commander was present in person, and the invasion was more successful than the two attempts commanded by General Franklin had been. Banks landed at the mouth of the Rio Grande, and for the first and only time his army was able to occupy Texas soil for the remainder of the war. Following the capture of Brownsville, Banks's advance up the coast went well, and soon there was a strip of land a few miles wide and several hundred miles long that he could claim as Union-controlled territory. All of this was of little value, however, unless he could occupy the populous areas of east Texas; specifically, Galveston and Houston. In December, after Banks had left Texas, his field commander, General Washburn, wanted to continue the advance toward Galveston. However, rather than help his commander on the scene with reinforcements from General Dana at Brownsville and encourage him to continue the army's advance, Banks ordered General Washburn to halt pending arrival of reinforcements from Louisiana. As a result General Magruder had ample time to strengthen and solidify his defensive position near Velasco.

While Washburn waited at Pass Cavallo, there was no discussion of flanking the Confederates out of their position by advancing inland up the Caney River, or by using the Union navy and the available army transports to land troops on the coast behind the enemy to attack their position from the rear. Although the action subsequent to his assuming command in Texas had not tested his military abilities, General Washburn had done well against Fort Esperanza and had an extraordinarily competent subordinate in General Ransom. Because Magruder had not yet completed his defensive preparations, it is possible that these officers could have captured the enemy positions at the mouth of the Brazos River and continued their move up the coast had they been given the authority to do so after the fall of Fort Esperanza. However, Banks did not entrust his field commander in Texas with the authority to pursue the stated mission of the coastal invasion, and Magruder was never attacked. Instead, Banks soon began removing men from Texas in order to chase Halleck's dream of establishing a line of defense along the Red River and invading Texas from some point along that line. Ultimately the entire invasion of the Texas coast proved to be a waste of time and effort, and finally, late in June 1864, the last of the Federal occupation force of about 1,200 men withdrew to Brazos Island.[6] Even Banks's one successful invasion of Texas turned out to be incomplete.

With this history behind him, Banks then proceeded to fashion another of the great military blunders of the war. The idea of conducting a rapid raid on enemy headquarters in Shreveport, with the intent of disrupting the Confederate chain of command and destroying equipment and supplies, thereby crippling the ability of the enemy to fight west of the Mississippi, was militarily reasonable. Had Banks authorized a combined operation for this purpose, to be executed under competent leadership such as that of Porter and Sherman, there would have been every reason to anticipate success. Instead, Banks undertook to lead the Red River expedition himself and as a result was able to practice "exercising his talents for mismanagement to the utmost."[7] In retrospect, it would have been better for Banks to resign his commission than to allow himself to be prodded into the expedition by General Halleck.

Banks was confused about the objectives of the Red River expedition from the beginning. After capturing Shreveport, he had some conception of returning A. J. Smith and his men to Sherman and having General Steele take over occupation of the city. Then he, Banks, would either chase Taylor's army into Texas or return to New Orleans and prepare to move against Mobile. In addition, there was the option of implementing one of the original objectives of the expedition, as described by Halleck, which was to establish a base at Shreveport for operations in Texas. However, Halleck's role in the Federal command structure was de facto changed by Grant's promotion to lieutenant general. By Grant's orders of March 30, 1864, the Red River expedition was not to establish a base for operations in Texas. In light of this fact it would have been proper for the commander in the field to reconsider his plans for the expedition. This did not happen, and Banks appeared to have no clear idea as to how any of the desired outcomes of the campaign were to occur.

Tactical confusion is a great weakness in a military commander, and to this Banks added indecisiveness. Several times during the expedition he called together his subordinates, who in many cases did not even measure up to his own, low standards of military competence, to advise him on military decisions. As is frequently the case when decisions are made by committee, as a group these subordinates seemed doomed to offer bad advice. Banks apparently could no more distinguish good advice from bad advice than good subordinates from bad subordinates, and he consistently listened to, and acted on, this bad advice. When to this he added his own inflated imagination and mental anxieties, he produced a recipe for disaster. As pointed out by Ludwell Johnson in his study of the Red River campaign, Banks was completely unprepared for the "imagination and aggressiveness displayed by Richard Taylor in contending against the Federals' overwhelming numerical and material superiority."[8]

The overland advance of the Gulf army from the town of Franklin to Alexandria in March 1864 went rather smoothly. Porter's advance up the Red, with A. J. Smith's troops in escort, entailed the capture and destruction of Fort De Russy. A few days later Mower's successful attack and capture of most of Taylor's 2nd Louisiana Cavalry at Henderson's Hill cleared the way for an easy advance to Natchitoches and beyond, if only the gunboats could cross the rapids at Alexandria. The decision at this point to continue the expedition despite the low stage of water in the river was reasonable. During the spring runoff it was rare for the water level to stay as low as the navy found it in March, and it was justifiable to anticipate a rise. The task of getting almost the entire fleet over the falls in just ten days was Herculean, and the navy deserved much credit for the determination and endurance it demonstrated.

Things began to unravel at Grand Ecore. After the battle at Sabine Crossroads Porter mentioned the presence of a road leading north along the river, but there is no indication that anyone either alerted Banks to the existence of this road or investigated how far the road extended upstream. Loyalist residents of Natchitoches and Grand Ecore apparently made no mention of the road to the Union military leadership, which may well indicate that it did not offer a viable route to Shreveport. Porter's flowery, postbattle description of a river road to Shreveport was self-serving and at best was probably misleading.[9] However, even if the existence of the road were communicated to General Banks, and even if the road did continue to Shreveport, the commander would not likely have chosen to use it for his advance. Banks did not believe the enemy would fight, and therefore there was no need for the army to remain close to the river. The main road led to Mansfield, and Banks almost certainly would have taken it under any circumstances.

There can be no doubt that the structure of the column that departed Grand Ecore April 7 en route to Shreveport was poorly suited for an advance through a dense forest, deep in enemy territory, in the face of an enemy army led by a commander known to be both competent and aggressive. The presence of the long train of wagons immediately in the rear of the cavalry, separating the cavalry from the infantry, meant that the leading element of the army could not retreat in the face of an enemy attack without risking loss of their train and artillery and that the infantry could not provide ready support to the cavalry under the same event. Thus, the two obvious contingencies available to the cavalry in the event of a strong enemy stand—fall back on the infantry or have the infantry join them at the front—were at best substantially handicapped, and at worst prohibited, by the organization of the column.

Had Taylor structured Banks's column for his own purpose, he could hardly have done a better job than General Franklin managed to do.

The fight at Wilson's plantation might have tipped a commander wiser than General Banks or General Franklin to the fact that there was some possibility of encountering major enemy resistance up the road and that it was time to consider a reorganization of the advancing column. Not only did that affair indicate that the Union commanders could be incorrect in assuming that the enemy would not fight before reaching Shreveport but it also provided irrefutable proof that the column as then constituted was poorly suited for the conditions under which the advance was proceeding. Franklin started to send infantry help to Lee before Franklin was told that the enemy had withdrawn. If he had stopped to think, Franklin would have realized that had the ambush been a major attack, the delay attendant to his reinforcements getting to the front could have resulted in the loss of much of the cavalry and cavalry train. Instead, he seemed to take the attitude that Lee's request for help was a false alarm and that everything was under control. Furthermore, after the fight at Wilson's plantation he appeared to change his mind about whether infantry support should be forwarded to the cavalry. He now decided this should not be done under any circumstances.

During the night of April 7 Lee again requested help from the infantry. This time Franklin refused but was subsequently ordered by Banks to send troops forward. In 1865 Franklin testified before the Joint Committee on the Conduct of the War concerning this order from Banks. In his testimony Franklin stated that the defeat at Sabine Crossroads was caused by the reinforcements sent to the cavalry. Without infantry support, he claimed, Lee's cavalry would never have advanced as far as it did April 8, and in any case a significant attack by the enemy would have resulted in the retreat of the cavalry. Therefore, in his eyes, the army would have been safe had his decision not to forward the infantry support to General Lee been sustained. He did not comment on the probable fate of the cavalry train should Lee have been forced to retreat.

If Franklin really believed that sending infantry reinforcements forward was dangerous, why did he not tell Banks of his concern and protest Banks's order of April 7 to the best of his ability? Even had Banks taken no action in response to such a protest, as commander of the column Franklin could have taken measures to compensate somewhat for the situation. Instead, professing to believe that the cavalry alone could not get into trouble but with infantry help would almost certainly do so, he forwarded the infantry reinforcements apparently without complaint, as ordered. He then made no change in the advancing column. One is inclined to believe that Franklin did not, in fact, predict the disaster that befell the advance, that he was as much in the dark about what he was doing as was his commander, and that his ex post facto remarks to the Joint Committee were rationalizations directed at undermining General Banks and leaving himself blameless.

Banks walked blindly into Taylor's trap at Mansfield and suffered accordingly. The results of the pandemonium, caused by the routed advance encountering the cavalry wagons that congested the only line of escape from the battlefield, could have been predicted. Twenty cannon, several hundred wagons, and many hundreds of men were captured by the enemy. The panicked Union troops dashed madly around the wagons and down the road with the enemy close behind, until they encountered General Emory's men. There the disciplined troops under that competent commander stopped the enemy in a bloody, hand-to-hand fight. It was a close thing, however, and a little delay in General Franklin's notifying Emory of the problem at the front and ordering him forward, or a little delay in Emory's advance against the routed throng, could have led to Emory's force being routed, captured, or destroyed. As often happens in war, it took a bit of luck as well as a lot of determination for Emory to halt Taylor's juggernaut.

At Pleasant Hill Banks's army settled the issue of its survival. Despite the amount of time available to prepare their position, the Union commanders did not mount a well-organized defense. The gaps in the line between Dwight and Shaw, Shaw and Benedict, and Benedict and Mower were major defects. Cameron received ambiguous orders, and his force was not on the field during the battle. However, the outcome was not changed by these omissions, and with fierce fighting and the field leadership of Mower and A. J. Smith the Union troops turned back Taylor's Confederates. Although Taylor's fighting spirit was not dampened by this setback, the size of his army was subsequently reduced by Kirby Smith, and thereafter Taylor was unable to mount a successful offensive.

A. J. Smith had come to Banks's aid at Pleasant Hill, and a victory was won, but Banks failed to take advantage of this tactical gain. Taylor's bold actions had overwhelmed the insecure Union commander, who, following the battle and on the advice of his subordinates, ordered his army to retreat and assume the defensive against a heavily outnumbered foe. Had Banks followed the victory at Pleasant Hill with an advance by the troops of A. J. Smith up the Mansfield Road the next day, it seems reasonably certain that Taylor would have been driven back or at least would have been fixed in position until the Union army was resupplied and preparations were made for another move on Shreveport. However, by this time such an aggressive act was impossible for Banks.

Despite Banks's personal bravery and his vainglorious statement made immediately following the battle at Pleasant Hill regarding his intent to resume the advance, the commanding general had completely lost his offensive mindset, along with whatever confidence his subordinates had in his leadership. Furthermore, he had already sent his supply train to Grand Ecore. After the battle at Pleasant Hill was won, he found that he had virtually locked himself into a retreat, and so retreat he did. In fact, he soon dedicated himself to retreating and thereby contrived the most undignified Union retreat of the Civil War. The image of Banks's army of some 25,000 men, plus artillery, wagons, teamsters, and hangers-on, fleeing from Taylor's 5,000 lean and hungry Confederates conjures a sense more of comedy than drama. Banks was mentally beaten, and the only thought on his mind was to escape from his enemy.

Except for the engagements at Monett's Ferry, Avoyelles Prairie, Belle Prairie, and Yellow Bayou, the fighting during Banks's escape from General Taylor was more like a running skirmish than a battle. Monett's Ferry was a classic example of the use of a flanking maneuver to force an enemy out of a strong position. Thanks to the leadership of Emory and the determination and fighting spirit of Fessenden and Birge, unlike Grover's efforts at Irish Bend the maneuver at Monett's Ferry was executed promptly and effectively. Because of the decision by General Bee to retire from his position on the right bank of the Cane, the maneuver also met with total success. The affair at Avoyelles Prairie was quickly resolved by another flank movement on the part of the Federals. The standoff at Belle Prairie was more pageantry than fighting, and its outcome was never in doubt. At Yellow Bayou Mower's troops met the enemy face-to-face in a stand-up battle and stopped them with hard fighting. The real drama in the retreat was not the fighting, but the building of the dams at Alexandria.

The testy and insecure Joseph Bailey possessed the knowledge and ability necessary to bring the plan of building wing dams to increase the water level over the falls at Alexandria to the attention of his superiors and to carry the plan through to completion once it was approved. Whether from arrogance or jealousy, he refused to listen to good advice from his fellow engineers; although he was not the only one to think of the idea of wing dams and although his plan had to be modified to achieve final success, he got the job done. Saving Porter's fleet from being stranded above the rapids, and thus preventing it from being exposed either to destruction or capture, was an outstanding accomplishment. The work required to save the fleet was performed in the field under trying conditions using only the tools and facilities at hand. The resolve demonstrated by the Engineers, the Pioneers, the officers, and the soldiers who built the Red River dams during the first part of May 1864, not to mention the resolve of the commanding general who ordered it done, equaled in its own way many of the battlefield actions that occurred during the war. For the Union it was the highlight of the Red River expedition.

Banks's efforts as a general were not without some useful product for the Union cause, and overall he did better than most of the other political generals that served either the Union or the Confederacy during the war. On a good day he could outshine many of the professional officers of the army, and he gained a level of positive notoriety from his actions at Cedar Mountain and Port Hudson that was unmatched by the majority of the other Union major generals. On a bad day, however, what distinguished General Banks from most Union officers of his grade was not so much the fact that he failed to achieve his military objectives, which was a common enough occurrence, but that he failed in such a spectacular manner. He seemed to have a talent for getting himself and his army not just into trouble, which might require maneuver or retreat in order to recoup losses or to regroup, but into a position of imminent destruction. There never seemed to be a normal setback or withdrawal for General Banks. Almost every time his army was checked or repulsed by the enemy, his retreat seemed to turn into a rout.

Several shortcomings in Banks's military psyche led to his spectacular failures as a commander. First, during the Civil War most military commanders did not hesitate to remove subordinates when they felt such subordinates lacked the ability to do the job that was required. Banks, however, almost never questioned the abilities of his subordinates. Apart from the single case of General Sherman at Port Hudson, it was only after the battle at Pleasant Hill that he took even rudimentary steps to replace some of his officers. Although he would have been fully justified in removing General Grover from command after the battle at Irish Bend, he did not do so. Fortunately for him this failure was of little consequence since Grover did not play an important role in the subsequent actions in the department. On the other hand, leaving General Franklin in a command position despite his repeated demonstrations of incompetence was inexcusable. This lack of action on Banks's part was extremely costly both to the commanding general of the Gulf Department and to the Union cause.

Second, Banks suffered from incurable self-importance. He continually reported to his superiors that whatever action he or his department was engaged in, or was planning at the moment, was the "key" to success, the "best" line of action, the move that would quickly be followed by overwhelming victory. In Banks's view his every undertaking was vital to the Union cause and was "certain" of success. His failures, which were repeatedly highlighted against these brash declarations, and the fact that the predicted dire consequences of failure did not develop, undercut his credibility in Washington.

Third, Banks seemed to lack imagination and was frequently beset by indecision. He could not conceive of his enemies doing anything but what he wanted or expected them to do. When surprised by enemy actions, he quickly became overwhelmed and could not decide whether to advance or retreat, to stay where he was or move somewhere else. The more critical the situation he found himself in, the worse his reaction. When a portion of his army was routed by the unexpected attack at Sabine Crossroads during the Red River expedition, he forfeited his command authority and allowed his subordinate officers to make military decisions for him. Once proved wrong in his belief that the enemy would not fight, he became confused and uncertain, and he soon showed that he was thoroughly beaten mentally if not physically.

Kirby Smith, in an article published in 1888, addressed the condition of the Confederate forces in Louisiana following the battles at Mansfield and Pleasant Hill: "Our repulse at Pleasant Hill was so complete and our command was so disorganized that had Banks followed up his success vigorously he would have met with but feeble opposition to his advance on Shreveport. . . . Our troops were completely paralyzed and disorganized by the repulse at Pleasant Hill."[10] There is some question as to the complete accuracy of this statement since Taylor's forces were still elated by the victory at Mansfield and were still able to fight. But whether or not Taylor's troops were "paralyzed and disorganized" is irrelevant. Although after Kirby Smith withdrew Churchill and Walker, Banks faced little real opposition from Taylor, Banks was hoodwinked by Taylor's aggressive tactics and took council of his fears. Seldom has a commander been so thoroughly "outgeneraled." Following the removal of Banks from field command, Lincoln admitted to Secretary of the Navy Welles that he had "cousined" up to Banks but that Banks had failed him.[11] It took Lincoln rather a long time to accept this fact and make corrections.

In association with Union military activities conducted in Louisiana, the Union troops committed a vast amount of unauthorized foraging, marauding, and pillaging. Many soldiers actively pursued the theft or destruction of the property of local residents along and near their line of march. Looting and burning of business establishments, private dwellings, barns, and other structures occurred continuously while the army was in enemy territory. Although these activities did not start with Banks's arrival in the Department of the Gulf, they reached their peak while he was in command. Banks opposed unauthorized foraging and theft or destruction of private property, but his orders forbidding such were consistently ignored; and he, along with many other officers of like mind in the army, was either unable or unwilling to take the steps necessary to stop it.[12]

The devastation inflicted on the defenseless populace in the Trans-Mississippi region of the Confederacy during 1864 might be seen as part of the pattern of destructiveness practiced by the Union armies late in the war. This pattern included Sherman's raid on Meridian, the same general's March to the Sea through Georgia and advance through South Carolina, and Sheridan's occupation of the Shenandoah Valley.[13] These latter activities have been described as "economic warfare" because the destruction they entailed emphasized the elimination of enemy resources required for continuing the war. As concluded by Mark Grimsley in his study of Union military policy toward Southern civilians, the strategy of raids intended to destroy systematically the Southern war resources "had done a great deal to defeat the Confederacy. . . . Yet such results, important as they were, were less decisive than what the raids did to Southern morale and perceptions. Even at the end of the war, Confederate troops still possessed weapons and ammunition. . . . What they did not possess was confidence that they could continue the struggle effectively. They could not prevent Union troops from roaming at will and visiting hardship and destruction upon places throughout the South."[14]

The destruction brought about in Louisiana by Banks's army was not done as a pattern of living off the land or of systematic destruction of economic assets. Except for a few instances, such as the destruction of the salt works at Marsh Island, the destruction in Louisiana was directed against targets of opportunity. By this stage of the war the soldiers had learned that their officers at worst would not punish them for plundering and marauding, and at best endorsed such activities. Although in Louisiana it was said that the worst of the destruction was practiced by stragglers, or "bummers," which may have been true, much of the destruction was performed by organized units while officers either participated or deliberately failed to intervene. Some of the destruction may have been committed under direct orders. Regardless of who was responsible and what constituted the motivation—belief of military necessity, revenge, frustration, boredom, or simple malice—Banks's men, not to mention those of A. J. Smith, were second to none in the Union armies in the devastation they left in their wake, and the suffering of the local populace during the movements of the Union army in Louisiana was great.[15]

For the Union troops there was little recognition to be had in fighting west of the Mississippi, especially toward the end of the war. To the individual soldiers, defeat while fighting in this region was particularly bitter, and this may have been conducive to the vigorous, wanton destruction of private property that occurred in Banks's department. As Captain Hebard of the 1st Vermont Battery stated, "A man gets no credit for fighting in this department—if he gets killed and his ghost comes back to earth it will see his name misspelt in the newspapers and that is all."[16] Surgeon John Homans of Massachusetts believed that "any life lost in battle west of the Mississippi River after January, 1864, was an unnecessary sacrifice, and that the real theatre of war was east of the river, and the operations west of it only a side-show."[17]

Despite all of the errors made by Banks while commanding the Department of the Gulf, there was some feeling among the men of his army that their general's character may have been incorrectly impugned. Elias Porter Pellet of the 114th New York stated, "A single success is proof of Napoleonic genius; a single defeat, of total incompetency. General Banks was not an exception to the rule."[18] On May 8, 1864, George Templeton Strong wrote in his diary: "Poor Banks! Why will men of ability and reputation in civil affairs let themselves be deluded into the notion that they can handle armies?"[19] Concerning whether Banks took part in the cotton dealings that were continually going on around him, General Hubbard, in his memorial presentation to the Minnesota Commandery in 1892, stated with some sense of respect that Banks had neither sponsored nor condoned the acquisition of privately owned cotton.[20]

Other participants in the campaigns in the Gulf Department recognized merit in their commanding officer that went beyond his shortcomings as a general. Pellet stated that "what General Banks lacks in being a great General, he makes up in being a philanthropist, a humanitarian, a statesman and a gentleman."[21] Richard B. Irwin, who perhaps best understood Banks as a man, said, "General Banks is not a great general, but he is a man of great personal bravery, too apt, indeed, to run into needless exposure. And I am sure that neither gold nor cotton, which is worse than gold, can corrupt him. His thirst is not for money, but for power."[22] Phlegmatist, conciliationist, and practical politician that he was, Banks inadvertently stated his philosophy best when he wrote, "Wise men will do what they can when they cannot do what they would. It is the law of success."[23]

Whatever could be said about the Union army commander in the Gulf Department and his abilities as a military leader, it was certain that the foe in western Louisiana was no pushover. Porter stated after the war:

> The rebs in this quarter were a saucy and independent set of fellows, and the prospect of punishment didn't seem to make them a bit more respectful. I rather admired them for their independent spirit; they were foemen worthy of our steel, and can be relied on now to defend our country, if necessary, against the world combined.
>
> Their valor was equal to that of the Northern soldiers, and their endurance, I think, greater. Had they been the people of any other nation, our troops would have walked over them without much difficulty.[24]

Porter added, "I am certain of one thing, and that is, if General A. J. Smith and myself had been there alone with the forces we had, we would have gone to Shreveport without any trouble."[25] He was perhaps correct in this assertion.

Banks wound up with little to show for his immense effort in the west. Following the capture of Port Hudson essentially nothing of value to the war effort resulted from all of the struggle, the fighting, and the casualties incurred by the Union army and navy in Louisiana. Despite the continuing attempts by the Gulf army, and the civilian speculators accompanying it, to obtain cotton for the mills in New England, relatively little survived the torches of the Southern troops. Banks's desire to recruit loyal Texans for the Union army while he was in that state was also largely a failure. Only 2,164 white troops from Texas enlisted in the Union ranks, excluding those Texans who enlisted in units from states other than Texas.[26]

Banks pushed his conciliatory position to the limit and succeeded in establishing a loyalist state government in Louisiana that met Lincoln's 10 percent requirement. Lincoln sought acceptance by Congress of the new government, and after General Canby arrived in New Orleans, Banks came to Washington to support the president in his attempt to gain this acceptance. In his last public address, April 11, 1865, Lincoln offered arguments in favor of accepting the new Louisiana free-state government as the legitimate government of the state and of allowing this government to resume its "proper practical relation with the Union." He argued that

> the question is not whether the Louisiana government, as it stands, is quite all that is desirable. The question is "Will it be wiser to take it as it is, and help to improve it; or to reject, and disperse it?" "Can Louisiana be brought into proper practical relation with the Union *sooner* by *sustaining*, or by *discarding* her new State Government?" . . . Concede that the new government of Louisiana is only to what it should be as the egg is to the fowl, we shall sooner have the fowl by hatching the egg than by smashing it?[27]

Unfortunately for Lincoln and Banks, one of the newly elected representatives from Louisiana, A. P. Field, had an altercation with radical representative William D. Kelley, a strong opponent of the president's Reconstruction effort in Louisiana, in which Kelley received a slight knife wound. This action essentially eliminated any chance that the House would seat the Louisiana delegation sent to Washington by Banks's reconstructed state government. On the Senate side, the Judiciary Committee recommended that the newly elected senators from Louisiana be seated provided Congress passed a joint resolution recognizing the legitimacy of the new state government. When this motion reached the floor of the Senate, Charles Sumner initiated a filibuster and essentially single-handedly blocked its passage.[28] Thus, as a final parting blow to General Banks the free state's elected representatives were not seated.

Banks retained a sympathy for Southerners throughout the war, and after the war he continued to favor conciliation in relations with the former seceded states. Speaking of the radicals and their Reconstruction policies, he stated that "I am not the enemy of southern men. I recognize them as brothers, and Americans. I know that we must live together. . . . I do not clamor for their punishment."[29] Banks argued that because secession was illegal, the Southern states were never out of the Union. Therefore, they should be readmitted to full participation in the national government as soon as they established pro-Union state governments.[30] Banks came eventually to agree with the radicals' position on suffrage for the former slaves and free blacks, and as a congressman after the war he voted in favor of military rule in the South. Some radicals even began to speak favorably of the labor system that Banks had instituted in Union-controlled Louisiana while he was the Gulf Department commander.

Subsequent to the Red River expedition no military operations of significance were undertaken by either side in Louisiana. The new department commander, General Canby, directed his attention toward keeping the Mississippi free from harassment by small enemy units that periodically took positions along the river in an attempt to disrupt shipping. Small bands of Confederates roamed through western Louisiana, occasionally causing excitement and concern that Kirby Smith might send reinforcements across the river to assist Southern forces east of the Mississippi. This never happened, however, and "Kirby-Smithdom" operated essentially in isolation from the rest of the Confederacy.

The Confederate trade through Mexico continued even while Union forces occupied Brownsville. The wagonloads of cotton and other goods now had to travel west to Laredo or Eagle Pass before crossing the Rio Grande, then move down the right bank of the river to Matamoros or Bagdad. Though the new route was less convenient than the old, the trade by means of ships from Europe and other countries, including in some cases the United States, was not greatly disturbed. Unfortunately for the Confederacy, most of the goods received in exchange for cotton and other commodities never reached the armies struggling east of the Mississippi because of the thorough and effective patrolling of the Mississippi by the Union navy. The trade became a hollow and irrelevant activity that benefited only a few.

After watching the Federals disappear into the woods across the Atchafalaya in May 1864, Taylor gave up the chase. He did so not because he wanted to but because he was finally forced to face the reality of his supply shortages and the exhaustion of his troops. As the last of the Union forces moved across Bailey's plank bridge, Kirby Smith was still focusing on Arkansas and Missouri, and he ordered Taylor north. Taylor, by taking every opportunity to complain of the situation both to Smith and to the government authorities in Richmond, continued his attempts to affect the policies of his superior.

As Taylor pursued his relentless criticism of Kirby Smith, his remarks became increasingly derogatory. General Smith did not want to lose his talented subordinate; however, after ignoring or excusing this criticism for several weeks, Smith had to take action against Taylor in order to maintain his leadership of the Trans-Mississippi. On June 10 Smith had Taylor arrested for insubordination. This arrest did not stop Taylor's criticism, nor did it have any effect on Richmond's attitude toward this new Confederate hero.[31] Taylor had, after all, stopped a major invading Yankee army and saved western Louisiana and eastern Texas from Union occupation. As a reward for these actions he was promoted to lieutenant general and reassigned to the command of the Department of Alabama, Mississippi, and East Louisiana. Shortly thereafter he crossed the Mississippi River and assumed his new command, released at last from the authority of Kirby Smith. In the spring of 1865 Taylor's were the last Confederate troops to surrender east of the Mississippi.

Following his escape from the Red River, Porter was appointed commander of the North Atlantic Blockading Squadron. In that capacity, leading the largest American fleet assembled to that time, he assisted the Provisional Corps of Maj. Gen. A. H. Terry in capturing Fort Fisher near Wilmington, North Carolina, in January 1865. This action closed the last functioning Confederate port on the Atlantic. By the end of the war Porter carried the grade of rear admiral. In 1870 he was promoted to full admiral, the second officer, after Farragut, to achieve that grade in the U.S. Navy.

A. J. Smith, with his detachment from the Army of the Tennessee, embarked for Vicksburg May 22. In subsequent operations Smith commanded the right wing of Maj. Gen. George H. Thomas's forces in the Battle of Nashville and participated in the capture of Mobile. The 1st Brigade, XIII Corps, left Louisiana May 25, bound for Virginia to join Emory, who, along with a detachment of the XIX Corps, had previously been sent east. The 3rd Division, XIX Corps, and most of the original XIII Corps detachment remained in Louisiana as the Reserve Corps (Gulf). Ironically, the activities undertaken by General Canby in his new position were probably not different from those that would have been undertaken by Banks had the latter been allowed to stay in command. Offensive engagements were essentially limited to the capture of the forts protecting Mobile Bay, in August 1864, and the capture of the city of Mobile, in April 1865.

Apart from raids along the coast, the only Union incursions into the territory of the state of Texas throughout the Civil War were Renshaw's brief residence in Galveston Bay and Banks's coastal invasion, the latter ultimately resulting in the occupation of a small amount of territory near Brownsville. To some extent this was the result of the limited resources of the North, the remote location of Texas relative to the major population centers of the country, the limited ground transportation routes available in the western parts of the Confederacy, and the paucity of military ability in the Union commanders who were assigned the responsibility of invading the state. However, even these factors would have been insufficient for the protection of the state had it not been for the leadership of the defensive forces available in Texas and Louisiana. Richard Taylor, John Magruder, Thomas Green, and Richard Dowling were leaders who placed themselves and the forces they commanded in the path of the Union army and, with determination and military skill, sent it reeling.

Banks, though he remained for a while head of the Department of the Gulf, never commanded a military force in the field following his return from the Red River. It seemed a tragic end to a gallant gentleman who had striven mightily to be a good general but who was clearly trying to do a job that was beyond his capacity. Eventually Banks resigned from the army and returned to Massachusetts. There he was elected to six more terms in the U.S. House of Representatives, five times as a Republican and once as an independent; and to one term in the Massachusetts Senate.

Unfortunately, his appalling performance as a general, as well as his political position as a moderate, left Banks without a following at the national level. He had no military reputation or standing that would command public admiration, and he was at odds with the radicals in Congress. As a result, though respected by most of his peers in the House, he never regained a position of leadership in that body. In one of the ironies of the war, Banks, the consummate Speaker, parliamentarian, and statesmanlike politician, almost Lincolnesque in his sympathy and concern for the defeated South and in his desire to reunite the nation in equanimity and a spirit of forgiveness, was left without a major role in molding the nation's future.

APPENDIX

Composition of the Union Army, Department of the Gulf, during the Red River Expedition

Roster as of March 31, 1864.[1]

Department Commander, Maj. Gen. Nathaniel P. Banks
- XIII Army Corps (Detachment), Brig. Gen. Thomas E. G. Ransom
  - 3rd Division, Brig. Gen. Robert A. Cameron
    - 1st Brigade, Lt. Col. Aaron M. Flory
      - 46th Indiana, Capt. William M. DeHart
      - 29th Wisconsin, Maj. Bradford Hancock
    - 2nd Brigade, Col. William H. Raynor
      - 24th Iowa, Maj. Edward Wright
      - 28th Iowa, Col. John Connell
      - 56th Ohio, Capt. Maschil Manring
    - Artillery
      - 1st Missouri Light, Battery A, Lt. Elisha Cole
      - Ohio Light, 2nd Battery, Lt. William H. Harper
  - 4th Division, Col. William J. Landram
    - 1st Brigade, Col. Frank Emerson
      - 77th Illinois, Lt. Col. Lysander R. Webb
      - 67th Indiana, Maj. Francis A. Sears
      - 19th Kentucky, Lt. Col. John Cowan
      - 23rd Wisconsin, Maj. Joseph E. Greene
    - 2nd Brigade, Col. Joseph W. Vance
      - 97th Illinois, Col. Friend S. Rutherford
      - 130th Illinois, Maj. John B. Reid
      - 48th Ohio, Lt. Col. Joseph W. Lindsey
      - 83rd Ohio, Lt. Col. William H. Baldwin
      - 96th Ohio, Lt. Col. Albert H. Brown
    - Artillery
      - Chicago Mercantile Battery, Lt. Pinckney S. Cone
      - Indiana Light, 1st Battery, Capt. Martin Klauss
- XIX Army Corps, Maj. Gen. William B. Franklin
  - 1st Division, Brig. Gen. William H. Emory

1st Brigade, Brig. Gen. William Dwight
29th Maine, Col. George L. Beal
114th New York, Lt. Col. Henry B. Morse
116th New York, Col. George M. Love
153rd New York, Col. Edwin P. Davis
161st New York, Lt. Col. William B. Kinsey
2nd Brigade, Brig. Gen. James W. McMillan
13th Maine, Col. Henry Rust Jr.
15th Maine, Col. Isaac Dyer
160th New York, Lt. Col. John B. Van Petten
47th Pennsylvania, Col. Tilghman H. Good
3rd Brigade, Col. Lewis Benedict
30th Maine, Col. Francis Fessenden
162nd New York, Lt. Col. Justus W. Blanchard
165th New York, Lt. Col. Gouverneur Carr
173rd New York, Col. Lewis M. Peck
Artillery, Capt. George T. Hebard
New York Light, 25th Battery, Lt. Irving D. Southworth
1st United States, Battery L, Lt. Franck E. Taylor
Vermont Light, 1st Battery, Capt. George T. Hebard
2nd Division, Brig. Gen. Cuvier Grover
2nd Brigade, Col. Edward L. Molineux
13th Connecticut, Col. Charles D. Blinn
1st Louisiana, Col. William O. Fiske
90th New York (three companies), Maj. John C. Smart
159th New York, Lt. Col. Edward L. Gaul
3rd Brigade, Col. Jacob Sharpe
38th Massachusetts, Lt. Col. James P. Richardson
128th New York, Col. James Smith
156th New York, Capt. James J. Hoyt
175th New York (three companies), Capt. Charles McCarthey
Artillery, Capt. George W. Fox
Massachusetts Light, 7th Battery (or Battery G), Capt. Newman W. Storer
New York Light, 26th Battery, Capt. George W. Fox
1st United States, Battery F, Lt. Hardman P. Norris
2nd United States, Battery C, Lt. John I. Rodgers

Cavalry
3rd Maryland, Col. C. Carroll Tevis
Artillery Reserve, Capt. Henry W. Closson
Delaware Light, 1st Battery, Capt. Benjamin Nields
1st Indiana Heavy (two companies), Capt. William S. Hinkle
Corps D'Afrique, 1st Brigade, 1st Division, Col. William H. Dickey
1st Infantry (73rd U.S. Colored Troops),[2] Maj. Hiram E. Perkins
3rd Infantry (75th U.S. Colored Troops), Col. Henry W. Fuller
12th Infantry (84th U.S. Colored Troops), Capt. James H. Corrin
22nd Infantry (92nd U.S. Colored Troops), Col. Henry N. Frisbie
Cavalry, Brig. Gen. Albert L. Lee
1st Brigade, Col. Thomas J. Lucas
16th Indiana Infantry (mounted), Lt. Col. James H. Redfield
2nd Louisiana Infantry (mounted), Maj. Alfred Hodsdon
6th Missouri, Capt. Sidney A. Breese (6th Missouri Howitzer Battery attached, Capt. Herbert H. Rottaken)
14th New York, Maj. Abraham Bassford
3rd Brigade, Col. Harai Robinson
87th Illinois Infantry (mounted), Lt. Col. John M. Crebs
1st Louisiana, Maj. Algernon S. Badger
4th Brigade, Col. Nathan A. M. Dudley
2nd Illinois, Maj. Benjamin F. Marsh Jr.
3rd Massachusetts, Lt. Col. Lorenzo D. Sargent
31st Massachusetts Infantry (mounted), Capt. Elbert H. Fordham
2nd New Hampshire (combined with 8th New Hampshire Infantry [mounted]), Lt. Col. George A. Flanders
5th Brigade, Col. Oliver P. Gooding
2nd New York Veteran, Col. Morgan H. Chrysler
18th New York, Col. James J. Byrne
3rd Rhode Island (detachment), Maj. George R. Davis
Artillery
Massachusetts Light, 2nd Battery (or Battery B), Capt. Ormand F. Nims

5th United States, Battery G, Lt. Jacob B. Rawles
Army of the Tennessee (detachment), Brig. Gen. Andrew J. Smith
1st Division, XVI Army Corps, Brig. Gen. Joseph A. Mower
2nd Brigade, Col. Lucius F. Hubbard
47th Illinois, Col. John D. McClure
5th Minnesota, Maj. John C. Becht
8th Wisconsin, Lt. Col. John W. Jefferson
3rd Brigade, Col. Sylvester G. Hill
35th Iowa, Lt. Col. William B. Keeler
33rd Missouri, Lt. Col. William H. Heath
3rd Division, XVI Army Corps, Brig. Gen. Andrew J. Smith
1st Brigade, Col. William F. Lynch
58th Illinois, Maj. Thomas Newlan
119th Illinois, Col. Thomas J. Kinney
89th Indiana, Col. Charles D. Murray
2nd Brigade, Col. William T. Shaw
14th Iowa, Lt. Col. Joseph H. Newbold
27th Iowa, Col. James I. Gilbert
32nd Iowa, Col. John Scott
24th Missouri, Maj. Robert W. Fyan
3rd Brigade, Col. Risdon M. Moore
49th Illinois, Maj. Thomas W. Morgan
117th Illinois, Lt. Col. Jonathan Merriam
178th New York, Col. Edward Wehler
Artillery, Capt. James M. Cockefair
Indiana Light, 3rd Battery, Capt. James M. Cockefair
Indiana Light, 9th Battery, Capt. George R. Brown
Provisional Division, XVII Army Corps, Brig. Gen. T. Kilby Smith
1st Brigade, Col. Jonathan B. Moore
41st Illinois, Lt. Col. John H. Nale
3rd Iowa, Lt. Col. James Tullis
33rd Wisconsin, Maj. Horatio H. Virgin
2nd Brigade, Col. Lyman M. Ward
81st Illinois, Lt. Col. Andrew W. Rogers
95th Illinois, Col. Thomas W. Humphrey
14th Wisconsin, Capt. Carlos M. G. Mansfield
Artillery
1st Missouri Light, Battery M, Lt. John H. Tiemeyer

NOTES

Abbreviations used in notes:

B&L—R. U. Johnson and C. C. Buel, eds., *Battles and Leaders of the Civil War* (New York: Century Press, 1887–88).

CCW—*Report of the Joint Committee on the Conduct of the War,* 38th Cong., 2nd sess., vol. 2, "Red River Expedition" (Washington, D.C.: U.S. Government Printing Office, 1865).

CWL—Roy P. Basler, Marion Dolores Pratt, and Lloyd A. Dunlap, eds., *Collected Works of Abraham Lincoln* (New Brunswick, N.J.: Rutgers University Press, 1953).

LOC—Library of Congress.

MHI—U.S. Army Military History Institute, Carlisle, Penn.

OR—*The War of the Rebellion: A Compilation of the Official Records of the Union and Confederate Armies,* 70 vols. in 128 pts., compiled by Robert N. Scott (Washington, D.C.: U.S. Government Printing Office, 1880–1901).

OR Navies—*Official Records of the Union and Confederate Navies in the War of the Rebellion,* 30 vols. (Washington, D.C.: U.S. Government Printing Office, 1894–1922).

PROLOGUE

1. P. F. Parsiot, *Reminiscences of a Texas Missionary* (San Antonio: Johnson Bros., 1899), 56. See Robert L. Kerby, *Kirby Smith's Confederacy* (New York: Columbia University Press, 1972), 182.

2. See Frank L. Owsley, *King Cotton Diplomacy,* 2nd ed. rev. by Harriet C. Owsley (Chicago: University of Chicago Press, 1959); Robert E. May, ed., *The Union, the Confederacy, and the Atlantic Rim* (West Lafayette, Ind.: Purdue University Press, 1995), 5; Ephraim Douglass Adams, *Great Britain and the American Civil War* (New York: Longmans, Green, 1925; repr., New York: Russell & Russell, n.d.), 2:7; Nathan Rosenburg, "The Economic Consequences of Technological Change, 1830–1880," in *Technology in Western Civilization,* ed. Melvin Kranzberg and Carroll W. Pursell Jr. (New York: Oxford University Press, 1967), 1:520; James M. McPherson, *Battle Cry of Freedom, the Civil War Era* (New York: Oxford University Press, 1988), 39.

3. E. Merton Coulter, *History of the South,* vol. 7, *The Confederate States of America 1861–1865* (Baton Rouge: Louisiana State University Press, 1950), 241–42, gives the number of bales for 1861 as 4.5 million. E. B. Long, *The Civil War Day by Day* (Garden City, N.Y.: Doubleday, 1971), 722, cites production in the South of 5,192,744.5 ginned cotton bales for the year 1860. McPherson, *Battle Cry of Freedom,* 100, cites 4 million bales as nominal annual production for the late 1850s. Adams, *Great Britain,* 2:7, refers to "nearly four million bales" produced in 1860, "the largest on record."

4. McPherson, *Battle Cry of Freedom,* 383–86, 548. According to McPherson, "The cotton famine from which the South expected so much did not really take hold until the summer of 1862. By then the Confederacy had scuttled its embargo and was trying desperately to export cotton through the tightening blockade to pay for imported supplies" (ibid., 386). See also Richard H. Abbott, *Cotton & Capital, Boston Businessmen and Antislavery Reform, 1854–1868* (Amherst: University of Massachusetts Press, 1991), 80; Dean B. Mahin, *One War at a Time* (Washington, D.C.: Brassey's, 1999), 83–86; George Winston Smith, "The Banks Expedition of 1862," *Louisiana Historical Quarterly* 26 (April 1943): 347.

5. Lincoln was not the only one bothered by cotton speculators. See W. S. Oldham, letter to J. Davis, January 4, 1864, *The War of the Rebellion: A Compilation of the Official Records of the Union and Confederate Armies* (hereafter cited as *OR,* with series I understood unless otherwise indicated), comp. Robert N. Scott, vol. 34, pt. 2 (Washington, D.C.: U.S. Government Printing Office, 1880–1901), 820–21; Joseph Howard Parks, *General Edmund Kirby Smith, C.S.A.* (Baton Rouge: Louisiana State University Press, 1954), 289.

6. Quoted by Abbott, *Cotton & Capital,* 38. For a discussion of the issue related to cotton and Texas, see Ludwell H. Johnson, *Red River Campaign* (Baltimore, Md.: The Johns Hopkins Press, 1958), 5–11.

7. Frederick Law Olmsted, letters to the New York *Daily Times,* emphasis in original; F. L. Olmsted, *A Journey through Texas, or a Saddle-Trip on the Southwestern Frontier,* ed. John H. Olmsted (New York: Dix, Edwards, 1857; repr., Austin: University of Texas Press, 1978); F. L. Olmsted, *The Cotton Kingdom,* ed. Arthur M. Schlesinger (New York: Alfred A. Knopf, 1953), xl–xli. See also Laura Wood Roper, *FLO, a Biography of Frederick Law Olmsted* (Baltimore, Md.: Johns Hopkins University Press, 1973), 96–97.

8. See Abbott, *Cotton & Capital,* 47–48.

9. J. A. Andrew, letter to G. V. Fox, November 27, 1861, *OR,* 15:412–13. See also Abbott, *Cotton & Capital,* 78; Cecil D. Eby Jr., ed., *A Virginia Yankee in the Civil War, the Diaries of David Hunter Strother* (Chapel Hill: University of North Carolina Press, 1961), 130.

10. See J. G. Randall, *Lincoln the President* (New York: Dodd, Mead, 1945–55), 1:161; Ralph A. Wooster, *Texas and Texans in the Civil War* (Austin: Eakin Press, 1995), 114; Richard N. Current, *Lincoln's Loyalists, Union Soldiers from the Confederacy* (New York: Oxford University Press, 1992), 93–103; Dudley G. Wooten, ed., *A Comprehensive History of Texas 1685 to 1897* (Dallas: William G. Scarff, 1898; repr., Austin: Texas State Historical Association, 1986), 2:563–70.

11. See Richard B. McCaslin, *Tainted Breeze: The Great Hanging at Gainesville, Texas, 1862* (Baton Rouge: Louisiana State University Press, 1994); Wooster, *Texas and Texans,* 115; B. P. Gallaway, ed., *Texas, the Dark Corner of the Confederacy,* 3rd ed. (Lincoln: University of Nebraska Press, 1994), 109–24.

12. L. Pierce Jr., letters to W. H. Seward, March 1 and May 5, 1862, *OR,* 9:674, 684–85; C. B. H. Blood, letter to W. H. Seward, May 23, 1862, *OR,* 9:685–86. See also Charles Hunter, letter to W. H. Seward, June 16, 1862, *OR,* 15:522.

13. A brief summary of the events leading to this action can be found in J. G. Randall and Richard N. Current, *Lincoln the President* (New York: Dodd, Mead, 1955), 4:64. See also Carl Sandburg, *Abraham Lincoln, the War Years* (New York: Charles Scribner's Sons, 1939), 1:655; Joan Haslip, *The Crown of Mexico: Maximilian and His Empress Carlota* (New York: Holt, Rinehart and Winston, 1971), 155–68; Mahin, *One War at a Time,* 101, 111, 115, 118.

14. Napoleon III, letter to E. Forney, July 3, 1862. Quoted by Thomas Schoonover, "Napoleon Is Coming! Maximilian Is Coming? The International History of the Civil War in the Caribbean Basin," in May, *Union, the Confederacy,* 117. See also John G. Nicolay and John Hay, *Abraham Lincoln, a History* (New York: Century, 1890), 6:33–34; Allan Nevins, *The War for the Union,* vol. 2, *War Becomes Revolution 1862–1863* (New York: Charles Scribner's Sons, 1960), 259–60; Mahin, *One War at a Time,* 220.

15. This treaty was formally termed the "Convention between Great Britain, Spain, and France, Relative to Combined Operations against Mexico," signed in London October 31, 1861. The United States was invited to join the pact but refused. See Edward Hertslet, *A Complete Collection of the Treaties and Conventions, and Reciprocal Regulations, at Present Subsisting between Great Britain and Foreign Powers* (Edinburgh: Morrison & Gibb, 1905), 12:474–76; Adams, *Great Britain,* 1:259–62; Jay Monaghan, *Diplomat in Carpet Slippers, Abraham Lincoln Deals with Foreign Affairs* (New York: Bobbs-Merrill, 1945), 151–54, 204–11; Howard Jones, *Union in Peril, the Crisis over British Intervention in the Civil War* (Chapel Hill: University of North Carolina Press, 1992), 76–77, 114–15; Alfred J. Hanna and Kathryn A. Hanna, *Napoleon III and Mexico: American Triumph over Monarchy* (Chapel Hill: University of North Carolina Press, 1971), 42–45.

16. Leopold I, letter to Maximilian, October 25, 1861. The quotation is from James M. McPherson, "The Whole Family of Man, Lincoln and the Last Best Hope Abroad," in May, *Union, the Confederacy,* 138. See also A. R. Tyrner-Tyrnauer, *Lincoln and the Emperors* (New York: Harcourt, Brace & World, 1962), 69; Mahin, *One War at a Time,* 220; Monaghan, *Diplomat in Carpet Slippers,* 355. Maximilian did not arrive in Mexico until May 28, 1864.

17. See Sandburg, *Abraham Lincoln, the War Years* 2:395–96; David Herbert Donald, *Lincoln* (New York: Simon & Schuster, 1995), 320–23.

18. J. M. Mason, letter to J. P. Benjamin, November 8, 1862, *Official Records of the Union and Confederate Navies in the War of the Rebellion* (hereafter cited as *OR Navies,* with series I understood unless otherwise indicated) (Washington, D.C.: U.S. Government Printing Office, 1894–1922), ser. II, 3:602–3; Henry Hotze, letter to J. P. Benjamin, November 22, 1862, ibid., 610–11. See also Randall and Current, *Lincoln the President,* 4:55; Adams, *Great Britain,* 2:62; Mahin, *One War at a Time,* 136, 220–23.

19. G. B. McClellan, letter to A. Lincoln, August 2, 1861, *The Civil War Papers of George B. McClellan,* ed. Stephen W. Sears (New York: Ticknor & Fields, 1989), 71–75. Lincoln read this letter to his cabinet on August 3. For a discussion of other early proposals for military campaigns in Texas, see Smith, "Banks Expedition of 1862," 341–42. Related proposals came from former Whig congressman Edward S. Hamlin and Post-

master General Montgomery Blair, as well as from Gens. Benjamin F. Butler and John C. Frémont.

20. G. B. McClellan, letter to D. Hunter, in Sears, *Civil War Papers,* 144–45, 157–58. Lincoln wrote Stanton January 31, 1862, indicating that the "expedition commonly called the 'Lane Expedition' shall be as much as promised . . . *and not any more.* I have not intended, and do not now intend that it shall be *a great exhausting affair;* but a snug, sober column of 10,000 or 15,000" (Roy P. Basler, Marion Dolores Pratt, and Lloyd A. Dunlap, eds., *Collected Works of Abraham Lincoln* [New Brunswick, N.J.: Rutgers University Press, 1953] [hereafter cited as *CWL*], 5:115–16, emphasis in original).

21. See Nicolay and Hay, *Abraham Lincoln,* 4:298–303; Rowena Reed, *Combined Operations in the Civil War* (Annapolis, Md.: United States Naval Institute, 1978), 5–10; Shelby Foote, *The Civil War—a Narrative,* vol. 1, *Fort Sumter to Perryville* (New York: Random House, 1958), 11–13; James M. McPherson, *Ordeal by Fire* (New York: Alfred A. Knopf, 1982), 206–207; T. Harry Williams, *Lincoln and His Generals* (New York: Alfred A. Knopf, 1952), 15–16.

CHAPTER 1

1. As a general assertion, this was proven wrong repeatedly during the war, but by the time the lesson was learned, it was too late to change the early appointments. See H. W. Halleck, letter to W. T. Sherman, April 29, 1864, *OR,* vol. 34, pt. 3, 333; *OR Navies,* 26:56; Smith, "Banks Expedition of 1862," 351–52; Stephen B. Oates, *With Malice toward None* (New York: Harper & Row, 1977), 239.

2. Williams, *Lincoln and His Generals,* 8. According to Williams, the appointment of politicians to military command was "completely political but completely sound in a military sense" because the president's use of such military patronage helped unite the North in support of the war.

3. Biographical information on Banks can be found in Fred Harvey Harrington, *Fighting Politician: Major General N. P. Banks* (Philadelphia: University of Pennsylvania Press, 1948); and James G. Hollandsworth Jr., *Pretense of Glory, the Life of General Nathaniel P. Banks* (Baton Rouge: Louisiana State University Press, 1998). For additional information on Banks's prewar career, see David M. Potter, *The Impending Crisis 1848–1861* (New York: Harper & Row, 1976), 256–59. See also Michael F. Holt, *Political Parties and American Political Development from the Age of Jackson to the Age of Lincoln* (Baton Rouge: Louisiana State University Press, 1992); and William E. Gienapp, *The Origins of the Republican Party, 1852–1856* (New York: Oxford University Press, 1987).

4. Boston *Evening Post,* May 26, 1851. See Harrington, *Fighting Politician,* 14. The Massachusetts House unanimously passed a resolution of thanks to Banks for the "eminent ability, impartiality, and courtesy with which the duties of the chair have been administered" (Boston *Evening Post;* see Hollandsworth, *Pretense of Glory,* 14).

5. N. P. Banks, letter to Mary Banks, May 3, 1853, N. P. Banks Papers, Library of Congress (hereafter cited as LOC; a microfilm copy of the Banks Papers, formerly at the Essex Institute in Salem, Massachusetts, is now in the Ramsdell Collection at the Center

for American History, University of Texas at Austin). Regarding the motivation behind the Massachusetts constitutional convention, see David Donald, *Charles Sumner and the Coming of the Civil War* (New York: Alfred A. Knopf, 1961), 244–45.

6. Edward L. Pierce, *Memoir and Letters of Charles Sumner* (Boston: Roberts Brothers, 1877–93), 3:420.

7. Quoted by Hollandsworth, *Pretense of Glory,* 17. See Harrington, *Fighting Politician,* 16–17. Unfortunately for the delegates who had worked so hard on the document, the new constitution was rejected by the voters November 11, 1853.

8. During the contest for Speaker there was an undercurrent of violence that apparently included bringing arms into the House chamber. It was in this environment that Albert Rust of Arkansas physically attacked Horace Greeley of the New York *Tribune* (L. D. Ingersoll, *The Life of Horace Greeley* [Philadelphia: John E. Potter, 1874], 302–303; Hollandsworth, *Pretense of Glory,* 26).

9. Quoted by Ingersoll, *Life of Horace Greeley,* 303–304. Ingersoll added: "In after years he [Banks] became the most influential man on the floor, and the only member of the XLIId Congress—1871–73—who always received universal attention the moment he pronounced 'Mr. Speaker.'" For other complimentary references to Banks as Speaker, including that of Alexander H. Stephens, who called him "the most impartial Speaker I ever saw," see Harrington, *Fighting Politician,* 31–32; Hollandsworth, *Pretense of Glory,* 28.

10. See *CWL,* 4:147–48. George S. Boutwell told Banks that "had you remained in New England there would be no second man thought of" (G. Boutwell to N. P. Banks, March 3, 1861; quoted by Harrington, *Fighting Politician,* 52–53; Hollandsworth, *Pretense of Glory,* 43; see Randall, *Lincoln the President,* 1:261–62).

11. There is some controversy over the exact ranking of Lincoln's early appointments to major general. McClellan and Frémont were appointed to the grade of major general in the Regular Army to rank from May 14, 1861. John A. Dix, Benjamin F. Butler, and N. P. Banks, in that order, were appointed major generals of volunteers to rank from May 16, 1861. These latter nominations were all sent to the Senate July 29 for approval; Dix and Banks were confirmed August 3, and Butler was confirmed August 5 (see *CWL,* 4:370, 463; John H. Eicher and David J. Eicher, *Civil War High Commands* [Stanford, Calif.: Stanford University Press, 2001], 32–34, 702–703; Sears, *Civil War Papers,* 546 [see prologue, n. 19]; Frank Moore, ed., *The Rebellion Record: A Diary of American Events* [New York: D. Van Nostrand, 1862–71], 7:340).

12. David D. Porter, *Incidents and Anecdotes of the Civil War* (New York: D. Appleton, 1885), 218–19.

13. Eby, *Virginia Yankee,* 147. Banks summed up his attitude succinctly when he wrote, "The universe is the patrimony of patient men" (N. P. Banks, *The Reconstruction of States, Letter of Major-General Banks to Senator Lane* [New York: Harper & Brothers, 1865], 6).

14. Boston *Semi-Weekly Journal,* October 31, 1865. See Harrington, *Fighting Politician,* 60, 125–26. See also Eby, *Virginia Yankee,* 22; *American Annual Cyclopedia and Register of Important Events* (New York: D. Appleton, 1861), 1:451, 576; W. B. Hessel-

tine, *Lincoln and the War Governors* (New York: Alfred A. Knopf, 1948), 109, 111; General Orders No. 26, *OR*, 5:747; F. H. Harrington, "A Peace Mission of 1863," *American Historical Review* 46 (1940): 76–86; Hollandsworth, *Pretense of Glory*, 254–57.

15. See Sears, *Civil War Papers*, 344 (see prologue, n. 19). For a detailed discussion of the policy of conciliation, see Mark Grimsley, *The Hard Hand of War, Union Military Policy toward Southern Civilians 1861–1865* (New York: Cambridge University Press, 1995), esp. chap. 2. See also Banks, *Reconstruction of States*, 14.

16. For biographical information on Frémont, see Tom Chaffin, *Pathfinder: John Charles Frémont and the Course of American Empire* (New York: Hill & Wang, 2002); Allan Nevins, *Frémont, Pathmarker of the West* (New York: D. Appleton-Century, 1939). For biographical information on Butler, see Chester G. Hearn, *When the Devil Came Down to Dixie* (Baton Rouge: Louisiana State University Press, 1997); Dick Nolan, *Benjamin Franklin Butler* (Novato, Calif.: Presidio Press, 1991); Hans L. Trefousse, *Ben Butler* (New York: Twayne Publishers, 1957); Robert S. Holzman, *Stormy Ben Butler* (New York: Macmillan, 1954).

17. See, e.g., General Orders No. 26, March 13, 1862, *OR*, 5:747; Harrington, *Fighting Politician*, 64–65.

18. N. P. Banks, dispatch to E. M. Stanton, April 30, 1862, *OR*, vol. 12, pt. 3, 118.

19. The strength of the opposing forces is discussed by several historians of the Valley campaign. Regarding the Union forces, see N. P. Banks, dispatch to E. M. Stanton, May 21, 1862, *OR*, 15:523. See also Matthew F. Steele, *American Campaigns* (Harrisburg, Penn.: Military Service Publishing, 1949), 1:226; William Allen, *Stonewall Jackson's Valley Campaign* (Boston: Houghton Mifflin, 1892; repr., New York: Smithmark Publishers, 1995), 249.

20. N. P. Banks, letter to Mary Banks, May 28, 1862, Banks Papers, LOC.

21. Harrington, *Fighting Politician*, 78; Hollandsworth, *Pretense of Glory*, 69. Both biographers conclude that Banks showed "unwillingness" to learn from experience.

22. Thomas L. Livermore, *Numbers & Losses in the Civil War* (Boston: Houghton Mifflin, 1901; repr., Bloomington: Indiana University Press, 1957), 87–88; Robert K. Krick, *Stonewall Jackson at Cedar Mountain* (Chapel Hill: University of North Carolina Press, 1990), 45. See also Mark M. Boatner III, *The Civil War Dictionary*, rev. ed. (New York: David McKay, 1988), 102, who gives slightly different numbers.

23. Harrington, *Fighting Politician*, 84. Horace Greeley attributed the loss to Jackson's superior numbers: "We were not so much beaten as fairly crowded off the field" (*The American Conflict: A History of the Great Rebellion in the United States of America, 1860–65* [Hartford, Conn.: O. D. Case, 1866], 2:177).

24. Henry Kid Douglas, *I Rode With Stonewall* (Chapel Hill: University of North Carolina Press, 1940), 50.

CHAPTER 2

1. Eby, *Virginia Yankee*, 77. N. P. Banks, letter to Mary Banks, August 16, 1862, Banks Papers; also undated manuscript, "How Banks Was Injured," Banks Papers, LOC.

2. N. P. Banks, General Orders No. 1, September 8, 1862, *OR*, vol. 19, pt. 2, 214;

R. B. Irwin, *History of the Nineteenth Army Corps* (New York: G. P. Putnam's Sons, 1892), 55; Hollandsworth, *Pretense of Glory,* 81–82.

3. E. D. Townsend, General Orders No. 184, November 8, 1862, *OR,* 15:590.

4. See *CWL,* 5:485; H. W. Halleck, letter to N. P. Banks, November 9, 1862, *OR,* 15:590–91. See also *Report of the Joint Committee on the Conduct of the War,* 38th Cong., 2nd sess., vol. 2, "Red River Expedition" (Washington, D.C.: U.S. Government Printing Office, 1865 [hereafter cited as *CCW*]), iii–iv.

5. H. W. Halleck, letter to N. P. Banks, November 9, 1862, *OR,* 15:590–91.

6. E. M. Stanton, letter to Governors of New York, Massachusetts, Connecticut, Vermont, Rhode Island, Maine, and New Hampshire, October 28, 1862, *OR,* ser. III, 2:692. See Smith, "Banks Expedition of 1862," 351–54; Eby, *Virginia Yankee,* 127–28.

7. John L. Waller, *Colossal Hamilton of Texas: A Biography of Andrew Jackson Hamilton* (El Paso: Texas Western Press, 1968), 22–23; Eicher and Eicher, *Civil War High Commands,* 275.

8. Harrington, *Fighting Politician,* 134; *OR,* 15:201.

9. *CWL,* 5:505–506. See also A. Lincoln, letter to N. P. Banks, November 22, 1862, *OR,* ser. III, 2:862.

10. H. W. Halleck, dispatch to N. P. Banks, November 22, 1862, and N. P. Banks, dispatch to H. W. Halleck, of the same date, *OR,* ser. III, 2:863. Excessive paraphernalia was a common problem in the Union army. On October 18, 1862, in General Orders No. 160, by order of General Halleck, the adjutant general's office placed restrictions on army trains and baggage (*OR,* ser. III, 2:671–72).

11. N. P. Banks, letter to A. Lincoln, November 24, 1862, *OR,* ser. III, 2:865. T. Harry Williams noted that the weak excuse Banks offered to Lincoln over this incident was "a measure of the man" (Williams, *Lincoln and His Generals,* 188).

12. For a description of some of the vessels that were assembled, see George H. Hepworth, *The Whip, Hoe and Sword or, The Gulf-Department in '63* (Boston: Walker, Wise, 1864; repr., Baton Rouge: Louisiana State University Press, 1979), 213–14; William B. Stevens, *History of the Fiftieth Regiment of Infantry, Massachusetts Volunteer Militia in the Late War of the Rebellion* (Boston: Griffith-Stillings Press, 1907), 43–44.

13. Eby, *Virginia Yankee,* 134–35.

14. James Parton, *General Butler in New Orleans* (New York: Mason Brothers, 1863), 599. According to Parton, General Butler "gave General Banks a cordial and brilliant reception. At Fort Jackson, the arriving general, much to his surprise, was saluted by the number of guns which, by regulation, announce the presence of the commander of the department."

15. Benjamin F. Butler, *Private and Official Correspondence of General Benjamin F. Butler during the Period of the Civil War,* ed. Jessie Ames Marshall (Norwood, Mass.: Plimpton Press, 1917), 2:149. See also Benjamin F. Butler, *Butler's Book, Autobiography and Personal Reminiscences of Major-General Benjamin F. Butler* (Boston: A. M. Thayer, 1892), 526; Parton, *General Butler in New Orleans,* 593, 596–99; Holzman, *Stormy Ben Butler,* 103; Hearn, *When the Devil Came Down,* 213.

16. N. P. Banks, report to E. M. Stanton, April 6, 1865, *OR,* vol. 26, pt. 1, 7–8.

17. Irwin, *History of the Nineteenth Army Corps,* 266–67. These numbers were high but, except for greatly overestimating the size of General Taylor's force in western Louisiana, were not unreasonable (E. K. Smith, report to J. Davis, June 16, 1863, *OR,* vol. 22, pt. 2, 871; Parks, *General Edmund Kirby Smith,* 254–57; *OR,* 15:391, 932).

18. N. P. Banks, report to H. W. Halleck, January 7, 1863, *OR,* 15:639.

19. N. P. Banks, letter to Mary Banks, January 3, 1863, Banks Papers, LOC.

20. See Harrington, *Fighting Politician,* 92–96; Hollandsworth, *Pretense of Glory,* 95–98.

21. General Orders No. 8, January 12, 1863, *OR,* 15:643–45. See also N. P. Banks, dispatch to H. W. Halleck, December 24, 1862, with enclosure, *OR,* 15:616.

22. Eby, *Virginia Yankee,* 145. For a discussion of the bribery and other illegal activity involving cotton speculation and trading while Banks was commander of the Gulf Department, see Johnson, *Red River Campaign,* 53–57.

23. N. P. Banks, letter to Mary Banks, January 16, 1863, Banks Papers, LOC; Harrington, *Fighting Politician,* 135; Hollandsworth, *Pretense of Glory,* 158.

24. The induction of blacks into the Union army in Louisiana was the brainchild and product of the radical abolitionist from Vermont, Brig. Gen. John W. Phelps (James G. Hollandsworth Jr., *The Louisiana Native Guards: The Black Military Experience during the Civil War* [Baton Rouge: Louisiana State University Press, 1991], esp. 13–17; Parton, *General Butler in New Orleans,* 495–516; Peyton McCrary, *Abraham Lincoln and Reconstruction: The Louisiana Experiment* [Princeton, N.J.: Princeton University Press, 1978], 85–87; see also Butler, *Private and Official Correspondence,* 2:125–27, 142–46; B. F. Butler, letter to E. M. Stanton, June 18, 1862, with enclosure from J. W. Phelps, *OR,* 15:485–90; Lincoln's comments can be found in *CWL,* 5:342–43; Butler's General Orders No. 63 can be found in *OR,* 15:556–57).

25. General Orders No. 40, May 1, 1863, *OR,* 15:716–17.

26. There was friction between white troops and black officers, and Banks actively sought to get the black officers to resign or otherwise to remove them from their positions. N. P. Banks, dispatch to L. Thomas, February 12, 1863, *OR,* ser. III, 3:46; *OR,* vol. 26, pt. 1, 689. See also Hollandsworth, *Louisiana Native Guards,* 71–78; Irwin, *History of the Nineteenth Army Corps,* 49–50; *OR,* vol. 26, pt. 1, 688–89; Harrington, *Fighting Politician,* 110–11; Joseph T. Glatthaar, *Forged in Battle, the Civil War Alliance of Black Soldiers and White Officers* (New York: Free Press, 1990), 36; Hollandsworth, *Pretense of Glory,* 148–49.

27. General Orders No. 12, January 29, 1863, *OR,* 15:666–67. See McCrary, *Abraham Lincoln and Reconstruction,* 115–20.

28. T. Harry Williams, *Lincoln and the Radicals* (Madison: University of Wisconsin Press, 1965), 275. Banks was aware of the imperfections of this labor system but was convinced that it was the best that could be offered under the circumstances (*OR,* 15:667).

29. Harrington, *Fighting Politician,* 94. See Wickham Hoffman, *Camp Court and Siege* (New York: Harper & Brothers, 1877), 111. The term "dancing master" may also have

been a reference to Banks's conciliatory policy. See John Beatty, *The Citizen-Soldier; or, Memoirs of a Volunteer* (Cincinnati: Wilstach, Baldwin, 1879), 152; Grimsley, *Hard Hand of War,* 85; P. Drayton, letter, April 8, 1864, *Naval Letters from Captain Percival Drayton, 1861–1865,* printed from the original manuscripts presented to the New York Public Library by Gertrude L. Hoyt, New York, 1906, 48–49.

30. In late 1862 Butler held elections to fill the seats in two Louisiana congressional districts that were within the area of Union control. The Union voters elected Michael Hahn and Benjamin F. Flanders to fill the vacancies. After being initially rejected by the House, both of these men eventually took their seats in Congress (John D. Winters, *The Civil War in Louisiana* [Baton Rouge: Louisiana State University Press, 1963], 133–34; McCrary, *Abraham Lincoln and Reconstruction,* 102–107; Amos E. Simpson and Vaughn Baker, "Michael Hahn: Steady Patriot," *Louisiana History* 13 [1972]: 229–33).

31. Stewart Sifakis, *Who Was Who in the Civil War* (New York: Facts on File, 1988), 586–87; Parton, *General Butler in New Orleans,* 336–40, 371. A discussion of the appointment of treasury agents by Chase, and the related political ambitions of the latter during the 1864 presidential election, is presented by Randall and Current, *Lincoln the President,* 4:104–10; and by John Niven, *Salmon P. Chase, A Biography* (New York: Oxford University Press, 1995), 315–20.

32. While leaving Shepley's civil responsibilities intact, Banks removed certain military functions from his purview. See Joseph G. Dawson III, *Army Generals and Reconstruction* (Baton Rouge: Louisiana State University Press, 1982), 12–14.

CHAPTER 3

1. See, e.g., Chester G. Hearn, *The Capture of New Orleans 1862* (Baton Rouge: Louisiana State University Press, 1995); Charles L. Dufour, *The Night the War Was Lost* (Garden City, N.Y.: Doubleday, 1960).

2. *CWL,* 5:495; *OR Navies,* 19:342.

3. D. G. Farragut, dispatch to H. H. Bell, December 22, 1862, *OR Navies,* 19:421.

4. See Harold B. Simpson, "The Battle of Sabine Pass," in *Battles of Texas,* ed. Seymour Connor, 141–42 (Waco: Texian Press, 1967); Donald S. Frazier, *Cottonclads! The Battle of Galveston and the Defense of the Texas Coast* (Abilene, Tex.: McWhiney Foundation Press, McMurry University, 1998), 27–34; Edward T. Cotham Jr., *Battle on the Bay, the Civil War Struggle for Galveston* (Austin: University of Texas Press, 1998), 69. See also Charles Lee Lewis, *David Glasgow Farragut, Our First Admiral* (Annapolis, Md.: United States Naval Institute, 1943), 148–50.

5. N. P. Banks, dispatch to H. W. Halleck, January 7, 1863, *OR,* 15:200–201.

6. For background information on this regiment, see Cotham, *Battle on the Bay,* 73–79; Charles P. Bosson, *History of the Forty-second Regiment Infantry, Massachusetts Volunteers, 1862, 1863, 1864* (Boston: Mills, Knight, 1886).

7. W. B. Renshaw, report to D. G. Farragut, October 8, 1862, *OR Navies,* 19:259–60, 317–18.

8. Isaac S. Burrell, dispatch to N. P. Banks, December 29, 1862, *OR,* 15:204–205.

9. For biographical data on Magruder, see Paul D. Casdorph, *Prince John Magruder, His Life and Campaigns* (New York: John Wiley & Sons, 1996).

10. "Cottonclad" refers to the "armoring" of a boat by stacking bales of cotton on the deck to provide protection from enemy gunfire. This technique for strengthening river craft was used frequently by the Confederates. See Frazier, *Cottonclads!* 48–50.

11. X. B. Debray, *A Sketch of the History of Debray's (26th) Regiment of Texas Cavalry* (Austin: E. Von Boeckmann, 1884), 7. See also X. B. Debray, "A Sketch of Debray's Twenty-sixth Regiment of Texas Cavalry, Paper No. 1," *Southern Historical Society Papers* 12 (1885): 551.

12. Wooten, *Comprehensive History of Texas,* 2:532; Cotham, *Battle of the Bay,* 120–22.

13. W. L. Burt, report to N. P. Banks, January 7, 1863, *OR Navies,* 19:455–57.

14. Frank J. Welcher, *The Union Army 1861–1865,* vol. 2, *The Western Theater* (Bloomington: Indiana University Press, 1993), 55; Frazier, *Cottonclads!* 82–83; Cotham, *Battle on the Bay,* 126–29. See also General Orders No. 38, January 7, 1863, *OR Navies,* 19:463–64. Fox gave this response to these events in Galveston: "It is too cowardly to place on paper. Poor Wainwright did well. Renshaw—bah—he is dead" (Letter to D. D. Porter, February 6, 1863, in *Confidential Correspondence of Gustavus Vasa Fox,* ed. Robert M. Thompson and Richard Wainwright [New York: Naval History Society, 1920], 2:156; Lewis, *David Glasgow Farragut, Our First Admiral,* 157).

15. *OR,* 15:200–220; *OR Navies,* 19:457–62; *OR,* vol. 26, pt. 1, 7; Eicher and Eicher, *Civil War High Commands,* 91, 265, 360. Magruder and others also received the thanks of the Texas legislature (*OR,* 15:221).

16. Wooten, *Comprehensive History of Texas,* 2:533; Cotham, *Battle on the Bay,* 140–41.

17. N. P. Banks, report to H. W. Halleck, January 7, 1863, *OR,* 15:200–201. The comments by Farragut to which Banks refers were made in a letter to General Butler dated October 14, 1862 (*OR Navies,* 19:300). Regarding Butler's plan to send a force to Galveston, see *OR,* 15:588, 591–92. See also Current, *Lincoln's Loyalists,* 98; Johnson, *Red River Campaign,* 28.

18. T. M. Buchanan, report to B. F. Butler, November 4, 1862, *OR,* 15:183–85. See also *OR Navies,* ser. II, 1:251. The *Cotton* was occasionally, and incorrectly, referred to as the *J. A. Cotton* (see, e.g., *OR,* 15:89, 234, 1087). The latter name, or alternatively *Cotton II,* was applied to the tender *Mary T* (Gary Dillard Joiner, *One Damn Blunder from Beginning to End, the Red River Campaign of 1864* [Lanham, Md.: SR Books, 2003], 18).

19. Ezra J. Warner, *Generals in Blue: Lives of the Union Commanders* (Baton Rouge: Louisiana State University Press, 1964), 548–49; Sifakis, *Who Was Who,* 703; Patricia L. Faust, ed., *Historical Times Illustrated Encyclopedia of the Civil War* (New York: Harper & Row, 1986), 812. See Hearn, *When the Devil Came Down,* 195, 208.

20. Sifakis, *Who Was Who,* 461; Eicher and Eicher, *Civil War High Commands,* 400–401; Ezra J. Warner, *Generals in Gray: Lives of the Confederate Commanders* (Baton

Rouge: Louisiana State University Press, 1959), 222–23; John Dimitry, "Louisiana," in *Confederate Military History,* ed. Clement A. Evans (Atlanta: Confederate Publishing, 1899), 10:311–13.

21. G. Weitzel, dispatch to N. P. Banks, January 15, 1863, *OR,* 15:234. For descriptions of this engagement, see ibid., 234–37; Winters, *Civil War in Louisiana,* 212–14; Richard Taylor, *Destruction and Reconstruction: Personal Experiences of the Late War* (New York: D. Appleton, 1879), 119–21; Alvin M. Josephy Jr., *The Civil War in the American West* (New York: Alfred A. Knopf, 1991), 168; T. Michael Parrish, *Richard Taylor, Soldier Prince of Dixie* (Chapel Hill: University of North Carolina Press, 1992), 264; Morris Raphael, *The Battle in the Bayou Country* (Detroit: Harlo Press, 1975), 67–73.

22. Extract from the Houston *Tri-Weekly Telegraph,* February 2, 1863, *OR Navies,* 19:525. The destruction wrought by Federal troops during a previous incursion along Bayou des Allemands was so flagrant that General Taylor sent a message to General Butler stating that if such plundering continued, he would treat the marauders as robbers rather than as prisoners of war (Taylor, *Destruction and Reconstruction,* 111–12). In his reply to Taylor, Butler stated, "I need not say that acts such as you describe are neither ordered nor tolerated by the Government or by myself" (B. F. Butler, letter to R. Taylor, September 10, 1862, *OR,* 15:565–67).

23. N. P. Banks, letter to H. W. Halleck, February 28, 1863, *OR Navies,* 19:640. According to Farragut, "The Army of General Banks will attack by land or make a reconnaissance in force at the same time that we run the batteries" (D. G. Farragut, letter to G. Welles, March 2, 1863, ibid., 644).

24. Winters, *Civil War in Louisiana,* 214.

25. N. P. Banks, letter to Mary Banks, March 14, 1863, Banks Papers, LOC.

26. See N. P. Banks, report to H. W. Halleck, March 21, 1863, *OR,* 15:251–57; see also *OR Navies,* 19:665–69. The Farragut quote is from Alfred Thayer Mahan, *Admiral Farragut* (New York: D. Appleton, 1892), 213.

27. Banks blamed his inability to assist Farragut on poor maps, the absence of a road, and a lack of warning from Farragut (N. P. Banks, report to H. W. Halleck, March 21, 1863, *OR,* 15:253; see also letter from T. A. Jenkins, quoted by James R. Soley, "Naval Operations in the Vicksburg Campaign," in *Battles and Leaders of the Civil War,* ed. R. U. Johnson and C. C. Buel [New York: Century Press, 1887–88; hereafter cited as *B&L*], 1:566n).

28. Eby, *Virginia Yankee,* 158. See also James K. Hosmer, *The Color Guard: Being a Corporal's Notes of Military Service in the Nineteenth Army Corps* (Boston: Walker, Wise, 1864), 103.

29. G. Weitzel, dispatch to R. B. Irwin, January 18, 1863, *OR,* 15:655–56; Irwin, *History of the Nineteenth Army Corps,* 85–87.

30. N. P. Banks, letter to H. W. Halleck, February 12, 1863, *OR,* 15:240–42. This water route had apparently been suggested by Farragut to facilitate attacking Port Hudson from the north (Eby, *Virginia Yankee,* 148).

31. For biographical information on Taylor, see Parrish, *Richard Taylor;* see also Taylor, *Destruction and Reconstruction.*

32. See Jefferson Davis Bragg, *Louisiana in the Confederacy* (Baton Rouge: Louisiana State University Press, 1941), 253.

33. Douglas Southall Freeman, *Lee's Lieutenants* (New York: Charles Scribner's Sons, 1942), 1:668.

CHAPTER 4

1. N. P. Banks to U. S. Grant, April 10, 1863, Inclosure, *OR,* 15:296. See also Hollandsworth, *Pretense of Glory,* 109; R. Taylor, report to W. R. Boggs, April 23, 1863, *OR,* 15:388–96. Taylor estimated his total force as "less than 4,000," including the detachment sent to Grand Lake (*OR,* 15:391; Taylor, *Destruction and Reconstruction,* 120, 129).

2. G. Weitzel, letter to C. C. Augur, February 15, 1863, *OR,* 15:676–77. Weitzel had tried a similar scheme under Butler in October 1862. See B. F. Butler, dispatch to H. W. Halleck, October 24, 1862, *OR,* 15:159–60. See also G. Weitzel, report to G. C. Strong, October 29, 1862, *OR,* 15:168–70; *OR Navies,* 19:330; John W. De Forest, *A Volunteer's Adventures: A Union Captain's Record of the Civil War* (New Haven, Conn.: Yale University Press, 1946), 66–73.

3. Frank M. Flinn, *Campaigning with Banks in Louisiana, '63 and '64, and with Sheridan in the Shenandoah Valley in '64 and '65* (Lynn, Mass: Thomas P. Nichols, 1887), 41.

4. Colonel Greenleaf and Church's journal, 52nd Massachusetts, quoted by J. F. Moors, *History of the Fifty-second Regiment Massachusetts Volunteers* (Boston: George H. Ellis, 1893), 111–12, 118. The 24th and 25th Connecticut, the 52nd Massachusetts, and Nims's 2nd Massachusetts Battery were all on one of the transports, the *St. Mary.* In addition, there were many horses and a large volume of supplies aboard.

5. C. Grover, report to R. B. Irwin, May 2, 1863, *OR,* 15:357–62; Irwin, *History of the Nineteenth Army Corps,* 106–107. See Donald S. Frazier, "Texans on the Teche: The Texas Brigade at the Battle of Bisland and Irish Bend, April 12–14, 1863," *Louisiana History* 32 (1991): 419–20.

6. Taylor, *Destruction and Reconstruction,* 134. On the other hand, the Southern retreat was apparently conducted with both energy and vigor. See Diary of Lt. Col. A. W. Hyatt, reproduced by Napier Bartlett, *Military Record of Louisiana,* pt. III, "The Trans-Mississippi" (Baton Rouge: Louisiana State University Press, 1964), 9, 11. The retreating Confederates stopped Banks's navy escort by burning and sinking an unfinished ironclad, the *Stevens,* sideways across the channel of the Teche.

7. W. Dwight, dispatch to J. Hibbert, April 27, 1863, *OR,* 15:373.

8. Eby, *Virginia Yankee,* 168–69.

9. Colonel Greenleaf, 52nd Massachusetts, quoted by Moors, *History of the Fifty-second Regiment,* 113.

10. Harris H. Beecher, *Record of the 114th Regiment, NYSV: Where It Went, What It Saw, What It Did* (Norwich, N.Y.: J. F. Hubbard Jr., 1866), 149.

11. D. C. Edmonds, ed., *The Conduct of Federal Troops in Louisiana during the Invasions of 1863 and 1864 . . .* (Lafayette, La.: Acadiana Press, 1988), 15–16. One resident reported, "I can only say it was bedlam let loose" (ibid., 6).

12. Beecher, *Record of the 114th Regiment,* 169–70.

13. General Orders No. 29, *OR,* 15:705–706.

14. N. P. Banks, dispatch to H. W. Halleck, May 2, 1863, *OR,* 15:305–306. In pursuance of General Orders No. 29 General Dwight executed Pvt. Henry Hamill of the 131st New York for "quitting his colors to plunder and pillage" (*OR,* 15:1119; see also *OR,* 15:22–23; Butler, *Private and Official Correspondence,* 2:233).

15. Winters, *Civil War in Louisiana,* 232; Kerby, *Kirby Smith's Confederacy,* 70; Bragg, *Louisiana in the Confederacy,* 83–84, 227. General Taylor had long worried about protecting these valuable salt works (Taylor, *Destruction and Reconstruction,* 114; R. Taylor, dispatch to S. Cooper, November 9, 1862, *OR,* 15:174–76; see also Ella Lonn, *Salt as a Factor in the Confederacy* [New York: W. Neale, 1933], 32–33, 192–93, 208).

16. C. Grover, report to R. B. Irwin, May 2, 1863, *OR,* 15:361. See also W. K. Kimball, report to Captain Hibbert, April 21, 1863, *OR,* 15:382.

17. See David C. Edmonds, *Yankee Autumn in Acadiana* (Lafayette, La.: Acadiana Press, 1979), 85–88; Irwin, *History of the Nineteenth Army Corps,* 124–25.

18. From "J. K. H." and Church's journal, 52nd Massachusetts; quoted by Moors, *History of the Fifty-second Regiment,* 124, 128.

19. R. B. Irwin, dispatch to C. C. Augur, April 18, 1863, *OR,* 15:704.

20. Corporal Hosmer, 52nd Massachusetts, quoted by Moors, *History of the Fifty-second Regiment,* 138–39.

21. N. P. Banks, letter to Mary Banks, May 3, 1863, Banks Papers, LOC.

22. For example, on March 23 Grant indicated his willingness to reinforce Banks with 20,000 men to take Port Hudson and then move to the Black River (*OR,* 15:300). On April 10 Banks told Grant he would "return to Baton Rouge to cooperate with you against Port Hudson. I can be there easily by May 10" (*OR,* 15:296).

23. D. G. Farragut, dispatch to N. P. Banks, May 4, 1863, *OR,* 15:718.

24. De Forest, *Volunteer's Adventures,* 86, 92. According to A. W. Hyatt of Louisiana's Crescent Regiment, the retreat by the Confederate army was "a regular race from the enemy" (Bartlett, *Military Record of Louisiana,* pt. III, "The Trans-Mississippi," 10).

25. N. P. Banks, report to E. M. Stanton, April 5, 1865, *OR,* vol. 26, pt. 1, 11.

26. Howard K. Beale, ed., *The Diary of Gideon Welles* (New York: W. W. Norton, 1960), 1:88, 157. The Porter family included Commodore David Porter, David Dixon Porter's father and naval hero of the war of 1812; Commodore William David Porter, David Dixon's brother; David Glasgow Farragut, David Dixon's foster brother; and Fitz-John Porter, David Dixon's cousin.

27. *CCW,* 27; N. P. Banks, report to H. W. Halleck, May 4, 1863, *OR,* 15:309–11. One observer of these activities wrote, "Cotton is king for the army is doing nothing else but gathering cotton" (Flinn, *Campaigning with Banks in Louisiana,* 62, 65).

28. E. K. Smith, dispatch to T. H. Holmes, May 16, 1863, *OR,* vol. 22, pt. 2, 840.

29. Concerning the number of troops, N. P. Banks, dispatch to U. S. Grant, April 10, 1863, *OR,* 15:295.

30. N. P. Banks, dispatch to S. B. Holabird, May 12, 1863, ibid., 727–28.

31. N. P. Banks, dispatch to U. S. Grant, May 13, 1863, ibid., 732. See also ibid., 300.

32. Special Orders No. 115, May 13, 1863, *OR,* 53:558.

33. M. W. Merrick, *From Desert to Bayou, the Civil War Journal and Sketches of Morgan Wolfe Merrick* (El Paso: Texas Western Press, University of Texas at El Paso, 1991), 43.

34. Quoted by Kerby, *Kirby Smith's Confederacy,* 110. For the reaction of the advancing Confederates to this destruction, see Richard Lowe, *Walker's Texas Division C.S.A., Greyhounds of the Trans-Mississippi* (Baton Rouge: Louisiana State University Press, 2004), 77.

35. N. P. Banks, dispatch to H. W. Halleck, June 4, 1863, *OR,* vol. 26, pt. 1, 535.

36. Ibid., May 30, 1863, 44.

37. Beecher, *Record of the 114th Regiment,* 182. According to Beecher, "Upon the east side of the Teche, Colonel Chickering seized and carried off all the available property, particularly the slaves, while Colonel Per Lee performed the same duty upon the west side." See also Edmonds, *Yankee Autumn,* 106; Edmonds, *Conduct of Federal Troops,* 106–14; A. W. Bergeron Jr., ed., *The Civil War Reminiscences of Major Silas T. Grisamore, C.S.A.* (Baton Rouge: Louisiana State University Press, 1993), 123; Hepworth, *Whip, Hoe, and Sword,* 30.

38. H. W. Halleck, dispatches to N. P. Banks, May 19 and May 23, 1863, *OR,* vol. 26, pt. 1, 494, 500. See Irwin, *History of the Nineteenth Army Corps,* 150–51.

39. N. P. Banks, dispatch to H. W. Halleck, October 16, 1863, *OR,* vol. 26, pt. 1, 767; see also *CCW,* xxi.

40. H. W. Halleck, dispatch to N. P. Banks, June 27, 1863, *OR,* vol. 26, pt. 1, 603. See also ibid., 503, 535, 564–65.

41. Edward Cunningham, *The Port Hudson Campaign, 1862–1863* (Baton Rouge, Louisiana State University Press, 1963), 70, 120–21. In addition to Confederate soldiers there were about 1,100 civilians inside the fort during the siege. The number of Union troops involved varied widely over the period of the siege. Livermore estimates 13,000 Union and 4,192 Confederate troops were engaged in the assault of May 27; 6,000 Union and 3,487 Confederate troops on June 14, 1863 (*Numbers & Losses in the Civil War,* 101 [see chap. 1, n. 23]).

42. N. P. Banks, dispatch to G. Weitzel, May 27, 1863, *OR,* vol. 26, pt. 1, 509–10.

43. N. P. Banks, dispatch to D. G. Farragut, June 12, 1863, *OR Navies,* 20:228.

44. Winters, *Civil War in Louisiana,* 268–73; Cunningham, *Port Hudson Campaign,* 82–93.

45. Public Resolution No. 7, *OR,* vol. 26, pt. 1, 66, 911.

46. See, e.g., Harrington, *Fighting Politician,* 125; Hollandsworth, *Pretense of Glory,*

133; J. Cutler Andrews, *The North Reports the Civil War* (Pittsburgh: University of Pittsburgh Press, 1955), 403.

CHAPTER 5

1. *CWL,* 5:357; 3:499. The most influential of the Texas loyalists were E. J. Davis, J. L. Haynes, and A. J. Hamilton. See Current, *Lincoln's Loyalists,* 95; Waller, *Colossal Hamilton of Texas,* 39–40; Wooster, *Texas and Texans,* 110, 112; Jerry Thompson and Lawrence T. Jones III, *Civil War & Revolution on the Rio Grande Frontier* (Austin: Texas State Historical Association, 2004), 55.

2. For biographical information about Halleck, see John F. Marszalek, *Commander of All Lincoln's Armies, a Life of General Henry W. Halleck* (Cambridge, Mass.: Belknap Press of Harvard University Press, 2004); Stephen E. Ambrose, *Halleck: Lincoln's Chief of Staff* (Baton Rouge: Louisiana State University Press, 1962); Curt Anders, *Henry Halleck's War* (Zionsville: Guild Press of Indiana, 1999).

3. Ambrose, *Halleck,* 65–66. Despite his many shortcomings, Halleck certainly made positive contributions to the war effort in his new position. See, e.g., ibid., 65, 106, 160.

4. Marszalek, *Commander of All Lincoln's Armies,* 158. Marszalek interpreted Halleck's rejection of leadership as a search for a father figure: "During the Civil War, Halleck had power over generals such as McClellan, yet he could not issue orders to them. So he reverted to being a subordinate who did not have to make decisions" (ibid., 252).

5. A. W. Alexander, quoted by Stanley F. Horn, *The Army of Tennessee* (Norman: University of Oklahoma Press, 1941), 160. See also Warner, *Generals in Blue,* 196.

6. Beale, *Diary of Gideon Welles,* 1:364 (see chap. 4, n. 26). See also Joiner, *One Damn Blunder,* 8–9; Tyler Dennett, ed., *Lincoln and the Civil War in the Diaries and Letters of John Hay* (New York: Dodd, Mead, 1939), 164; Jean Edward Smith, *Grant* (New York: Simon & Schuster, 2001), 286. According to Earl Schenck Miers, "With justification Halleck could be called an ambitious schemer, a malicious gossip, a dangerous juggler of the truth, and a man who often mistook his hulking shadow for the image of his innate ability, but no fair-minded critic could call Halleck a fool" (*The Web of Victory* [Baton Rouge: Louisiana State University Press, 1955], 11).

7. *CWL,* 6:364. See also Mahin, *One War at a Time,* 223–25 (see prologue, n. 4).

8. H. W. Halleck, dispatch to N. P. Banks, August 6, 1863, *OR,* vol. 26, pt. 1, 672; see also *CCW,* iv; *CWL,* 6:366. On the same day Halleck sent a similar message to Grant deflecting a proposal from the latter for a campaign against Mobile (*OR,* vol. 24, pt. 3, 558; see also ibid., 584).

9. H. W. Halleck, dispatch to N. P. Banks, August 10, 1863, *OR,* vol. 26, pt. 1, 673; see also *CCW,* iv–v.

10. Irwin, *History of the Nineteenth Army Corps,* 257–58.

11. See Warner, *Generals in Blue,* 159–60; Sifakis, *Who Was Who,* 227–28; Faust, *Historical Times Illustrated Encyclopedia,* 285; Boatner, *Civil War Dictionary,* 303–304; Eicher and Eicher, *Civil War High Commands,* 243.

12. Randall, *Lincoln the President,* 2:63–64. See Bruce Tap, *Over Lincoln's Shoulder, the Committee on the Conduct of the War* (Lawrence: University Press of Kansas, 1998), 24. Franklin published a scathing diatribe against the committee: *A Reply of Maj. Gen. William B. Franklin* (New York: D. Van Nostrand, 1863).

13. H. W. Halleck, dispatch to N. P. Banks, July 31, 1863, *OR,* vol. 26, pt. 1, 664; U. S. Grant, letter to N. P. Banks, August 7, 1863, *OR,* vol. 24, pt. 3, 580; Special Orders No. 214, *OR,* vol. 24, pt. 3, 581.

14. Irwin, *History of the Nineteenth Army Corps,* 258.

15. Beecher, *Record of the 114th Regiment,* 255–56.

16. George Crooke, *The Twenty-first Iowa Volunteer Infantry* (Milwaukee: King, Fowle, 1891), 117. See also De Forest, *Volunteer's Adventures,* 38; Hepworth, *Whip, Hoe, and Sword,* 31, 34.

17. Letter, D. G. Farragut to H. H. Bell, January 30, 1863, *OR Navies,* 19:589–90. According to one student of these events, Farragut mentioned his plan to Banks in July 1863 (Frank X. Tolbert, *Dick Dowling at Sabine Pass, a Texas Incident in the War between the States* [New York: McGraw-Hill, 1962], 57). Farragut may have been referring to such a discussion when, in a message dated July 30, he told the senior officer at Berwick Bay that "Captain Crocker has a little project on hand for the Sachem, which I think well of" (*OR Navies,* 20:428).

18. Edward T. Cotham Jr., *Sabine Pass, the Confederacy's Thermopylae* (Austin: University of Texas Press, 2004), 28–31. Union naval actions along the Texas coast are discussed by Wooster, *Texas and Texans,* 46–47, 62; Lester N. Fitzhugh, "Saluria, Fort Esperanza, and Military Operations on the Texas Coast, 1861–1864," *Southwestern Historical Quarterly* 61 (1958): 74–80.

19. H. H. Bell, report to G. Welles, September 4, 1863, *OR Navies,* 20:515.

20. N. P. Banks, dispatch to H. W. Halleck, August 15, 1863, *OR,* vol. 26, pt. 1, 682–83. In this message Banks also presaged an overland expedition to Texas: "The enemy fears only an attack from the land, via Niblett's Bluff, the route I propose, or Alexandria. From that point our success is certain."

21. N. P. Banks, report to E. M. Stanton, April 6, 1865, *OR,* vol. 26, pt. 1, 18. See also Cotham, *Sabine Pass,* 94–95; Tolbert, *Dick Dowling at Sabine Pass,* 58.

22. N. P. Banks, dispatch to H. W. Halleck, August 26, 1863, *OR,* vol. 26, pt. 1, 696. See also *CCW,* xx–xxi.

23. Terrence J. Winschel, ed., *The Civil War Diary of a Common Soldier, William Wiley of the 77th Illinois Infantry* (Baton Rouge: Louisiana State University Press, 2001), 75. See John Y. Simon, ed., *The Papers of Ulysses S. Grant* (Carbondale: Southern Illinois University Press, 1967–2000), 9:n. 222; Ulysses S. Grant, *The Personal Memoirs of U. S. Grant* (New York: Charles L. Webster, 1885), 1:581; Geoffrey Perret, *Ulysses S. Grant, Soldier & President* (New York: Random House, 1997), 268–69. See also Bruce Catton, *Grant Takes Command* (Boston: Little, Brown, 1968), 26.

24. *CWL,* 6:366.

25. H. H. Bell, dispatch to G. Welles, September 4, 1863, *OR Navies,* 20:515–16.

26. Beale, *Diary of Gideon Welles,* 1:441–42 (see chap. 4, n. 26).

27. James A. L. Fremantle, *The Fremantle Diary,* ed. Walter Lord (London: Andre Deutsch, 1956), 56. See William T. Block, "The Ghostly Silent Guns of Galveston: A Chronicle of Colonel J. G. Kellersberger, Confederate Chief Engineer of East Texas," *East Texas Historical Journal* 33, no. 2 (1995): 23–34. Cotham attributes much of the Confederate success at Sabine Pass to these foreign-born engineers (*Sabine Pass,* 193).

28. Simpson, "Battle of Sabine Pass," 147; Tolbert, *Dick Dowling at Sabine Pass,* 86; Cotham, *Sabine Pass,* 81. The marksmanship of Dick Dowling and the Jeff Davis Guards had been instrumental in the capture of the blockading vessels at Sabine Pass in January 1863 (Cotham, *Sabine Pass,* 52).

29. R. W. Dowling, report to F. H. Odlum, September 9, 1863, *OR,* vol. 26, pt. 1, 311–12. See Simpson, "Battle of Sabine Pass," 138; Lenoir Hunt, *Bluebonnets and Blood* (Houston: Texas Books, 1938), 287. The 42 men are listed by name in O. M. Roberts, "Texas," in Clement A. Evans, *Confederate Military History* (Atlanta: Confederate Publishing, 1899), 11:110–11.

30. N. P. Banks, report to H. W. Halleck, September 5, 1863, *OR,* vol. 26, pt. 1, 286.

31. N. P. Banks, orders to W. B. Franklin, August 31, 1863, ibid., 287–88; Irwin, *History of the Nineteenth Army Corps,* 267. See also Welcher, *Union Army,* 2:56.

32. Cotham, *Sabine Pass,* 27–28; Tolbert, *Dick Dowling at Sabine Pass,* 61–62.

33. N. P. Banks, orders to W. B. Franklin, August 31, 1863, *OR,* vol. 26, pt. 1, 287.

34. W. B. Franklin, report to N. P. Banks, September 11, 1863, ibid., 284–98. See also H. H. Bell, dispatch to G. Welles, September 4, 1863, *OR Navies,* 20:515–16.

35. J. Madigan, dispatch to G. Welles, October 15, 1863, *OR Navies,* 20:539.

36. F. Crocker, Report to G. Welles, April 21, 1865, ibid., 20:544–45. The steamer observed by Lamson was the *Ossipee,* which was en route to Galveston.

37. Beecher, *Record of the 114th Regiment,* 247.

38. W. B. Franklin, report to N. P. Banks, September 11, 1863, *OR,* vol. 26, pt. 1, 284.

39. Beecher, *Record of the 114th Regiment,* 248. See Cotham, *Sabine Pass,* 130. Dowling's report can be found in *OR,* vol. 26, pt. 1, 311–12. See also *OR,* vol. 26, pt. 1, 307–10. Two volunteers, Lt. N. H. Smith from Louisiana and George Bailey, assistant surgeon, aided the gunners during the engagement. The garrison was also augmented by Capt. F. H. Odlum, commander of the post, and Col. Leon Smith, commander of the Marine Department of Texas. With Lieutenant Dowling there were 47 men inside the fort during the Federal attack.

40. Beecher, *Record of the 114th Regiment,* 248–49.

41. F. Crocker, report to H. H. Bell, September 12, 1863, *OR,* vol. 26, pt. 1, 301–302. Lieutenant Crocker prepared his report of the battle while a prisoner in Houston.

42. W. B. Franklin, report to N. P. Banks, September 11, 1863, ibid., 297; *OR Navies,* 20:529. Weitzel must share the blame for not landing troops. However, as pointed out by Simpson, Weitzel's report of the battle is confusing "and it is difficult to assess his role in the debacle" ("Battle of Sabine Pass," 163). Weitzel stated that the *Clifton* was

blocking his intended point of landing but that he had "just given orders to attempt the landing, nevertheless," when "a few moments afterward I was ordered to retire" (G. Weitzel, report to W. Hoffman, September 11, 1863, *OR,* vol. 26, pt. 1, 298–99). In the opinion of one reviewer General Weitzel lost his nerve and failed to obey orders to land (Cotham, *Sabine Pass,* 150–52).

43. Simpson, "Battle of Sabine Pass," 162; James R. Soley, "Gulf Operations in 1862 and 1863," in Johnson and Buel, *B&L,* 3:571; see also Josephy, *Civil War in the American West,* 180–84; J. Thomas Scharf, *History of the Confederate States Navy* (New York: Rogers & Sherwood, 1887; repr., New York: Gramercy, 1996), 526; Roberts, "Texas," 111; Cotham, *Sabine Pass,* 147.

44. N. P. Banks, report to H. W. Halleck, September 13, 1863, *OR,* vol. 26, pt. 1, 288–89. In a letter to his wife dated September 22, 1863, Banks referred to the "ignorance" of the naval officers involved in the expedition (see Johnson, *Red River Campaign,* 39). In 1882 Jefferson Davis stated that the "battle at Sabine Pass was more remarkable than the battle of Thermopylae" ("A Grand Meeting in New Orleans," *Southern Historical Society Papers* 10, no. 5 [May 1882]: 223–33, quote on 229; see also Cotham, *Sabine Pass,* 3–4).

45. Horace Greeley declared that Franklin had achieved "the distinction of being the first American General [for Renshaw was not a General] who managed to lose a fleet in a contest with land batteries alone" (*American Conflict,* 2:339, bracketed remark in original).

CHAPTER 6

1. Banks's orders are given in *OR,* vol. 24, pt. 2, 562.

2. E. K. Smith, to the people of Arkansas, Louisiana, and Texas, n.d., *OR,* vol. 26, pt. 2, 581.

3. See Edmonds, *Yankee Autumn,* 84–87.

4. N. P. Banks, dispatch to H. W. Halleck, October 9, 1863, *OR,* vol. 26, pt. 1, 756–57; J. H. McLeary, "History of Green's Brigade," in Wooten, *Comprehensive History of Texas,* 2:721.

5. N. P. Banks, letter to A. Lincoln, October 26, 1863, *OR,* vol. 26, pt. 1, 292.

6. Beecher, *Record of the 114th Regiment,* 261.

7. John A. Bering and Thomas Montgomery, *History of the Forty-eighth Ohio Vet. Vol. Inf.* (Hillsboro, Ohio: Highland News Office, 1880), 108–109.

8. Caroline E. Whitcomb, *History of the Second Massachusetts Battery (Nimms Battery) of Light Artillery, 1861–1865* (Concord, N.H.: Rumford Press, 1912), 57. Judge Edmund Davis had recruited his cavalry in Matamoros (Kerby, *Kirby Smith's Confederacy,* 16–17; Wooten, *Comprehensive History of Texas,* 2:565).

9. See Edmonds, *Yankee Autumn,* 165–72.

10. E. K. Smith, dispatch to R. Taylor, October 20, 1863, *OR,* vol. 26, pt. 2, 341.

11. W. B. Franklin, dispatch to C. P. Stone, October 23, 1863, *OR,* vol. 26, pt. 1, 340.

12. Alvin P. Hovey Manuscripts, Lilly Library (24th Indiana), University of Indiana, 78.

13. Roberts, "Texas," 199–200; McLeary, "History of Green's Brigade," 721–22.

14. S. G. Burbridge, report to W. H. Morgan, November 7, 1863, *OR*, vol. 26, pt. 1, 359–61. See Alwyn Barr, "The Battle of Bayou Bourbeau, November 3, 1863: Colonel Oran M. Roberts' Report," *Louisiana History* 6 (Winter 1965): 83–91.

15. J. T. Woods, *Services of the Ninety-sixth Ohio Volunteers* (Toledo: Blade Printing and Paper, 1874), 43–44. See also R. B. Scott, *The History of the 67th Regiment Indiana Infantry Volunteers, War of the Rebellion* (Bedford, Ind.: Herald Book and Job Print, 1892), 51–52.

16. Thomas H. Bringhurst and Frank Swigart, *History of the Forty-sixth Regiment, Indiana Volunteer Infantry* (Logansport, Ind.: Committee of the Regimental Association, Press of Wilson, Humphreys, 1888), 78. See also Hovey Manuscripts, 80.

17. T. Green, report to E. Surget, November 4, 1863, *OR*, vol. 26, pt. 1, 394; McLeary, "History of Green's Brigade," 723.

18. Hovey Manuscripts, 81; see also Frank McGregor Papers, Correspondence, March 4–May 30,1864 (83rd Ohio) U.S. Army Military History Institute Manuscript Collection (hereafter cited as MHI).

19. Houston *Tri-Weekly Telegraph*, November 11, 1863; Lowe, *Walker's Texas Division*, 146; Edmonds, *Yankee Autumn*, 311.

20. C. P. Stone, dispatch to W. B. Franklin, November 13, 1863, *OR*, vol. 26, pt. 1, 799.

21. Quoted by Edmonds, *Yankee Autumn*, 352. See Winschel, *Civil War Diary*, 81–82.

22. Richard Lowe, *The Texas Overland Expedition of 1863* (Abilene, Tex.: McWhiney Foundation Press, 1998), 110. Lowe concluded that "General Banks's refusal to give Franklin specific instructions about the move toward Texas, Franklin's own timidity, both generals' lack of imaginative solutions to the supply problem, and the stinging defeat on the Bourbeau all spelled failure for the Texas overland campaign" (ibid.).

CHAPTER 7

1. Warner, *Generals in Blue*, 111–12; Sifakis, *Who Was Who*, 166–67; Boatner, *Civil War Dictionary*, 221; Eicher and Eicher, *Civil War High Commands*, 198–99.

2. N. P. Banks, report to H. W. Halleck, November 7, 1863, *OR*, vol. 26, pt. 1, 397. See also ibid., 425; Chester Barney, *Recollections of Field Service with the Twentieth Iowa Infantry Volunteers* (Davenport: Printed for the author at Gazette Job Rooms, 1865), 243. For another account of the crossing, see Nannie M. Tilley, ed., *Federals on the Frontier, the Diary of Benjamin F. McIntyre 1862–1864* (Austin: University of Texas Press, 1963), 240.

3. "The Texan Expedition, a National Account," November 2, 1863, in Moore, *Rebellion Record*, 8:146.

4. J. Bruce, report to N. B. Baker, December 1, 1863, *OR*, vol. 26, pt. 1, 425; *OR Navies*, 20:647. See also Tilley, *Federals on the Frontier*, 242–43; J. Irvine Dungan, *History of the Nineteenth Regiment, Iowa Volunteer Infantry* (Davenport: Luse & Griggs, 1865), 116; Barney, *Recollections of Field Service*, 243.

5. Moore, *Rebellion Record*, 8:146.

6. J. H. Strong, report to H. H. Bell, November 3, 1863, *OR Navies,* 20:645–46.

7. Moore, *Rebellion Record,* 8:146.

8. N. P. Banks, dispatch to C. P. Stone, November 2, 1863, *OR,* vol. 26, pt. 1, 396. A similar dispatch was sent by Banks to the president November 3, 1863 (ibid.).

9. Tilley, *Federals on the Frontier,* 251, 253.

10. N. P. Banks, dispatch to H. W. Halleck, November 4, 1863, *OR,* vol. 26, pt. 1, 398.

11. Fredericka Meiners, "The Texas Border Cotton Trade, 1862–1863," *Civil War History* 23, no. 4 (December 1977): 293–306. See also E. J. Warner, *Generals in Gray,* 24–25; Sifakis, *Who Was Who,* 45; Faust, *Historical Times Illustrated Encyclopedia,* 52–53; Robert W. Delaney, "Matamoros, Port for Texas during the Civil War," *Southwestern Historical Quarterly* 58 (April 1955): 473–87; Fremantle, *Fremantle Diary,* 23; Thompson and Jones, *Civil War & Revolution,* 34, 56–60.

12. N. P. Banks, report to H. W. Halleck, November 6, 1863, *OR,* vol. 26, pt. 1, 399–401; H. P. Bee, report to E. P. Turner, November 8, 1863, ibid., 434–35. See also Josephy, *Civil War in the American West,* 186.

13. Tilley, *Federals on the Frontier,* 257; N. J. T. Dana, dispatch to N. P. Banks, November 21, 1863, *OR,* vol. 26, pt. 1, 415.

14. W. H. Seward, letter to N. P. Banks, November 23, 1863, ibid., 815.

15. As has often been the case in Mexico's tumultuous history, these were troubled times for that country. See *OR,* vol. 26, pt. 1, 399–409, 844; *OR,* vol. 34, pt. 1, 81–84. See also Jerry D. Thompson, ed., *Juan Cortina and the Texas-Mexico Frontier 1859–1877* (El Paso: Texas Western Press, 1994), 31–47; Wooten, *Comprehensive History of Texas,* 2:540–41.

16. N. P. Banks, dispatch to A. Lincoln, November 9, 1863, *OR,* vol. 26, pt. 1, 405.

17. N. P. Banks, letter to Mary Banks, November 15, 1863, Banks Papers, LOC, emphasis in original.

18. Allan Nevins, *War for the Union,* vol. 3, *The Organized War 1863–1864* (New York: Charles Scribner's Sons, 1971), 366. See also *OR,* vol. 34, pt. 2, 890; *OR,* vol. 34, pt. 4, 467; Thompson and Jones, *Civil War & Revolution,* 40–44.

19. N. J. T. Dana, report to N. P. Banks, November 21, 1863, *OR,* vol. 26, pt. 1, 414–15. See Thompson and Jones, *Civil War & Revolution,* 66–67.

20. Barney, *Recollections of Field Service,* 273. In addition, numbers of former slaves were mustered into the Corps d'Afrique at Brownsville (*OR,* vol. 26, pt. 1, 830–31; *OR,* vol. 34, pt. 2, 296).

21. N. P. Banks, letter to Mary Banks, November 15, 1863, Banks Papers, LOC. See Harrington, *Fighting Politician,* 133. The troops remaining with Dana at Brownsville continued the tradition of pillaging and destroying civilian property. Dana declared, "I wish to kill, burn, and destroy all the Rebels own that cannot be taken and secured" (*OR,* vol. 26, pt. 1, 865). Union cavalry sacked the King Ranch, "fired several shots into the house, killed one man, broke open trunks, and took what they wanted." According to Richard King, the house was "a complete wreck" (Bruce S. Cheeseman, "Let Us Have 500 Good Determined Texans," *Southwestern Historical Quarterly* 101 [July 1997]: 91, 93).

22. Warner, *Generals in Blue,* 389–90; Sifakis, *Who Was Who,* 532; Faust, *Historical Times Illustrated Encyclopedia,* 614–15; Boatner, *Civil War Dictionary,* 679–80; Eicher and Eicher, *Civil War High Commands,* 446.

23. U. S. Grant, dispatch to G. H. Thomas, January 19, 1864, *OR,* vol. 32, pt. 2, 141.

24. N. P. Banks, dispatch to H. W. Halleck, November 18, 1863, *OR,* vol. 26, pt. 1, 409–10.

25. N. P. Banks, letter to A. Lincoln, December 4, 1863, ibid., 832. See also A. J. Hamilton, letter to E. M. Stanton, December 19, 1863, Correspondence of the War Department, H, 123/124, Box 301, National Archives; *OR,* vol. 26, pt. 1, 865–67; Waller, *Colossal Hamilton of Texas,* 50–51.

26. *OR,* 1:562. See also Albert G. Hartje, *Van Dorn* (Nashville: Vanderbilt University Press, 1967), 85.

27. Marcus J. Wright, *Texas in the War 1861–1865,* ed. Harold B. Simpson (Hillsboro, Tex.: Hill Junior College Press, 1965), 143; Fitzhugh, "Saluria, Fort Esperanza," 96–98. For background information on Bradfute, see Fitzhugh, "Saluria, Fort Esperanza," 86–88.

28. H. D. Washburn, report to W. H. Clark, December 3, 1863, *OR,* vol. 26, pt. 1, 421.

29. C. C. Washburn, dispatches to N. P. Banks, November 30 and December 1, 1863, ibid., 416–17. See also ibid., 421; *OR,* vol. 26, pt. 2, 458; Fitzhugh, "Saluria, Fort Esperanza," 97–98; Francis R. Lubbock, *Six Decades in Texas, or Memoirs of Francis Richard Lubbock, Governor of Texas in War-Time, 1861–63,* ed. C. W. Raines (Austin: Ben C. Jones, 1900), 530; *OR,* vol. 26, pt. 2, 517–18, 523–24.

30. H. P. Bee, dispatch to E. P. Turner, November 19, 1863, *OR,* vol. 26, pt. 1, 436–7; *OR,* vol. 26, pt. 2, 460–62. At the end of the year Magruder reported that he had 9,700 Confederate and state troops located near Velasco (Casdorph, *Prince John Magruder,* 263).

31. C. P. Stone, dispatch to C. C. Washburn, December 5, 1863, *OR,* vol. 26, pt. 1, 420.

32. C. C. Washburn, dispatch to N. P. Banks, January 2, 1864, ibid., 481.

33. S. D. Yancey, dispatch to H. P. Bee, September 1, 1863, *OR,* vol. 26, pt. 2, 196–97. One student of these events termed Magruder's conclusion that the loss of Saluria would place Galveston at risk "tactically preposterous" and attributed the conjecture to "excited reasoning" and "those odd deficiencies" in the general's military makeup (Fitzhugh, "Saluria, Fort Esperanza," 89, and n68).

34. John Griffith Jones Papers (23rd Wisconsin), letter dated January 3, 1864, typescript translation from the original Welsh Cymric, LOC; Bering and Montgomery, *History of the Forty-eighth Ohio,* 112–13; William H. Bentley, *History of the 77th Illinois Volunteer Infantry* (Peoria, Ill.: Edward Hine Printer, 1883), 234; Winschel, *Civil War Diary,* 85–86.

35. Bentley, *History of the 77th Illinois,* 235. See also Winschel, *Civil War Diary,* 87.

36. N. P. Banks, dispatch to H. W. Halleck, January 15, 1864, *OR,* vol. 34, pt. 2, 82. See also N. J. T. Dana, report to E. O. C. Ord, February 9, 1864, ibid., 277–78.

37. N. J. T. Dana, report to E. O. C. Ord, January 18, 1864, *OR,* vol. 34, pt. 2, 103. See also E. J. Davis, report to E. O. C. Ord, February 10, 1864, ibid., 287.

38. N. J. T. Dana, report to W. B. Scates, January 28, 1864, *OR,* vol. 34, pt. 1, 98–99. See also S. A. Dupree, ed., *Campaigning with the 67th Indiana 1864* (New York: iUniverse, 2006), 21–22; *OR,* vol. 34, pt. 1, 100.

39. H. W. Halleck, dispatch to N. P. Banks, December 7, 1863, *OR,* vol. 26, pt. 1, 834–35. See also *CCW,* xxii.

40. N. P. Banks, dispatch to H. W. Halleck, December 23, 1863, *OR,* vol. 26, pt. 1, 871. See also *CCW,* xxiii.

41. H. W. Halleck, dispatch to N. P. Banks, January 4, 1864, *OR,* vol. 26, pt. 2, 15. See also *CCW,* xxiv.

42. Beecher, *Record of the 114th Regiment,* 284.

43. *CWL,* 7:1–2.

44. Ibid., 7:90–91. See also Ted Tunnell, *Crucible of Reconstruction: War, Radicalism, and Race in Louisiana, 1862–1877* (Baton Rouge: Louisiana State University Press, 1984), 43.

45. *CWL,* 7:89–90, emphasis in original.

46. Abraham Lincoln, "Annual Message to Congress," December 8, 1863, *CWL,* 7:36–53, quote from 52. The proclamation, which was transmitted as a document separate from the annual message, is given in ibid., 53–56.

47. See John C. Waugh, *Reelecting Lincoln* (New York: Crown Publishers, 1997), 68–71; Eric Foner, *Reconstruction* (New York: Harper & Row, 1988), 35–37; McCrary, *Abraham Lincoln and Reconstruction,* 4–9, 186–94; Phillip Shaw Paludan, *The Presidency of Abraham Lincoln* (Lawrence: University Press of Kansas, 1994), 250–52; Donald, *Lincoln,* 471–74; Randall and Current, *Lincoln the President,* 4:6–10, 188; Abbott, *Cotton & Capital,* 83.

48. *CWL,* 7:123–24, emphasis in original. Banks sent two identical letters to Lincoln, that dated December 30, referred to here, and another dated December 27 (ibid.).

49. See, e.g., McCrary, *Abraham Lincoln and Reconstruction,* 203–207; T. Harry Williams, "General Banks and the Radical Republicans in the Civil War," *New England Quarterly* 12 (June 1939): 274.

50. Quoted by McPherson, *Battle Cry of Freedom,* 704.

51. *CWL,* 7:123–24. See also McCrary, *Abraham Lincoln and Reconstruction,* 227–28.

52. Proclamation of General Banks, January 11, 1864, *OR,* ser. III, 4:23; Moore, *Rebellion Record,* 8:331–32. See Williams, *Lincoln and the Radicals,* 295.

53. Letter, N. P. Banks to G. Boutwell, December 11, 1863, Banks Papers, LOC. Regarding this letter, see McCrary, *Abraham Lincoln and Reconstruction,* 225, n.30.

54. Letter, N. P. Banks to A. Lincoln, August 25, 1863, *OR,* ser. III, 4:133–34. Hahn received 54 percent of the vote.

CHAPTER 8

1. *CCW,* 5.

2. N. P. Banks, dispatch to H. W. Halleck, December 30, 1863, *OR,* vol. 26, pt. 1, 889. See also *CCW,* xxiv.

3. H. W. Halleck, dispatches to N. P. Banks, January 4 and January 11, 1864, *OR*, vol. 34, pt. 2, 16, 55.

4. W. T. Sherman, dispatch to A. J. Smith, January 6, 1864, *OR*, vol. 32, pt. 2, 36.

5. W. T. Sherman, dispatch to N. P. Banks, January 16, 1864, *OR*, vol. 34, pt. 2, 431. See also *CCW*, xxvi.

6. W. T. Sherman, dispatch to H. W. Halleck, February 29, 1864, *OR*, vol. 32, pt. 2, 498.

7. See John F. Marszalek, *Sherman, a Soldier's Passion for Order* (New York: Free Press, 1993), 248–56; Herman Hattaway and Archer Jones, *How the North Won: A Military History of the Civil War* (Urbana: University of Illinois Press, 1983), 520.

8. N. P. Banks, dispatch to H. W. Halleck, January 23, 1864, *OR*, vol. 34, pt. 2, 133.

9. *CCW*, 14.

10. N. P. Banks, dispatch to C. Grover, March 31, 1864, *OR*, vol. 34, pt. 2, 796; *CCW*, 20, 341.

11. N. P. Banks, dispatch to H. W. Halleck, January 29, 1864, *OR*, vol. 34, pt. 2, 178–79. See also *CCW*, xxvii.

12. W. T. Sherman, letter to N. P. Banks, January 31, 1864, *OR*, vol. 34, pt. 2, 266–67. See also W. T. Sherman, *Memoirs of General William T. Sherman* (New York: D. Appleton, 1875; repr., Bloomington: Indiana University Press, 1957), 1:393.

13. W. T. Sherman, dispatch to N. P. Banks, January 31, 1864, *OR*, vol. 34, pt. 2, 267. See also *CCW*, xxvii–xxviii.

14. H. W. Halleck, dispatch to N. P. Banks, February 1, 1864, *OR*, vol. 34, pt. 2, 211. See also *CCW*, xxviii.

15. The present interpretation of Halleck's pressure on Banks to move up the Red River differs from that of Ambrose, who provides a Jominian argument, "modified for political reality," to explain Halleck's actions (Ambrose, *Halleck*, 146–47).

16. H. W. Halleck, dispatch to N. P. Banks, February 11, 1864, *OR*, vol. 34, pt. 2, 293.

17. H. W. Halleck, dispatch to U. S. Grant, February 16, 1864, ibid., 340. See also *CCW*, xxx.

18. H. W. Halleck, dispatch to U. S. Grant, February 17, 1864, *OR*, vol. 34, pt. 2, 351.

19. N. P. Banks, letter to D. D. Porter, February 20, 1864, Banks Papers, LOC.

20. N. P. Banks, dispatch to H. W. Halleck, February 25, 1864, *OR*, vol. 34, pt. 2, 416. See also *CCW*, xxxi.

21. See, e.g., McCrary, *Abraham Lincoln and Reconstruction*, 237; Winters, *Civil War in Louisiana*, 327; Johnson, *Red River Campaign*, 83–84.

22. Sherman, *Memoirs*, 1:397.

23. On March 10 Sherman wrote to his wife, "I wanted to go up Red River but as Banks was to command in person I thought it best not to go" (Brooks D. Simpson and Jean V. Berlin, eds., *Sherman's Civil War* [Chapel Hill: University of North Carolina Press, 1999], 607).

24. W. T. Sherman, letter to N. P. Banks, March 4, 1864, *OR*, vol. 34, pt. 2, 494. See also Sherman, *Memoirs*, 1:402.

25. A. J. Smith, report to W. T. Sherman, September 26, 1865, *OR,* vol. 34, pt. 1, 304.

26. *CCW,* 275.

27. Ibid., 6. For Banks's comments regarding his lack of authority over A. J. Smith, see N. P. Banks, report to E. M. Stanton, April 6, 1865, *OR,* vol. 34, pt. 1, 216–17.

28. D. D. Porter, letter to W. T. Sherman, April 16, 1864, *OR,* vol. 34, pt. 3, 174; *OR Navies,* 25:747–48.

29. *OR Navies,* 26:24–25. See also Moore, *Rebellion Record,* 8:429.

30. St. Louis *Daily Missouri Republican,* March 26, 1864, in Moore, *Rebellion Record,* 8:430. See also Andrews, *The North Reports,* 498.

31. Bell Irvin Wiley, *The Life of Billy Yank: The Common Soldier of the Union* (New York: Bobbs-Merrill, 1951), 346–47; Grady McWhiney and Perry D. Jamieson, *Attack and Die* (Tuscaloosa: University of Alabama Press, 1982), 181–82.

32. The motivation for the marauding and for the theft and destruction of civilian property by Union troops was complex. These actions, which grew worse as the war continued, have been attributed to (1) a continual shortage of supplies for the Union armies in the west, (2) the fact that Confederate soldiers practiced similar acts of theft and destruction on their own citizens, and (3) the belief that such acts were proper punishment for Southern citizens for initiating and supporting the rebellion (Grimsley, *Hard Hand of War,* 99).

33. F. Steele, dispatch to H. W. Halleck, March 12, 1864, *OR,* vol. 34, pt. 2, 576. See also *CCW,* xxxi–xxxii; Stephen Z. Starr, *The Union Cavalry in the Civil War,* vol. 3, *The War in the West, 1861–1865* (Baton Rouge: Louisiana State University Press, 1985), 489.

34. Taylor, *Destruction and Reconstruction,* 156.

CHAPTER 9

1. J. G. Chandler, report to M. C. Meigs, December 26, 1864, *OR,* vol. 34, pt. 1, 236.

2. Winters, *Civil War in Louisiana,* 218. See also Phillip Cuccia, "'Gorillas' and White Glove Gents: Union Soldiers in the Red River Campaign," *Louisiana History* 36 (1995): 423–25. The failure of Union soldiers to obey orders against unauthorized foraging was widespread (see Grimsley, *Hard Hand of War,* 39–45).

3. Bentley, *History of the 77th Illinois,* 248. See also Grimsley, *Hard Hand of War,* 99.

4. Bering and Montgomery, *History of the Forty-eighth Ohio,* 129, parenthetical remark in original. See also Beecher, *Record of the 114th Regiment,* 237. The biblical reference to pillars of smoke and fire was not uncommon in descriptions of advances through Confederate territory by Union soldiers. See, e.g., Grimsley, *Hard Hand of War,* 203.

5. D. D. Porter, report to G. Welles, March 16, 1864, *OR Navies,* 26:29. See also Moore, *Rebellion Record,* 8:518.

6. Affidavit of E. R. Biossant, December 5, 1864, in Edmonds, *Conduct of Federal Troops,* 174.

7. Ed Steers, ed., "Garrison Duty in Alexandria: The Red River Campaign Letters of Lt. Charles W. Kennedy, 156th New York Volunteer Infantry," *Civil War Regiments* 4, no. 2 (1994): 107–108.

8. Montgomery Family Papers, letter, Frank Henry Peck (13th Conn.), March 21–28, 1864, LOC.

9. Richard S. West Jr., *Gideon Welles, Lincoln's Navy Department* (New York: Bobbs-Merrill, 1943), 247. See also Affidavit of E. R. Biossant, December 5, 1864, in Edmonds, *Conduct of Federal Troops,* 175.

10. D. D. Porter, letter to S. H. Treat, March 24, 1864, *OR Navies,* 26:35.

11. T. Kilby Smith, letter to his mother, March 24, 1864, in Walter G. Smith, *Life and Letters of Thomas Kilby Smith, Brevet Major-General United States Volunteers* (New York: G. P. Putnam's Sons, 1898), 362.

12. Cloyd Bryner, *The Story of the Illinois 47th* (Springfield, Ill.: Phillips Bros., Printer and Binders, 1905), 100. See also David C. Ashley, letter, March 23, 1864, Ashley Family Collection, Civil War Miscellaneous Collection (2nd New York Cavalry), MHI.

13. J. A. Mower, dispatch to J. Hough, March 24, 1864, *OR,* vol. 34, pt. 1, 315–16. See also report of A. J. Smith, September 26, 1865, ibid., 306–307; W. B. Keeler, letter to H. Hoover, March 24, 1864, ibid., 332–33; R. Taylor, dispatch to W. R. Boggs, March 22, 1864, ibid., 501; Joseph P. Blessington, *The Campaigns of Walker's Texas Division, by a Private Soldier* (New York: Lange, Little, 1875; repr., Austin: State House Press, 1994), 177–78; *OR,* vol. 34, pt. 1, 225, 315; Lowe, *Walker's Texas Division,* 178–80.

14. R. Taylor, dispatch to W. R. Boggs, March 23, 1864, *OR,* vol. 34, pt. 1, 505.

15. E. K. Smith, dispatch to R. Taylor, March 31, 1864, ibid., 516.

16. H. W. Halleck, dispatch to F. Steele, March 13, 1864, *OR,* vol. 34, pt. 2, 587.

17. U. S. Grant, dispatch to F. Steele, March 15, 1864, ibid., 616. The difference between the command authority assumed by Grant (as illustrated by this citation) and that assumed by Halleck (as illustrated by the suggestion cited in the previous note) is apparent.

18. West, *Gideon Welles,* 247. See also *CCW,* 177; Johnson, *Red River Campaign,* 104–105.

19. St. Louis *Daily Missouri Republican,* April 17, 1864, in Andrews, *The North Reports,* 502–503.

20. Elias Porter Pellet, *History of the 114th Regiment, New York State Volunteers* (Norwich, N.Y.: Telegraph & Chronicle Power Press Print, 1866), 182.

21. Lucius F. Hubbard, "Minnesota in the Red River Expedition, 1864" and "The Campaign of Mobile, 1865," papers read before the monthly meeting of the Executive Council, November 11, 1907, and February 10, 1908, Minnesota Historical Society, Paper III, 270, St. Paul, 1908. See also Lucius F. Hubbard, "The Red River Expedition," in *Glimpses of the Nation's Struggle, Second Series, Minnesota Commandery of the Military Order of the Loyal Legion of the United States (MOLLUS), 1887–1889* (St. Paul: St. Paul Book & Sta. Co., 1890), 578. Some authors refer to A. J. Smith's men as "Smith's Gorillas" as opposed to "Guerrillas" (see Cuccia, "'Gorillas' and White Glove Gents," 418–25; Joiner, *One Damn Blunder,* 63).

22. New York *World,* April 16, 1864, in Andrews, *The North Reports,* 504.

23. Ashley Family Collection, letter, March 23, 1864, MHI.

24. Return for March 31, *OR,* vol. 34, pt. 1, 167–68. See also Irwin, "Red River Campaign," in Johnson and Buel, *B&L,* 4:366; Johnson, *Red River Campaign,* 100. Banks's 30,000 soldiers included at least two women (Lauren Cook Burgess, ed., *An Uncommon Soldier, the Civil War Letters of Sarah Rosetta Wakeman* [New York: Oxford University Press, 1994], 67).

25. There were rumors that the Confederates deliberately reduced the flow in the Red River to thwart the Union advance. Evidence of the construction of a dam on Tone's Bayou, and destruction of the dam in combination with the sinking of the *New Falls City* to block the channel and divert part of the flow of the Red into Bayou Pierre, has been presented by Joiner, *One Damn Blunder,* 23–26, 66–67.

26. *CCW,* 8–9. Porter claimed that he had said his boats could go anywhere it was a little damp "a half-dozen times in joke, for we had gone into a great many queer places" (ibid., 275).

27. U. S. Grant, dispatch to N. P. Banks, March 15, 1863, *OR,* vol. 34, pt. 2, 610–11.

28. Irwin, "Red River Campaign," in Johnson and Buel, *B&L,* 350–51.

29. G. B. Drake, Field Orders No. 4, March 26, 1864, *OR,* vol. 34, pt. 2, 735. See also *CCW,* xxxvi; *OR,* vol. 34, pt. 1, 197, 768; C. G. Hearn, *Ellet's Brigade* (Baton Rouge: LSU Press), 1995, 223–24.

30. R. Taylor, dispatch to W. R. Boggs, March 30, 1864, *OR,* vol. 34, pt. 1, 514–15. See McLeary, "History of Green's Brigade," 725.

31. The gunboats brought over the falls are listed in *OR Navies,* 26:50.

32. N. P. Banks, dispatch to H. W. Halleck, April 2, 1864, *OR,* vol. 34, pt. 1, 179–80.

33. Nicolay and Hay, *Abraham Lincoln, a History,* 8:291 (see prologue, n. 14); Sandburg, *Abraham Lincoln, the War Years,* 3:13 (see prologue, n. 13).

34. According to Col. Charles Dwight, "I heard General Franklin once say that the only announcement of the plan of the campaign which he ever heard from the commanding general was in these words, 'One bound to Alexandria, one bound to Shreveport, one bound to the Gulf'" (*CCW,* 400).

35. New York *Herald,* April 16, 1864, in Harrington, *Fighting Politician,* 154.

36. U. S. Grant, report to E. M. Stanton, July 22, 1865, *OR,* vol. 34, pt. 1, 11. See also *OR,* vol. 46, pt. 1, 14.

37. F. Steele, report to H. W. Halleck, April 17, 1864, *OR,* vol. 34, pt. 1, 661–62. See also S. Price, report to W. R. Boggs, May (n.d.), 1864, ibid., 779.

38. F. Steele, dispatch to W. T. Sherman, April 22, 1864, *OR,* vol. 34, pt. 1, 662–63.

39. *CCW,* 8. For Farragut's comments on Banks's assistance in passing Port Hudson, see his response, p. 33.

CHAPTER 10

1. For a first-person description of the fleet's advance, see Lawrence Van Alstyne, *Diary of an Enlisted Man* (New Haven, Conn.: Tuttle, Morehouse and Taylor, 1910), 297.

2. D. D. Porter, letter to W. T. Sherman, April 15, 1864, *OR Navies,* 26:60.

3. *CCW,* 35.

4. Ibid., 286–87.

5. Johnson, *Red River Campaign,* 113–15.

6. Joiner, *One Damn Blunder,* 76–78.

7. William Riley Brooksher, *War along the Bayous, the 1864 Red River Campaign in Louisiana* (Washington, D.C.: Brassey's, 1998), 75, 232.

8. Thomas Ayres, *Dark and Bloody Ground, the Battle of Mansfield and the Forgotten Civil War in Louisiana* (Dallas: Taylor Trade Publishing, 2001), 217.

9. Curt Anders, *Disaster in Damp Sand, the Red River Expedition* (Indianapolis: Guild Press of Indiana, 1997), 45–48.

10. Taylor, *Destruction and Reconstruction,* 161.

11. By following the main road across the island formed by the Cain and the Bon Dieu, Banks's army had been separated from Porter's gunboats, but only for a short while. Using the Mansfield road, on the other hand, involved a lengthy separation with no expectation of a reunion before reaching Shreveport.

12. N. P. Banks, letter to Mary Banks, April 4, 1863, Banks Papers, LOC; Johnson, *Red River Campaign,* 116. According to Col. John Clark, the opinion that the enemy would not fight was prevalent at General Franklin's headquarters (*CCW,* 194, 196).

13. N. P. Banks, report to E. M. Stanton, April 6, 1865, *OR,* vol. 34 pt. 1, 198.

14. *CCW,* 58.

15. *OR Navies,* 26:51. See also Moore, *Rebellion Record,* 8:520. The transports are identified in *OR,* vol. 34, pt. 1, 379–80.

16. Porter, *Incidents and Anecdotes,* 232.

17. A. L. Lee, report to G. B. Drake, April 29, 1864, *OR,* vol. 34, pt. 1, 454; *CCW,* 58.

18. In testimony to the Joint Committee, Lee admitted having "from 320 to 350 wagons." However, see *OR,* vol. 34, pt. 1, 454. For further discussions, see *CCW,* 32, 49, 58, 183; *OR,* vol. 34, pt. 1, 237, 240.

19. Chandler claimed a total of 900 wagons for the cavalry and infantry, of which about 250 were cavalry (*OR,* vol. 34, pt. 1, 237, 240). Franklin claimed the infantry baggage train consisted of 700 wagons (*CCW,* 58).

20. J. G. Chandler, report to M. C. Meigs, December 26, 1864, *OR,* vol. 34, pt. 1, 237.

21. The paper-collar stories were widespread. See St. Louis *Daily Missouri Republican,* May 7, 1864, in Andrews, *The North Reports,* 516–17; Henry A. Shorey, *The Story of the Maine Fifteenth . . .* (Bridgton, Maine: Press of the Bridgton News, 1890), 90; John Scott, *Story of the Thirty Second Iowa Infantry Volunteers* (Nevada, Iowa: Published by the author, 1896), 136. According to Porter, Smith had only two wagons for his whole command. Porter stated that "if he [Smith] had soldiers that couldn't find a restaurant in the Desert of Sahara, and a comfortable bed in the swamps of Louisiana, he wanted to swap them off for those who could." He added that Smith "did not interfere with their disposition to forage on occasion" (Porter, *Incidents and Anecdotes,* 217–18).

22. *CWL,* 5:505–506; *OR,* vol. 3, pt. 2, 862. See also Lincoln's reply, p. 18–19.

23. Sylvanius Cadwallader, *Three Years with Grant* (Lincoln: University of Nebraska Press, 1996), 175.

24. D. S. Stanley, report to W. D. Whipple, February 25, 1865, *OR,* vol. 45, pt. 1, 114.

25. For these and more comparisons, see *Wilderness-Spotsylvania Staff Ride Briefing Book* (Carlisle, Penn.: U.S. Army Center of Military History, n.d.), 12.

26. General Orders No. 160, *OR,* vol. 3, pt. 2, 671–72.

27. U. S. Grant, dispatch to G. G. Meade, April 9, 1864, *OR,* 33:828. See John D. Billings, *Hard Tack and Coffee* (Boston: George M. Smith, 1887), 362–63; Smith, *Grant,* 305.

28. *CCW,* 26–27.

29. Hubbard, "Minnesota in the Red River Expedition," 578, 582.

30. See Irwin, "Red River Campaign," in Johnson and Buel, *B&L,* 352. Irwin did not participate in the expedition and received his information secondhand.

31. E. Kirby Smith, "The Defense of the Red River," in Johnson and Buel, *B&L,* 4:371.

32. S. A. Smith, letter to J. Davis, August 21, 1864, *OR,* vol. 34, pt. 1, 485. For a less sympathetic opinion of Kirby Smith's intent, see W. R. Boggs, *Military Reminiscences of Gen. Wm. R. Boggs, C.S.A.,* ed. William K. Boyd (Durham, N.C.: Seeman Printery, 1913), 75–76. See also Johnson, *Red River Campaign,* 123–24.

33. Scott, *History of the 67th Regiment,* 70.

34. Charles Oscar Torrey Papers (27th Iowa), letter, April 14, 1864, LOC. See also Henry Nathaniel Fairbanks, "The Red River Expedition of 1864," in *MOLLUS, Maine Commandery War Papers* (Portland, Maine: B. Thurston, 1898), 1:181.

35. Lee described the action nine months later in *CCW,* 58. See Irwin, *History of the Nineteenth Army Corps,* 296–97.

36. N. P. Banks, dispatch to U. S. Grant, April 13, 1864, *OR,* vol. 34, pt. 1, 181.

37. *CCW,* 32.

38. W. Hoffman, dispatch to A. L. Lee, April 7, 1864, *OR,* vol. 34, pt. 1, 455. See also *CCW,* xxxvii.

39. *CCW,* 36.

40. Ibid., 194–95. See also ibid., 29, 59. Using hindsight, Lee declared later that "I was laughed at for insisting that we would have a fight before we got to Shreveport" (ibid., 64).

41. Ibid., 11.

42. W. B. Franklin, dispatch to T. E. G. Ransom, April 7, 1864, *OR,* vol. 34, pt. 1, 264, 290.

43. Moore, *Rebellion Record,* 8:552. For comments about the line of march, see Bentley, *History of the 77th Illinois,* 248–49. The statement attributed to Ransom is strange in that it apparently assumes A. J. Smith would pass the infantry wagons to join the XIII and XIX Corps, and somehow the combined column would then advance along the narrow roadway and attack Taylor. It is difficult to believe that Ransom would have considered such a movement feasible based on the information available to him at the time.

44. C. E. Dickey, dispatch to W. J. Landram, April 7, 1864, *OR,* vol. 34, pt. 1, 290.

45. *CCW,* viii.

46. Ibid., 33. See also ibid., 39–40.

47. Testimony of J. S. Clark, ibid., 193–94.

48. Harrington, *Fighting Politician,* 153.

49. Joiner, *One Damn Blunder,* 88.

50. Kerby, *Kirby Smith's Confederacy,* 303. The length of Lee's wagon train is not accurately known but almost certainly exceeded the two miles cited by Kerby. The number of troops under Lee indicated by Kerby presumably includes Emerson's brigade.

51. Johnson, *Red River Campaign,* 144.

52. *National Tribune,* March 26, 1891. Quoted by John M. Stanyan, *A History of the Eighth Regiment of New Hampshire Volunteers . . .* (Concord, N.H.: Ira C. Evans, Printer, 1892), 396.

53. Scott, *History of the 67th Regiment,* 70. For Davis's text calling for a day of fasting and prayer, see Moore, *Rebellion Record,* 8:458.

54. Bentley, *History of the 77th Illinois,* 249. See also Winschel, *Civil War Diary,* 100–102.

55. Dupree, *Campaigning with the 67th Indiana,* 52.

CHAPTER 11

1. In 1865 Franklin claimed he "directed General Ransom to go with it [the 2nd Brigade] to the front, and see that it was not put in alongside of the first brigade, but really relieved it" (*CCW,* 30).

2. Frank McGregor Papers, letter, April 12, 1864, MHI.

3. *CCW,* 10, 11. See also ibid., xxxvii.

4. G. B. Drake, dispatch to W. B. Franklin, April 8, 1864, *OR,* vol. 34, pt. 3, 473. See also *CCW,* 30.

5. N. P. Banks, report to E. M. Stanton, April 6, 1865, *OR,* vol. 34, pt. 1, 198.

6. *CCW,* 11.

7. R. A. Cameron, report to W. Hoffman, April 16, 1864, *OR,* vol. 34, pt. 1, 273.

8. For Ransom's description of the situation at the front, see T. E. G. Ransom, report to W. Hoffman, June 11, 1864, *OR,* vol. 34, pt. 1, 265.

9. Frank McGregor Papers, letter, April 12, 1864, MHI.

10. Quoted by Stanyan, *History of the Eighth Regiment,* 403.

11. The Missouri *Republican,* letter dated April 13, 1864, dateline Grand Ecore, in Moore, *Rebellion Record,* 8:542; Greeley, *American Conflict* 2:541. For an analogous Confederate opinion, see Theophilus Noel, *A Campaign from Santa Fe to the Mississippi: Being a History of the Old Sibley Brigade* (Raleigh, N.C.: Charles R. Sanders Jr., 1961), 86.

12. A. W. Hyatt, quoted by Bartlett, *Military Record of Louisiana,* pt. III, "The Trans-Mississippi," 13; Bergeron, *Civil War Reminiscences,* 191. See also Arthur W. Bergeron Jr., "A Colonel Gains His Wreath: Henry Gray's Louisiana Brigade at the Battle of Mansfield, April 8, 1864," *Civil War Regiments* 4, no. 2 (1994): 19.

13. Corporal Charles B. Maxwell, 2nd Massachusetts Light Artillery, quoted by Whitcomb, *History of the Second Massachusetts Battery,* 68–69.

14. See Alwyn Barr, *Polignac's Texas Brigade* (Houston: Texas Gulf Coast Historical Association, 1964; repr., College Station: Texas A&M University Press, 1998), 29–30.

15. Frederick H. Dyer, *A Compendium of the War of the Rebellion* (Des Moines, Iowa: Dyer Publishing, 1908), pt. 3, 1100, 1519; *OR,* vol. 34, pt. 1, 267; Bering and Montgomery, *History of the 48th Ohio,* 132.

16. Frank McGregor Papers, letter, April 12, 1864, MHI. See also Flinn, *Campaigning with Banks in Louisiana,* 106.

17. Frank McGregor Papers, letter, April 12, 1864, MHI. McGregor probably saw Banks and Ransom instead of Banks and Franklin since Franklin was not on the field at the time of this attack.

18. T. E. G. Ransom, report to W. Hoffman, June 11, 1864, *OR,* vol. 34, pt. 1, 266–67. See also Greeley, *American Conflict,* 2:541.

19. *CCW,* 31.

20. Franklin's left arm was broken when he fell from his horse (Joiner, *One Damn Blunder,* 102).

21. Bringhurst and Swigart, *History of the Forty-sixth Regiment,* 89.

22. *Chicago Tribune,* quoted by Greeley, *American Conflict,* 2:542.

23. Frank McGregor Papers, letter, April 12, 1864, MHI.

24. Ibid., emphasis in original. See also Scott, *History of the 67th Regiment,* 72.

25. "A. W. M.," correspondent for the Chicago *Tribune,* April 11, 1864, dateline Grand Ecore, in Moore, *Rebellion Record,* 8:559. See also Flinn, *Campaigning with Banks in Louisiana,* 108–109.

26. Irwin, *History of the Nineteenth Army Corps,* 306. The twenty guns were Nims's 2nd Massachusetts Battery (six); Chicago Mercantile Battery (six); 1st Indiana Battery (four); Rawles's Battery G of the 5th U.S. Artillery (two); and 6th Missouri howitzer battery (two).

27. Lt. Tyler M. Shattuck, quoted by Stanyan, *History of the Eighth Regiment,* 404–405.

28. Parrish, *Richard Taylor,* 349. See also Greeley, *American Conflict,* 2:540–41.

29. John Russell Young, *The Press,* Philadelphia, April 25, 1864, dateline Grand Ecore, April 10, 1864, in Moore, *Rebellion Record,* 8:546, 48. See also Andrews, *North Reports the Civil War,* 507–508, 518–19; Greeley, *American Conflict,* 2:540.

30. See, e.g., Wiley, *Life of Billy Yank,* 90; *OR,* vol. 34, pt. 3, 153, 172; Starr, *Union Cavalry,* 3:498.

31. William Barr Papers, letter, April 17, 1864, Joseph J. Riggs Collection (33rd Wisconsin), MHI.

32. J. H. Snyder, quoted by Bentley, *History of the 77th Illinois,* 253–54.

33. N. P. Banks, report to U. S. Grant, April 13, 1864, *OR,* vol. 34, pt. 1, 182.

34. Fairbanks, "Red River Expedition of 1864," 181–82.

35. Pellet, *History of the 114th Regiment,* 195.

36. Chatman's Bayou was also known as Six Mile Creek, or Six Mile Bayou. Alwyn Barr, "William T. Mechling's Journal of the Red River Campaign," *Texana* 1 (1963): 365.

37. Pellet, *History of the 114th Regiment,* 196–97. See also Beecher, *Record of the 114th Regiment,* 311.

38. Frank McGregor Papers, letter, April 12, 1864, MHI, emphasis in original.

39. Irwin, *History of the Nineteenth Army Corps,* 309.

40. Chicago *Tribune,* quoted by Greeley, *American Conflict,* 2:542. See also Pellet, *History of the 114th Regiment,* 197.

41. James Sherwood Diary, Civil War Miscellaneous Collection (114th New York), MHI. There is no punctuation in the original; periods have been added for clarity; word repetition in original.

42. N. P. Banks, report to E. M. Stanton, April 6, 1865, *OR,* vol. 34 pt. 1, 201. See also Frank McGregor Papers, letter, April 12, 1864, MHI, dateline Grand Ecore.

43. James Sherwood Diary, MHI.

44. Banks maintained later that he planned to advance the next day but was talked out of it by his officers, who were convinced that the army must retreat because of lack of water for men and animals (N. P. Banks, report to E. M. Stanton, April 6, 1865, *OR,* vol. 34, pt. 1, 202). Franklin supported Dwight in urging retreat (*CCW,* 77, 179). Sources for the interpretation of this situation, some of which interpretations differ from that given here, include Johnson, *Red River Campaign,* 146–47; Hollandsworth, *Pretense of Glory,* 190; Harrington, *Fighting Politician,* 157; Anders, *Disaster in Damp Sand,* 65–66; Brooksher, *War along the Bayous,* 107–108; Ayres, *Dark and Bloody Ground,* 233; Winters, *Civil War in Louisiana,*. 347; Joiner, *One Damn Blunder,* 107; Bergeron, "Colonel Gains His Wreath," 21.

45. The conjecture that Banks's self-reliance was slipping at this point in the campaign, which led to the council of war at Pleasant Grove, was made by Anders, *Disaster in Damp Sand,* 65.

46. Beecher, *Record of the 114th Regiment,* 313. See also Bentley, *History of the 77th Illinois,* 257.

47. *OR,* vol. 34, pt. 1, 167, 263–64, 273, 292, 295, 421. See also Johnson, *Red River Campaign,* 140.

48. Taylor claimed to have captured 250 wagons (Taylor, *Destruction and Reconstruction,* 164), whereas Lee stated that 156 wagons were lost (*OR,* vol. 34, pt. 1, 452). Johnson concluded, "Apparently there was a large number of private wagons with Lee's train that were not listed in quartermaster records since they were not owned by the government" (Johnson, *Red River Campaign,* 141, n. 156).

CHAPTER 12

1. Adolphus P. Wolfe Letters, letter, April 18, 1864, Civil War Times Illustrated Collection (117th Illinois), MHI.

2. A. J. Smith, report to W. T. Sherman, September 26, 1865, *OR,* vol. 34, pt. 1, 307.

3. *CCW,* 77, 179.

4. Frank McGregor Papers, letter, April 12, 1864, MHI. See also Winschel, *Civil War Diary,* 106.

5. J. R. Young, Philadelphia *Press,* April 10, 1864, dateline Grand Ecore, in Moore, *Rebellion Record,* 8:549.

6. Col. J. G. Wilson, *CCW,* 77.

7. Ibid., 13. Richard Irwin later argued that the lack of sufficient water in the area caused Banks to order his wagons to withdraw (*History of the Nineteenth Army Corps,* 314; see also *OR,* vol. 34, pt. 1, 238–39, 249–50, 452, 459).

8. Sgt. J. M. Boyd, quoted by Scott, *Story of the Thirty Second,* 137.

9. Charles Oscar Torrey Papers, letter, April 14, 1864, LOC.

10. W. T. Shaw, report to J. B. Sample, April 15, 1864, *OR,* vol. 34, pt. 1, 354.

11. Some observers reported that the battery was positioned in front as "bait." Others saw it as a serious weakness in the army's defensive formation. See Moore, *Rebellion Record,* 8:550–52.

12. New Orleans *Era,* April 15, 1864, dateline New Orleans, in Moore, *Rebellion Record,* 8:556. The correspondent was apparently not present during the battle (see ibid., 554). The *Era* was closely associated with Banks and his programs (McCrary, *Abraham Lincoln and Reconstruction,* 166).

13. *OR,* vol. 34, pt. 1, 355. See postwar comments by Shaw in Scott, *Story of the Thirty Second Iowa,* 181–86. See also Pellet, *History of the 114th Regiment,* 208.

14. R. A. Cameron, report to W. Hoffman, April 16, 1864, *OR,* vol. 34, pt. 1, 272–74. See also ibid., 269–72.

15. Hubbard, "Minnesota in the Red River Expedition," 579. For a more pessimistic assessment, see "Battle of Pleasant Hill," quoted by Moore, *Rebellion Record,* 8:536.

16. Taylor, *Destruction and Reconstruction,* 166–67. See *OR,* vol. 34, pt. 1, 566–67. See also Hamilton P. Bee, "Battle of Pleasant Hill—an Error Corrected," *Southern Historical Society Papers* 8 (1880): 184.

17. W. T. Shaw, report to J. B. Sample, April 15, 1864, *OR,* vol. 34, pt. 1, 355. In 1865 Shaw bitterly criticized Southworth. However, the passing of time changed his perspective, and in 1888 he was a bit more understanding (Scott, *Story of the Thirty Second Iowa,* 182).

18. Fairbanks, "Red River Expedition of 1864," 184.

19. Capt. William S. Burns, recollections published in the Philadelphia *Times,* 1879; quoted by Scott, *Story of the Thirty Second Iowa,* 229.

20. William Barr, letter, April 16, 1864, Joseph J. Riggs Collection (33rd Wisconsin), MHI. Barr's information concerning the events at Pleasant Hill is secondhand. Barr was aboard the transport steamer *Rob Roy* at the time.

21. Adolphus P. Wolfe, letter, April 18, 1864, MHI.

22. Pellet, *History of the 114th Regiment,* 210.

23. William F. Lynch, report to J. B. Sample, April 13, 1864, *OR,* vol. 34, pt. 1, 341–42.

24. Scott (*Story of the Thirty Second Iowa,* 193) disputes Taylor's claim that he, Taylor, remained on the field (*OR,* vol. 34, pt. 1, 568) although Taylor is corroborated by Bee ("Battle of Pleasant Hill," 184–86). See also Parrish, *Richard Taylor,* 368. For an assessment of Taylor's performance at Pleasant Hill, see Parrish, *Richard Taylor,* 367.

25. Alwyn Barr, "William T. Mechling's Journal," 368. See also Debray, *Sketch of*

the History of Debray's Regiment, 19 (see chap. 3, n. 11); X. B. Debray, "A Sketch of Debray's Twenty-Sixth Regiment of Texas Cavalry, Paper No. 2—Conclusion," *Southern Historical Society Papers* 13 (1885): 159; Bee, "Battle of Pleasant Hill," 185.

26. James Sherwood Diary, MHI. See also Hubbard, "Minnesota in the Red River Expedition," 579.

27. Livermore (*Numbers & Losses in the Civil War in America,* 116 [see chap. 1, n. 23]) cites the Union force at Pleasant Hill as 12,647 and the Confederate force at 14,300. Because Livermore gives no numbers for the battles at Sabine Crossroads and Pleasant Grove, and because the numbers he attributes to Pleasant Hill are high, presumably his results are meant to include all three engagements. However, see Winters, *Civil War in Louisiana,* 355; McLeary, "History of Green's Brigade," 730.

28. Quoted by Kenneth P. Williams, *Lincoln Finds a General* (New York: Macmillan, 1959), 5:46–47; Josephy, *Civil War in the American West,* 209. See also Pellet, *History of the 114th Regiment,* 212.

29. Taylor, *Destruction and Reconstruction,* 171.

30. *OR,* vol. 34, pt. 1, 309. See also Johnson, *Red River Campaign,* 167; Brooksher, *War along the Bayous,* 135; Anders, *Disaster in Damp Sand,* 72.

31. For criticism of Taylor, see Johnson, *Red River Campaign,* 167–68; Parrish, *Richard Taylor,* 367; Brooksher, *War along the Bayous,* 136–37.

32. N. P. Banks, report to U. S. Grant, April 13, 1864, *OR,* vol. 34, pt. 1, 185.

33. *CCW,* 13, 35, 221.

34. Irwin, *History of the Nineteenth Army Corps,* 313.

35. Hollandsworth, *Pretense of Glory,* 193–94; Harrington, *Fighting Politician,* 158; Joiner, *One Damn Blunder,* 119–20. See also T. P. Savas, "A Death at Mansfield: Col. James Hamilton Beard and the Consolidated Crescent Regiment," *Civil War Regiments* 4, no. 2 (1994), 97; Greeley, *American Conflict,* 2:545.

36. Johnson, *Red River Campaign,* 162–66, 165–66; Brooksher, *War along the Bayous,* 141; Parrish, *Richard Taylor,* 368–69; Winters, *Civil War in Louisiana,* 356. See also Lowe, *Walker's Texas Division,* 212.

37. Lowe argues that the engagement at Pleasant Hill was a tactical stalemate but agrees that the subsequent retreat of the Union army produced a strategic Confederate victory (*Walker's Texas Division,* 210).

38. *CCW,* 13.

39. N. P. Banks, report to E. M. Stanton, April 6, 1865, *OR,* vol. 34, pt. 1, 202–204. See also Hoffman, *Camp, Court and Siege,* 92–93.

40. A. J. Smith, report to W. T. Sherman, September 26, 1865, *OR,* vol. 34, pt. 1, 309. See Hoffman, *Camp, Court and Siege,* 96–97; John Homans, "The Red River Expedition," in *The Mississippi Valley Tennessee, Georgia, Alabama 1861–1864, Papers of the Military Historical Society of Massachusetts* (Boston: The Military Historical Society of Massachusetts, 1910), 8:86–87; Johnson, *Red River Campaign,* 164. For additional discussions of this event, see St. Louis *Republican,* May 7, 1864; Scott, *Story of the Thirty Second Iowa,* 231–38; New York *Times,* May 10, 1864, in Andrews, *North Reports the Civil War,* 516.

41. A. J. Smith, report to W. T. Sherman, September 26, 1865, *OR,* vol. 34, pt. 1, 309–10. In January 1865 Banks claimed, "Our dead were buried. The wounded men were brought in and placed in the best hospitals we could organize, and surgeons were left with them with provisions, medicines and supplies" (*CCW,* 13). One of the surgeons remaining behind was Benjamin Fordyce of the 160th New York, who described his experience in 1886: "With sixteen other surgeons I was . . . immediately paroled to assist in the care and treatment of our wounded prisoners and will add that I was treated with great kindness and . . . was furnished with the facilities they had in this part of the country" (Lydia P. Hecht, ed., *Echoes, from the Letters of a Civil War Surgeon* [Sarasota, Fla.: Bayou Publishing, 1996], 246).

42. Charles Oscar Torrey Papers, letter, April 14, 1864, LOC.

43. Irwin, *History of the Nineteenth Army Corps,* 323.

44. Hubbard, "Minnesota in the Red River Expedition," 580.

45. Winschel, *Civil War Diary,* 107.

46. Smith, "Defense of the Red River," 372. Smith's arguments for moving against Steele instead of pursuing Banks are given in *OR,* vol. 34, pt. 1, 480–82, 485–87. See also Albert Castel, *General Sterling Price and the Civil War in the West* (Baton Rouge: Louisiana State University Press, 1965), 184.

CHAPTER 13

1. Porter, *Incidents and Anecdotes,* 232. See Joiner, *One Damn Blunder,* 26.

2. D. D. Porter, letter to W. T. Sherman, April 16, 1864, *OR,* vol. 34, pt. 3, 169–74; *OR Navies,* 26:60; Richard S. West, *The Second Admiral, a Life of David Dixon Porter 1813–1891* (New York: Coward-McCann, 1937), 251–52. Joiner argues that because of faulty maps, Porter did not in fact know where he was when he claimed to have reached Loggy Bayou (Joiner, *One Damn Blunder,* 140–41).

3. N. P. Banks, dispatch to D. D. Porter, April 9, 184, *OR Navies,* 26:48. See also *OR,* vol. 34, pt. 1, 452; pt. 3, 98–99.

4. D. D. Porter, letter to G. Welles, April 14, 1864, *OR Navies,* 26:45–49. Porter's opinion of Banks's military ability was summed up in his conclusion that the army's defeat was "owing to a blind security and mismanagement and a contempt for the enemy—three things that should always be avoided by a good general" (ibid., 47).

5. William Truman Diary, entry dated April 10, Joseph J. Riggs Collection, MHI.

6. *CCW,* 95. See also Taylor, *Destruction and Reconstruction,* 172.

7. New York *Daily Tribune,* April 30, 1864, in Andrews, *The North Reports,* 512.

8. G. B. Drake, report to R. B. Irwin, April 11, 1864, *OR,* vol. 34, pt. 3, 128; Irwin, *History of the Nineteenth Army Corps,* 327–27; *OR,* 53:592.

9. G. D. Robinson, report to D. C. Houston, June 13, 1864, *OR,* vol. 34, pt. 1, 250.

10. N. P. Banks, report to U. S. Grant, April 13, 1864, ibid., 185.

11. Pellet, *History of the 114th Regiment,* 221.

12. On April 12 Porter ordered the town of Coushatta burned because of enemy fire emanating from nearby. See *OR,* vol. 34, pt. 1, 388; *OR Navies,* 26:51.

13. See Scott, *Story of the Thirty Second Iowa,* 243.

14. A. J. Smith, report to W. T. Sherman, September 26, 1865, *OR,* vol. 34, pt. 1, 310. See Hubbard, "Minnesota in the Red River Expedition," 581–82.

15. Sherman, *Memoirs,* 2:13; Marszalek, *Sherman,* 262.

16. Dispatch, W. T. Sherman to N. P. Banks, April 3, 1864, *OR,* vol. 36, pt. 3, 24.

17. See Lloyd Lewis, *Sherman, Fighting Prophet* (New York: Harcourt, Brace, 1932), 350.

18. N. P. Banks, report to U. S. Grant, April 17, 1864, *OR,* vol. 34, pt. 1, 188.

19. N. P. Banks, dispatch to U. S. Grant, April 18, 1864, ibid., 189.

20. G. B. Drake, Field Orders No. 23, April 18, 1864, *OR,* vol. 34, pt. 3, 211. Arnold's assignment is in ibid., 294. See Starr, *Union Cavalry,* 3:499. Shortly after returning to New Orleans, both Lee and Dudley were relieved of all command in the cavalry. See Banks's comments in *CCW,* 17.

21. Frank McGregor Papers, letter, April 16, 1864, MHI.

22. U. S. Grant, dispatch to N. P. Banks, March 31, 1864, *OR,* vol. 34, pt. 1, 11; *OR,* vol. 36, pt. 1, 15; *OR,* vol. 38, pt. 1, 3; *OR,* vol. 56, pt. 1, 14. Grant cited this dispatch in a letter to Sherman on April 4, 1864, from which the quote is taken (*OR,* vol. 33, pt. 3, 245–46; see also ibid., 306).

23. U. S. Grant, confidential dispatch to G. G. Meade, April 9, 1864, *OR,* 33:827–29.

24. Grant, *Personal Memoirs,* 2:130. For discussions of Grant's strategy for 1864, see, e.g., Richard E. Beringer, Herman Hattaway, Archer Jones, and William N. Still Jr., *Why the South Lost the Civil War* (Athens: University of Georgia Press, 1986), 309–11; Hattaway and Jones, *How the North Won,* 518–24.

25. Dispatch, U. S. Grant to G. G. Meade, April 9, 1864, *OR,* 33:827.

26. N. P. Banks to U. S. Grant, dispatch dated April 30, 1864, *OR,* vol. 34, pt. 1, 189–92.

27. N. P. Banks, letter to Mary Banks, April 20, 1864, Banks Papers, LOC.

28. General Orders No. 39, April 21, 1863, *OR,* vol. 34, pt. 3, 244.

29. Hubbard, "Minnesota in the Red River Expedition," 583.

30. Beecher, *Record of the 114th Regiment,* 336–37. See also chap. 9, note 4.

31. James Kendall Ewer, *The Third Massachusetts Cavalry in the War for the Union* (Maplewood, Mass.: Wm. G. J. Perry Press, 1903), 169.

32. Philadelphia *Press,* June 1, 1864, in Andrews, *The North Reports,* 514. See also Barr, "William T. Mechling's Journal," 379.

33. Pellet, *History of the 114th Regiment,* 225.

34. Sarah A. Dorsey, *Recollections of Henry Watkins Allen: Brigadier General, Confederate States Army; Ex-Governor of Louisiana* (New York: M. Doolady, 1866), 278–79.

35. De Forest, *Volunteer's Adventures,* 99.

36. Dupree, *Campaigning with the 67th Indiana,* 56. Porter claimed the army covered forty miles that day (*OR Navies,* 26:76).

37. Johnson, *Red River Campaign,* 223. See also Orton S. Clark, *The 116th Regiment of New York Volunteers* (Buffalo: Matthews & Warren, 1868), 167.

38. Diary of T. C. Prescott, quoted by Stanyan, *History of the Eighth Regiment,* 438.

39. Taylor, *Destruction and Reconstruction,* 193. On April 27 AAG Wickham Hoffman issued General Orders No. 43, which offered a reward for the conviction of soldiers guilty of incendiarism (*OR,* vol. 34, pt. 3, 307).

40. Barr, "William T. Mechling's Journal," 373.

41. John L. Waller, "Colonel George Wythe Baylor," *Southwestern Social Science Quarterly* 24, no. 1 (June 1943): 23–35. Baylor, who typically used both given names, was the brother of John Robert Baylor, at one time the self-declared governor of Confederate Arizona.

42. N. P. Banks, report to E. M. Stanton, April 6, 1865, *OR,* vol. 34, pt. 1, 207. See Pellet, *History of the 114th Regiment,* 228.

43. Henry Rust Papers, letter, April 16, 1864, Gregory A. Coco Collection, Harrisburg Civil War Round Table (13th Maine), MHI.

44. N. P. Banks, report to E. M. Stanton, April 6, 1865, *OR,* vol. 34, pt. 1, 207. See Pellet, *History of the 114th Regiment,* 227.

45. Barr, "William T. Mechling's Journal," 374; Noel, *Campaign from Santa Fe,* 83–84; Debray, "Sketch of Debray's Twenty-sixth Regiment . . . Paper No. 2," 161. Taylor stated that the distance between Monett's Ferry and Beasley's was thirty miles (Taylor, *Destruction and Reconstruction,* 182; R. Taylor, "Unpublished After-Action Reports," *Civil War Regiments* 4, no. 2 [1994]: 121; see also McLeary, "History of Green's Brigade," 722–23).

46. *OR,* vol. 34, pt. 1, 190, 432–35, 611. See also Johnson, *Red River Campaign,* 232–33.

47. Pellet, *History of the 114th Regiment,* 229.

48. Fairbanks, "Red River Expedition of 1864," 188.

49. W. B. Franklin, report to G. B. Drake, April 29, 1864, *OR,* vol. 34, pt. 1, 263. Regarding Franklin's offer of a reward for the arrest and conviction of the perpetrators, see note 39 in this chapter.

50. R. Taylor, report to S. S. Anderson, April 24, 1864, *OR,* vol. 34, pt. 1, 581.

CHAPTER 14

1. E. Cort Williams, "Recollections of the Red River Expedition," in *Sketches of War History 1861–1865, Papers Read before the Ohio Commandery . . .* (Wilmington, N.C.: Broadfoot Publishing, 1991), 2:108.

2. David D. Porter, report to G. Welles, April 28, 1864, *OR Navies,* 26:94. See D. D. Porter, *The Naval History of the Civil War* (New York: Sherman Publishing 1886; repr., Secaucus, N.J.: Castle, 1984), 524.

3. D. D. Porter, report to G. Welles, April 28, 1864, marked "Confidential," *OR Navies,* 26:92–95. See also *CCW,* 250–51.

4. D. D. Porter, report to G. Welles, April 14, 1864, *OR Navies,* 26:47.

5. U. S. Grant, dispatch to D. Hunter, April 17, 1864, with enclosure to N. P. Banks, *OR,* vol. 34, pt. 3, 190–92.

6. N. P. Banks, dispatch to U. S. Grant, April 30, 1864, *OR,* vol. 34, pt. 1, 191–92.

7. U. S. Grant to H. W. Halleck, April 26, 1864, *OR,* vol. 34, pt. 3, 293–94.

8. H. W. Halleck, letter to U. S. Grant, May 3, 1864, marked "Confidential," *OR,* vol. 34, pt. 3, 409. See also ibid., 252–53.

9. D. Hunter to U. S. Grant, April 28, 1864, ibid., 390.

10. H. W. Halleck to N. P. Banks, April 26, 1864, ibid., 306–307. See capture of the *City Belle,* pp. 159–60.

11. Debray, "Sketch of Debray's Twenty-sixth Regiment . . . Paper No. 2," 162. See Beecher, *Record of the 114th Regiment,* 339. Debray was acting brigadier general prior to April 13, 1864 (Bruce S. Allardice, *More Generals in Gray* [Baton Rouge: Louisiana State University Press, 1995], 75).

12. D. D. Porter, dispatch to G. Welles, April 17, 1864, *OR Navies,* 26:71; Moore, *Rebellion Record,* 8:522.

13. Williams, "Recollections of the Red River Expedition," 112.

14. See Taylor, *Destruction and Reconstruction,* 186.

15. K. R. Breeze, report to D. D. Porter, May 4, 1864, *OR Navies,* 26:105; Jerry Frey, *Grandpa's Gone, the Adventures of Daniel Buchwalter in the Western Army, 1862–1865* (Shippensburg, Penn.: Burd Street Press, 1998), 95–98. See also *OR Navies,* 26:107–108; Winters, *Civil War in Louisiana,* 371; Taylor, *Destruction and Reconstruction,* 186.

16. R. Taylor, report to S. S. Anderson, May 10, 1864, *OR,* vol. 34, pt. 1, 590. See also Bergeron, *Civil War Reminiscences of Major Silas T. Grisamore,* 154.

17. Hubbard, "Minnesota in the Red River Expedition," 585–86.

18. R. Taylor, postscript in dispatch to S. S. Anderson, May 7, 1864, *OR,* vol. 34, pt. 1, 589.

19. Warner, *Generals in Blue,* 14–15; Faust, *Historical Times Illustrated Encyclopedia,* 33; Sifakis, *Who Was Who,* 26; *OR,* vol. 34, pt. 1, 209; Cunningham, *Port Hudson Campaign,* 47. See also A. A. Hoehling, *Damn the Torpedoes! Naval Incidents of the Civil War* (Winston-Salem, N.C.: John F. Blair, 1989), 91–103; Hoffman, *Camp, Court and Siege,* 84–86. Bailey frequently signed his personal correspondence "Jo" rather than "Joseph."

20. J. Bailey, report to W. Hoffman, May 17, 1864, *OR,* vol. 34, pt. 1, 403. See also U. B. Pearsall, comp., "The Official Reports of Building the 'Red River Dam,'" in *The History of the Union and Confederate Armies* (Washington, D.C.: War Department, 1882), ser. 61, 34:11.

21. Porter, *Incidents and Anecdotes,* 247, emphasis and exclamation point in original. See also James G. Wilson, "The Red River Dam," in *Personal Recollections of the War of the Rebellion, Commandery of the Loyal Legion of the United States, 1883–1891,* ed. James Grant Wilson and Titus Munson Coan (New York: New York Commandery, 1891), 80.

22. D. D. Porter, dispatch to G. Welles, May 16, 1864, *OR,* vol. 34, pt. 1, 219.

23. Wilson, "Red River Dam," 80.

24. J. Bailey, report to W. Hoffman, May 17, 1864, *OR,* vol. 34, pt. 1, 404.

25. U. B. Pearsall, report to G. B. Drake, August 1, 1864, ibid., 256. See also Frederick W. Cron, "Colonel Bailey's Red River Dams," *The Military Engineer* 29, no. 168 (November–December 1937): 422.

26. Although credit for the first idea for the dams appears to be properly assigned to Bailey, the origin of the idea for a dam, as well as ideas for the specific number and locations of any dams, is disputed. See *OR Navies,* 26:95–96; *CCW,* 223; Beecher, *Record of the 114th Regiment,* 341; Homer B. Sprague, *History of the 13th Infantry Regiment of Connecticut Volunteers during the Great Rebellion* (Hartford, Conn.: Case, Lockwood, 1876), 205.

27. J. Bailey, report to W. Hoffman, May 17, 1864, *OR,* vol. 34, pt. 1, 403.

28. N. P. Banks, dispatch to D. D. Porter, April 29, 1864, *OR,* vol. 34, pt. 3, 333.

29. *CCW,* 16.

30. Wilson, "Red River Dam," 82–83.

31. See Pearsall, "Official Reports of Building the 'Red River Dam.'" See also Cron, "Colonel Bailey's Red River Dams," 423; Josephy, *Civil War in the American West,* 219.

32. Cron, "Colonel Bailey's Red River Dams," 423.

33. U. S. Grant, report to E. M. Stanton, July 22, 1865, *OR,* vol. 38, pt. 1, 3.

34. D. D. Porter, report to G. Welles, June 13, 1864, *OR,* vol. 34, pt. 1, 220; Wilson, "Red River Dam," 81; *OR Navies,* 26:136. See also Cron, "Colonel Bailey's Red River Dams," 423; *OR,* vol. 34, pt. 1, 254.

CHAPTER 15

1. *CCW,* 16; *OR,* vol. 34, pt. 1, 209–10. See also Wilson, "Red River Dam," 88–89.

2. N. P. Banks, dispatch to D. D. Porter, May 9, 1864, *OR Navies,* 26:136.

3. H. Allan Gosnell, *Guns on the Western Waters, the Story of River Gunboats in the Civil War* (Baton Rouge: Louisiana State University Press, 1949), 15, 246–66; John D. Milligan, *Gunboats down the Mississippi* (Annapolis, Md.: United States Naval Institute, 1965), 6–11.

4. Porter, *Incidents and Anecdotes,* 248–49. Porter has used poetic license here since silence was unlikely in the presence of the roaring water and pounding steamboat. It is also unlikely that 30,000 people were watching the event. See also *OR,* vol. 34, pt. 1, 210; Williams, "Recollections of the Red River Expedition," 116–17; Wilson, "Red River Dam," 85.

5. Porter, *Incidents and Anecdotes,* 249.

6. *CCW,* 83.

7. D. D. Porter, report to G. Welles, May 19, 1864, *OR Navies,* 26:156. See also Moore, *Rebellion Record,* 8:532.

8. Hoffman, *Camp, Court and Siege,* 102.

9. U. B. Pearsall, report to G. B. Drake, August 1, 1864, *OR,* vol. 34, pt. 1, 255.

10. Ibid., 256. See also *CCW,* 22; *OR Navies,* 26:140–41, 144–45.

11. J. Bailey, report to W. Hoffman, May 17, 1864, *OR,* vol. 34, pt. 1, 404. See also *OR Navies,* 26:112, 137. Porter's recollections of the construction of the dam are given in Porter, *Incidents and Anecdotes,* 248. Porter's statement that the barges were emplaced after the tree dam was complete is contradicted by photographic evidence (see Pearsall, "Official Reports of Building the 'Red River Dam,'" 18).

12. James P. Jones and Edward F. Keuchel, eds., *Frank L. Church, Civil War*

Marine, a Diary of the Red River Expedition, 1864 (Washington, D.C.: History and Museums Division, Headquarters, U.S. Marine Corps, 1975), 56.

13. See Hoffman, *Camp, Court and Siege,* 101–102.

14. Taylor, *Destruction and Reconstruction,* 188–90; Parrish, *Richard Taylor,* 385. See comments by Ayres, *Dark and Bloody Ground,* 256; Johnson, *Red River Campaign,* 261–62, 280–81; Hollandsworth, *Pretense of Glory,* 201; Anders, *Disaster in Damp Sand,* 129; Brooksher, *War along the Bayous,* 210–11.

15. Wilson, "Red River Dam," 87.

16. D. D. Porter, dispatch to G. Welles, May 16, 1864, *OR,* vol. 34, pt. 1, 221. See Wilson, "Red River Dam," 88.

17. D. D. Porter, dispatch to G. Welles, May 16, 1864, *OR,* vol. 34, pt. 1, 220–21. Congress offered its thanks to Bailey on June 11, 1864 (ibid., 406; see also Eicher and Eicher, *Civil War High Commands,* 88–89).

18. J. Bailey, report to W. Hoffman, May 17, 1864, *OR,* vol. 34, pt. 1, 403.

19. G. D. Robinson, report to D. C. Houston, June 13, 1864, ibid., 253.

20. These writers give credit to Bailey: Gary D. Joiner and Charles E. Vetter, "The Union Naval Expedition on the Red River, March 12–May 22, 1864," *Civil War Regiments* 4, no. 2 (1994): 64–65; Joiner, *One Damn Blunder,* 164–68; Anders, *Disaster in Damp Sand,* 126–28, 133, 135; Hollandsworth, *Pretense of Glory,* 201; Harrington, *Fighting Politician,* 159; Ayres, *Dark and Bloody Ground,* 252, 255–56; Winters, *Civil War in Louisiana,* 369–70. Winters mentions the contribution of Colonel Robinson. Johnson (*Red River Campaign,* 249–50, 260–66) and Brooksher (*War along the Bayous,* 209–13) give credit to Pearsall.

21. Bailey-Stroud Papers, letter, July 12, 1864, MHI.

22. Hoffman, *Camp, Court and Siege,* 99.

23. J. Bailey, letter to P. Stroud, July 12, 1864, Bailey-Stroud Papers, MHI. See also Milwaukee *Journal,* November 23, 1972 (copy in Bailey-Stroud Papers, MHI).

24. D. D. Porter, dispatch to E. R. S. Canby, June 13, 1864, *OR,* vol. 34, pt. 1, 223.

25. Edmonds, *Conduct of Federal Troops,* 149. See Banks's report to Stanton, April 6, 1865, *OR,* vol. 34, pt. 1, 212; Banks's testimony to the Joint Committee, *CCW,* 23.

26. G. B. Drake, dispatch to R. Arnold, May 9, 1864, *OR,* vol. 34, pt. 3, 521. See *CWL,* 7:335. The Unionist residents of the area were also distraught at the thought of Confederates returning to power following Banks's departure.

27. N. P. Banks, report to E. M. Stanton, April 6, 1865, *OR,* vol. 34, pt. 1, 214. See *CCW,* 45; Sprague, *History of the 13th Infantry,* 206–207; *OR,* vol. 34, pt. 3, 532; Chicago *Daily Tribune,* July 23, 1864; St. Louis *Daily Missouri Republican,* May 29, 1864; Andrews, *The North Reports,* 517; Williams, "General Banks and the Radical Republicans," 277; Scott, *Story of the Thirty Second Iowa,* 252.

28. Jones and Keuchel, *Frank L. Church,* 56; New York *Daily Tribune,* June 3, 1864; St. Louis *Daily Missouri Republican,* June 10, 1864; Andrews, *The North Reports,* 520; Philadelphia *Press,* June 14, 1864. See Van Alstyne, *Diary of an Enlisted Man,* 320–21. Banks later expressed regret for this destruction (*CCW,* 23).

29. N. P. Banks, dispatch to D. D. Porter, May 13, 1864, *OR Navies,* 26:146–47.

30. Bringhurst and Swigart, *History of the Forty-sixth Regiment,* 95. See also Van Alstyne, *Diary of an Enlisted Man,* 325–26.

31. Ewer, *Third Massachusetts Cavalry,* 169. See Starr, *Union Cavalry,* 3:500.

32. Frey, *Grandpa's Gone,* 105 (see chap. 14, n. 15).

33. Beecher, *Record of the 114th Regiment,* 350–51. See also Sprague, *History of the 13th Infantry,* 212.

34. Hubbard, "Minnesota in the Red River Expedition," 586; Taylor, "Unpublished After-Action Reports," 125 (see chap. 13, n. 45). See Fairbanks, "Red River Expedition of 1864," 189–90; Montgomery Family, Perkins Family Papers, letter, May 18, 1864, LOC.

35. Hubbard, "Minnesota in the Red River Expedition," 587.

36. Bringhurst and Swigart, *History of the Forty-sixth Regiment,* 95. This bridge caught portions of Porter's fleet below Simmesport and temporarily blocked their return passage upstream (W. Smith, report to D. D. Porter, May 18, 1864, *OR Navies,* 26:153).

37. Van Alstyne, *Diary of an Enlisted Man,* 329. See Henry S. Commager, ed., *The Blue and the Gray* (New York: Bobbs-Merrill, 1950), 399.

38. General Green was killed during an attack on several of Porter's gunboats on the Red River. See Anne J. Bailey, *Between the Enemy and Texas, Parsons's Texas Cavalry in the Civil War* (Fort Worth: Texas Christian University Press, 1989), 171–78; Selfridge, letter to Porter, June 2, 1880, Thomas O. Selfridge, *Memoirs of Thomas O. Selfridge, Jr., Rear Admiral, U.S.N.* (New York: G. P. Putnam's Sons, 1924), 102–103; see also Porter, *Naval History of the Civil War,* 514–15; Diary of Alexander Porter Morse, quoted by Smith, *Life and Letters of Thomas Kilby Smith,* 118; Taylor, *Destruction and Reconstruction,* 178.

39. Alwyn Barr, *Polignac's Texas Brigade,* 45–46.

40. T. J. Kinney, report to J. B. Sample, May 20, 1864, *OR,* vol. 34, pt. 1, 347–48.

41. A. J. Smith, report to W. T. Sherman, September 26, 1864, ibid., 311.

42. Hubbard, "Minnesota in the Red River Expedition," 587.

43. Taylor, "Unpublished After-Action Reports," 126 (see chap. 13, n. 45).

44. Max L. Heyman Jr., *Prudent Soldier: A Biography of Major General E. R. S. Canby 1817–1873* (Glendale, Calif.: Arthur H. Clark, 1959), 201–202.

CHAPTER 16

1. For a sympathetic examination of the problems facing Banks when he took over the Gulf Department, see Harrington, *Fighting Politician,* 90–92. According to Harrington, "So varied and so serious were the problems [faced by Banks] that no administrator could have solved them all, and many men would have broken down under the strain" (ibid., 90).

2. H. W. Halleck, letter to N. P. Banks, November 9, 1862, *OR,* 15:590–91. See Halleck's orders, pp. 16–17.

3. Parrish, *Richard Taylor,* 443.

4. Hollandsworth, *Pretense of Glory,* 255–56.

5. Lowe, *Texas Overland Expedition,* 105–107.

6. See John S. Ford, *Rip Ford's Texas,* ed. Stephen B. Oates (Austin: University of Texas Press, 1963), 342–75; Wooster, *Texas and Texans,* 136–37, 180–81; Phillip T. Tucker, *The Final Fury* (Mechanicsburg, Penn.: Stackpole Books, 2001); Faust, *Historical Times Illustrated Encyclopedia,* 556.

7. Williams, *Lincoln and His Generals,* 308–309.

8. Johnson, *Red River Campaign,* 277.

9. D. D. Porter, letter to W. T. Sherman, April 15, 1864, *OR Navies,* 26:60.

10. Smith, "Defense of the Red River," 372. See Irwin, *History of the Nineteenth Army Corps,* 321.

11. Beale, *Diary of Gideon Welles,* 2:26 (see chap. 4, n. 26).

12. See, e.g., O. O. Howard's General Field Orders No. 26, dated November 22, 1864, *OR,* 64:521.

13. Johnson drew a parallel between the destruction left behind by the Federal troops during the retreat from Mansfield to that levied on Mississippi during the Meridian expedition: "The stellar role in this drama was played by the troops of A. J. Smith. They had not long ago returned from the Meridian expedition, in the course of which they made 'a swath of desolation fifty miles broad across the State of Mississippi'" (Johnson, *Red River Campaign,* 223–25; the quote is from ibid., 224; the embedded quote is from Lewis, *Sherman, Fighting Prophet,* 333 [see chap. 13, n. 17]).

14. Grimsley, *Hard Hand of War,* 203, 208.

15. As one student of the destructive acts against Southern civilians has stated, "If the desolation inflicted on the South possesses significance, it is also significant that it was not far worse. . . . [I]t was conducted not by brutes but by men from good families, with strong moral values that stayed their hands as often as they impelled retribution" (Grimsley, *Hard Hand of War,* 204).

16. Quoted by Wells, Frank Wells Papers, letter, April 15, 1864, MHI. The reaction of the troops to the defeat at Sabine Crossroads is mentioned by Johnson, *Red River Campaign,* 206, 283.

17. Homans, "Red River Expedition," 71.

18. Pellet, *History of the 114th Regiment,* 235.

19. George Templeton Strong, *Diary of the Civil War 1860–1865,* ed. Allan Nevins (New York: Macmillan, 1962), 443.

20. Hubbard, "Minnesota in the Red River Expedition," 588.

21. Pellet, *History of the 114th Regiment,* 241.

22. "The Red River Campaign," in *The United States Service Magazine* 2 (New York: Charles B. Richardson, 1864), 430. According to Pellet (*History of the 114th Regiment,* 238–39), the author of the article is Richard Irwin.

23. General Orders No. 12, *OR,* 15:667.

24. Porter, *Incidents and Anecdotes,* 240. See Gosnell, *Guns on the Western Waters,* 254.

25. Porter, *Incidents and Anecdotes,* 237. See also Hubbard, "Minnesota in the Red River Expedition," 588; Hubbard, "Red River Expedition," 267.

26. Current, *Lincoln's Loyalists,* 103. According to *OR,* ser. III, 4:1269, the number of Texans that ultimately served in the Union army was 1,965.

27. *CWL,* 8:403–404, emphasis in original.

28. Donald, *Charles Sumner,* 197–205 (see chap. 1, n. 5). See Williams, *Lincoln and the Radicals,* 357–59; McCrary, *Abraham Lincoln and Reconstruction,* 287–302; Joe Gray Taylor, *Louisiana Reconstructed, 1863–1877* (Baton Rouge: Louisiana State University Press, 1974), 53–58.

29. Springfield *Daily Republican,* October 21, 1865, quoted by Harrington, *Fighting Politician,* 172.

30. See Hollandsworth, *Pretense of Glory,* 227.

31. William R. Geise, "Military Command and the Campaigns of 1864 in the Trans-Mississippi Department," *Military History of Texas and the Southwest* 16, no. 1 (1980): 61–66. On June 10 Taylor received the Thanks of the Confederate Congress for his success against Banks (Eicher and Eicher, *Civil War High Commands,* 91, 523).

APPENDIX

1. The roster as of March 31, 1864, is given in *OR,* vol. 34, pt. 1, 167–76. See also "The Opposing Forces in the Red River Campaign," in Johnson and Buel, *B&L,* 4:367–68.

2. The assignments to USCT are given in General Orders No. 51, *OR,* vol. 34, pt. 3, 221–22.

BIBLIOGRAPHY

MANUSCRIPT COLLECTIONS

Library of Congress

Banks, N. P. Papers (microfilm copy at Center for American History, University of Texas, Austin).

Franklin, W. B. Papers.

Jones, John Griffith. Papers (23rd Wisconsin).

Montgomery Family–Perkins Family Papers (13th Connecticut).

Torrey, Charles Oscar. Papers (27th Iowa).

U.S. Army Military History Institute

Ashley, David C. Papers. Ashley Family Collection, Civil War Miscellaneous Collection (2nd New York Cavalry).

Bailey-Stroud Papers. Joseph Bailey (4th Wisconsin).

Barr, William. Papers. Joseph J. Riggs Collection (33rd Wisconsin).

Douglass, Thomas B. Papers. Civil War Miscellaneous Collection (24th Iowa).

McGregor, Frank. Papers. Correspondence, March 4–May 30, 1864 (83rd Ohio).

Mitchell, Theodore L. Diary (165th New York).

Polignac, Camille. Diary. Civil War Times Illustrated Collection.

Rust, Colonel Henry. Report of Battle at Cane River Crossing, La., April 26, 1864. Gregory A. Coco Collection, Harrisburg Civil War Round Table (13th Maine).

Sherwood, James. Diary. Civil War Miscellaneous Collection (114th New York).

Truman, William. Diary. Joseph J. Riggs Collection (33rd Wisconsin).

Wells, Frank. Northwest Corner Civil War Round Table Collection (13th Connecticut).

Wolf, Adolphus P. Letters, August 31, 1862–May 17, 1865. Civil War Times Illustrated Collection (117th Illinois).

University of Indiana

Hovey, Alvin P. Hovey Manuscripts. Lilly Library (24th Indiana).

Kirkman, George D. Kirkman Manuscripts. Lilly Library (24th Indiana).

U.S. GOVERNMENT PUBLICATIONS

Abstract of Infantry Tactics; including Exercises and Manoeuvres of Light-Infantry and Riflemen. Philadelphia: Moss Brothers, 1861.

Atlas to Accompany the Official Records of the Union and Confederate Armies. Compiled by Capt. Calvin D. Cowles. Washington, D.C.: U.S. Government Printing Office, 1891–95.

The Field Manual for the Use of the Officers on Ordnance Duty, Ordnance Bureau. Richmond, Va.: Ritchie and Dunnavant Printers, 1862.

Official Records of the Union and Confederate Navies in the War of the Rebellion. 30 vols. Washington, D.C.: U.S. Government Printing Office, 1894–1922.

Report of the Joint Committee on the Conduct of the War. 38th Cong., 2nd sess. Vol. 2, "Red River Expedition." Washington, D.C.: U.S. Government Printing Office, 1865.

U.S. Infantry Tactics for the Instruction, Exercise, and Manoeuvres of the United States Infantry, including Infantry of the Line, Light Infantry, and Riflemen. Philadelphia: L. B. Lippincott, 1861.

The War of the Rebellion: A Compilation of the Official Records of the Union and Confederate Armies. 70 vols. in 128 pts. Compiled by Robert N. Scott. Washington, D.C.: U.S. Government Printing Office, 1880–1901.

PRIMARY SOURCES—ARTICLES

Bee, Hamilton P. "Battle of Pleasant Hill—an Error Corrected." *Southern Historical Society Papers* 8 (1880): 184–86.

Debray, X. B. "A Sketch of Debray's Twenty-sixth Regiment of Texas Cavalry, Paper No. 1." *Southern Historical Society Papers* 12 (1885): 547–54.

———. "A Sketch of Debray's Twenty-sixth Regiment of Texas Cavalry, Paper No. 2—Conclusion." *Southern Historical Society Papers* 13 (1885): 153–65.

Donnan, William G. "A Reminiscence of the Last Battle of the Red River Expedition." *Annals of Iowa* 6 (January 1904): 241–47.

Drake, F. M. "Campaign of General Steele." In *War Sketches and Incidents, Military Order of the Loyal Legion of the United States, Iowa,* 1:60–73. Des Moines: Kenyon, 1893.

Fairbanks, Henry Nathaniel. "The Red River Expedition of 1864." In *Military Order of the Loyal Legion of the United States, Maine Commandery War Papers,* vol. 1, B, 181–90. Read before the Commandery March 2, 1892. Portland, Maine: B. Thurston, 1898.

Homans, John. "The Red River Expedition." In *The Mississippi Valley Tennessee, Georgia, Alabama, 1861–1864, Papers of the Military Historical Society of Massachusetts,* 8:65–97. Paper read before the society January 3, 1893. Boston: The Military Historical Society of Massachusetts, 1910.

Hubbard, Lucius F. "Minnesota in the Red River Expedition, 1864" and "The Campaign of Mobile, 1865." Papers read before the monthly meeting of the Executive Council, November 11, 1907, and February 10, 1908. Paper III, 531–638. St. Paul: Minnesota Historical Society, 1908.

———. "The Red River Expedition." In *Glimpses of the Nation's Struggle, Second Series, Minnesota Commandery of the Military Order of the Loyal Legion of the United States (MOLLUS), 1887–89,* 267–79. St. Paul: St. Paul Book & Sta. Co., 1890. Reprint, Wilmington, N.C.: Broadfoot Publishing, 1992.

Irwin, Richard B. "The Capture of Port Hudson." In *Battles and Leaders of the Civil War,* edited by R. U. Johnson and C. C. Buel, 3:586–98. New York: Century Press, 1887–88.

———. "The Red River Campaign." In *Battles and Leaders of the Civil War,* edited by R. U. Johnson and C. C. Buel, 4:346–62. New York: Century Press, 1887–88.

———. "The Red River Campaign." *The United States Service Magazine* 2 (November 1864): 417–31. New York: Charles B. Richardson.

Maury, Dabney H. "Reminiscences of General Taylor." *Appleton's Journal* 6 (June 1879): 567–69.

———. "Sketch of General Richard Taylor." *Southern Historical Society Papers* 7 (July 1879): 343–45.

Meredith, William T. "Farragut's Capture of New Orleans." In *Battles and Leaders of the Civil War,* edited by R. U. Johnson and C. C. Buel, 2:70–73. New York: Century Press, 1887–88.

Palfrey, John C. "Port Hudson." *The Mississippi Valley Tennessee, Georgia, Alabama, 1861–1864, Papers of the Military Historical Society of Massachusetts,* 8:21. Read before the society, February 6, 1891. Boston: The Military Historical Society of Massachusetts, 1910.

Parkhurst, Charles H. "Incidents of Cavalry Service in Louisiana." Paper read before the Rhode Island Soldiers and Sailors Historical Society, 1st ser., no. 7. Providence: S. S. Rider, 1879.

Pearsall, U. B., comp. "The Official Reports of Building the 'Red River Dam.'" In *The History of the Union and Confederate Armies* (Washington, D.C.: War Department, 1882), ser. 61, 34:1–13. (Pamphlet contained in report E173P18no201pam12, Army War College Library, Carlisle, Penn.)

"Polignac's Diary." Pts. I and II. *Civil War Times Illustrated* 19 (August 1980): 14–18; and (October 1980): 34–41.

Porter, David D. "The Mississippi Flotilla in the Red River Expedition." In *Battles and Leaders of the Civil War,* edited by R. U. Johnson and C. C. Buel, 4:366. New York: Century Press, 1887–88.

———. "The Opening of the Lower Mississippi." In *Battles and Leaders of the Civil War,* edited by R. U. Johnson and C. C. Buel, 2:22–55. New York: Century Press, 1887–88.

Selfridge, Thomas O. "The Navy in the Red River." In *Battles and Leaders of the Civil War,* edited by R. U. Johnson and C. C. Buel, 4:362–66. New York: Century Press, 1887–88.

Smith, E. Kirby. "The Defense of the Red River." In *Battles and Leaders of the Civil War,* edited by R. U. Johnson and C. C. Buel, 4:369–74. New York: Century Press, 1887–88.

Soley, James Russell. "Closing Operations in the Gulf and Western Rivers." In *Battles and Leaders of the Civil War,* edited by R. U. Johnson and C. C. Buel, 4:412. New York: Century Press, 1887–88.

———. "Gulf Operations in 1862 and 1863." In *Battles and Leaders of the Civil War,* edited by R. U. Johnson and C. C. Buel, 3:571. New York: Century Press, 1887–88.

———. "Naval Operations in the Vicksburg Campaign." In *Battles and Leaders of the*

Civil War, edited by R. U. Johnson and C. C. Buel, 3:551–70. New York: Century Press, 1887–88.

Williams, E. Cort. "Recollections of the Red River Expedition." In *Sketches of War History 1861–1865, Papers Read before the Ohio Commandery of the Military Order of the Loyal Legion of the United States,* 2:96–120. Cincinnati: Robert Clarke, 1888. Reprint, Wilmington, N.C.: Broadfoot Publishing, 1991. (Separately bound and slightly different version at MHI E464W54, Army War College Library, Carlisle: Penn.)

Wilson, James Grant. "The Red River Dam." In *Personal Recollections of the War of the Rebellion, Commandery of the Loyal Legion of the United States, 1883–1891,* edited by James Grant Wilson and Titus Munson Coan, 78–95. New York: New York Commandery, 1891. Reprint, Wilmington, N.C.: Broadfoot Publishing, 1992. (See also *Journal of the Military Service Institution of the United States* 12 [1891]: 589–600.)

PRIMARY SOURCES—BOOKS

Andrews, J. Cutler. *The North Reports the Civil War.* Pittsburgh: University of Pittsburgh Press, 1955.

Bacon, Edward. *Among the Cotton Thieves.* Detroit: Free Press Steam Book and Job Printing House, 1867.

Banks, N. P. *The Reconstruction of States, Letter of Major-General Banks to Senator Lane.* New York: Harper & Brothers, 1865.

Barney, Chester. *Recollections of Field Service with the Twentieth Iowa Infantry Volunteers.* Davenport, Iowa: Printed for the author at the Gazette Job Rooms, 1865.

Bartlett, Napier. *Military Record of Louisiana.* Baton Rouge: Louisiana State University Press, 1964.

Bartlett, Robert F. *Roster of the Ninety-sixth Regiment, Ohio Volunteer Infantry, 1862 to 1865.* Columbus, Ohio: Press of Hann & Adair, 1895.

Basler, Roy P., Marion Dolores Pratt, and Lloyd A. Dunlap, eds. *Collected Works of Abraham Lincoln.* New Brunswick, N.J.: Rutgers University Press, 1953.

Beecher, Harris H. *Record of the 114th Regiment, NYSV: Where It Went, What It Saw, What It Did.* Norwich, N.Y.: J. F. Hubbard Jr., 1866.

Behlendorff, Frederick. *The History of the Thirteenth Illinois Cavalry Regiment, Volunteers U.S. Army, from September, 1861 to September, 1865.* Grand Rapids, Mich.: Major, Lothar, Lippert, 1888.

Bentley, William H. *History of the 77th Illinois Volunteer Infantry.* Peoria, Ill.: Edward Hine Printer, 1883.

Bergeron, Arthur W., Jr., ed. *The Civil War Reminiscences of Major Silas T. Grisamore, C.S.A.* Baton Rouge: Louisiana State University Press, 1993.

Bering, John A., and Thomas Montgomery. *History of the Forty-eighth Ohio Vet. Vol. Inf.* Hillsboro, Ohio: Highland News Office, 1880.

Billings, John D. *Hard Tack and Coffee.* Boston: George M. Smith, 1887.

Blessington, Joseph P. *The Campaigns of Walker's Texas Division, by a Private Soldier.* New York: Lange, Little, 1875. Reprint, Austin: State House Press, 1994.

Bringhurst, Thomas H., and Frank Swigart. *History of the Forty-sixth Regiment, Indiana Volunteer Infantry.* Logansport, Ind.: Committee of the Regimental Association, Press of Wilson, Humphreys, 1888.

Bryner, Cloyd. *The Story of the Illinois 47th.* Springfield, Ill.: Phillips Bros., Printer and Binders, 1905.

Butler, Benjamin F. *Butler's Book, Autobiography and Personal Reminiscences of Major-General Benjamin F. Butler.* Boston: A. M. Thayer, 1892.

———. *Private and Official Correspondence of General Benjamin F. Butler during the Period of the Civil War.* Edited by Jessie Ames Marshall. Norwood, Mass.: Plimpton Press, 1917.

Carpenter, George N. *History of the Eighth Regiment Vermont Volunteers, 1861–1865.* Boston: Press of Deland & Barta, 1886.

Chenery, William H. *The Fourteenth Regiment Rhode Island Heavy Artillery (Colored).* New York: Negro University Press, 1969.

Clark, Orton S. *The 116th Regiment of New York Volunteers.* Buffalo, N.Y.: Matthews & Warren, 1868.

Crooke, George. *The Twenty-first Iowa Volunteer Infantry.* Milwaukee: King, Fowle, 1891.

Dana, Charles A. *Recollections of the Civil War.* New York: D. Appleton, 1902. Reprint, Lincoln: University of Nebraska Press, 1996.

De Forest, John William. *A Volunteer's Adventures: A Union Captain's Record of the Civil War.* New Haven, Conn.: Yale University Press, 1946.

Duffy, Edward. *History of the 159th Regiment, N.Y.S.V.* New York, 1890. Reprinted from *Hudson Gazette,* 1865. Microfilm Division, Library of Congress.

Eby, Cecil D., Jr., ed. *A Virginia Yankee in the Civil War, the Diaries of David Hunter Strother.* Chapel Hill: University of North Carolina Press, 1961.

Edmonds, David C., ed., *The Conduct of Federal Troops in Louisiana during the Invasions of 1863 and 1864, Official Report. Compiled from Sworn Testimony under Direction of Governor Henry W. Allen. Shreveport, April 1865.* Lafayette, La.: Acadiana Press, 1988.

Ewer, James Kendall. *The Third Massachusetts Cavalry in the War for the Union.* Maplewood, Mass.: Wm. G. J. Perry Press, 1903.

Flinn, Frank M. *Campaigning with Banks in Louisiana, '63 and '64, and with Sheridan in the Shenandoah Valley in '64 and '65.* Lynn, Mass.: Thomas P. Nichols, 1887. (Portions duplicate George W. Powers, *The Story of the Thirty Eighth Regiment of Massachusetts Volunteers* [Cambridge, Mass.: Dakin and Metcalf, 1866].)

Fowler, Philemon H. *Memorials of William Fowler.* New York: A. D. F. Randolph, 1875.

Fremantle, James A. L. *The Fremantle Diary.* Edited by Walter Lord. London: Andre Deutsch, 1956.

Gould, John Meade. *History of the First—Tenth—Twenty-ninth Maine Regiment.* Portland, Maine: S. Berry, 1871.

Grant, U. S. *The Personal Memoirs of U. S. Grant.* New York: Charles L. Webster, 1885.

Hall, Henry. *Cayuga in the Field: A Record of the 19th N.Y. Volunteers, and 3d New York Artillery.* New York: Truair, Smith, 1873.

Hanaburgh, David H. *History of the One Hundred and Twenty-eighth Regiment, New York Volunteers (U.S. Infantry) in the Late Civil War.* Poughkeepsie, N.Y.: Press of Enterprise Publishing, 1894.

Haskins, William L. *The History of the First Regiment of Artillery.* Portland, Maine: B. Thurston, 1879.

Hatch, Carl E., ed. *Dearest Susie, a Civil War Infantryman's Letters to His Sweetheart.* New York: Exposition Press, 1971.

Hepworth, George H. *The Whip, Hoe and Sword or, The Gulf-Department in '63.* Boston: Walker, Wise, 1864. Reprint, Baton Rouge: Louisiana State University Press, 1979.

An Historical Sketch of the 162nd Regiment NY Vol. Infantry (3d Metropolitan Guard), 19th Army Corps, 1862–1865. New York: Weed, Parsons, 1867.

Hoffman, Wickham. *Camp, Court and Siege.* New York: Harper & Brothers, 1877.

Hughes, Nathaniel Cheairs, Jr., ed. *Liddell's Record.* Dayton, Ohio: Morningside House, 1985.

Irwin, Richard B. *History of the Nineteenth Army Corps.* New York: G. P. Putnam's Sons, 1892.

Jones, James P., and Edward F. Keuchel, eds. *Frank L. Church, Civil War Marine, a Diary of the Red River Expedition, 1864.* Washington, D.C.: History and Museums Division, Headquarters, U.S. Marine Corps, 1975.

Jones, S. C. *Reminiscences of the Thirty-second Iowa Volunteer Infantry.* Iowa City, Iowa: N.p., 1907.

Jones, William. *The Military History of the One Hundred & Sixty-first New York Volunteers, Infantry.* Bath, Maine: Hull & Barnes, Printers, 1865.

Knox, Thomas W. *Camp-Fire and Cotton Field.* New York: Blelock, 1865.

Lester, Robert E., and Gary Hoag, eds. *Civil War Unit Histories.* Bethesda, Md.: University Publications of America, 1991. (Copies of many pertinent unit histories and memoirs can be found in this microfiche set, which is available in the Library of Congress microfilm reading room.)

Lubbock, Francis R. *Six Decades in Texas, or Memoirs of Francis Richard Lubbock, Governor of Texas in War-Time, 1861–63.* Edited by C. W. Raines. Austin: Ben C. Jones, 1900.

Lufkin, Edwin B. *History of the Thirteenth Maine Regiment from Its Organization in 1861 to Its Muster Out in 1865.* Bridgton, Maine: H. A. Shorey & Son, 1898.

Marshall, T. B. *History of the Eighty-third Ohio Volunteer Infantry: The Greyhound Regiment.* Cincinnati: Eighty-third Ohio Volunteer Infantry Association, 1912.

Merrick, Morgan Wolfe. *From Desert to Bayou, the Civil War Journal and Sketches of Morgan Wolfe Merrick.* El Paso: Texas Western Press, University of Texas at El Paso, 1991.

Moore, Frank, ed. *The Rebellion Record: A Diary of American Events.* 12 vols. New York: D. Van Nostrand, 1862–71.

Moors, J. F. *History of the Fifty-second Regiment Massachusetts Volunteers.* Boston: George H. Ellis, 1893.

Morris, Gouverneur. *The History of a Volunteer Regiment, Being a Succinct Account of the Organization, Services, and Adventures of the Sixth Regiment New York Volunteers Infantry.* New York: Veteran Volunteer Publishing, 1891.

Newsome, Edmund. *Experience in the War of the Great Rebellion, by a soldier of the Eighty-first Regiment Illinois Volunteer Infantry.* Carbondale, Ill.: Printed by the author, 1879.

Noel, Theophilus. *A Campaign from Santa Fe to the Mississippi; Being a History of the Old Sibley Brigade.* Raleigh, N.C.: Charles R. Sanders Jr., 1961.

Pellet, Elias Porter. *History of the 114th Regiment, New York State Volunteers.* Norwich, N.Y.: Telegraph & Chronicle Power Press Print, 1866.

Porter, David D. *Incidents and Anecdotes of the Civil War.* New York: D. Appleton, 1885.

———. *The Naval History of the Civil War.* New York: Sherman Publishing, 1886. Reprint, Secaucus, N.J.: Castle, 1984.

Post, Lydia Minturn, ed. *Soldiers' Letters, from Camp, Battlefield and Prison.* New York: Published for the U.S. Sanitary Commission by Bunce & Huntington, 1865.

Powers, George W. *Story of the Thirty-eighth Regiment of Massachusetts Volunteers.* Cambridge, Mass.: Dakin and Metcalf, 1866.

Scott, John. *Story of the Thirty Second Iowa Infantry Volunteers.* Nevada, Iowa: Published by the author, 1896.

Scott, R. B. *The History of the 67th Regiment Indiana Infantry Volunteers, War of the Rebellion.* Bedford, Ind.: Herald Book and Job Print, 1892.

Selfridge, Thomas O. *Memoirs of Thomas O. Selfridge, Jr., Rear Admiral, U.S.N.* New York: G. P. Putnam's Sons, 1924.

Sherman, W. T. *Memoirs of General William T. Sherman by Himself.* New York: D. Appleton, 1875. Reprint, Bloomington: Indiana University Press, 1957.

Shorey, Henry A. *The Story of the Maine Fifteenth, Being a Narrative of the More Important Events in the History of the Fifteenth Maine Regiment.* Bridgton, Maine: Press of the Bridgton News, 1890.

Sperry, A. F. *History of the 33rd Iowa Infantry Volunteer Regiment, 1863–6.* Des Moines, Iowa: Mills, 1866.

Sprague, Homer B. *History of the 13th Infantry Regiment of Connecticut Volunteers during the Great Rebellion.* Hartford, Conn.: Case, Lockwood, 1876.

Stanyan, John M. *A History of the Eighth Regiment of New Hampshire Volunteers, including Its Service as Infantry, Second N.H. Cavalry, and Veteran Battalion in the Civil War of 1861–1865.* Concord, N.H.: Ira C. Evans, Printer, 1892.

Stevens, William B. *History of the Fiftieth Regiment of Infantry, Massachusetts Volunteer Militia in the Late War of the Rebellion.* Boston: Griffith-Stillings Press, 1907.

Taylor, Richard. *Destruction and Reconstruction: Personal Experiences of the Late War.* New York: D. Appleton, 1879.

Tiemann, William F. *The 159th Regiment of Infantry, New York State Volunteers, in the War of the Rebellion, 1862–1865.* Brooklyn: Printed by the author, 1891.

Tilley, Nannie M., ed. *Federals on the Frontier, the Diary of Benjamin F. McIntyre 1862–1864.* Austin: University of Texas Press, 1963.

Van Alstyne, Lawrence. *Diary of an Enlisted Man.* New Haven, Conn.: Tuttle, Morehouse and Taylor, 1910.

Welles, Gideon. *Civil War and Reconstruction, Selected Essays by Gideon Welles.* Compiled by Albert Mordell. New York: Twayne Publishers, 1959–60.

———. *Diary.* Edited by Howard K. Beale. 2 vols. New York: W. W. Norton, 1960.

Wells, Carol, ed. *War, Reconstruction and Redemption on Red River, the Memoirs of Dosia Williams Moore.* Ruston: Department of History, Louisiana Tech University, 1990.

Williams, J. M. *"The Eagle Regiment," 8th Wisconsin Infantry Volunteers: A Sketch of Its Marches, Battles, and Campaigns from 1861–1865.* Belleville, Wis.: Recorder Print, 1890.

Williams, Thomas J. *An Historical Sketch of the 56th Ohio Volunteer Infantry during the Great Civil War from 1861 to 1866.* Columbus, Ohio: Lawrence Press, 1899.

Winschel, Terrence J., ed. *The Civil War Diary of a Common Soldier, William Wiley of the 77th Illinois Infantry.* Baton Rouge: Louisiana State University Press, 2001.

Woods, J. T. *Services of the Ninety-sixth Ohio Volunteers.* Toledo, Ohio: Blade Printing and Paper, 1874.

Wook, Wales W. *A History of the Ninety-fifth Regiment, Illinois Infantry Volunteers.* Chicago: Tribune Company's Book and Job Printing Office, 1865.

SECONDARY SOURCES—ARTICLES

Abbott, John S. C. "Heroic Deeds of Heroic Men, Part V. Military Adventures beyond the Mississippi." *Harper's New Monthly Magazine* 30 (March 1865): 575–93.

Allardice, Bruce S. "Curious Clash at Blair's Landing." *America's Civil War* 10 (July 1997): 58–64.

Bailey, Anne J. "Chasing Banks out of Louisiana: Parson's Texas Cavalry in the Red River Campaign." *Civil War Regiments* 3 (1993): 212–35.

Barr, Alwyn. "The Battle of Blair's Landing." *Louisiana Studies* 2 (Winter 1963): 204–12.

———. "Civil War Diary of James Allen Hamilton." *Texana* (Summer 1964): 132–45.

———. "Sabine Pass, September 1863." *Texas Military History* 2 (February 1962): 17–22.

———. "Texas Coastal Defense, 1861–1865." *Southwestern Historical Quarterly* 65 (1961): 1–31.

———. "Texas Losses in the Red River Campaign, 1864." *Texas Military History* 3 (Summer 1963): 103–10.

———. "William T. Mechling's Journal of the Red River Campaign." *Texana* 1 (1963): 363–79.

———, ed. "The Battle of Bayou Bourbeau, November 3, 1863: Colonel Oran M. Roberts' Report." *Louisiana History* 6 (Winter 1965): 83–91.

Bergeron, Arthur W., Jr. "A Colonel Gains His Wreath: Henry Gray's Louisiana Brigade at the Battle of Mansfield, April 8, 1864." *Civil War Regiments* 4, no. 2 (1994): 1–25.

Block, W. T. "Sabine Pass in the Civil War." *East Texas Historical Journal* 9 (October 1971): 129–36.

Buenger, Walter L. "Unionism on the Texas Frontier, 1859–1861." *Arizona and the West* 22 (Autumn 1980): 237–54.

Cron, Frederick W. "Colonel Bailey's Red River Dams." *The Military Engineer* 29, no. 168 (November–December 1937): 421–24.

Cuccia, Phillip. "'Gorillas' and White Glove Gents: Union Soldiers in the Red River Campaign." *Louisiana History* 36 (1995): 413–30.

Cumberland, Charles C. "The Confederate Loss and Recapture of Galveston, 1862–1863." *Southwestern Historical Quarterly* 51 (October 1947): 109–30.

Czech, Kenneth P. "Gunboats up the River." *America's Civil War* 3 (May 1990): 42–48.

Delaney, Robert W. "Matamoros, Port for Texas during the Civil War." *Southwestern Historical Quarterly* 58 (April 1955): 473–87.

Dohrman, H. G. "Diplomacy and Inland Naval Warfare." *The Military Engineer* 26, no. 147 (May–June 1934): 212–15.

Edmonds, David C. "Surrender on the Bourbeau: Honorable Defeat or Incompetency under Fire?" *Louisiana History* 18 (Winter 1977): 63–86.

Elliot, Claude. "Union Sentiment in Texas, 1861–1865." *Southwestern Historical Quarterly* 50 (April 1947): 449–77.

Erickson, Edgar L., ed. "Hunting for Cotton in Dixie: From the Civil War Diary of Captain Charles E. Wilcox." *Journal of Southern History* 4 (1938): 493–513.

Ewing, Floyd E. "Origins of Unionist Sentiment on the West Texas Frontier." *West Texas Historical Association Yearbook* 32 (October 1956): 21–29.

———. "Unionist Sentiment on the Northwest Texas Frontier." *West Texas Historical Association Yearbook* 33 (October 1957): 58–70.

Fitzhugh, Lester N. "Saluria, Fort Esperanza, and Military Operations on the Texas Coast, 1861–1864." *Southwestern Historical Quarterly* 61 (July 1958): 66–100.

———. "Texas Forces in the Red River Campaign, March–May 1864." *Texas Military History* 3 (1963): 15–22.

Frazier, Donald S. "Texans on the Teche: The Texas Brigade at the Battle of Bisland and Irish Bend, April 12–14, 1863." *Louisiana History* 32 (Fall 1991): 417–35.

Geise, William Royston. "Military Command and the Campaigns of 1864 in the Trans-Mississippi Department." *Military History of Texas and the Southwest* 16, no. 1 (1980): 55–76.

Gill, Samuel T. "The Pain of Pyrrhic Victory." *Civil War Times Illustrated* 23 (May 1984): 8–15, 42–43.

Groce, William Wharton. "Major General John A. Wharton." *Southwestern Historical Quarterly* 19 (January 1916): 271–78.

Hailston, Earl B. "Joint Operations in the Civil War: The Mississippi." Carlisle, Penn.: Army War College Paper, 1898.

Holmes, Jack D. L. "The Battle of Sabine Crossroads." *Civil War Times Illustrated* 1 (November 1962): 14–19.

Houghton, Edgar P. "History of Company I, Fourteenth Wisconsin Infantry from October 15, 1861, to October 9, 1865." *Wisconsin Magazine of History* 11 (September 1927): 26–49.

Huffstodt, James T. "Ransom at the Crossroads: One Man's Ruin on the Red River." *Civil War Times Illustrated* 19 (December 1980): 8–17.

Joiner, Gary D., and Charles E. Vetter. "The Union Naval Expedition on the Red River, March 12–May 22, 1864." *Civil War Regiments* 4, no. 2 (1994): 26–67.

Jones, Ernest. "The Battle of Sabine Pass, September 8, 1863." *Blue & Gray Magazine* 4 (September 1986): 19–53.

Jones, Virgil C. "The Battle of Galveston Harbor." *Civil War Times Illustrated* 5 (February 1967): 28–38.

Lale, Max S. "New Light on the Battle of Mansfield." *East Texas Historical Journal* 25 (Fall 1987): 34–41.

Landers, H. L. "Wet Sand and Cotton—Banks' Red River Expedition." *Louisiana Historical Quarterly* 19 (1936): 150–95.

Leaf, William N. "War in the Second New Orleans District." *The Military Engineer* 30, no. 171 (1938).

Longacre, Edward G. "Rescue on Red River." *Civil War Times Illustrated* 16, no. 6 (October 1975): 4–9.

McArthur, Henry S. "A Yank at Sabine Pass." *Civil War Times Illustrated* 12 (December 1973): 38–43.

McLeary, J. H. "History of Green's Brigade." In *A Comprehensive History of Texas 1685 to 1897,* edited by Dudley G. Wooten, 2:695–740. Dallas: William G. Scarff, 1898. Reprint, Austin: Texas State Historical Association, 1986.

McPherson, James M. "The Whole Family of Man, Lincoln and the Last Best Hope Abroad." In *The Union, the Confederacy, and the Atlantic Rim,* edited by Robert E. May, 131–58. West Lafayette, Ind.: Purdue University Press, 1995.

Magee, Kenneth J. "Most Disgraceful Affair." *America's Civil War* 5, no. 6 (January 1993): 50–56.

Martin, David P. "The *Harriet Lane.*" *Southwestern Historical Quarterly* 39 (July 1935): 15–20.

Meiners, Fredericka. "Hamilton P. Bee in the Red River Campaign." *Southwestern Historical Quarterly* 78, no. 1 (July 1974): 21–44.

———. "The Texas Border Cotton Trade, 1862–1863." *Civil War History* 23, no. 4 (December 1977): 293–306.

Michot, Stephen S. "In Relief of Port Hudson: Richard Taylor's 1863 Lafourche Offensive." *Military History of the West* 23 (Fall 1993): 103–34.

Milbourn, Curtis W. "Brigadier General Thomas Green of Texas." *East Texas Historical Journal* 32 (Spring 1994): 3–11.

Muir, Andrew Forest. "Dick Dowling and the Battle of Sabine Pass." *Civil War History* 4 (December 1958): 399–428.

Roberts, A. S. "The Federal Government and Confederate Cotton." *American Historical Review* 32 (January 1927): 262–75.

Roots, William H. "The Experiences of a Federal Soldier in Louisiana in 1863." *Louisiana Historical Quarterly* 19 (July 1936): 635–67.

Sandefer, H. L., and Archie P. McDonald. "Sabine Pass: David and Goliath." *Texana* 7 (Fall 1969): 177–88.

Savas, Theodore P. "A Death at Mansfield: Col. James Hamilton Beard and the Consolidated Crescent Regiment." *Civil War Regiments* 4, no. 2 (1994): 68–103.

Schoonover, Thomas. "Napoleon Is Coming! Maximilian Is Coming? The International History of the Civil War in the Caribbean Basin." In *The Union, the Confederacy, and the Atlantic Rim,* edited by Robert E. May, 101–30. West Lafayette, Ind.: Purdue University Press, 1995.

Simpson, Harold B. "The Battle of Sabine Pass." In *Battles of Texas,* edited by Seymour Connor et al., 137–69. Waco: Texian Press, 1967.

Smith, George Winston. "The Banks Expedition of 1862." *Louisiana Historical Quarterly* 26 (April 1943): 341–60.

Smyrl, Frank H. "Texans in the Union Army, 1861–1865." *Southwestern Historical Quarterly* 65 (October 1961): 233–50.

———. "Unionism in Texas." *Southwestern Historical Quarterly* 68 (October 1964): 172–95.

Steers, Ed, ed. "Garrison Duty in Alexandria: The Red River Campaign Letters of Lt. Charles W. Kennedy, 156th New York Volunteer Infantry." *Civil War Regiments* 4, no. 2 (1994): 104–17.

Sutherland, Daniel E. "1864: 'A Strange, Wild Time.'" In *Rugged and Sublime: The Civil War in Arkansas,* edited by Mark K. Christ, 105–44. Fayetteville: University of Arkansas Press, 1994.

Taylor, Richard. "Unpublished After-Action Reports from the Red River Campaign." *Civil War Regiments* 4, no. 2 (1994): 118–35.

Tregle, Joseph G., Jr. "Thomas J. Durant, Utopian Socialism, and the Failure of Presidential Reconstruction in Louisiana." *Journal of Southern History* 45, no. 4 (November 1979): 485–512.

Trexler, H. A. "The *Harriet Lane* and the Blockade of Galveston." *Southwestern Historical Quarterly* 35 (October 1931): 109–23.

Tucker, Philip C., III. "The United States Gunboat *Harriet Lane.*" *Southwestern Historical Quarterly* 21 (April 1918): 360–80.

Tyler, Ronnie C. "Cotton on the Border, 1861–1865." *Southwestern Historical Quarterly* 73 (April 1970): 456–77.

Tyson, Carl P. "Highway of War." *Red River Historical Review* 3 (Summer 1978): 28–56.

Waller, John L. "Colonel George Wythe Baylor." *Southwestern Social Science Quarterly* 24 (June 1943): 23–35.

Waterfall, Richard T. "The Battle of Pleasant Hill, Louisiana, April 9, 1864." In *Civil War Battles in the West,* edited by LeRoy H. Fischer. Manhattan, Kans.: Sunflower University Press, 1981.

Williams, T. Harry. "General Banks and the Radical Republicans in the Civil War." *New England Quarterly* 12 (June 1939): 268–80.

Wilson, James Grant. "The Red River Dam, with Comments on the Red River Campaign." *Journal of the Military Service Institution of the United States* 12 (1891): 589–600.

Young, Jo. "The Battle of Sabine Pass." *Southwestern Historical Quarterly* 52 (April 1949): 398–409.

SECONDARY SOURCES—BOOKS

Abbott, Richard H. *Cotton & Capital, Boston Businessmen and Antislavery Reform, 1854–1868.* Amherst: University of Massachusetts Press, 1991.

Abbot, Willis J. *The Naval History of the United States.* New York: Peter Fenelon Collier, 1890.

Adams, Ephraim Douglass. *Great Britain and the American Civil War.* New York: Longmans, Green, 1925. Reprint: New York: Russell & Russell, n.d.

Ambrose, Stephen E. *Halleck: Lincoln's Chief of Staff.* Baton Rouge: Louisiana State University Press, 1962.

Anders, Curt. *Disaster in Damp Sand, the Red River Expedition.* Indianapolis: Guild Press of Indiana, 1997.

Ayres, Thomas. *Dark and Bloody Ground, the Battle of Mansfield and the Forgotten Civil War in Louisiana.* Dallas: Taylor Trade Publishing, 2001.

Bailey, Anne J. *Between the Enemy and Texas, Parsons's Texas Cavalry in the Civil War.* Fort Worth: Texas Christian University Press, 1989.

Barr, Alwyn. *Polignac's Texas Brigade.* Houston: Texas Gulf Coast Historical Association Publication Series, 1964. Reprint, College Station: Texas A&M University Press, 1998.

Bearss, Edwin C. *Steele's Retreat from Camden and the Battle of Jenkins Ferry.* Little Rock: Arkansas Civil War Centennial Commission and Pioneer Press, 1965.

Beringer, Richard E., Herman Hattaway, Archer Jones, and William N. Still Jr. *Why the South Lost the Civil War.* Athens: University of Georgia Press, 1986.

Biesele, Rudolph L. *The History of the German Settlements in Texas.* Austin: Von Boeckmann-Jones, 1930.

Boatner, Mark M., III. *The Civil War Dictionary.* New York: David McKay, 1959. Rev. ed. New York: David McKay, 1988.

Bragg, Jefferson Davis. *Louisiana in the Confederacy.* Baton Rouge, Louisiana State University Press, 1941.

Brooksher, William Riley. *War along the Bayous, the 1864 Red River Campaign in Louisiana.* Washington, D.C.: Brassey's, 1998.

Burgess, Lauren Cook, ed. *An Uncommon Soldier, the Civil War Letters of Sarah Rosetta Wakeman.* New York: Oxford University Press, 1994.

Casdorph, Paul D. *Prince John Magruder, His Life and Campaigns.* New York: John Wiley & Sons, 1996.

Castel, Albert. *General Sterling Price and the Civil War in the West.* Baton Rouge: Louisiana State University Press, 1965.

Christ, Mark K., ed. *Rugged and Sublime, the Civil War in Arkansas.* Fayetteville: University of Arkansas Press, 1994.

Cornish, Dudley Taylor. *The Sable Arm, Black Troops in the Union Army, 1861–1865.* Lawrence: University Press of Kansas, 1987.

Cotham, Edward T., Jr. *Battle on the Bay, the Civil War Struggle for Galveston.* Austin, University of Texas Press, 1998.

———. *Sabine Pass, the Confederacy's Thermopylae.* Austin: University of Texas Press, 2004.

Cunningham, Edward. *The Port Hudson Campaign, 1862–1863.* Baton Rouge: Louisiana State University Press, 1963.

Current, Richard Nelson. *Lincoln's Loyalists, Union Soldiers from the Confederacy.* New York: Oxford University Press, 1992.

Dimitry, John. "Louisiana." In *Confederate Military History,* vol. 10, edited by Clement A. Evans. Atlanta: Confederate Publishing, 1899.

Donald, David Herbert. *Lincoln.* New York: Simon & Schuster, 1995.

Duffy, James P. *Lincoln's Admiral, the Civil War Campaigns of David Farragut.* New York: John Wiley & Sons, 1997.

Dupree, Stephen A., ed. *Campaigning with the 67th Indiana 1864.* New York: iUniverse, 2006.

Edmonds, David C. *The Guns of Port Hudson.* 2 vols. Lafayette, La.: Acadiana Press, 1983–84.

———. *Yankee Autumn in Acadiana.* Lafayette, La.: Acadiana Press, 1979.

Eicher, John H., and David J. Eicher. *Civil War High Commands.* Stanford, Calif.: Stanford University Press, 2001.

Farragut, Loyall. *The Life of David Glasgow Farragut.* New York: D. Appleton, 1879.

Faulk, Odie B. *Tom Green: Fightin' Texan.* Waco: Texian Press, 1963.

Faust, Patricia L., ed. *Historical Times Illustrated Encyclopedia of the Civil War.* New York: Harper & Row, 1986.

Ferguson, John L., ed. *Arkansas and the Civil War.* Little Rock: Pioneer Press, 1965.

Finch, L. Boyd. *Confederate Pathway to the Pacific: Major Sherod Hunter and Arizona Territory, C.S.A.* Tucson: Arizona Historical Society, 1996.

Fite, Emerson David. *Social and Industrial Conditions in the North during the Civil War.* New York: Macmillan, 1910.

Fitzhugh, Lester N. *Texas Batteries, Battalions, Regiments, Commanders and Field Officers Confederate States Army, 1861–1865.* Midlothian, Tex.: Mirror Press, 1959.

Foote, Shelby. *The Civil War—a Narrative.* Vol. 2, *Fredericksburg to Meridian.* New York:

Random House, 1963; Vol. 3, *Red River to Appomattox.* New York: Random House, 1974.

Frazier, Donald S. *Cottonclads! The Battle of Galveston and the Defense of the Texas Coast.* Abilene, Tex.: McWhiney Foundation Press, McMurry University, 1998.

Glatthaar, Joseph T. *Forged in Battle, the Civil War Alliance of Black Soldiers and White Officers.* New York: Free Press, 1990.

Gosnell, H. Allen. *Guns on the Western Waters, the Story of River Gunboats in the Civil War.* Baton Rouge: Louisiana State University Press, 1949.

Greeley, Horace. *The American Conflict: A History of the Great Rebellion in the United States of America, 1860–'65.* Hartford, Conn.: O. D. Case, 1866.

Grimsley, Mark. *The Hard Hand of War, Union Military Policy toward Southern Civilians 1861–1865.* New York: Cambridge University Press, 1995.

Hamilton, James K. "The Battle of Mansfield." Master's thesis, University of Southwestern Louisiana, 1994.

Harrington, Fred Harvey. *Fighting Politician: Major General N. P. Banks.* Philadelphia: University of Pennsylvania Press, 1948.

Hattaway, Herman, and Archer Jones. *How the North Won, a Military History of the Civil War.* Urbana: University of Illinois Press, 1983.

Hearn, Chester G. *The Capture of New Orleans 1862.* Baton Rouge: Louisiana State University Press, 1995.

———. *Ellet's Brigade, the Strangest Outfit of All.* Baton Rouge: Louisiana State University Press, 2000.

———. *When the Devil Came Down to Dixie.* Baton Rouge: Louisiana State University Press, 1997.

Hewitt, Lawrence L. *Port Hudson: Confederate Bastion on the Mississippi.* Baton Rouge: Louisiana State University Press, 1987.

Hill, Jim Dan. *Sea Dogs of the Sixties.* Minneapolis: University of Minnesota Press, 1935.

Hollandsworth, James G., Jr. *The Louisiana Native Guards: The Black Military Experience during the Civil War.* Baton Rouge: Louisiana State University Press, 1991.

———. *Pretense of Glory, the Life of General Nathaniel P. Banks.* Baton Rouge: Louisiana State University Press, 1998.

Holzman, Robert S. *Stormy Ben Butler.* New York: Macmillan, 1954.

Johnson, Ludwell H. *Red River Campaign, Politics & Cotton in the Civil War.* Baltimore, Md.: Johns Hopkins Press, 1958. Reprint, Kent, Ohio: Kent State University Press, 1993.

Joiner, Gary Dillard. *One Damn Blunder from Beginning to End, the Red River Campaign of 1864.* Lanham, Md.: SR Books, 2003.

Jones, Howard. *Union in Peril, the Crisis over British Intervention in the Civil War.* Chapel Hill: University of North Carolina Press, 1992.

Jones, Virgil Carrington. *The Civil War at Sea.* Vol. 3, *The Final Effort.* New York: Holt, Rinehart and Winston, 1962.

Jordan, Terry L. *German Seed in Texas Soil.* Austin: University of Texas Press, 1966.

Josephy, Alvin M., Jr. *The Civil War in the American West.* New York: Alfred A. Knopf, 1991.

Kerby, Robert L. *Kirby Smith's Confederacy.* New York: Columbia University Press, 1972.

Lewis, Charles Lee. *David Glasgow Farragut, Admiral in the Making.* Annapolis, Md.: United States Naval Institute, 1941.

———. *David Glasgow Farragut, Our First Admiral.* Annapolis, Md.: United States Naval Institute, 1943.

Lonn, Ella. *Salt as a Factor in the Confederacy.* New York: W. Neale, 1933.

Lowe, Richard. *The Texas Overland Expedition of 1863.* Abilene, Tex.: McWhiney Foundation Press, McMurry University, 1998.

———. *Walker's Texas Division C.S.A., Greyhounds of the Trans-Mississippi.* Baton Rouge: Louisiana State University Press, 2004.

Macartney, Clarence Edward Nobel. *Mr. Lincoln's Admirals.* New York: Funk & Wagnalls, 1956.

McCrary, Peyton. *Abraham Lincoln and Reconstruction: The Louisiana Experiment.* Princeton, N.J.: Princeton University Press, 1978.

McPherson, James M. *Battle Cry of Freedom, the Civil War Era.* New York: Oxford University Press, 1988.

Mahan, Alfred Thayer. *Admiral Farragut.* New York: D. Appleton, 1892.

———. *The Gulf and Inland Waters.* New York: Charles Scribner's Sons, 1883.

Marszalek, John F. *Commander of All Lincoln's Armies, a Life of General Henry W. Halleck.* Cambridge, Mass.: Belknap Press of Harvard University Press, 2004.

———. *Sherman, a Soldier's Passion for Order.* New York: Free Press, 1993.

May, Robert E., ed. *The Union, the Confederacy, and the Atlantic Rim.* West Lafayette, Ind.: Purdue University Press, 1995.

Milligan, John D. *Gunboats down the Mississippi.* Annapolis, Md.: United States Naval Institute, 1965.

Monaghan, Jay. *Diplomat in Carpet Slippers, Abraham Lincoln Deals with Foreign Affairs.* New York: Bobbs-Merrill, 1945.

Nevins, Allan. *Fremont, Pathmarker of the West.* New York: D. Appleton-Century, 1939.

Niven, John. *Gideon Welles, Lincoln's Secretary of the Navy.* New York: Oxford University Press, 1973.

Oates, Stephen B. *Confederate Cavalry West of the River.* Austin: University of Texas Press, 1961.

Paludan, Phillip Shaw. *The Presidency of Abraham Lincoln.* Lawrence: University Press of Kansas, 1994.

Parks, Joseph Howard. *General Edmund Kirby Smith, C.S.A.* Baton Rouge: Louisiana State University Press, 1954.

Parrish, T. Michael. *Richard Taylor: Soldier Prince of Dixie.* Chapel Hill: University of North Carolina Press, 1992.

Parton, James. *General Butler in New Orleans.* New York: Mason Brothers, 1863.

Perret, Geoffrey. *Ulysses S. Grant, Soldier & President.* New York: Random House, 1997.

Plummer, Alonzo H. *Confederate Victory at Mansfield: Including Federal Advance from and Retreat to Natchitoches.* Mansfield, La.: Kate Beard Chapter, UDC, Ideal Printing Company, 1969.

Potter, David M. *The Impending Crisis 1848–1861.* New York: Harper & Row, 1976.

Pratt, Fletcher. *Civil War on Western Waters.* New York: Henry Holt, 1956.

Randall, J. G. *Lincoln the President.* 4 vols. (Vol. 4 with Richard N. Current). New York: Dodd, Mead, 1945–55.

Raphael, Morris. *The Battle in the Bayou Country.* Detroit: Harlo Press, 1975.

Roberts, O. M. "Texas." In *Confederate Military History,* vol. 11, edited by Clement A. Evans. Atlanta: Confederate Publishing, 1899.

Roland, Charles P. *Louisiana Sugar Plantations during the Civil War.* Leiden, The Netherlands: E. J. Brill, 1957. Reprint, Baton Rouge: Louisiana State University Press, 1997.

Savas, Theodore P., David A. Woodbury, and Gary D. Joiner, eds. *The Red River Campaign, Union and Confederate Leadership and the War in Louisiana.* Shreveport: Parabellum Press, 2003. (Contains reprints of the Red River Campaign articles from *Civil War Regiments* 4 [1994].)

Scharf, John Thomas. *History of the Confederate States Navy.* New York: Rogers & Sherwood, 1887. Reprint, New York: Gramercy Books, 1996.

Schmidt, Lewis G. *A Civil War History of the 47th Regiment of Pennsylvania Veteran Volunteers: "The Wrong Place at the Wrong Time."* Allentown, Penn.: Published by the author, 1986.

Sellers, John R. *Civil War Manuscripts, a Guide to Collections in the Manuscript Division of the Library of Congress.* Washington, D.C.: Library of Congress, 1986.

Sifakis, Stewart. *Who Was Who in the Civil War.* New York: Facts on File, 1988.

Smith, Jean Edward. *Grant.* New York: Simon & Schuster, 2001.

Smith, Myron J. *The U.S. Gunboat* Carondelet, *1861–1865.* Manhattan, Kans.: Sunflower University Press, 1982.

Smith, Walter G. *Life and Letters of Thomas Kilby Smith, Brevet Major-General United States Volunteers.* New York: G. P. Putnam's Sons, 1898.

Soley, James Russell. *Admiral Porter.* New York: D. Appleton, 1903.

Starr, Stephen Z. *The Union Cavalry in the Civil War.* Vol. 3, *The War in the West, 1861–1865.* Baton Rouge: Louisiana State University Press, 1985.

Tap, Bruce. *Over Lincoln's Shoulder, the Committee on the Conduct of the War.* Lawrence: University Press of Kansas, 1998.

Thompson, Jerry. *Henry Hopkins Sibley: Confederate General of the West.* Natchitoches, La.: Northwestern State University Press, 1987.

Thompson, Jerry, and Lawrence T. Jones III. *Civil War and Revolution on the Rio Grande Frontier, a Narrative and Photographic History.* Austin: Texas State Historical Association, 2004.

Tolbert, Frank X. *Dick Dowling at Sabine Pass, a Texas Incident in the War between the States.* New York: McGraw-Hill, 1962.

Waller, John L. *Colossal Hamilton of Texas: A Biography of Andrew Jackson Hamilton.* El Paso: Texas Western Press, 1968.

Warner, Ezra J. *Generals in Blue: Lives of the Union Commanders.* Baton Rouge: Louisiana State University Press, 1964.

———. *Generals in Gray: Lives of the Confederate Commanders.* Baton Rouge: Louisiana State University Press, 1959.

Welcher, Frank J. *The Union Army 1861–1865.* Vol. 2, *The Western Theater.* Bloomington: Indiana University Press, 1993.

West, Richard S., Jr. *Gideon Welles, Lincoln's Navy Department.* New York: Bobbs-Merrill, 1943.

———. *The Second Admiral, a Life of David Dixon Porter 1813–1891.* New York: Coward-McCann, 1937.

Whitcomb, Caroline E. *History of the Second Massachusetts Battery (Nimms Battery) of Light Artillery, 1861–1865.* Concord, N.H.: Rumford Press, Concord, 1912.

Wiley, Bell Irvin. *The Life of Billy Yank: The Common Soldier of the Union.* New York: Bobbs-Merrill, 1951.

Williams, T. Harry. *Lincoln and His Generals.* New York: Alfred A. Knopf, 1952.

———. *Lincoln and the Radicals.* Madison: University of Wisconsin Press, 1965.

Winters, John D. *The Civil War in Louisiana.* Baton Rouge: Louisiana State University Press, 1963.

Wooster, Ralph A. *Texas and Texans in the Civil War.* Austin: Eakin Press, 1995.

Wooten, Dudley G., ed. *A Comprehensive History of Texas 1685 to 1897.* Dallas: William G. Scarff, 1898. Reprint, Austin: Texas State Historical Association, 1986.

Wright, Marcus J. *Texas in the War 1861–1865.* Edited by Harold B. Simpson. Hillsboro, Tex: Hill Junior College, 1965.

INDEX